AMERICAN PUBLIC OPINION:

Its Origins, Content, and Impact

AMERICAN PUBLIC OPINION:

Its Origins, Content, and Impact

SECOND EDITION

Robert S. Erikson
Professor of Political Science
University of Houston

Norman R. Luttbeg
Professor of Political Science
Texas A&M University

Kent L. Tedin
Associate Professor of Political Science
University of Houston

JOHN WILEY & SONS
New York . Chichester . Brisbane . Toronto

Library of Congress Cataloging in Iudlication Data:

Erikson, Robert S
    American public opinion.

    Includes bibliographical references and indexes.
    1. Public opinion—United States. I. Luttbeg, Norman R., joint author. II. Tedin, Kent L.,
joint author. III. Title.

HN90.P8E74   1980   301.15'4'0973   79−17806
ISBN 0−471−03139−9

Printed in the United States of America

10 9 8 7 6 5 4 3 2

PREFACE

Our purpose in this second edition, as in the first, is to present the best available data on the origin, content, and impact of public opinion in America. We hope this volume provides valuable source material for students of public opinion.

The knowledge that permits this effort is based not only on the research and thoughts of others but, most importantly, on the existence of data conscientiously gathered and made available to the scholarly community by the Center for Political Studies of the University of Michigan. And without the public opinion data gathered by the Gallup and Harris polls, our conclusions would be far more tenuous.

This edition has also been vastly improved by the kind personal efforts of friends and colleagues. We particularly thank Alan Monroe and John L. Sullivan who read the manuscript in its entirety and provided many valuable criticisms and insights. We also thank the adopters of the first edition who guided our revision by completing our questionnaire regarding their experiences with it. Finally, our thanks to Charlotte Jones and Maggie Banks without whose typing and editorial skills this book would have been much delayed.

Our work obviously benefits from the efforts of others. Three classic studies of the American electorate—Campbell, Converse, Miller, and Stokes' *The American Voter*, V. O. Key's *Public Opinion and American Democracy,* and Key's provocative little book *The Responsible Electorate* stand as the scholarly heritage most valuable to our thinking. In many ways our efforts here are an updating of their thoughts and data to include findings through the late 1970s. To this understanding of American political behavior we add evidence of the origins of public opinion that has been gleaned from the studies of political socialization and media impact. We also add studies of the interaction between the public and their representatives that achieve congruence between public opinion and public policy.

Robert S. Erikson
Norman R. Luttbeg
Kent L. Tedin

CONTENTS

6. GROUP DIFFERENCES IN POLITICAL OPINIONS

7. ELECTIONS AS INSTRUMENTS OF POPULAR CONTROL

8. THE PUBLIC AND ITS ELECTED REPRESENTATIVES

9. PARTIES AND PRESSURE GROUPS: MEDIATING INSTITUTIONS AND REPRESENTATION

10. PUBLIC OPINION AND THE PERFORMANCE OF DEMOCRACY

APPENDIX A. THE THEORY OF SAMPLING POLITICAL OPINIONS

APPENDIX B. SURVEY RESEARCH CENTER/ CENTER FOR POLITICAL STUDIES OPINION ITEMS

CHAPTER 1

Public Opinion in Democratic Societies

"Support the Equal Rights Amendment!" "Make your beliefs count, send your contributions to Save Our Schools today!" "Write your congressional representative and say, 'I'm against gun control.' " "Oppose legalized abortion!" "Stop pollution!" "No matter how you vote—VOTE!" Americans are continually exhorted to be active in governing our cities, schools, county, state, and nation. In a typical year we could express ourselves politically six times just in our choice for various public offices. And voting is not the sole political act. Government bodies call occasional public meetings; candidates seek both workers and contributions; friends cajole us into participating in political causes; groups call for public outcries; and late some evening, our anger may urge us to write a letter to what's-his-name—our representative in Congress. In short, political activities continually call for our attention and participation. A person who feels strongly about political candidates and issues could clearly become so involved in politics that his or her interest could seriously infringe on earning a living, raising a family, or enjoying leisure. Political activity seems limited more by the time and energies people wish to commit to it than by the lack of opportunity to get involved.

Although continually urged to be concerned with politics, Americans, like people everywhere, are more concerned with events that affect them personally in an immediate sense than they are about relatively remote political questions. Examples of the former are personal health, one's job, how the children are doing in school, or paying for the new camper. This outlook is reflected in a series of polls conducted about the hopes and fears of Americans. These surveys show that concern with family, health, and living standards are uppermost in Americans' thoughts about the future. In 1976, for example, the most frequently mentioned fear (28 percent) was loss of personal health. The most frequently mentioned hope (31 percent) was a better standard of living. However, 15 percent mentioned peace in the world as their fondest hope, and 16 percent expressed a fear of economic instability. These are events over which the government presumably has some control.

When asked specifically to focus on fears and hopes of national significance, public responses center on concern about war. But immediate political items are also mentioned. For example, 10 percent hoped to get a better president, and 13 percent feared the threat of communism.[1] Thus, although personal needs are of the greatest concern to Americans, political questions are not considered trivial. One might speculate that the importance of politics increases as it begins to affect economic well-being. During the Great Depression of the 1930s, political questions may have occupied the thoughts of substantially more Americans than they do today.

Of course, a person can be politically inactive and still be a concerned spectator of political events. When Gallup Polls ask national samples to name "the most important problem facing this country," most people will mention some problem, such as crime, pollution, or unemployment. But this is a very nondemanding sort of question. Americans are seldom queried as to what they would do if they were government officials, but the responses to a question asked in 1943 suggest that Americans are indeed not preoccupied with government matters. When asked, "If you were elected to Congress this fall what laws would you want to have passed?" more than 47 percent responded that they had no opinions. Furthermore, when questioned, "Can you think of any problem which you feel a congressional committee should investigate," only 38 percent could think of such a problem.[2] More recent surveys indicate little change in this pattern. In 1970, just prior to the congressional election, 54 percent of a national sample claimed that candidates' stands on issues were the most important reasons for their voting decision. However, only 22 percent could name an issue that motivated their choice in the local congressional election.[3] Another example is from 1976, when a national sample was asked if they felt that more issues should be decided by voters in public referendums—68 percent responded positively. But less than a majority could think of any issue they would like to consider in such a poll.[4] Although Americans subscribe to the notion that the public must take an active role in a democracy, few are sufficiently motivated to become politically involved—or for that matter, even well informed.

If the public showed low interest in nonpolitical social activities such as birdwatching, further inquiry into the motives and quality of this behavior would not merit our attention. But politics is not like other activities. The role of the public in a democracy is crucial.

1-1 PUBLIC OPINION AND DEMOCRACY

After an extensive review of contemporary and classic definitions of public opinion, V. O. Key, Jr., defined public opinion as ". . . those opinions held by private persons which governments find it prudent to heed."[5] We prefer to expand that notion somewhat and define public opinion as *the combined personal opinions of adults toward issues of relevance to government.* Public opinion as a concept derives its importance from its use as a standard for judging the popularity of government decisions and, hence, the likelihood of whether those decisions will be obeyed. It is, in addition, important as an indicator of desires by the mass public for action (or inaction) on some particular issue. However, the study of public opinion also includes many facets not immediately apparent from our simple definition. Important questions include whether decision makers correctly perceive public opinion, whether they find it "prudent to heed" those perceived opinions, whether failure to do so leads to electoral defeat, and whether policies enacted garner public compliance.

Prior to the twentieth century, public opinion was not directly assessable and, therefore, was measured by after-the-fact reactions to events. For example, the defeat of William Jennings Bryan in the election of 1896 was interpreted as support among the electorate for the gold standard rather than the silver standard. The victory of Franklin Roosevelt over Herbert Hoover in 1932 was interpreted as a call for government action in the economic sphere. Obviously, elected officials and party workers would prefer to discover that they are not doing well before an election (when corrections can be made) rather than afterward (when it is too late). Two twentieth-century technologies, probability theory and survey research, now make that possible; they allow us to assess directly at any time the political views of the public.

Probability Theory and Survey Research

The development of probability theory and procedures for probability sampling makes it possible to analyze the opinions of the mass public after only a small number of persons have been asked their opinions. Sampling theory tells us the probability that some characteristic of a carefully drawn sample is similar to that of the entire population. If only 10 percent of a randomly drawn sample are redheads, we can conclude that it is highly probable that close to 10 percent of the entire population has red hair. Similarly, if 29 percent of a 1500-person sample say that the president is doing a good job, we can be fairly certain that between 26 and 32 percent of the entire American public would express the same opinion (see Appendix A).

Survey research is based on the straightforward notion that people will, if asked, answer with candor questions put to them by an interviewer. What is asked may range, for example, from the respondent's height to what he or she would do if faced by a mugger with a gun. The only apparent limits are the intelligibility of the questions and the respondent's willingness to answer.

What People Say and What They Do

One of the enduring issues in the study of verbal opinions is the nature of the link between those opinions and overt behavior. To what extent do people behave consistently with their answers to survey questions? The problem was first investigated in the now classic study by LaPiere.[6] After touring the country with a Chinese couple and being only once refused service by restaurants and motels, he found most of these same restaurants and motels responded negatively to an inquiry as to whether they would accept members of the Chinese race as guests. In other words, although the various managers indicated verbally (or in writing) that they would not accept Chinese as guests, the Chinese couple were in fact not turned away. We shall be able to touch the extensive literature dealing with this problem only briefly.[7] One point made in this literature is that the context of the expressed opinion should closely correspond to that of the behavior being studied. For example, if one were concerned with representation and voting, an example of a question closely linking opinion to behavior might be: What actions by your representative on this issue would cause you to vote against him? A second point made in this literature concerns social desirability. People often want to present themselves in the best possible light. It is a norm in American culture that good citizens vote. Thus people will often report having voted in the last election when in fact they did not do so. This overreporting often amounts to as much as 10 percent. A final problem involves "doorstep opinions." Somewhat disturbingly, people are inclined to answer almost any questions put to them. Perhaps out of the flattery in being asked or to avoid appearing uninformed, they answer. In Chapter 2 we discuss this problem in some depth and suggest some possible ways to counteract it.

1-2 LEVELS OF POLITICAL PARTICIPATION

Americans greatly underutilize opportunities for political participation. Consider the frequency with which people engage in the act of voting, an important but relatively easy form of political activity. In the 1976 presidential election only about 55 percent of those over age 18 went to the polls. Recent midterm elections have drawn around 35 percent. In primary, state, and local elections, the proportion drops even further.

Political activities that extend beyond the act of voting attract even fewer participants. Table 1-1 shows the frequencies with which survey respondents report engaging in various forms of political activity during recent presidential campaigns. While about three-fourths claim to have voted, only about one-third report that they tried to convince others how to vote. Other forms of campaign activity, such as wearing campaign buttons, putting political bumper stickers on cars, making campaign contributions, attending

Table 1-1.   Percent of Americans Professing to Having Taken Various Political
Actions, 1952–1976

Activity	1952	1956	1960	1964	1968	1972	1976
Belong to political club	2	3	3	4	3	a	a
Work for political party	3	3	6	5	5	5	4
Attend political rally or meeting	7	10	8	9	9	9	6
Contribute money to campaign	4	10	12	11	9	10	9
Use political sticker or button	a	16	21	16	15	14	8
Give political opinions	27	28	33	31	30	32	37
Vote in election	73	73	74	78	75	73	72

Sources. John P. Robinson, Jerrold G. Rusk, and Kendra B. Head, *Measures of Political Attitudes*
(Ann Arbor: Survey Research Center, 1968), p. 591 and (for 1968, 1972, and 1976) Center for
Political Studies data made available through the Interuniversity Consortium for Political Research.
aNot   asked.

political rallies, and working for political parties, are even less popular. None-
lectoral forms of political participation also attract few Americans. About one
in three is active in a community organization that involves a community
problem. Only about one in five has ever contacted a local government official
about an issue or problem. However, we do not want to leave the impression
that rates of political participation in America are atypically low compared
with other countries. As Table 1-2 indicates, levels of political activity in the
United States are about the same as in other nations.

The Costs of Participation

When we ask why people do not participate in political activities in greater
numbers, we should keep in mind that participation has its costs as well as
its benefits. In fact, if we imagine potential participants as being solely motivated by their anticipated gains from participation, we may wonder why
people participate at all. Consider the decision whether or not to vote in an
election. The costs of voting include factors such as the expense of traveling
to the polling place, the time spent standing in line, and the lost opportunity
to have engaged in some other activity. If a person's vote were the decisive
factor in determining the outcome of an election, the benefits would usually
outweigh the slight costs. Thus the rational individual would vote. But a
single voter cannot control an election except in the extremely unlikely instance where an election is decided by one ballot. By abstaining, the nonvoter
will have virtually no effect on the chances of victory of his or her favorite
candidate. Why then do so many people vote? Apparently individuals obtain
psychological satisfaction from voting apart from any consideration of
whether their vote can be decisive. Political scientists often refer to this
motivation as a "sense of citizen duty." As Table 1-3 shows, a person's

Table 1–2. Percentages of Citizens Active in Various Ways in Seven Countries

	Austria	India	Japan	Netherlands	Nigeria	United States	Yugoslavia
Voting							
Regular voters	85	48	93	77	56	63	82
Campaign activity							
Members of a party or political organization	28	5	5	13	a	8	15
Worked for a party	10	6	25	10	a	25	45
Attended a political rally	27	14	50	9	a	19	45
Communal activity							
Active members in a community action organization	9	7	11	15	34	32	39
Worked with a local group on a community problem	3	18	15	16	35	30	22
Helped form a local group on a community problem	6	5	5	a	26	14	a
Contacted an official in the community on some social problem	5	4	1	6	2	13	11
Contacted an official outside the community on a social problem	3	2	5	7	3	11	a
Particularized contacting							
Contacted a local official on a personal problem	15	12	7	38	2	6	20
Contacted an official outside the community on a personal problem	10	6	3	10	1	6	a
Number of cases	1769	2637	2657	1746	1799	2544	2995

Source. Sidney Verba and Norman H. Nie, "Political Participation," in Fred Greenstein and Nelson W. Polsby, eds., *Handbook of Political Science* (Reading, Mass.: Addison-Wesley, 1974), Vol. 4,, pp. 24-25. Some information on the construction of this table included in the original is not reproduced here.

anot asked.

Table 1-3. Relationship Between Voting and Sense of Civic Duty, 1976

	Sense of Civic Duty				
	Low				High
Percent voting	25	35	47	73	85
Percent of sample	4	4	9	36	47 N = 1909

Source. Center for Political Studies, 1976 Election Study.

score on a scale measuring citizen duty is a very good predictor of whether or not the person will vote. In fact, civic duty seems to be the single most important motivation for casting the ballot.[8]

Who Participates

Some people participate in politics more than others. Whether we are considering only the act of voting or include more complex forms of participation, two basic generalizations can be made about differential rates of participation. First, participation is greatest among those who are are high in socioeconomic status, that is, among the most educated, the wealthy, and those with the most prestigious occupations. Second, people are more likely to participate at certain stages of their life than at others.

The most important determinant of political participation is socioeconomic status (SES). The effects of this variable can clearly be seen by looking at voting rates within different categories of education. As Table 1-4 demonstrates, only 44 percent of those with less than an eighth-grade education reported voting in the 1976 presidential election. As education increases, so does the frequency of voting. At the high extreme, 74 percent of those with education beyond high school cast their ballot. Similar effects, although not as strong, exist for family income and occupational status. People high in socioeconomic status are also those most frequently found to participate in activities that extend beyond the act of voting. Verba and Nie offer graphic evidence in this regard: among the 13 percent of Americans who are the *most active* in politics, 57 percent are in the *upper third* SES category. In contrast, among the 13 percent who are *least active*, 59 percent are in the *lower third* SES category.[9]

Why is it that upper status persons are the most politically active? The answer is rather obvious, but more complex than one might think. Upper status persons tend to be the most concerned about political problems, and they also tend to feel that their political activity can be genuinely effective. In addition, they have the advantage of available time, money, and skills that allow them to be politically influential. Another commonly advanced explanation is that the well-to-do participate because they have a greater stake in political outcome (the protection of their advantaged position). Re-

Table 1-4. Percentage of Different Groups Voting in the 1976 Presidential Election

Voters	Percent voting
	25% 50% 75% 100%
Education: Past H.S.	74%
Family Income: $15,000 and over	70%
Age: 45–64 years	69%
Residence: Northcentral	65%
Age: 35–44 years	63%
Age: 65 years or over	62%
Employed	62%
White	61%
Male	60%
Female	60%
Residence: Northeast	60%
Family Income: $10,000–14,999	60%
Residence: West	59%
Education: At least some H.S.	56%
Residence: South	55%
Age: 25–34 years	55%
Family Income: $5,000–9,999	53%
Blacks	49%
Family Income: Under $5,000	46%
Age: 21–24 years	46%
Unemployed	44%
Education: 8 years or less	44%
Age: 18–20 years	38%
Spanish Origins	32%

Source. U.S. Bureau of the Census, *Current Population Survey,* 1976.

gardless, this upper class bias would certainly seem to operate in a fashion likely to lessen the political influence of the more disadvantaged classes.

Beside socioeconomic status, the other important variable in predicting a person's level of political participation is position in the life-cycle. Again, the reasons are fairly obvious. Young adults enter the electorate without political experience or the habit of prior participation. They generally are preoccupied with personal matters such as finding a mate and a good job. Also, they are not likely to be well integrated into their local community. Once married and with a stable job, however, an individual's political interest begins to increase. With the arrival of children (especially in the case of women), there occurs a depression in political activity. Participation picks up once again as a person's children begin school and remains at this relatively high level into the middle fifties. With the onset of old age, participation once again begins to decline.

Life-cycle effects are greatest among those with little education; conversely, they have the least impact on those with a college degree. There is relatively little difference between the voting habits of young and middle-aged college graduates. On the other hand, young adults with little education score particularly low on the political participation scale. Philip Converse and Richard Niemi offer this bleak description of the young, uneducated voter.

> They are functionally illiterate: They read little in totum and almost nothing of a serious nature. They appear furthermore to do quite an effective job of ignoring the more serious material which might confront them over the air waves. Their nonvoting is more than one symptom of a broader insulation from the public affairs of the society.[10]

Blacks participate less than whites; women participate somewhat less than men. But these differences can largely be explained by differences in socioeconomic status and placement in the life cycle. According to a U.S. Census survey, 61 percent of whites voted in the 1976 presidential election compared with only 49 percent of blacks.[11] This gap reflects the fact that blacks generally participate in politics less than whites. At one time, low black participation was the result of overt discrimination, particularly in the South. Today, however, the gap is basically due to socioeconomic differences between the races. For example, when the voting rates for blacks and whites are compared at the same level of education and income, the differential declines to a mere two percentage points.[12] Blacks actually participate more than whites, when this sort of comparison is extended to activities beyond voting.[13]

Today, considerable attention is being given to the activity of women in politics. Although women outnumber men, they are seldom found in political leadership positions. But women participate in more routine political activities at almost the same rate as men. Similarly, only trivial differences between males and females are found in forms of participation beyond voting.[14] These small differences are largely due to situational factors. Women who are low participators tend to be housewives or to be disadvantaged in terms of education.[15] At one time the participation gap between men and women was considerably wider than it is now.

Political leaders probably pay more attention to the viewpoints of the politically active as opposed to the noninvolved. To the extent that this is true, and to the extent that political attitudes among activists and nonactivists differ, there will be a bias in the political message that reaches the ears of government officials. The message will essentially be biased by an over-representation of educated, high-status whites.

1-3 POLITICAL PARTY IDENTIFICATION

Many voters approach elections with the decision-making guide of a long-standing loyalty to either the Republican or the Democratic party—what

Table 1-5. The Party Identification of the Electorate, 1952–1978

	1952	1954	1956	1958	1960	1962	1964	1966	1968	1970	1972	1974	1976	1978
Democrats	47%	47%	44%	47%	46%	47%	51%	45%	45%	43%	40%	38%	40%	39%
Independents	22	22	24	19	23	23	22	28	29	31	35	36	36	37
Republicans	27	27	29	29	27	27	24	25	24	24	23	22	23	20
Nothing, other don't know	4	4	3	5	4	3	2	2	2	1	1	4	1	3
Total	100%	100%	100%	100%	100%	100%	99%	100%	100%	99%	99%	100%	100%	99%
n =	1614	1139	1772	1269	3021	1317	1571	1291	1557	1507	2705	1522	2863	2297

Source. Survey Research Center/Center for Political Studies election data.

political scientists call "party identification." Since an individual's party identification is generally one of the most central and stable elements of his or her political beliefs, we refer to it extensively in subsequent chapters. As Table 1-5 shows, party identification was relatively constant from 1940 through the early 1960s. Independents usually accounted for about one-fifth of the public. However, during the late 1960s the number of Independents began to increase, and they now amount to more than one-third of the electorate. In fact, Independents currently outnumber Republicans, who have been the big losers in the partisan shift of recent years.

In the 1950s political scientists noted differences in voting and participation among people holding differing party identifications. These same patterns still exist, and are presented in Table 1-6, using the 1976 election data. Strong partisans are more likely to vote than are weak partisans, who vote more than those calling themselves "Independents." In addition, most partisans vote for the presidential candidate of the party with which they identify. In 1976, 83 percent of those identifying with a political party voted for the presidential candidate of that party. Loyalty to party has varied somewhat over the years, but it typically holds at about 80 percent. Clearly the party with the greatest number of identifiers has a real advantage.

Partisanship, like race and education, introduces a potential distortion in terms of which public opinions will be heard by elected officials. Partisans are more likely to be monitoring the activity of government, and certainly are more likely to make their opinions count by voting. Thus there is no necessary one-to-one connection between public opinion as heard by government personnel and public opinion as it really exists.

Table 1-6. Partisan Voting in 1976

	Voted Democrat (Percent)	Voted Republican (Percent)	Didn't Vote (Percent)	Total (Percent)
Strong Democrat	73	7	20	100
Weak Democrat	48	17	35	100
Leaning Democrat	51	16	33	100
Independent	21	29	50	100
Leaning Republican	10	62	28	100
Weak Republican	16	56	28	100
Strong Republican	2	88	9	99

$n = 2296.$

Source. Center for Political Studies, 1976 Election Study.

1-4 LINKAGE MODELS BETWEEN PUBLIC OPINION AND PUBLIC POLICIES

It is a normative position among democratic theorists that elected officials consider public opinion when making policy decisions. But what process, if any, links opinion with policies? In this final section we outline five models by which public opinion can be reflected in public policy. Note that earlier in the chapter we stressed the importance of public opinion as a standard in assessing the accountability of elected officials. As we will see, three of these models also offer a dynamic process by which elected officials are held accountable to the public for their policy enactments.

The Rational-Activist Model

This model is the basis for the widely accepted concept of the ideal citizen's role in a democracy. Voting on the basis of issues is at the heart of the Rational-Activist Model. By the standards of this model, individual citizens are expected to be informed politically, involved, rational, and, above all, active. On the basis of an informed and carefully reasoned set of personal preferences, and an accurate perception of the various candidates' positions, the voter is expected to cast a ballot for those candidates who best reflect the voter's issue preferences. The model suggests that elected officials who are not held accountable by an informed electorate will not responsibly enact public preferences into policy. Instead, such representatives may vote their own preferences or the preferences of limited segments of society, such as wealthy professional groups.

This model places great burdens on both elected officials and citizens, expecting both to be informed and to communicate with each other. In a complex and increasingly technical society, the task of the voter who seeks to be informed is indeed formidable. As we have noted, politics does not play a salient role in the lives of most Americans. Many people rarely or never vote. Those who do are often ill-informed, particularly when they participate in nonpresidential elections. In our search for methods by which political leaders can be held accountable, we must look beyond the Rational-Activist Model.

The Political Parties Model

The Political Parties Model greatly reduces the political demands placed on the citizen. This model depends on the desire of political parties to win elections as a mechanism for achieving popular control. According to the model the party states its positions on the various issues of the day in its platform. Because of their interest in winning elections, parties can be counted on to take stands that appeal to large segments of the electorate. The voter then selects among platforms, giving support to the candidate of the party whose platform most conforms to his or her personal preference. Instead of facing multiple decisions for the numerous offices up for election, the voter need only make a single decision among the available choice of parties.

A number of questions are raised by a consideration of this model. For example, do people simply adopt the party identification of their parents and loyally support that party throughout thier lives? Such loyalty violates the model's expectation that voters rationally chose the party most closely standing for issue positions preferred by the voters. Do Democratic victories reflect increasing public support for Democratic programs or merely the larger number of Democrats in our society?

The Pressure Groups Model

In the preceeding models we have emphasized the central importance of communication between elected officials and their constituents. For representatives to respond to public demands, they need to know what these demands are. For the public to achieve accountability from representatives, they need to know what the representatives have done, and what alternatives were available. Pressure groups can perform this function. They can serve as a link between the people and their representatives.

Numerous organized groups in society claim to speak for various segments of the electorate. Because they pressure government for their particular interests, they are called pressure groups (or interest groups). At one extreme, these groups could be so inclusive of individuals in our society, and could so accurately represent their members' opinions that representatives could achieve accountability merely by recording the choice of each group, weighing them by the number of voters they represent, and voting with the strongest pressure. This would be in accord with what might be called the Pressure Group Model of popular control.

Under ideal circumstances pressure groups might succeed in communicating public opinion to officials between elections and with greater clarity than election outcomes. However, to exert influence additional tactics might be necessary. Pressure groups may need to martial the votes they control during an election to defeat those who are not responding to the preferences of the group's membership. Pressure groups, like political parties, could simplify the choices for the individual voter, making it possible for an electorate that is largely disinterested in politics nevertheless to achieve accountability. Several questions arise out of the Pressure Groups Model. Do the opinions of those citizens within a pressure group seem highly similar, and do they differ from members of other groups? Does "group opinion," the somehow combined opinions of all those persons in the different pressure groups, coincide with public opinion? Or do the opinions carried to government by pressure groups reflect only the opinions of the wealthy or the business sector of our society?

The Role Playing Model

The remaining two models could be the basis for political linkage between opinion and policy, but neither assures that officials are accountable. The Role Playing Model builds on the sociological concept of role or widely shared beliefs about how people in various social positions should act. The judge is supposed to be judicious, the doctor both expert and comforting, and the representative willing to work to enact the preferences of his supporters.

If elected officials believe they should learn constituency opinion and enact it into public policy, public opinion may well reflect public policy. Even if the public behaved in an irrational fashion, such as voting for candidates and parties with no concern for their issue positions, public policy would still reflect public opinion because of the role orientation of the representative. He or she would attempt to learn public opinion and translate it into public policy regardless of the electorate's motives in casting the ballot. Questions that arise from the Role Playing Model are: Can an elected official accurately learn public opinion? What are the various roles a representative can adopt?

The Sharing Model

Because as a society we do not designate leaders early in life and hold them as a class apart throughout their early lives, it is unlikely that the personal opinions on the issues of the day held by elected officials differ diametrically from those held by the rest of the electorate. This possibility is the final of our models of political linkage—the Sharing Model. This model simply states that since many attitudes are broadly held throughout the public, elected leaders cannot help but satisfy public opinion to some degree, even if the public is totally apathetic. Unilateral disarmament, total government takeover of the economy, a termination of public education, and complete disregard for preservation of the environment are all examples of actions so contrary to broadly held American attitudes that they would be rejected by any set of government leaders. Even on issues that provoke substantial diagreement, the distribution of opinion among political leaders may be similar to that among the public. If so, even when leaders act according to personal preferences and are ignored by a disinterested electorate, their actions would often correspond to the viewpoint of the electorate. For this model, we need to consider how broadly opinions on national issues are shared, and how alike are elected officials' positions to those of the public.

1-5 PLAN OF THE BOOK

Necessarily, we order facts into various chapters that strike us as convenient. Chapter 2 discusses the difficulty in assessing public opinion and its content from opinion polls. Chapter 3 focuses on the role of "ideology" in shaping political beliefs. Chapter 4 evaluates data on broad public acceptance of certain attitudes that may be necessary for stable democratic government. Chapters 5 and 6 are discussions of the origins of political opinions. The former concerns the agents of adult and preadult socialization; the latter concerns the effects of group membership. Chapter 7 is an analysis of public opinion and elections. Chapter 8 analyzes the reverse aspect of political linkage—how elected officials respond to the views of their constituents. Chapter 9 considers the importance of political parties and pressure groups in achieving correspondence between public opinion and public policy. In the final chapter we assess the linkage models and draw conclusions about public opinion in the United States based on the data presented throughout the book.

FOOTNOTES FOR CHAPTER ONE

1. William Watts and Lloyd A. Free, *State of the Nation III* (Lexington, Mass: Lexington Books, 1978), pp. 170–173.

2. John C. Wahlke, "Public Policy and Representative Government: The Role of the Represented," a paper prepared for the Seventh World Congress of the International Political Science Association, Brussels, Belgium, 1967.

3. *The CBS News Poll*, 3, (October 30, 1970), p. 7.

4. David B. Hill and Norman R. Luttbeg, *Trends in American Electoral Behavior* (Itasca, Ill: Peacock, 1979).

5. V. O. Key, Jr., *Public Opinion and American Democracy* (New York: Knopf, 1967), p. 14.

6. Richard LaPiere, "Attitudes and Actions," *Social Forces* 13 (October 1934–May 1935), pp. 203–237.

7. See Irwin Deutscher, *What We Say/What We Do: Sentiments and Acts* (Glenview, Ill.: Scott, Foresman, 1973).

8. Angus Campbell, et al., *The American Voter* (New York: Wiley, 1960), p. 106.

9. Sidney Verba and Norman H. Nie, *Participation in America* (New York: Harper and Row, 1972), pp. 130–131.

10. Philip E. Converse and Richard Niemi, "Nonvoting Among Young Adults in the United States," in William J. Crotty, Donald M. Freeman, and Douglas S. Gatlin (eds.) *Political Parties and Political Behavior*, 2nd ed. (Boston: Allyn Bacon, 1971), p. 448.

11. United States Bureau of the Census, *Current Population Reports,* series P-20, no. 322, "Voting and Registration in the Election of November, 1976," p. 2.

12. Ibid., p. 3.

13. Verba and Nie, Chapter 10.

14. Susan Welch, "Women as a Political Animal: A Test of Some Explanations for Male-Female Political Participation Differences," *American Journal of Political Science*, 21 (Novem-

ber 1977), pp. 711–730; Kristi Anderson, "Working Women and Political Participation, 1952–1972," *American Journal of Political Science,* 19 (August 1975), pp. 439–451.

15. Kent L. Tedin, David W. Brady, and Arnold Vedlitz, "Sex Differences in Political Attitudes and Behavior: The Case for Situational Factors," *Journal of Politics,* 39 (May 1977), pp. 447–454; Welch, loc. cit.

CHAPTER 2

Opinion Polls and Public Opinion

Before the advent of the public opinion polls in the early 1930s, one had to rely on much more inexact measures of what the public was thinking. To understand his constituency's concerns, the political leader of the prepoll era had to choose from among several intuitive indicators of public opinion. He could consult his friends and assume that their thinking was representative of his constituency; he could have his staff make a count of the pro and con letters on given issues received in his office; he could make a similar count from letters to the editor in various newspapers; or he could try to assess a crowd's relative enthusiasm for different ideas during his speech. But the most relied upon method of assessing public opinion prior to the opinion poll was the interpretation of election results, and the occasional referendum that managed to find its way onto the ballot.

Until the development of scientific polling techniques, both practitioners and theorists of politics could not know the error in assessing public opinion in these manners. We know that most informal methods of assessing public opinion, such as those listed above, have a substantial bias built into them. For example, people who write letters to editors or congressmen on public issues tend to be more "extreme" in their opinion—and, on the whole, more conservative—than the bulk of the public.[1] Adding this to the fact that liberals tend to communicate with liberal politicians and conservatives with conservative politicians, we can expect that the impressions of public opinion that politicians receive are often greatly distorted, at least when compared with survey results.

Today, the results of numerous opinion polls continually inform interested politicians, scholars, and concerned citizens about the "pulse" of public opinion. On the basis of about 1500 carefully selected interviews, polling organizations can predict with remarkable accuracy how the American public as a whole would divide on the questions they ask. But polls can tell more than just the breakdown of mass opinion on a question at a given moment. They can, for example, reveal important opinion differences between various groups within society. They can be analyzed to discover the interrelations among the political attitudes that individuals hold. Data from polls can be examined to determine the extent to which voters are influenced

17

by certain issues in election campaigns. Moreover, historians have begun to comb the data archives of polling organizations to discover historical trends. In short, most of the information we now have about public opinion comes from the analysis of opinion poll data.

In addition to the familiar Gallup and Harris polls, various academic institutions conduct polls for scholarly purposes. Most prominent are the election surveys conducted on a biennial basis since 1952 by the Survey Research Center (SRC) at the University of Michigan. (Because the SRC changed its name in 1970 to the "Center for Political Studies" (CPS), we will refer to it as the "SRC/CPS".) Much of our current knowledge about public opinion results from polls taken by the SRC/CPS, which makes its data available to interested scholars.

Like other forms of opinion measurement, opinion surveys are far from perfect instruments for assessing public opinion. In this chapter, we take a preliminary look at some of the characteristics of American public opinion as revealed by polls. Our first task is an examination of the difficulties involved in interpreting survey results. Second, we look at how the American public has distributed itself—both recently and in the more distant past—on important political questions.

2-1 THE DEPTH OF OPINION HOLDING

We have already seen, in Chapter One, that the participation level of most Americans rarely extends beyond the act of voting. It is also true that most Americans are not very attentive observers of the political world. From the occasional information "quizzes" given the public in opinion surveys, we find that the citizen typically has little political information at his or her disposal. Indeed, careful analysis of data from opinion surveys indicates that many opinions people express are so shallow that extreme caution must be exercised in extracting significance from the tabulation of opinion breakdowns. Thus, before we attempt to find out what the public is thinking about political issues, we must first examine the extent of political inattentiveness and the problems this creates for the proper analysis of findings from opinion surveys.

How Politically Informed is the Public?

First, we examine the level of political information held by the mass public. In Table 2-1, an information scale is presented that gives the percentage of adults who could give the "correct" answer to various political information questions. The information varies from civics book knowledge to simple information about foreign governments. Although the results are for various years, it is reasonable to assume that the data are a fairly accurate representation of the public's information level at the present time. Since the lack of

Table 2-1. The Level of Political Information Among the Adult Public

		Year	Source
94%	Know the capital city of United States	1945	[AIPO]
94%	Know the president's term is four years	1951	[AIPO]
93%	Recognize photograph of the current president	1948	[AIPO]
89%	Can name governor of their home state	1973	[Harris]
80%	Know meaning of term "veto"	1947	[AIPO]
79%	Can name the current vice president	1978	[NORC]
78%	Know what initials "FBI" stand for	1949	[AIPO]
74%	Know meaning of the term "wiretapping"	1969	[AIPO]
70%	Can name their mayor	1967	[AIPO]
69%	Know which party has most members in U.S. House of Representatives	1978	[NORC]
68%	Know president limited to two terms	1970	[CPS]
63%	Know China to be Communist	1972	[CPS]
63%	Have some understanding of term "conservative"	1960	[SRC]
58%	Know meaning of term "open housing"	1967	[AIPO]
52%	Know that there are two U.S. senators from their state	1978	[NORC]
46%	Can name their congressman	1973	[Harris]
39%	Can name both U.S. senators from their state	1973	[Harris]
38%	Know Russia is not a NATO member	1964	[AIPO]
34%	Can name the current secretary of state	1978	[NORC]
30%	Know term of U.S. House member is two years	1978	[NORC]
31%	Know meaning of "no fault" insurance	1977	[AIPO]
28%	Can name their state senator	1967	[AIPO]
23%	Know which two nations involved in SALT	1979	[CBS/NYT]

Sources. American Institute of Public Opinion (Gallup); Center for Political Studies; Lou Harris and Associates; National Opinion Research Center; CBS/NYT.

an adequate benchmark of what, exactly, is a passing grade creates the danger of making too severe a judgment about the political capabilities of the average American, we merely suggest that many people are rather inattentive to the political world that dominates the front pages of the daily newspapers. One must, however, also notice that some people are, in fact, fairly knowledgeable.

The Frequency of Opinion Holding

The public's low level of political information implies that many Americans do not follow current events closely enough to develop concrete opinions on topical political issues. Typically, people are less able to offer opinions on specific government proposals than on broad issues. Occasionally a public opinion poll will reveal a striking example of this lack of opinion. One instance was the lack of opinion crystallizing over the complicated, but well publicized, 1969 Senate battle over President Nixon's controversial Antiballistic Missile (ABM) program. Informed observers generally agreed that the Senate vote over appropriations for Nixon's ABM program would vitally structure American defense policy and expenditure priorities for years to follow. When the showdown Senate vote came, Nixon's ABM program was approved by a margin of one vote. If we ask whether this outcome reflected the will of the majority of public opinion, the answer is difficult to determine for the simple reason that a sizeable majority of American adults apparently did not even have an opinion on the issue. Shortly before the Senate vote, Gallup asked this question: "Have you read or heard anything about the Antiballistic Missile program as submitted to Congress by President Nixon?" The 69 percent who indicated that they had read or heard something about it were then asked if they had an opinion on the program and, if so, whether they favored or opposed it. One quarter of these "informed" respondents indicated that they were "undecided" on the issue. The breakdown of the results, which indicates that only 41 percent held opinions on the ABM issue at the peak of the controversy, were:[2]

Aware of program and favor ABM program	23%	⎫
		⎬ 41% with opinion
Aware of program and oppose ABM program	18%	⎭
Aware of ABM program but undecided	28%	⎫
		⎬ 59% without opinion
Unaware of ABM program	31%	⎭
	100%	

The extremely low rate of opinion holding on ABM was largely because of the extreme complexity of the issue. But in public opinion polling, the number of respondents who fall in the "no opinion" category is not caused by the nature of the issue alone. One factor that can often influence the frequency of "no opinion" responses is the question format itself. Notice that, in the ABM survey, respondents were first asked if they were familiar with the issue and then whether they had opinions on it. Only those who indicated familiarity and also that they held an opinion were then asked for their opinions. This filtering device gave respondents considerable opportunity to place themselves in the category without opinions. Most likely, very few would have failed to offer an opinion if all respondents were simply asked one question in which a "no opinion" response would have to be volunteered, such as: "Do you favor or oppose the Antiballistic Missile program that was submitted to Congress by President Nixon?" The use of filter questions to screen out some of the haphazard "doorstep opinions" that might be offered by the disinterested and undecided is a frequent practice in public opinion research. One type of filter question is the information filter. The

"read or heard. . ." question in the ABM survey is an example. Sometimes, by means of a simple quiz it is possible to eliminate respondents who
are too ignorant to have a meaningful opinion. For example, in the fall of
1964 the Center for Political Studies surveyed attitudes toward admission of
Communist China to the United Nations, but asked opinions of only those
respondents who, in earlier questions, correctly identified mainland China as
having a Communist form of Government and as a nonmember of the UN.
The breakdown of responses to the question, "Do you think Communist
China should be admitted to the United Nations or do you think it should
not?" was:

China should be admitted   15% ⎫
                                                 ⎬ 60% with opinions
China should not be admitted   45% ⎭

Don't know   10% ⎫
                                                 ⎬ 40% without opinions
China not known to be Communist   ⎪
   and nonmember of UN   29% ⎭

On broad questions of policy (for example, school integration or foreign
aid) information filters are usually inappropriate. However, by being offered
the right encouragement, some respondents can still be induced to say they
have no opinion when they have none. For example, in recent Center for
Political Studies polls, respondents are generally asked whether they have an
opinion or "whether they have thought much about this [issue]." Only respondents who answer affirmatively are then asked their opinions. Generally,
about 20 percent of the respondents are found to be without opinions using
this technique. (Typically, an additional 20 percent or so will offer an opinion that puts them in the middle group on the issue—not preferring one side
over the other—if such an option is offered. We might hesitate, however, to
call these responses nonopinions.) Some examples of nonopinion rates on
selected issues from CPS surveys are given in Table 2-2.

From Table 2-2, some differences in the rate of opinion holding from
issue to issue can be noticed. In large part, these differences reflect the degree of difficulty in reacting to the particular issue in terms of direct personal
experience, perceived self-interest, or group-related attitudes. Most respondents have a ready opinion on busing, women's rights, and marijuana legalization. At the other extreme, relatively few respondents offer opinions on
foreign aid or trading with Communist nations for the reason that these foreign policy questions are remote from everyday experience. Two social welfare issues—medical care and a guaranteed standard of living—evoke
opinion rates that are in between these two extremes. But on the abstract
question of whether the federal government is getting too powerful, a
relatively low rate of opinion holding is found. Similarly, a high propor-

tion—about one-third—choose not to place themselves on the abstract liberalism-conservatism scale.

Despite the precautions taken to assure respondents that they are under no obligation to offer opinions when they have none, the fear of appearing uninformed causes many respondents to conjure up opinions even when they had not given the particular issue any thought prior to the interview. It is unavoidable that a large share of "opinions" that get counted in survey tabulations are of the "doorstep" variety. In fact, many respondents who give opinions in one interview will admit to having no opinion when interviewed at a later time. Similarly, many respondents who do offer opinions will change sides on an issue from one interview to the next.

Table 2-3 shows one example, from the Center for Political Studies 1976 election survey. In this survey, the same respondents were interviewed

Table 2-2. Rates of Opinion Holding on Selected Issues.

Issue	Percentage with Opinions	Percentage without Opinions
Should women "have an equal role with men in running business, industry, and government?" (1976)	91	9
Do you favor "busing children out to schools out of their own neighborhoods" to achieve racial integration? (1976)	89	11
Should "the use of marijuana be made legal?" (1976)	86	14
Should the government "see to it that every person has a job and a good standard of living?" (1976)	80	20
Should there "be a government insurance plan which would cover all medical and hospital expenses?" (1976)	79	21
Should our farmers and businessmen "be allowed to do business with Communist countries? (1968)	70	30
Is the government in Washington "getting too powerful for the good of the country?" (1976)	69	31
Should the U.S. "give aid to other countries if they need help?" (1968)	68	32
Where would you place yourself on a liberal to conservative scale? (1976)	67	33

Source. CPS election data. For the full questions, see Appendix B. For most items, the percent without opinions includes "haven't thought much about it" and "don't know." For the two 1968 items and the federal power item, the percent without opinions includes "don't know," "no interest," and "depends" responses.

Table 2-3. Opinion Consistency on Government Guarantee of a Job and Good Standard of Living[a]

	Preelection Responses, 1976		
	Govt. Should Guarantee Job and Good Standard of Living	In Between, No Opinion	Govt. Should Let Each Person Get Ahead on His Own
Postelection Responses, 1976			
Guarantee Job and Good Standard of Living	9%	5%	3%
In Between, No Opinion	9%	22%	11%
Let Each Get Ahead on Own	4%	10%	26%

Source. Center for Political Studies 1976 election data.
[a]Cell entries represent percentages of the entire sample.

shortly before and shortly after the 1976 election. In each of the two surveys, the respondents were asked their views on whether the federal government should guarantee everyone "a good job and a good standard of living" or whether the "government should let each person get ahead on his own." As Table 2-3 shows, only a minority of the respondents (35 percent) had a sufficiently firm opinion to take the same side (consistently pro or consistently con) in both interviews. A few (7 percent) changed sides completely from one interview to the next, and others (22 percent) gave no opinion in either interview. The remainder (35 percent) took sides in one interview but not the other.

The pattern shown in Table 2-3 is not a unique example. Other "panel surveys" (surveys in which the same people are interviewed more than once) show a high degree of response instability on opinion questions. The most elaborate panel studies have been conducted by the Center for Political Studies (CPS) and its predecessor, the Survey Research Center (SRC), at the University of Michigan. In its recent panel study, the CPS interviewed a constant group of respondents in three "waves"— in 1972, 1974, and again in 1976. Earlier, the SRC had interviewed a similar panel of respondents in 1956, 1958, and 1960. Although both of these "three-wave" panels display a high degree of response instability, it is the earlier SRC panel survey that to date has received the greatest attention from scholars.

In each of the three years of the 1956-58-60 panel study, the respondents were asked whether they agreed with the eight issue statements shown in Figure 2-1 below. On some issues examined in the 1956-58-60 panel study, more than one-half of the respondents admitted having no opinion in at least one of the three interviews. On no issue did as many as two-thirds offer an

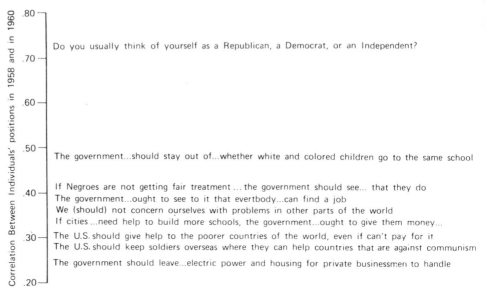

Figure 2-1. Temporal stability of different belief elements for individuals, 1958—1960. [*Source.* Reprinted with the permission of the Macmillan Company from Philip E. Converse, "The Nature of Belief Systems in Mass Publics," in David Apter [ed.], *Ideology and Discontent,* p. 240. Copyright © 1964 by The Free Press of Glencoe, a Division of the Macmillan Company.]

opinion at each of the three interviews. Respondents who did offer an opinion on an issue in each wave often shifted about from agreement to disagreement in a seemingly random fashion. For illustration, Table 2-4 shows the patterns of inconsistent responses found on two selected issues; government involvement in power and housing; and federal involvement in school integration.

In sharp contrast, the respondents were more consistent in their party identification, since under 5 percent of the sample made a complete switch from Democratic to Republican identification or vice versa between 1956 and 1960. Figure 2-1 ranks the opinion items (and the "party identification" question) according to the correlation or consistency of opinions over the 1958 to 1960 period.

One might be tempted to argue that the high degree of opinion turnover is evidence that voters are frequently changing their political opinions in a meaningful fashion, just as open-minded concerned citizens ought to be doing. However, a more acceptable interpretation is that most respondents who appear to have changed their minds actually gave changing responses because they lacked strong conviction on the particular issue. One reason for this interpretation is that although many "conversions" were found in the 1956 to 1960 study, the various pro-to-con changes canceled out those in the opposite direction, so that the distributions of opinions on the issues were quite stable over the time period. If, in fact, the high rate of opinion

Table 2—4. Distributions of Response Sequences in the 1956—58—60 Panel on Two Issues

			Power and Housing	School Segregation
			"The government should leave things like electric power and housing for private businessmen to handle"	"The government in Washington should stay out of the question whether white and colored children go to the same school"
1956	1958	1960		
Agree	Agree	Agree	214	217
Agree	Agree	Disagree	31	38
Agree	Disagree	Agree	26	36
Agree	Disagree	Disagree	20	68
Disagree	Agree	Agree	42	51
Disagree	Agree	Disagree	31	41
Disagree	Disagree	Agree	26	44
Disagree	Disagree	Disagree	59	202
(Avoids Taking Sides in at least One Interview)			681	433
Total Cases			1130	1130

Source. Survey Research Center 1956—58—60 Panel Data.

turnover had represented meaningful opinion change, the shift would probably have been largely in one direction or the other. A second reason for this interpretation is that turnover was found to be greatest on issues like "power and housing" which were rather quiet at the time, and least on the more hotly debated issues like school integration. This could hardly have been the pattern if most of the opinion "conversions" were provoked by highly visible political debates on the issues.

Although scholars agree that the response instability found in the SRC panel study was *not* due to respondents undergoing periodic opinion conversions, they do not agree what the unstable responses mean. By one ingenious interpretation of the data, developed by Philip Converse, virtually all respondents with responses on a given issue changing over time had no true convictions, but were instead expressing random responses or "nonattitudes." This "nonattitude" interpretation has been challenged by some scholars who prefer, what might be called, a "measurement error" interpretation. While the details of the opposing interpretations are too complex to receive full treatment here, we can present brief sketches of the competing points of view.

The "Nonattitudes" Explanation

After analyzing the pattern of responses, Converse suggests that most of the "opinion change" detected in this 1956 to 1960 survey may have been the result of respondents answering in random fashion rather than of meaningful opinion conversion.[3] Converse argues that if people who changed the direction of their opinion between 1956 and 1958 had undergone a real conversion, then their 1958 opinions should have been reasonably good predictors of their opinions in 1960. But, in fact, Converse found that the 1956 to 1958 "converts" were only slightly more likely to repeat their 1958 opinion in 1960 than they were to revert to their earlier 1956 opinion. On the foreign aid issue, for example, people who "switched" from anti-aid to pro-aid over the 1956–1958 period were only slightly more likely to respond favorably to foreign aid in 1960 than those who supported aid in 1956 but opposed it in 1958.

On the "power and housing" question, Converse found that the pattern of responses fit very closely with the results that would be expected if every opinion "changer" had actually been "guessing" or answering "randomly." For example, the two groups who "switched" in opposite directions over one time interval responded virtually alike at a third time. Thus it is possible that the portion of the sample who failed to respond consistently in the same direction over the three interviews were actually answering randomly. Moreover, this assumption that all "change" was actually random allowed Converse to calculate the additional percentage of the sample who answered "consistently" but randomly. Just as three tosses of a coin will yield all "heads" or all "tails" one-fourth of the time, about one-fourth of the people who answered randomly and without real opinions would appear "consistent" on the basis of chance alone. Calculating on the basis of this logic, Converse estimated that less than 20 percent of the adult public held meaningful opinions on the abstract issue of whether the government should leave things like housing and power plants to private enterprise, even though about two-thirds would venture a viewpoint on the matter when asked in a survey.[4]

The "Measurement Error" Explanation

If the "nonattitudes" explanation is correct, the reason why many people give unstable responses to opinion questions is that these individuals lack the amount of political sophistication that is necessary to form crystallized opinions. But contrary to this prediction, it has been found that response instability in the 1956-58-60 panel was equally high for respondents who appeared high in political sophistication and those who appeared low in political sophistication. For this reason, some scholars have suggested a "measurement error" explanation of response instability to survey questions about policy issues.[5] By this interpretation, the "blame" for the response instability is placed not so much on the capabilities of the respondents, as on the survey questions themselves. This is not to say that survey researchers do not know how to ask good questions. Rather, even the best survey question will produce some instability of responses from individuals who generally have weak (although not nonexistent) opinions on the particular issue. By this "measurement error" interpretation, the public is viewed neither as highly opinionated nor as largely void of meaningful opinions. Instead, this interpretation suggests that people generally—whether sophisticated or not— have opinions of sufficiently low intensity that they cannot be estimated with total reliability by simple survey questions.[6]

Knowledge, Intensity, and Opinion

Whether the unstable responses to policy questions are random behavior by nonattitude holders or are ambivalent responses by individuals with low intensity of convictions, the lack of depth to many of the "opinions" that get counted in surveys creates the possibility that the direction of opinion can be quite different among people with strong convictions or who are highly informed, than among people with weak convictions or who are not very informed. For some purposes, one might prefer to discount somewhat the views of the least knowledgeable respondents or of those who voice their opinons with the least intensity. But there is danger here. Imagine, for example, a legislative proposal designed to help the economically disadvantaged. We would probably find poor people more in favor of this proposal than the wealthy, but that poor people would have less understanding or involvement in the outcome than would the wealthy even though they may have the greater stake in the matter. Under such a circumstance, we would resist giving greater weight to the view of the more knowledgeable and intense opinions held disproportionately by wealthy individuals.

On issues that do not disproportionately affect the lives of the less informed or less involved individuals, we might be more willing to give special consideration to informed or involved opinion. Generally, however, the views of the more involved or more informed segments of the public do not clash markedly with those of the public as a whole. The debate over the Panama Canal treaty in 1977-1978 provides one example. While a Gallup poll showed that treaty supporters were more informed about the treaty's details than were the opponents,[7] a CBS-*New York Times* poll showed that treaty opponents were more willing to reward or punish their senators on the basis of their votes on the treaty than were the supporters.[8] Thus, it would have been difficult to argue that the views on one side or the other should have carried any special weight.

Polls only rarely ask respondents to express the intensity as well as the direction of their opinion. But when an intensity measure is available, one seldom finds the direction of "intense" opinion to be opposite of the direction of less intense opinion. This is true even on issues for which one might expect people on one side to have stronger convictions than people on the other. Table 2-5 shows examples on two issues: gun control and the Equal Rights Amendment (ERA). Although polls show most people favor gun control, states have been slow to regulate the sale of firearms. Similarly, although the ERA is apparently favored by a sizeable majority, as of this writing it has not been ratified by the necessary number of state legislatures. A popular explanation for these examples of legislative resistance is that the minorities on these issues have stronger convictions than the majorities. Yet as Table 2-5 shows, both gun control and the ERA draw majority support even from those who feel most strongly about these matters.[9] Cautious conclusions must be drawn from these examples, however. It is difficult to measure intensity of opinion with sufficient precision to identify the very small segment of the public for which a given issue is of such grave importance

Table 2–5. Direction of Opinion by Intensity of Opinion on Two Issues

Gun Control

How important is a candidate's position on permits for guns when you decide how to vote in a congressional election . . . ?

		One of the most important factors	A very important factor	Somewhat important	Not too important
"Would you favor or oppose a law which would require a person to obtain a police permit before he could buy a gun?"	Favor	58%	80%	82%	65%
	Oppose	42%	20%	18%	35%
(Number of Cases)		(31)	(158)	(238)	(170)

Equal Rights Amendment

		Strongly Favor or Strongly Oppose	Somewhat Favor or Somewhat Oppose
"Do you favor . . . or oppose [the Equal Rights] Amendment?"	Favor	68%	75%
	Oppose	32%	25%
(Number of Cases)		(389)	(809)

Sources. [Gun Control] adapted from Howard Schuman and Stanley Presser, "Attitude Measurement and the Gun Control Paradox," *Public Opinion Quarterly* 41 (Winter, 1977-8), pp. 427-438. [ERA] adapted from *General Social Sciences Cumulative Codebook 1972-1977* (Chicago: National Opinion Research Center, 1977), p. 149.

that it is the sole issue of their political concern. The views of such "single-issue" voters sometimes take on special importance to politicians, but it may be beyond the current capabilities of survey research to identify them.

"Doorstep Opinions" and Survey Results

One very real difficulty with interpreting opinion data from surveys is that since many people are responding to questions to which they have not given much previous thought, their replies can vary with even subtle differences in the way the question is worded. Of course, this is not a real problem with questions about voting preference, since there are only a limited number of ways to ask people how they will vote, and because most people do have crystallized preferences. But on policy questions, on which many people do not have crystallized opinions, the wording of the question can often determine the apparent majority position on the issue.

As an example, let us consider what the polls tell us about attitudes toward federal aid to education, an issue on which the bulk of the public has not had very strong convictions over the years. In a number of surveys taken from the late 1930s into the 1960s, the percentage of affirmative responses was generally about two-thirds to simple questions such as, "Do you think the federal government should give money to states to help local schools?"[10] But other questions on the issue that have been only slightly loaded have produced very different opinion breakdowns. For example, back in 1938, when 68 percent responded affirmatively to the simple question indicated above, the approval rate rose to 81 percent among a similar sample who were asked a question that emphasized aid on the basis of need: "Do you think the federal government should give money to help local schools in the poor communities?" On the other hand, when the question makes it clear that state and local responsibility is the alternative to spending federal tax money, majorities have been found to be opposed to federal aid. Thus, only 35 percent gave the pro-aid response to the Gallup Poll in 1947 when it asked: "Would you be willing to pay more taxes to the federal government to raise education levels in the poorer states of this country—or should the poorer states take this responsibility themselves?" Similarly, in 1964 when the Survey Research Center asked respondents to decide whether "the government in Washington should help towns and cities provide education for grade and high school children" or whether "this should be handled by the states and local communities," anti-aid responses outnumbered pro-aid responses by a ratio of three to two. In sharp contrast, an equally responsible poll taken the same year (1964) found the public to favor federal aid by a margin of over two to one when presented with the question:[11] "A broad general program of Federal Aid to education is under consideration, which would include Federal grants to help pay teachers' salaries. Would you be for or against such a program?"

Variations in the question format could not have influenced the distribution of opinion so greatly unless a sizeable portion of the public was so unconcerned or ambivalent on the issue that it could be swayed in different directions by slightly different versions of what was basically one question. Such people were reacting to the positive and negative symbols and images presented in the questions rather than on the basis of deeply felt conviction. Thus, if the question evokes the images of needy children, or if the question allows the issue to be viewed as a referendum on the value of education, many people will respond favorably to the principle of federal aid to education. But they may react negatively if the question evokes the image of tax money being spent or if the issue is presented as one of federal intervention versus the virtues of states rights and local responsibility.

The problem of different response distributions to slightly different questions is not limited only to the issues of lesser public concern, such as federal aid to education. Even on an issue as important as the war in Vietnam, the direction of public sentiment appeared to be quite different when measured by questions evoking different symbolic images. For example, fewer people appeared to be hawkish when asked whether "we did the right thing" getting into the war than when they were asked whether involvement was "a mistake."[12] The authors of an insightful book, *Vietnam and the Silent Majority,* offer the following caution about interpreting polls about public attitudes toward the war.[13]

> The fact that people do not hold very well-formed and thought-out opinions on public issues—even issues as important and well debated as the war in Indochina—explains many of the inconsistencies and seeming rapid changes in public opinion. The specific words that go into a question asked by a pollster may be positive or negative symbols to an individual. If a question is asked in which negative symbols are associated with withdrawal from the war, people sound quite "hawkish" in their responses. Thus people reject "defeat," "Communist take-overs," and "the loss of American credibility." On the other hand, if negative symbols are associated with a pro-war position, the American public will sound "dovish." They reject "killings," "continuing the war," and "domestic costs." Turning the matter upside down, we see the same thing. If positive symbols are associated with the war, the American public sounds "hawkish." They support "American prestige," "defense of democracy," and "support for our soldiers in Vietnam." On the other hand, if positive symbols are associated with "dovish" positions, the people sound "dovish." They come out in support of "peace", worrying about our own problems before we worry about the problems of other people," and "saving American lives."

Variation in question wording even yields evidence of public ambivalence on the crucial issue of pollution control. To a rather visible extent, the public has become conscious of the fact that some sort of environmental crisis exists. For example, between 1965 and 1970, the proportion of the public who would describe the local air-pollution problem as "serious" rose from 28 percent to 69 percent.[14] By 1971, "pollution control" became the area of federal spending that, except for aid to education, the public was least willing to see cut. Still, the public is not entirely convinced that new government programs to combat pollution are urgent. For example, in 1969 only 52 percent told Harris that "programs for improvement of the national environment now receive too little attention and support from the government." When people are reminded that their tax bill might expand to pay for pollution control, they become wary. For example, in 1971 only 59 percent said they were "willing to pay $15 a year more in taxes to finance a federal program to control air pollution." Another survey (in 1969) found only 22 percent "willing" to spend $200 more yearly to "solve our national problems of air and water pollution." Indeed, ordinary people may believe it unfair that they should be the ones to pay for the cleanup of industry-created pollution. If there ever is some taxpayer's revolt against the cost of fighting pollution, patriotic symbols may work as an antidote. For example, a plurality did respond favorably to the following question:

"As you may know, America faces serious pollution problems that will be very expensive to solve. One estimate said it might cost more than $1000 for each family in this country, in order to clean up existing pollution. Do you think that the American people can afford whatever it takes to clean up pollution, or can't they?"

Yes	48%
No	41%
Don't know	11%

Of course students of public opinion have long been aware of ways in which "question sensitivity" may contaminate survey results. It is known, for example, that "agree-disagree" types of items can produce different responses than questions presenting both sides of the issue. When people are asked to agree or disagree with a statement concerning a matter on which they do not have definite opinions, they tend to agree more often than disagree. Thus the percentage who agree with a statement will be greater than the percentage who disagree with a statement supporting the opposite point of view. For instance, compare the responses to two rather opposite statements about academic freedom that were presented to respondents in a 1968 California poll. When asked whether they agreed or disagreed with the statement, "professors in state supported institutions should have freedom to speak and teach the truth as they see it," Californians appeared to support academic freedom by a ratio of 52 to 39. But when opinions were sought on the statement, "professors who advocate controversial ideas or speak out against official policy have no place in a state supported college or university," the same ratio of 52 to 39 was found, but this time the majority was on the side favoring restrictions on academic freedom.[15] Taken out of context, the opinion distribution on either one of these statements would offer misleading evidence of where the majority stood on the right of professors to speak freely in the classroom. Taken together, these two opinion distributions suggest another case where a large portion of the public was without crystallized attitudes.

Another problem of question sensitivity is that if the question includes the hint of how the political parties are polarized on the issue, respondents will gravitate more than usual to their party's position. For example, in 1960 the SRC/CPS twice asked the same respondents whether they agreed or disagreed with the statement, "The government in Washington should see to it that everybody who is willing to work has a job." In one instance, but not the other, the query was prefaced by the obvious partisan cue: "Over the years most Democrats have said that the government in Washington ought to see to it that everyone who wants to work can find a job. Many Republicans do not agree that the government should do this." Table 2-6 shows that Democrats and Republicans in the sample diverged more in their opinions when they were told their parties' positions. Evidently opinions on the issue of full employment were so shallow that many people "shifted" when they "learned" which side of the issue a good Democrat and a good Republican would take.

In similar fashion, people without firm convictions on an issue are likely to support the side that they are led to believe is the "official" or existing policy. This may explain the considerable disparity in levels of support for capital punishment between California, Minnesota, and the nation as a whole, as shown in Table 2-7. Nationwide, the public was about evenly split in 1965 on whether death should be the penalty for murder. But in the California poll, in which people were told (correctly) that the state allowed the death penalty, capital punishment was supported by a 2 to 1 ratio. In the Minnesota poll, in which the sample was told (correctly) that the state had

Table 2−6.   The Impact of a Partisan Cue on "Guaranteed Job" Opinion

"The government should see to it that everyone who is willing to work can get a job."	No Party Cue		Told Democrats Are for and Republicans against	
	Democrats	Republicans	Democrats	Republicans
Percent Agree	78	61	81	42
Percent Disagree	22	39	19	58
	100	100	100	100
N	(498)	(304)	(495)	(305)

Source. Survey Research Center 1960 election data (unweighted sample). Nonopinion holders and undecided are excluded from analysis.

Table 2-7. Question Variation and Opinion on Capital Punishment

	For Capital Punishment	Against	No Opinion
Nationwide: 1965			
Are you in favor of the death penalty for persons convicted of murder?	45%	43%	12%
California: 1963			
As you know, this state has capital punishment—that is, execution—as a form of punishment for criminals. How do you personally feel about capital punishment—would you be in favor of doing away with the death sentence, or do you feel the death sentence should be kept as punishment for serious crimes, as it is now?	56	28	16
Minnesota: 1963			
Minnesota does not have the death sentence for any crime. Do you think Minnesota should or should not permit the death sentence for convicted murderers?	31	62	7

Source. Hazel Erskine, "The Polls: Capital Punishment," *Public Opinion Quarterly, 34* (Summer, 1970), pp. 291-296.

abolished the death penalty, the public came out 2 to 1 against capital punishment. The two states are not sufficiently different in political attitudes to expect such a large difference in opinion if the identical question had been asked in both states. Nor is it likely that most of the Californians or Minnesotans were aware of their states' policy toward capital punishment before the question was asked. Therefore it is probable that the pollsters' questions provided the cue that influenced respondents to support what they were told was the existing practice in their state.

2-2 DISTRIBUTIONS OF OPINION ON MAJOR ISSUES

The preceding discussion may create the erroneous impression that opinion polls are rather useless instruments for gauging public opinion. Our intent is simply to make the reader aware of some of the pitfalls that are involved in the interpretation of polls. Certainly, when they are interpreted with proper caution, polls are an extremely valuable source of information for the study of public opinion.

Sometimes little caution is necessary. For example, when 94 percent said that they "would like to see college administrators take a stronger stand on student unrest" at the same time when polls indicated "student unrest" to be most often stated as the "most important problem facing this country today," the conclusion that many Americans were concerned about the more extreme behavior of student activists is fairly well grounded. But normally, when the polls show that X percent appear to favor a certain policy at a given time, as based on a particular question, we need some anchor by which to measure the significance of the finding. We have already seen that by comparing the responses to similar questions with only slightly different wordings, we can determine whether opinion on the issue is either soft and malleable or rather hard and firm. Also, by comparing the responses to one question to those on slightly different but related issues, we can see what distinctions the public makes in the kinds of policies it is willing to support. Certainly the best anchor is to compare findings over the course of time. If the public displays a different level of support for some policy today than it did a few years ago when asked the same question, then we can say that we have located an important change in public opinion.

Unfortunately, the data that would allow the accurate assessment of trends in political opinion are not as available as one might expect. The reason is that although various polling organizations have been collecting vast amounts of opinion data over the years, it is not very often that they ask the same question in different years. Pollsters naturally ask questions on issues that are of current interest and since the issues that are salient change, so do the questions. For example, questions dealing with civil liberties were asked most often in the "McCarthy era" of the early 1950s when many people thought our basic liberties were threatened. Questions dealing with race relations were not often asked in the 1930s and 1940s when the aspirations of the black minority were given little thought. Today the public is not often polled on economic issues as frequently as had been the case in past decades when differences over the proper extent of government activity in the social welfare sphere comprised the dominant political cleavage of American politics.[16] Even when the polls monitor opinions on the same issue continually over a long time interval, they often vary their questions somewhat, so that the "trends" that develop may be functions of different question wordings.

In the following section we present a brief overview of what the polls do tell us about the distributions of public opinion—both today and in the past—on the broader long-standing political issues. Where possible, trend data are employed. We divided the issues into four broad issue domains: economic or "social welfare" issues, foreign policy, civil rights, and "social issues." Opinions in each of these four domains are examined separately.

Social Welfare

From New Deal days to the present, the American public has generally been receptive to government programs to accomplish social objectives. In fact, it is often said that on social welfare legislation mass opinion is usually well ahead of congressional action. For example, the earliest polls revealed an overwhelming majority in favor of "old-age pensions" prior to the adoption of Social Security in 1936.[17] Continually, majority approval has been found prior to each increase in the federal minimum wage.[18] Also, polls show that most people were at least mildly favorable to federal aid to education and Medicare long before these programs were finally enacted into law in 1965.

Most existing social welfare programs receive overwhelming public support. For example, Table 2-8 shows that in 1976 very few wanted reductions in federal programs to help the less fortunate obtain housing, education, medical care, or employment. Even for "welfare programs," the vast majority opposed reduced spending. The distributions in this table clearly demonstrate that there is little public sentiment for the extreme "conservative" position that the vast set of government social welfare programs should be dismantled. However, most people do not insist on a vigorous increase in the federal government's role either.

The questions shown in Table 2-8 refer to specific government programs or objectives. When asked whether federal spending for domestic programs *in general* should be increased, decreased, or kept at about the same level, people choose the middle category about as often as either extreme. Such a pattern can be seen in Table 2-9, which shows the results of two polls—one from 1964 and one from 1978. The most accurate statement about public attitudes toward federal social welfare legislation may be that the public tends to accept the existing role of the federal government and is somewhat favorably disposed toward the least controversial new proposals.

To the extent it is possible to evaluate trends by comparing the results of similarly worded questions that have been asked the public in different years, it appears that the level of mass support for social welfare legislation has been remarkably stable over recent decades. The clearest evidence is from poll questions on government subsidization of medical care. The stability of support for government help in paying medical expenses is illustrated in Figure 2-2. It shows that between 1956 and 1978, the portion of opinion holders who agreed that the government should "help people get doctors and hospital care at low cost" stayed fairly constant, within the range of 62 to 84 percent.[19] Polls also indicate that over the years a consistent majority has believed that the government has a responsibility to insure full employment. In several polls from 1935 to 1978, opinion holders were decidedly in favor of the notion that the government should insure "that everyone who wants to work has [or "can get" or "can find"] a job.[20] In 1964, 75 percent agreed that "the Federal Government has a responsibility to try to reduce unemployment," while only 18 percent dissented.[21]

However, this consensus in favor of government programs designed to give jobs to the unemployed does not extend to majorities in support of a

Table 2-8. Opinions on Selected Federal Social Welfare Programs, 1976 (in Percent)

[For each of these federal programs, indicate "whether you feel the amount of tax money being spent should be increased, kept at the present level, reduced, or ended altogether."]

	Increased	Kept at Present Level	Reduced	Ended Altogether	Don't Know
Programs to help the unemployed	43	36	14	4	3
Programs to provide adequate housing for all people including low income families	40	34	18	5	3
Federal programs to make a college education possible for deserving young people who could not otherwise afford it?	50	36	8	3	3
Programs to improve medical and health care for all Americans generally, including low income families?	50	35	10	2	3
Providing food stamps for low income families?	22	38	27	10	3
Welfare programs to help low income families?	22	39	14	4	3

Source. William Watts and Lloyd A. Free, *The State of the Nation III* (Lexington: Lexington Books, 1978) pp. 214-216.

Table 2–9. Opinion on Federal Government Power and Spending

Question	Percent
1964	
"Which one of the statements listed on this card comes closest to your own views about government power today?	
1. The Federal Government today has too much power	26
2. The Federal Government is now using just about the right amount of power for meeting today's needs.	36
3. The Federal Government should use its powers even more vigorously to promote the well being of all segments of the people."	31
4. Don't know	7
1978	
"Are you in favor of increasing government spending for domestic programs, reducing government spending, or keeping it about the same?"	
1. Decrease spending	34
2. Keep about same	28
3. Increase spending	28
4. No opinion	9

Sources: Lloyd A. Free and Hadley Cantril, *The Political Beliefs of Americans* (New York: Simon and Schuster, 1966), p. 19; CBS/*New York Times* poll, January 1978.

government responsibility to insure everybody a good standard of living or a guaranteed income. For example, when the SRC/CPS asks whether "the government in Washington should see to it that every person has a job and a good standard of living" or whether "the government should just let each person get ahead on his own," only about two-fifths of the opinion holders favor government assistance. The unwillingness of the public to support a guaranteed income is clearly revealed in the results of a 1969 Gallup Poll.[22]

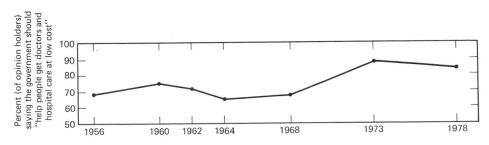

Figure 2-2. Opinion of government subsidation of medical expenses. *(Sources.* SRC/CPS, 1956–1968; NORC, 1973; CBS/*New York Times* poll, 1978.)

As you may know, there is talk about giving every family an income of at least $3200 a year, which would be the amount for a family of four. If the family earns less than this, the government would make up the difference. Would you favor or oppose such a plan?

Favor 32%   Oppose 62%   No Opinion 6%

In contrast, a followup question yielded the following results:

Another proposal is to guarantee enough work so that each family that has an employable wage earner would be guaranteed enough WORK each week to give him a wage of about $60 a week or $3200 a year. Would you favor or oppose such a plan?

Favor 79%   Oppose 16%   No Opinion 5%

Results such as these show that there are limits to the public's willingness to support innovative social welfare proposals. As innovative suggestions turn toward such matters as guaranteeing each family a minimum income, mass opinion is clearly lagging behind the thinking of reformers and government leaders. One reason for this resistance is the widespread mass belief that people who receive financial assistance ought to work for their money, even if the work they do is of little use. Also, when government programs are perceived as benefiting only the lowest income groups—slum dwellers, welfare recipients, and potential "rioters"—few people see themselves as beneficiaries of these policies. As a result, the bulk of the public now sometimes appears on the "conservative" side of current social welfare controversies. An additional factor is that as federal spending programs increase, Americans become less favorable to additional programs. Thus, between 1964 and 1978, the proportion who said "government has gone too far in regulating business and interfering with the free enterprise system" rose from 42 to 58 percent.[23] But such conservative manifestations do not necessarily mean that the public is reacting to specific proposals any differently than it did (or would have done) in the past. Instead, the change has been in the nature of the proposals rather than in public thinking. As the public welfare proposals that are the topic of public debate appear more and more "radical" from the mass perspective, the nonmoving public now sometimes appears to be more conservative than liberal on social welfare issues.

Civil Rights

Mass attitudes on racial questions are probably more highly crystallized than political attitudes on other kinds of issues. Yet if we attempt to locate majority sentiment on civil rights issues, very different opinion distributions can often be obtained with slight variations in the questions and issues put to respondents. For example, in 1968 the Survey Research Center asked people to choose which statement they agreed with most: "white people have a right to keep Negroes out of their neighborhoods if they want to," or "Negroes have a right to live wherevery they can afford to, just like white people." Since 78 percent of those venturing an opinion picked the second statement, there seemingly was a strong consensus in support of equal rights on the volatile issue of open housing. Yet, a year earlier (in 1967), when Gallup asked whether Congress should enact a national "open housing" law, only 35 percent of those who said they knew what the term "open housing" means favored it.[24]

On the issue of school integration too, estimates of the public mood depend on the particular question that is put to survey respondents. Some of this variation is shown in Table 2-10. If white parents are asked whether

Table 2–10. Opinion Distributions on Racial Integration of Schools (in Percent)

		Pro-Integration	Anti-Integration	No Opinion, Other
(1977)	Would you, yourself have any objection to sending your children to a school where a few of the children are blacks? (asked of whites only)	93	7	0
(1977)	Do you think white students and Negro students should go to the same schools or to separate schools?	85	13	2
(1972)	Should the government in Washington "see to it that white and black children go to the same schools . . . or stay out of this area as it is none of its business?"	37	44	19
(1969)	Do you think the racial integration of schools in the United States is going too fast or not fast enough?	22	44	34a
(1977)	In general, do you favor or oppose the busing of black and white children from one school district to another?	16	81	3

Sources. NORC 1977 General Social Survey (questions 1, 2, 5); Center for Political Studies (question 3); Gallup Poll News Release, August 17, 1969 (question 4).
[a]Includes "about right" response (volunteered).

they would object if their children are sent to a school where a few blacks attend, the vast majority say that they would go along. If the issue is whether in principle "white students and Negro students should go to the same schools" rather than "separate schools," more than 80 percent of all respondents give the integrationist response. But if the issue is federal activity—whether "the government in Washington should see to it that white and Negro children are allowed to go to the same school," the public is split about evenly. And if the issue is the pace of existing involvement—whether the federal government is pushing integration too fast, too slowly, or at about the right speed, those who say it is pushing "too fast" vastly outnumber those who say is is going "too slow." On school busing to achieve racial balance, there is overwhelming public opposition.

Whatever else can be concluded from the sampling of civil rights attitudes, polls clearly show that white America has at least rejected the prevalent "white supremacist" ideology that pervaded mass attitudes as recently as a few decades ago. Poll data from the 1930s and 1940s suggest that perhaps a majority of white Americans believed blacks to be intellectually inferior and underserving of equal status with whites. For example, in 1939 only 13 percent agreed that "Negroes should be allowed to live wherever they want to live, and there should be no laws and social pressures to keep them from it."[25] In 1944, only 42 percent of a national sample thought "Negroes should have as good a chance as white people to get any kind of job." By 1963 as evidence of change, 82 percent of adult whites were willing to agree with this statement.[26] A similar change can be seen in white estimates of black intelligence. While as late as 1944 only 44 percent believed that "Negroes are as intelligent as white people," the percentage had rise to 77 percent by 1956.[27]

The steady rise in support for racial integration is shown in Figure 2-3, which displays the rates of agreement with the pro-integration alternatives in three civil rights questions which were asked of white cross sections periodically between 1942 and 1970. On the basis of the three questions, public support for integration of schools, housing, and public transportation facilities all increased by over 30 percent over this period.[28] Other poll questions that have been continually asked since 1963 generally show that the rise in pro-integration sentiment has continued. For example, from 1963 to 1970 the percentage of white parents who said they would have objections to sending their children to "schools where half of the children are Negro" dropped from 33 percent to 24 percent in the North, and—more dramatically—from 78 to 43 percent in the South.[29] Similar declines can be found since 1963 in the percentages who would object to voting for a "qualified Negro" presidential candidate, who oppose the right of blacks to live in homes they can afford, and who say they favor "strict segregation of the races."[30]

Despite the clear decline in the frequency of explicitly "racist" sentiment expressed in surveys of the white public, this trend has not kept pace

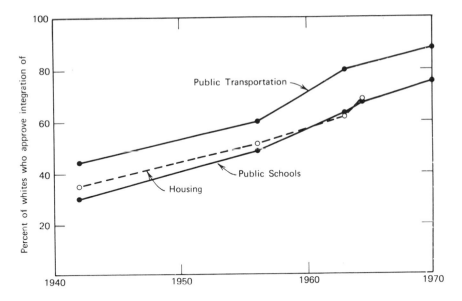

Figure 2-3. Trends in approval of school, housing, and transportation integration. [*Source.* Adapted from Paul B. Sheatsley, "White Attitudes toward the Negro," *Daedalus* (Winter 1966), pp. 219. 222, 235; Andrew M. Greeley and Paul B. Sheatsley, "Attitudes toward Racial Integration," *Scientific American*, 225 (December 1971), pp. 13–19.)

with the rise of black aspirations. One reason for this statement is that support for federal action in the civil rights sphere has remained at a lukewarm level over the years. For example, in the period following the 1954 Supreme Court ruling that school segregation was unconstitutional, public support for the decision in the Gallup poll rose only from 54 percent to 62 percent by 1961.[31] From 1956 to 1972, the public remained about evenly divided on whether the federal government should see to it that "white and Negro children go to the same schools."[32] Also, throughout the 1960s the proportion of the public who thought the federal government was moving "too fast" on integration remained at a fairly constant level.[33]

Polls show that one factor hindering a reduction in civil rights conflict is the persistently unfavorable attitude of most whites toward the civil rights movement. Even in the early 1960s, when black activism emerged in the form of nonviolent demonstrations against institutional segregation in the South, most whites reacted negatively to "demonstrations," "freedom rides," and "sit-ins."[34] As early as 1963, a year before the periodic outbreak of urban riots began, a majority of whites thought the civil rights movement was "more violent than peaceful." Polls taken in 1963 and thereafter have continually shown considerable, though declining, sentiment for the belief that civil rights leaders are pushing "too fast," and that the civil rights movement has "hurt more than helped" the black cause. This tendency can be seen in the poll results reported in Table 2-11.

There is, of course, some pattern to findings we have examined. By and large, most Americans give at least "lip service" to the principles of racial integration and equality. Yet far fewer believe that the federal government should do anything to implement these goals. Fewer still favor accelerations of federal civil rights activity. And the entire civil rights movement has been viewed with distrust by many Americans.

Foreign Policy

Because issues of foreign policy are quite removed from everyday experience, "foreign policy" attitudes are generally held less firmly than opinions on domestic policy. We have already examined the extent to which mass opinions were uncrystallized regarding the war in Vietnam. Taken out of context, responses to any one foreign policy question seldom provide an accurate portrayal of American opinion. For instance, one might believe most Americans favor a more belligerent foreign policy than our national leaders, from the fact that in 1964 the statement "the United States should take a firmer stand against the Soviet Union than it has in recent years" was approved by a ratio of 5 to 2. Yet in the same survey an even greater ratio of support was found for the milder, somewhat contrary view that the United States "should continue to negotiate with Russia with a view toward reducing armaments on both sides."[35] The "foreign aid" issue offers another instance of ambivalent opinion, since most Americans have only the

Table 2–11. Opinion on the Civil Rights Movement

Issue	1964	1968	1972
Some say that the civil rights people have been trying to push too fast. Others feel they haven't pushed fast enough. How about you: Do you think that civil rights leaders are trying to push too fast, are going too slowly, or are they moving about the right speed? (Percent too fast.)	71	65	48
During the past year or so, would you say that most of the actions Negroes have taken to get the things they want have been violent, or have most of these actions been peaceful? (Percent violent.)	64	74	48
Do you think the actions Negroes have taken have, on the whole, helped or, on the whole, have hurt their cause? (Percent hurt.)	64	69	48

Source. Center for Political Studies, Nonopinion holders are excluded from the percentages.

haziest notion about this subject. Table 2-12 shows how in the mid-1960s the opinion distribution on foreign aid varied with the question asked. Although most Americans say they support economic aid for needy countries and have a favorable image of "foreign aid" in general, polls continually reveal the public to be quite receptive to cuts in the foreign aid budget and unfavorably disposed to aiding nations that refuse to follow the U.S. lead in foreign policy.

Given variable results such as these, our understanding of foreign policy attitudes can best be served by following observable trends in opinion. On foreign policy questions, public opinion has undergone several visible shifts since the first days of opinion polls. Most dramatic is the change—precipitated by World War II—in majority sentiment from isolationism to an internationalist outlook regarding the United States' role in world affairs. A glimpse at the results of opinion polls from the late 1930s reveals the extent of isolationist sentiment in that decade and before. In 1937, 70 percent of opinion holders said the American entry in World War I had been a mistake.[36] The same year, 94 percent of opinion holders said the United States should "do everything possible to keep out of foreign wars" rather than "do everything possible to prevent war, even if it means threatening to fight

Table 2–12. Opinion Distributions on Foreign Aid (in Percent)

	Pro-Aid	Anti-Aid	No Opinion, Other
(1964) Should "we give aid to other countries if they need help?	52	19	29
(1966) In general, how do you feel about foreign aid—are you for it or against it?	53	35	12
(1964) And now, what about economic aid to foreign countries? Do you think government spending for this purpose should be kept at least at the present level, or reduced or ended altogether?	32	59[a]	9
(1966) Suppose another country—which is receiving aid from the United States— fails to support the United States in a major foreign policy decision, such as Vietnam. Do you think the United States should continue giving aid to that country, reduce aid, or cut off aid completely?	16	75[a]	9

Sources: Survey Research Center (question 1); *Gallup Opinion Index,* March 1966 (questions 2 and 4); Lloyd A. Free and Hadley Cantril, *The Political Beliefs of Americans* (New York: Simon and Schuster, 1968), p. 72 (question 3).

[a]Combination of responses favoring a reduction and those favoring an end to aid.

countries which fight wars."[37] Although only an infinitesimal number of American citizens supported the German or Japanese side when war broke out in 1939, only about 60 percent of those venturing opinions were willing to go as far as favoring aid to Britain and France "except at the risk of getting into war ourselves." Between 1939 and late 1941, the percentage who said they would vote in favor of entering the war against Germany rose only from 13 percent to 32 percent. By October 1941, 70 percent of voters with opinions considered it more important that Germany be defeated than that America stay out of the war, although the number saying it was "more important to help Britain win" than "keep out of war ourselves" had been only 36 percent 17 months before. Support for war with Japan prior to our entry was even lower: even a month before Pearl Harbor, only 19 percent felt "the United States should take steps to keep Japan from becoming too powerful, even if this means risking a war with Japan."

Once the Japanese attacked Pearl Harbor and we consequently entered World War II, Americans were unified behind the war effort—more so than during any other war in our history. Internationalist sentiment expressed in opinion polls naturally increased, and did not recede once the war was over. For example, between 1942 and 1954 the percentage agreeing that "we take an active part in world affairs" seldom strayed from the average of 71 percent.[38] Also, although a majority in the 1930s thought it would be a mistake for the United States to join the League of Nations, the postwar percentage favoring U.S. withdrawal from the United Nations has never risen above 1 in 8. The low point if isolationist feeling among the mass public probably occurred in the mid-1960s, just before full American involvement in the Vietnam conflict. In 1964, only 18 percent agreed with the "isolationist" statement that "the United States should mind its own business internationally and let other countries get along as best they can on their own."[39]

If the extent of support for the war in Vietnam is a valid indicator of the level of internationalism, then isolationist sentiment has increased once again. Between 1966 and 1971, the percentage who told Gallup that they thought our involvement in Vietnam was a mistake rose steadily from under one-third to a decisive majority. On foreign policy questions that do not deal directly with the war in Southeast Asia, support for the "isolationist" opinion has also been increasing. Whereas 74 percent of opinion holders, in 1964 told the SRC/CPS that the United States "should give aid to other countries if they need help," only 59 percent did so in 1968. Similarly, the proportion who said "It would be better for the United States to keep independent in world affairs" rather than "work closely with other nations" more than doubled—from 10 percent to 22 percent between 1963 and 1969.[40] By 1976, one respondent in three would say the United States should "stay out of world affairs" rather than "take an active part in world affairs."[41]

Of course, today the relevant foreign policy question may not be the extent of American involvement in world affairs so much as the manner in which the powerful United States conducts its foreign policy, particularly in relation to the Communist world. Through the years, mass attitudes toward the Soviet Union have generally followed the lead of foreign policy. During World War II, when the United States and Russia were allies, favorable attitudes toward the USSR grew until at war's end 55 percent said "Russia can be counted on to cooperate with us once the war is over." Such trust diminished rapidly thereafter; by October 1946 the percentage who thought Russia could "be trusted to cooperate with us during the next few years" dropped to 28 percent. By the late 1940s, most people thought it more important "to stop Soviet expansion in Europe and Asia than avoid major war." During the Korean War in the early 1950s, a majority of Americans polled said they expected a war with Russia during their lifetime.[42]

Since the mid-1950s, Americans have taken a more relaxed stand in respect to the Soviet threat. Decreasing minorities in the 1960s foresaw war with Russia in the near future. The melting of Cold War attitudes can be seen in the growing frequency with which Americans said they felt "favorable" toward the Soviet Union—from 7 percent in 1957 to 18 percent in 1967 and 34 percent in 1977.[43] Americans even began to reject the notion that

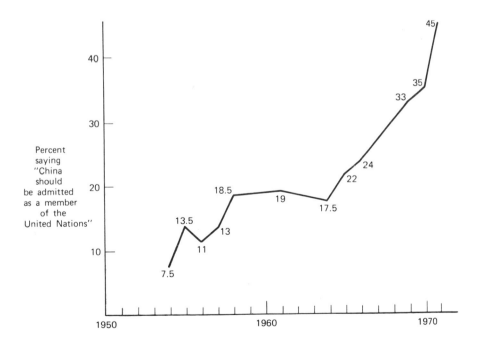

Figure 2-4. Increasing support for admitting China to the UN. *(Sources.* Hazel Erskine, "The Polls: Red China and the UN." *Public Opinion Quarterly*, 35 (Spring 1971), p. 125; *Gallup Opinion Index*, June, 1971, p. 16. For some years the results are the averages of more than one poll.

Communist nations always act in concert. For example, by 1967 most who ventured opinions thought that "if trouble ever broke out between the United States and China. . . Russia would be more likely to be on our side than on China's side." By the same date, China had replaced the Soviet Union as the major threat to world peace in the eyes of over 75 percent of the Opinion-holding public. Even so, support for admission of Red China to the United Nations has been rising steadily. As Figure 2-4 shows, support in Gallup Polls for Chinese admissions rose steadily between 1954 and 1971. This trend is perhaps the clearest indication from the polls of the long-term change in American attitudes toward the Communist world.

The "Social Issues"

In recent years, a new set of issues has entered the American political arena. We refer to the various components of what has been termed the "social issue" in American politics.[44] In its broadest context, the term "social issue" might apply to all conflicts between the forces of change and the forces of resistance to deviations from the "traditional moral values." Here we focus on the political aspects of the social issues: "law and order," "permissiveness," "dissent," "campus unrest," and the like.

The increasing public concern about these issues has been reflected in the kinds of questions the commercial polls have been asking in recent years. Some examples of the Gallup Poll's recent "social issue" questions and the responses are shown in Table 2-13. Overwhelmingly in some instances, the public clusters on the "conservative" side of these issues. A similar pattern is found in the results of a series of survey questions on protest and dissent that were asked the public in 1968 and 1970. As Table 2-14 shows, sizeable proportions of opinion holders unqualifiably disapproved of peaceful sit-ins, violating laws one feels to be unjust, and (in 1968) even lawful protest. The bulk of the remainder chose the option that their approval or disapproval of the kind of activity in question would "depend on the circumstances." This hostility to even the milder forms of political protest is consistent with earlier findings regarding the public's tolerance level for dissent. For example, in the early 1950s, majorities rejected the right of Communists, Socialists, or opponents of churches and religion to speak in their communities.[45]

Since most of the issues reflected in Tables 2-13 and 2-14 are relatively new, it is difficult to establish trends. Probably, if these questions had been asked of a national sample 20 years ago, the public would have responded even more conservatively. We do know from polls that attitudes regarding marijuana, pornography, and abortion have become somewhat more liberal or "permissive" throughout the 1970s. Similarly, as discussed in greater de-

Table 2-13. Opinion Distribution on "Social Issues" (in Percent)

		"Liberal"	"Conservative"
Divorce:	Should divorce in this country be easier or more difficult to obtain than it is now? (NORC, 1977)	Easier, 31	More Difficult, 51
Marijuana:	Do you think the use of marijuana should be legal or not? (Gallup, 1977)	Yes, 28	No, 66
Pornography:	Do you think the standards of this community regarding the sale of sexually explicit material should be stricter than they are now, not as strict, or kept as they are now? (Gallup, 1977)	Not as strict, 6	Stricter, 45
Abortion:	Would you favor [a constitutional amendment] which would prohibit abortions or would you oppose it? (Gallup, 1976)	Oppose, 49	Favor, 45
Gay Rights:	Do you think homosexual relations between consenting adults should or should not be legal? (Gallup, 1977)	Should, 43	Should not, 43

tail in Chapter 4, the public has grown more tolerant toward unpopular viewpoints.

On "law and order" issues, however, polls show a trend toward increasing conservatism. For example, between 1965 and 1977 the proportion who said that the courts in their area were "not harsh enough" rose from 48 percent to 88 percent.[46] Capital punishment is one "law and order" issue on which the public has been polled continuously over a long period of time. As Figure 2-5 shows, support for the death penalty declined steadily from the late 1930s into the 1960s but has noticeably grown since then. Perhaps because of its perceived social liberalism, the public prestige of the Supreme Court has declined. Between 1963 and 1969, the portion of the public who rated the Court as "excellent" or "good" dropped from 43 percent to 33 percent.[47]

Table 2-14. Opinion Distributions on the Right to Protest (in Percent)

Issue		Approve	Depends on Circumstances	Disapprove
How about taking part in protest meetings or marches that are permitted by the local authorities?	(1968)	19	27	54
	(1974)	16	43	41
How about refusing to obey a law that one thinks is unjust, if the person feels so strongly about it that he is willing to go to jail rather than obey the law?	(1968)	15	24	61
	(1974)	15	42	43
Suppose all the methods have failed and the person decides to try to stop the government from going about its usual activities with sit-ins, mass meetings, demostrations, and things like that?	(1968)	8	18	74
	(1974)	8	40	53

Source: Center for Political Studies. Nonopinion holders are excluded from the percentages.

2-3 STABILITY OF OPINION DISTRIBUTION OVER TIME

From the periodic fluctuations in presidential election results, it sometimes appears that the American public undergoes periodic swings of political mood, either from "liberal" to "conservative" or vice versa. An increase in the vote for the Democratic party is often interpreted as a sign that the voters

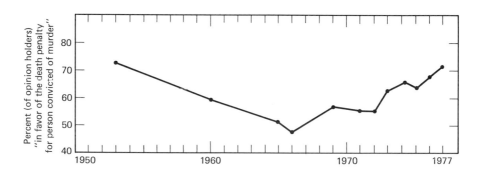

Figure 2-5. Changing attitudes toward capital punishment, *(Sources.* Recomputed from Gallup polls, 1953–1972; NORC polls, 1973–1977.)

are becoming more liberal, while a Republican trend in the vote is sometimes taken as a signal of increasing conservatism on the part of the electorate. In Chapter 1, we learned that the frequencies of Democratic and Republican party identification within the electorate remain relatively stable even when party fortunes in presidential contests undergo sharp changes. Similarly, we have found that trends in public opinion on policy issues are not nearly as volatile as short-term swings in the election fortunes of the two major parties would suggest. Our review of the results of opinion surveys has disclosed a few instances in which the distribution of opinion on an issue has changed somewhat over the course of time. But these shifts—such as the declines in white racist sentiment and in "cold war" attitudes—can best be

Table 2–15. Opinion on Eight Issues in 1972 and 1976

	Percent in 1972	Percent in 1976
Guaranteed Standard of Living		
government [should guarantee] job and good standard of living	41	36
government should let each person get ahead on his own	59	64
Medical Care		
government insurance plan	53	50
private insurance plan	47	50
Tax Reform		
increase the tax rate for high income	54	48
have the same tax rate for everyone	46	52
Aid to Minorities		
government should help minority groups	44	44
minority groups should help themselves	56	56
Busing		
bus to achieve school integration	10	11
keep children in neighborhood schools	90	89
Rights of Accused Criminals		
protect rights of accused	43	45
stop crime regardless of rights of accused	57	55
Marijuana		
make use of marijuana legal	24	31
set penalties higher than they are now	76	69
Women's Rights		
men and women should have equal role	61	69
women's place is in the home	39	31

Source. Center for Political Studies. For the full forms of the questions, see Appendix B.

seen over a span of many years. In the short run, opinion distribution on long standing issues is generally quite stable.

As a demonstration of this stability, Table 2-15 compares the distributions of policy preferences in 1972 and 1976 on eight long-standing issues of American politics. Respondents in the two years were asked the identical set of questions on eight issues. Despite the Democratic trend in presidential voting from 1972 to 1976, there was no tendency over this period toward an increase in "liberal" responses to the eight questions shown in Table 2-15. Nor was there a general shift in the conservative direction during this period when many commentators saw a shift in the public mood toward growing conservatism. A similar stability can be found in opinions from earlier four-year periods.

Seemingly the best way to locate trends of liberalism or conservatism on the part of the public would be simply to record changes in the degree to which people call themselves "liberals" or "conservatives." As shown in the next chapter, self-rankings as "liberals" or "conservatives" are of questionable value for the reason that many people lack adequate understanding of these terms. Yet we are obliged to note an obvious recent trend in self-placement on the liberal-conservative spectrum. In polls taken between the late 1930s and the mid-1960s, the public remained about evenly divided between people who called themselves "liberals" and self-declared "conservatives."[48] But then a "conservative" shift began, so by 1970 "conservatives" were outnumbering "liberals" as much as 2 to 1 (see table 2-16). This post-1964 shift in the "liberal-conservative" trend line is puzzling since, as we have seen, the public's stand on traditional political issues did not noticeably become more conservative over this period. Most likely, the sudden shift toward "conservatism" reflects the increasing public concern about the so-called "social issues," on which people are generally conservative. It used

**Table 2-16. The Trend in Self-Identification as "Liberal" and "Conservative,"
1964-1978**

	Very Liberal	Moderately Liberal	Middle of the Road	Moderately Conservative	Very Conservative	Don't Know
1964	6	20	34	24	6	10
1970	4	16[a]	35	31[a]	9	5
1972	8	18[a]	33	23[a]	14	4
1974	5	17	29	32	10	8
1976	6	19	31	31	9	4
1978	4	19	27	32	10	8

Sources: (1964) Lloyd Free and Hadley Cantril, *The Political Beliefs of Americans* (New York: Simon and Schuster, 1968), p. 222; (1970, 1972) *Gallup Opinion Index;* (1978) Adam Clymer, "More Conservatives Share 'Liberal' Views," *New York Times,* January 22, 1978; (1974-1976) Roper Poll cited by Clymer.
aWording in 1970 and 1972 was "fairly" liberal or conservative.

to be that the popular conception of the difference between liberals and conservatives involved the dimension of relative willingness to support federal programs on which the public gives relatively "liberal" responses. But, in recent years, the terms "liberal" and "conservative" have been more frequently applied to the dimensions of "tolerance" or "permissiveness" versus a more "strict" attitude on social issues on which people are generally conservative. Thus, in one sense, the relative "liberalism" of the public can shift with changes in the issues that are considered to be most important even though on particular issues there is no general shift of opinion.[49]

2-4 CONCLUSION

In this chapter we examine what can be learned from simply studying the distributions of opinion on political issues that are reported in the tabulation of survey results. We have seen that poll results are often contaminated by the responses of the many people who have less than well-informed opinions. Especially, we find that slight differences in the question wording can sometimes produce dramatic differences in the distribution of opinion. Because of this difficulty, the best way to analyze opinion breakdowns on policy issues is to follow opinion on a question over time. Doing this discloses some instances of opinion change. But, especially in the short run, the distributions of policy positions remain stable over time. That is, even though individuals often have opinions so underdeveloped that they seem to change their minds on political issues from one interview to the next, there is usually little change in the net breakdown of pro and con opinions from one time period to the next.

The findings in this chapter far from exhaust the kinds of information that can be extracted from opinion polls. By looking at the simple raw distributions of opinion we have only scratched the surface. For example, survey analysis allows us to examine the relationships between opinions on different issues, to locate group differences in opinions, and to examine the important question of the relationship between issue opinions and voting behavior. These and other topics that demand the employment of survey research are explored in the following chapters.

FOOTNOTES FOR CHAPTER 2

1. Philip E. Converse, Aage R. Clausen, and Warren E. Miller, "Electoral Myth and Reality, the 1964 Election." *American Political Science Review*, 59 (June 1965), pp. 332–335.

2. "Gallup Poll News Release," July 27, 1969.

3. Philip E, Converse, "The Nature of Belief Systems in Mass Publics," in David Apter (ed.), *Ideology and Discontent* (New York: The Free Press of Glencoe, 1964), pp. 238–245; Philip E. Converse, "Attitudes and Non-Attitudes: Continuation of a Dialogue," in Edward R. Tufte (ed.) *The Quantitative Analysis of Social Problems* (Reading, Mass: Addison Wesley, 1970), pp. 188–189.

4. Converse, "The Nature of Belief Systems," p. 239.

5. Christopher Achen, "Mass Political Attitudes and the Survey Response," *American Political Science Review*, 69 (December 1975), pp. 1218–1231; Robert S. Erikson, "The SRC Panel Data and Mass Political Attitudes," *British Journal of Political Science*, 9 (January 1979), pp. 89–114.

6. In the 1956-58-60 panel, politically sophisticated respondents were more likely to offer opinions. However, if one examines only those who offered opinions on a given issue in all three waves, the opinions offered by highly sophisticated respondents were no more stable over time than those offered by the less sophisticated (Erikson, "The SRC Panel Data". On the other hand, if the liberalism-conservatism of very sophisticated people is measured by a composite of several survey questions, long-term stability can be found. A long-term study of Bennington College students in the 1930s disclosed a remarkable consistency between the political attitudes they held during college and their attitudes 25 years later. See Theodore M. Newcomb et al, *Presistence and Change: Bennington College and its Students after Twenty-five Years* (New York: Wiley, 1967).

7. *Gallup Opinion Index*, December 1977, pp. 13, 14.

8. News Release, CBS News, *New York Times* Poll, Part 2, April 1978, p. 9.

9. For more information on the relationship between direction and intensity of opinion on the issue of gun control, see Howard Schuman and Stanley Presser, "Attitude Measurement and the Gun Control Paradox," *Public Opinion Quarterly*, 41, (Winter 1977–78), pp.

10. Except where noted, this and the following survey questions dealing with the subject of federal aid to education are from the Gallup Polls reported in Frank J. Munger and Richard F. Fenno, Jr., *National Politics and Federal Aid to Education* (Syracuse: Syracuse University Press, 1962), pp. 91–96.

11. Lloyd A. Free and Hadley Cantril, *The Political Beliefs of Americans* (New York: Simon and Schuster, 1968), p. 13.

12. John E. Mueller, "Trends in Popular Support for the Wars in Korea and Vietnam," *American Political Science Review*, 65 (June 1971), p. 363.

13. Milton J. Rosenberg, Sidney Verba, and Philip E. Converse, *Vietnam and the Silent Majority* (New York: Harper and Row, 1970), pp. 24–25.

14. This result and others reported in this paragraph are found in Hazel Erskine, "The Polls: Pollution and Its Cost," *Public Opinion Quarterly*, 36 (Spring 1972), pp. 120–135.

15. These questions are from the "Field Research Corporation's California Poll" of January 1968, as reported in *Gallup Opinion Index*, March 1968, p. 11.

16. A tabulation of some of the shifts in the types of questions that pollsters ask is found in Hazel Gaudet Erskine, "The Polls: Some Gauges of Conservatism," *Public Opinion Quarterly*, 28 (Spring 1964), pp. 154–155. The best discussion of opinion trends from 1936 through 1970 is Rita James Simon's *Public Opinion in America: 1936–1970* (Chicago: Rand McNally, 1974).

17. For example, in one of the first national polls on the subject (1935), 89 percent said that they were "in favor of old-age pensions for needy persons." *Source:* Hadley Cantril, *Public Opinion: 1935–1946* (Princeton: Princeton University Press, 1951), p. 541.

18. Hazel Gaudet Erskine, "The Polls: Attitudes toward Organized Labor," *Public Opinion Quarterly*, 26 (Summer 1962), p. 293; *Gallup Poll Index*, September 1965, p. 17.

19. The wording of the medical care question in 1964 and 1968 is slightly different from that of the other years shown in Figure 2-2. This may account for the slight dip in support for government aid in 1964 and 1968. In 1968, respondents were asked whether the government in Washington should "help people get doctors and hospital care at low cost" or whether the government should "stay out of this." In the other years, respondents were asked simply whether

they agreed or disagreed with the statement: "The government ought to help people get doctors and hospital care at low cost."

20. When asked whether the government should ensure that everyone who wants to work has a job, national samples have distributed themselves as follows:

	Should	Should Not	No Opinion, Other
1935 (Fortune)	77	20	3
1939 (Fortune)	61	32	7
1956 (SRC)	56	27	17
1958 (SRC)	57	26	17
1960 (SRC)	59	24	17
1973 (NORC)	43	26	31
1978 (CBS/NYT)	74	22	4

21. Free and Cantril, p. 14.

22. *Gallup Opinion Index*, January 1969, pp. 20–21.

23. Adam Clymer, "More Conservatives Share 'Liberal' Views," *New York Times*, January 22, 1978.

24. *Gallup Opinion Index*, April 1967, p. 15.

25. Hazel Erskine, "The Polls: Negro Housing," *Public Opinion Quarterly*, 31 (Fall 1967).

26. Hazel Erskine, "The Polls: Negro Employment," *Public Opinion Quarterly*, 32 (Spring 1968), p. 132.

27. Hazel Gaudet Erskine, "The Polls: Race Relations," *Public Opinion Quarterly*, 26 (Spring 1962), p. 138.

28. The exact forms of these questions were: "Do you think white and Negro students should go to the same schools, or to separate schools?" "If a Negro with the same income and education as you have moved into your block, would it make any difference to you?" "Generally speaking, do you think there should be separate sections for Negroes in streetcars and buses?" In some instances in Figure 2-3, the results of more than one survey taken in the same years are averaged together.

29. *Gallup Opinion Index*, May 1970, p. 5.

30. The proportion who said they would vote for their party's presidential nominee if he were a "well-qualified man" and "happened to be a Negro" rose from 47 percent in 1963 to 67 percent in 1969. *(Source: Gallup Opinion Index*, April 1969, p. 6.) According to Center for Political Studies data, the percentage of opinion holders who agreed that "Negroes have a right to live wherever they can afford to, just like white people" rose from 69 percent in 1964 to 78 percent in 1970. Between 1964 and 1976, the percentages of opinion holders telling the Center for Political Studies that they favored "strict segregation" (rather than "desegregation" or "something in between") declined from 23 percent to 10 percent. Over the same period, the percentage favoring "desegregation" rose slightly from 32 percent to 41 percent.

31. Erskine, "The Polls: Race Relations," p. 140.

32. Questions asked on this subject by the SRC/CPS have varied somewhat. In 1956, 1958, and 1960, the percentages of opinion holders who disagreed with the statement "the government in Washington should stay out of the question of whether white and colored children go to the same school" were, respectively, 47 percent, 48 percent, and 51 percent. In 1962, the percentage agreeing with the statement "the government in Washington should see to it that white

and colored children are allowed to go to the same school'' was 61 percent. In later surveys, respondents were asked whether the government should "see to it that white and black [Negro] children go to the same schools'' or whether the government should "stay out of this area as it is none of the government's business.'' The percentages of opinion holders giving a response in favor of integration were 52 percent in 1964, 58 percent in 1966, 47 percent in 1968, 57 percent in 1970, and 48 percent in 1972. In 1976, only 38 percent of the responses were favorable, but much of the opposition that year was in the context of the busing issue.

33. See the tabulations reported in Hazel Erskine, "The Polls," *Public Opinion Quarterly*, 32 (Fall 1968), pp. 513–514, and (Winter 1968–1969), p. 702. The question was: "Do you think the Kennedy [Johnson] administration is pushing racial integration too fast, or not fast enough?''

34. A summary of poll results on public attitudes toward racial demonstrations is found in Hazel Erskine, "The Polls: Demonstrations and Race Riots.'' *Public Opinion Quarterly*, 31 (Winter 1967–1968), pp. 654–677.

35. Free and Cantril, pp. 83–84.

36. Ibid., p. 62

37. This and the remaining findings reported in this paragraph are from the unpublished paper by Alfred O. Hero, Jr., "Public Reactions to Federal Policy: Some Comparative Trends.''

38. William R. Caspary, "The Mood Theory: A Study of Public Opinion and Foreign Policy," *American Political Science Review*, 64 (June 1970), pp. 536–537.

39. Free and Cantril, p. 64.

40. *Gallup Opinion Index*, March 1969, p. 21.

41. National Opinion Research Center, 1976 General Social Survey.

42. Hero, "Public Reactions.''

43. *Gallup Opinion Index*, July 1972; Gallup Poll Release, May 8, 1967; National Opinion Research Center, 1977 General Social Survey.

44. See especially the popular treatment by Richard M. Scammon and Ben J. Wattenberg; *The Real Majority* (New York: Coward-McCann, 1970).

45. Samuel Stouffer, *Communism, Conformity, and Civil Liberties* (Garden City: Doubleday, 1955).

46. *Gallup Opinion Index*, March 1969, p. 12; National Opinion Research Center, 1977 General Social Survey.

47. Gallup Poll Release, June 15, 1969.

48. Results of polls from 1938 to 1962 that asked the public to pick between the "liberal" and "conservative" choice are summarized in Erskine, "The Polls: Some Gauges of Conservatism," pp. 155–158.

49. We can see evidence of the changing meanings of the terms "liberal" and "conservative" from the dramatic changes in the self-ranking tendencies of different groups. Southerners were once more inclined to call themselves "liberals," while the reverse is true today. Similarly, reflecting the former impact of economic issues, self-declared "liberals" were most frequently found among the least educated. However this relationship is also reversed today. Although there once was little tendency for the young to be more "liberal" than their elders in self-identification, this gap has increased markedly since the early 1960s.

CHAPTER 3

Ideology and Political Opinions: the Search for Consistency in Public Opinion

Although the term "ideology" is elusive in meaning, it is generally assumed that a person's "political ideology" is his set of beliefs about the proper order of society and how it can be achieved.[1] One can think of a strong ideology as a "prism" that filters a person's view of the political world: the central elements of a person's belief system restrict or constrain the individual's views on specific political issues. The role of ideology is most apparent when we examine the set of beliefs held by people with viewpoints so unusual that they are labeled political "extremists." For example, the devout members of the John Birch Society are forced by their belief that there is a pervasive internal Communist conspiracy toward the conclusion that the American involvement in Vietnam was actually a Communist plot.[2] On the other hand, strict adherents to Marxist ideology interpret the Vietnam conflict as a war of capitalistic imperialism. To most Americans both views appear to go against the grain of reality.

Although few Americans have ideological outlooks of either the far left or the far right, it is often assumed that there exists a more modest division of the American people between "liberals" and "conservatives." This distinction has considerable meaning when one describes the opinions or behavior of very politically active people. For example, an individual's political opinions on even widely disparate subjects (such as a foreign policy issue and a domestic policy issue) are somewhat predictable from one another, if one is talking about delegates to national political conventions[3] or congressional candidates.[4] The same appears to be true for people such as syndicated political columnists. If one knows a columnist's bias toward most political issues, one can often successfully predict what he would write about other issues.

   This chapter takes the reader on a search for patterns of consistency among the political opinions held by members of the public. Chapter 2 showed that the public does not display strong opinions on most political issues. Consistent with this pattern, most Americans are largely indifferent to the liberal versus conservative battles fought among members of the more activist strata. To be sure, a respectable portion of the public understands the common meaning of the terms "liberal" and "conservative." Yet people do not normally behave as self-conscious liberals or conservatives, aligning their beliefs according to a general ideological commitment. Partisanship, as we shall see, plays a slightly greater role in shaping political opinions, since many people do achieve some consistency between their issue stances and those that predominate among the leaders of their favored political party.

3-1 IDEOLOGY AS LIBERALISM-CONSERVATISM: ARE AMERICANS IDEOLOGUES?

To what do the ideological terms "liberal" and "conservative" actually refer? At the philosophical level, political thinkers who have reputations as liberals or conservatives depart from each other in several, somewhat overlapping ways. Conservatives view society as a control for man's intrinsically base impulses; liberals view man's condition as relative to the quality of his society. Conservatives consider men to be inherently unequal and due unequal rewards; liberals are equalitarian. Conservatives venerate tradition and—most of all—order and authority; liberals believe planned change brings the possibility of improvement.[5] Of course, people who are liberal or conservative in their practical politics need not be strict adherents to the "philosophy about man" that is associated with their particular ideological label. Nevertheless, we can see the implications of these philosophical distinctions at work in the common application of the ideological labels to particular political points of view. Conservatives are more afraid than liberals of "big government" except on matters of law and order; in foreign policy, conservatives are more aggressive than liberals in their Cold War posture and are more afraid of Communism. Conservatives are more likely to see harmful consequences of government attempts to help the disadvantaged, while liberals see the advantages.[6]

   These kinds of relative distinctions are familiar to people who follow politics closely. But does the language of ideology have any meaning for the general public? When asked in a survey, most people will categorize themselves as either liberal or conservative, since few will refuse such labels when given forced-choice questions. But since many people respond arbitrarily to survey questions, the significance of the apparent willingness of people to give themselves ideological labels may be cast in doubt. Indeed, when people are also given the safe "middle of the road" alternative, about one-third will choose it. Moreover, when people are asked whether they feel "warm," "cold," or "neutral" toward "liberals" and "conservatives," only about 20 percent clearly differentiate between the two ideological groups by responding "warm" toward one, but "cold" toward the other.

Knowledge of the Ideological Terms

To learn whether the mass public has much understanding of the ideological terms, we can examine what people say the terms stand for, and whether, in fact, self-classification as liberal or conservative is a good predictor of the opinions a person will express on particular issues. Actually, many people seem capable of assigning the correct meanings to the ideological terms. For example, a study by Louis Harris showed that substantial percentages of the American public correctly perceived the conservative and liberal positions on various issues of the day. Forty-four percent versus 22 percent interpreted the desire to "stop being permissive with student protesters" to be the conservative rather than liberal position, and "getting tougher on the subject of crime and law and order" was thought to be a conservative position (48 percent to 23 percent). Liberal positions may be more clearly seen. The statement "help[ing] blacks move faster toward equality" was thought to be liberal by 54 percent, with only 17 percent thinking it was a conservative position; and 51 percent versus 19 percent thought "increasing federal programs to help the poor" to be liberal.[7]

These percentages can be viewed in two ways. Majorities or near majorities can correctly identify the liberal and conservative sides of major political issues. But one must also recognize that some 20 percent were persistently incorrect in their labeling, and another 30 percent claimed not to know. Also, on some additional issues (for example, Vietnam and taxing corporations), Harris found no public consensus on how the ideological terms should be applied.

Table 3-1. Public Views of Presidential Candidates' Political Ideologies, 1972 and 1976

	1972		1976	
	Nixon	McGovern	Ford	Carter
Conservative	42%	6%	43%	11%
Moderate	15	6	11	12
Liberal	9	53	8	38
Don't Know[a]	32	35	38	40
	98%	100%	100%	101%

Source: CPS 1972 and 1976 Election data.
[a]Includes respondents who "haven't thought much about" ideological labels.

Although there is a considerable amount of "guessing," people tend to apply the correct ideological labels to visible political figures and to issue stances. During presidential campaigns, many people are able to associate the presidential candidates with appropriate ideological labels. Table 3-1 shows some examples from recent presidential elections. In the "ideological" elections of 1972, voters displayed a clear tendency to rate McGovern as a liberal and a lesser tendency to rate Nixon as a conservative. Even in the less ideological 1976 contest, voters generally saw Carter as liberal or moderate and Ford as conservative or moderate. Correct rating of a politican on the liberal-conservative scale is not an isolated phenomenon peculiar to recent elections. Back in 1939, over 90 percent of a Gallup sample could label President Roosevelt as "liberal" or "radical" and correctly tag former President Hoover with the "conservative" label.[8]

In a 1960 study, described by Converse, people were asked which party they, or most people, considered to be more conservative.[9] People who responded with an answer (or a guess) were then asked what "people have in mind when they say that the Republicans (Democrats) are more conservative than the Democrats (Republicans)?" From the responses, the "maximum estimate of reasonable recognition" of the ideological labels and their proper association with the two major political parties was put at slightly more than 50 percent.[10] This figure represents the percentage who said the Republicans were considered more conservative and who gave some sort of "correct" definition of the term "conservative." Thus, it is estimated that about half the public recognizes ideological labels. But, rather than raising questions of "broad philosophy," most of the "correct" answers focused on narrow issues, such as unemployment compensation or highway building. Many focused on the somewhat narrow distinction that conservatives save money and liberals spend it. Typical respondents said the Republicans were more conservative because "they vote against the wild spending sprees the Democrats get on," and because "they pay as you go."[11] In Converse's study, respondents were classified as able to conceptualize the "conservative" label in terms of broad philosophical distinctions if they touched on postures toward such matters as change, the welfare state, the power of the federal government, or the relationship between the government and the individual. Only 17 percent of the sample associated the conservative label, by some correct philosophical definition of the term, with the Republic party. Perhaps the lesson to be learned from this analysis is that people find it easier to apply the ideological terms to policy positions that are emphasized in the political rhetoric of the moment than to longstanding or abstract philosophical orientations. In 1960, the year of the survey we have been discussing, it was easy to apply ideological terms to government spending versus balancing budgets. During the unrest of the late 1960s, the ideas that conservatives are firm on "law and order," while liberals are more "soft" or "permissive" entered into the public's conceptualization of the terms.

A 1978 CBS/*New York Times* poll shows the extent to which the public's views of the ideological labels have shifted.[12] Respondents were asked for their interpretation of "the biggest difference between liberal views and conservative views." Predictably, only about half (53 percent) ventured an answer. Only 19 percent responded in terms of government spending or government control. Seven percent answered in terms of liberal vs. conservative differences in attitude toward change. Seventeen percent gave responses that were categorized as involving differences between the "personality characteristics" of liberals and conservatives. We can see that over the years the public has altered its conception of the meaning of conservative and liberal. These changes may indeed parallel actual distinctions among liberal and conservative senators and representatives. All of the prominent public conceptions of what these words mean would seem to have some validity although the valid distinctions are held by only a minority of the public.

When survey respondents are asked to classify themselves on the liberal-conservative spectrum, are they reasonably correct in how they do so? That is, can one predict that self-identified liberals will take liberal viewpoints on particular issues, and that the opposite stands will be taken by those who call themselves conservatives? The limited evidence on this subject does show an association of this kind. Some examples of the relationships between ideological self-placement and positions on specific issues are shown in Table 3-2. Although it is not surprising to find that self-declared "liberals" take more liberal positions than do self-declared "conservatives," the strength of these relationships suggests that at least to a substantial minority of the public, the liberal-conservative continuum has genuine meaning. The tendency for ideological self-identification to correspond to actual issue positions can be seen more clearly when issue positions are measured as a composite over several issues. Table 3-3 shows this. As measured by their composite stands over several issues, people who are very liberal overwhelmingly identify themselves as liberals, and people who are very conservative overwhelmingly identify themselves as conservatives. It may also be noted that people who cannot identify themselves as liberal, moderate, or conservative tend to cluster in the center of the political spectrum as measured by their stands on specific issues.[13]

The historical trend regarding the way self-described liberals and conservatives divide on issues suggests that the meanings of the liberal and conservative concepts among the mass public have undergone considerable evolution. According to Hero's extensive analysis of historical poll data, it was during the New Deal Era of the 1930s that self-declaration as a liberal or conservative was the best indicator of one's social welfare opinions.[14] But it is only relatively recently that the liberal-conservative distinction has been

Table 3-2. Ideological Preference and Opinions on Selected Policy Issues, 1976

Belief	Support Among Self-Declared Liberals	Support Among Self-Declared Conservatives
The government should guarantee "that every person has a job and a good standard of living"	55%	17%
"There should be a government insurance plan which would cover all medical and hospital expenses"	73%	30%
The government "should make every possible effort to improve the social and economic position of blacks and other minority groups"	67%	28%
"To protect the legal rights of those accused of committing crimes is more important than to stop criminal activity"	61%	32%
"The use of marijuana should be made legal"	69%	23%

Source: Center for Political Research, 1976 election data. For the full text of the opinion questions, see Appendix B.

Table 3-3. Correspondence of Ideological Self-Ratings and Summary of Positions on Ten Issues, 1976

Ideological Self-Rating	Summary of Positions on Ten Issues[a]				
	Very Liberal	Liberal	Center	Conservative	Very Conservative
Liberal	81%	41%	15%	6%	4%
Moderate	8	21	30	24	20
Conservative	4	11	19	41	61
Don't Know[b]	6	27	37	29	15
	99%	100%	101%	100%	100%
(percent of total sample)	(3)	(13)	(47)	(31)	(6)

Source: Center for Political Studies, 1976 election data.
[a]Summary scores are based on responses to the ten issues used to construct the index shown in Figure 3-2, below. The categorization is: very liberal, -10 to -7; liberal, -6 to -3; moderate, -2 to +2; conservative, +3 to +6; very conservative +7 to +10.
[b]"Don't Know" categories includes responses of "haven't thought much about it."

connected in the public mind with civil rights or foreign policy. Prior to the Supreme Court's outlawing of segregated schools in 1954, people with pro-integration views called themselves liberals at an only slightly higher than average rate. But by the late 1960s, self-declared liberalism or conservatism had become almost as good an indicator of a person's views on civil rights as on social welfare. As a stark indication of the change, the South had once been the region with the greatest percentage of self-declared liberals.[15] Correlations between self-declared liberalism or conservatism and foreign policy views have always been weak, since most people do not associate the terms with stands on international problems; but these correlations have been increasing since the 1930s when they were virtually nonexistent.[16] Variations in the definitions of ideological terms can cause the public to rate itself differently on the ideological spectrum although actual mass opinion on the issues of the day has not shifted. For example, as discussed in Chapter 2, the sudden gravitation of the public toward the "conservative" label in the late 1960s appears to be caused by the public's realization that the label fits the popular pro "law and order" position rather than changes of opinion on particular issues.

Use of Ideological Language

Although the ideological terms are within the vocabularies of a large share of the American public, few actually employ them to defend their choices of parties and candidates, such as by arguing that some candidate is "too liberal" or "too conservative." During the 1956 presidential campaign, the Survey Research Center's interviewers asked persons in its national sample to describe what they disliked and liked about both political parties and their presidential candidates, Eisenhower and Stevenson. The profile of the public's responses to these questions is reported in *The American Voter,* a classic study of American voting behavior.[17] The researchers were interested not only in the individuals' images of the parties and candidates but also in the conceptual *sophistication* of the responses. Respondents who spontaneously and knowledgeably evaluated the parties and candidates in terms of their placement on the liberal-conservative spectrum were labeled "ideologues." Even with a generous definition of what the ideologue response would demand (to include what *The American Voter* calls "near-ideologues"), only 12 percent of the 1956 sample fit the ideologue category. A typical ideologue response was that of an Ohio woman who, when asked what she liked about the Democratic party, answered "nothing, except it being a more liberal party, and I think the Republicans as being more conservative and interested in big business." A weaker ideologue response was given by a Texan: "I think the Democrats are more concerned with all the people . . . they put out more liberal legislation for all the people."[18]

An added 42 percent of the 1956 sample expressed their likes and dislikes about the candidates and parties in terms of the groups they represent. Farmers often expressed their "group-benefits" orientation to explain their partisan preferences. Typical was the response of an Ohio farm woman when asked what she liked about the Democrats: "I think they have always helped the farmers. To tell you the truth, I don't see how any farmer could vote for Mr. Eisenhower."[19] Most group-benefits responses were somewhat class related, evoking the notion that Republicans favor "big business" while the Democrats favor "the little man." Whereas most ideologues were Republican in preference, most group benefits respondents were Democrats. Though not ideologues, the people who give the most sophisticated group-benefits responses may be said to operate from an "ideology by proxy." They do often express a set of opinions that are consistent with their group interest, but only when this group interest is an obvious guide to their responses. On issues for which their group identifications cannot be a valuable cueing device, they do not behave in an ideologically predictable way.

At a lower level of conceptualization, another 24 percent in 1956 referred to "the nature of the times" the different parties are associated with when in power. Nature of the times voters do not evaluate the parties and candidates in terms of their policies or their group benefits. But they are guided by past performance indicators, such as which party brings economic prosperity or which party keeps most of its "promises." However, many nature of the times responses are simply rationalizations of party preference. An interesting example is that of a Kentucky woman. When asked what she liked about the Democrats, she responded: "I like the good wages my husband makes." When the interviewer pointed out that the Republicans were then in power, she replied, "I know, and it's sort of begun to tighten up since the Republicans got in."[20]

Finally, 23 percent were found to offer no issue content whatsoever when asked to describe their partisan and candidate likes and dislikes. Typical was the North Carolina man who answered as follows (with interviewer questions abbreviated):[21]

(Like about the Democrats?)	"No Ma'am, not that I know of."
(Dislike?)	"No Ma'am but I've always been a Democrat, just like my daddy."
(Like about the Republicans?)	"No."
(Dislike?)	"No."

This distribution of how people conceptualize partisan politics may be interpreted to mean that the American public is not very ideological, and in one sense this would be correct. The authors of *The American Voter* account for the scarcity of ideologues in terms of the public's "cognitive limitations," such as the lack of intellectual ability to think in terms of ideological abstractions.[22] But our knowledge that the public knows the liberal-conservative terms and can apply them to issue positions suggests the alternative interpretation that the American public simply does not find the ideological terms particularly useful to describe their partisan likes and dislikes. Consistent with this argument, the use of ideological language increases when the ideological differences between political candidates become magnified. Researchers have discovered that ideological references increased dramatically during the 1964 presidential campaign contested by Johnson and Goldwater, a campaign that commentators saw as more clearly defined on ideological grounds than any others of recent times.[23] Table 3-4 shows that the percentage of people classified as ideologues jumped dramatically between 1956 and 1964—from 12 percent to 27 percent. From the distributions, it appears that the new ideologues were added from the ranks of the kinds of people who previously gave group benefits responses. Since the percentages in the lower two conceptual strata did not decline, the ideologue increase does not represent a general uplifting of political sophistication from the 1956 pattern. Rather, the extensive use of the "liberal" and "conservative" terminology by the candidates and mass media during the 1964 campaign was picked up by the public to defend their choices of parties and candidates.

Has the increase in the public's willingness to volunteer ideological terminology when describing their likes and dislikes about parties or presidential candidates been a gradual change or did the increase take place suddenly? As documented by *The Changing American Voter* (a recent book challenging many interpretations of the earlier *The American Voter*) the change was rather sudden.[24] *The Changing American Voter* authors look for ideological responses to the likes/dislikes questions in SRC/CPS surveys for all presidential elections from 1952 to 1972. They used an admittedly generous definition of what an ideologue or near-ideologue would be (the mere mention of the terms "liberal" or "conservative" was sufficient) and arrived at

Table 3–4. Levels of Political Conceptualization in 1956 and 1964

Conceptual Level	1956	1964
Ideologue[a]	12%	27%
Group interest	42	27
Nature of times	24	20
No issue content	23	26
Total	101%	100%
N	1684	1564

Sources: For 1956, Angus Campbell, et al., *The American Voter* (New York: Wiley, 1960), p. 249; and, for 1964, recomputed from John C. Pierce, "Party Identification and the Changing Role of Ideology in American Politics," *Midwest Journal of Political Science,* 14 (February, 1970), p. 35.
[a]Including "near ideologues."

the graph shown in Figure 3-1. By *The Changing American Voter* calculation, in 1964 and thereafter virtually half the members of the electorate
were ideologues or near-ideologues by their definition: i.e., used some ideological language when telling the interviewer what they liked and disliked
about the parties and candidates. Even for the pre 1964 period, their generous ideologue definition results in the discovery of more ideologues than did
The American Voter with its stricter definition. Still, *The Changing American Voter* suggests there was a sudden surge in the frequency of ideologues
beginning in 1964. Perhaps as the authors speculate, Senator Barry Goldwater running for president as an explicit conservative caused the 1964 campaign to be unusually ideological. With Wallace's conservative candidacy in
1968 and with McGovern running as an explicit liberal in 1972, it is understandable that voters would respond to the cue of ideology in these elections
as well. The frequency of ideological comments in 1976 is not yet known,
although some evidence suggests the role of ideology was muted during the
1976 Ford-Carter contest.[25]

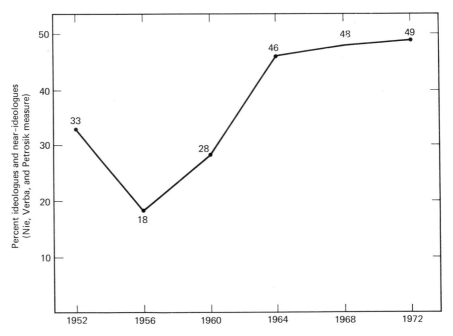

Figure 3-1. Ideological evaluation of candidates and parties, 1952–1972. *[Source.* Norman H.
Nie, Sidney Verba, and John R. Petrocik, *The Changing American Voter* (Cambridge: Harvard
University Press, 1976), Fig. 7-3, p. 115.]

Summary

Understanding the extent to which the public makes use of the ideological terms "liberal" and "conservative" is more limited than it might be. Scholars have been somewhat late to investigate the subject because the public's ability and willingness to use these terms has been greatly underestimated. Differing operationalizations of ideology have led to different estimates of the extent to which it exists. But all evidence suggests that since 1964 ideological thinking by the American public has been on the rise.

3-2 IDEOLOGY AS LIBERAL OR CONSERVATIVE CONSISTENCY

Do people have fundamental orientations toward politics (such as liberalism or conservatism) that link their judgments to several issues? One might suspect that many people are actually quite liberal or conservative by the opinions they express, even when they do not spontaneously choose these terms to describe their political orientation. But actually, relatively few people are consistently liberal or consistently conservative over a wide range of issues. Figure 3-2 shows one distribution of the American public's liberalism-conservatism "scores," as measured by their cumulative responses to ten opinion questions. (The issues are those shown in Table 3-7, below.) A person offering a liberal viewpoint on all ten issues would have a score of -10 whereas a person who expresses conservative outlooks on all eight issues would have a +10 score. Most respondents were near the midpoint of the

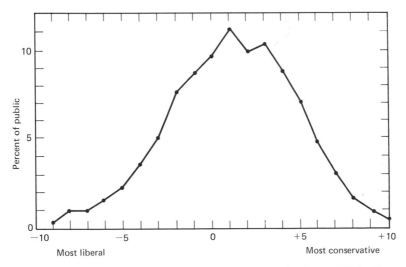

Figure 3-2. Distribution of composite opinion scores over ten policy issues, 1976. *(Source. SRC/CPS, 1976 election data.)* See the Appendix for opinion questions. Scores are the sum of conservative responses minus the sum of liberal responses.

Table 3-5. Correlations Between Opinions on Selected Issues, 1976

(a) Governmental Medical Insurance

		Pro	Con
Guaranteed Good Standard of Living	Pro	28%	10%
	Con	21%	41%

Q = .70

(b) Aid to Minorities

		Pro	Con
Busing	Pro	11%	2%
	Con	31%	56%

Q = .85

(c) Marijuana Legalization

		Pro	Con
Women's rights	Pro	31%	35%
	Con	3%	30%

Q = .77

(d) Marijuana Legalization

		Pro	Con
Guaranteed Good Standard of Living	Pro	13%	22%
	Con	21%	43%

Q = .10

(e) Tax Reform

		Pro	Con
Protect rights of Accussed	Pro	22%	19%
	Con	27%	31%

Q = .13

(f) More Domestic Spending

		Pro	Con
Cut military spending	Pro	15%	4%
	Con	64%	18%

Q = .00

Source: Center for Political Studies, 1976 election data. For the full texts of the opinion questions, see Appendix B.

scale, indicating that their liberal and conservative viewpoints balance each other out.

Since over a series of issues most people give some liberal and some conservative positions, there is the temptation to label the bulk of the public as political moderates. But these voters in the center cannot be grouped together as sharers of a common moderate ideology because they differ greatly in the pattern of their responses to individual issues. For example, one voter with "balanced" liberal and conservative views may be liberal on social welfare issues and civil rights, but conservative on foreign policy and law and order, while another with balanced views possess exactly the opposite opinions. Still a third person may have an overall score that is neither very conservative nor very liberal for the reason that he expresses few opinions at all.

Correlations Between Opinions

To what extent can one predict an individual's opinions on one political issue from his or her opinions on others? Only when issues are part of the same general policy domain do peoples' opinions tend to cluster into visible patterns of liberal or conservative consistency. For example, some consistency between peoples opinions on government subsidization of medical costs and on government efforts to provide everyone a job and a good standard of living is created by their general view (if they have one) of the proper involvement of government in social welfare activities. Table 3-5(a) shows that most people are either liberal or conservative on both of these issues. Since more people accept government and medical insurance than government guarantee of a good standard of living, there naturally must be some people who think government involvement in medical care is all right, but that guaranteeing a good standard of living is going too far. But very few are inconsistent in the opposite way. Table 3-5(b) shows another example. People's attitudes toward the government's role in helping blacks force a pattern of consistency between their views toward aid to minorities and their views toward busing school children for racial balance. Although some favor minority aid but oppose busing (a more unpopular step), very few hold the inconsistent position of favoring busing but opposing minority aid. Table 3-5(c) shows still another pattern of consistency between opinion on two so-called "social" issues—women's rights and marijuana legalization.

While the correlations presented in the top row of Table 3-5 are quite strong, we cannot carry the consistency argument too far. For example, the people who are most willing to support social welfare spending also tend to be the people who agree with the statement that "the government ought to cut taxes, even if it means putting off things that need to be done."[26] Since how much a government saves and how much it spends are obviously related, one ought to try to figure out the source of this inconsistency, rather than simply reject public opinion as being, in this instance, irrational. Per-

Table 3-6.   Medicare-Foreign Aid Consistency

	U.S. Senators (Roll-Call Votes)				SRC Public Sample (Opinions)		
	Foreign Aid Bill, 1964				Foreign Aid, 1964		
		Pro	Con			Pro	Con
1965 Medicare Bill	Pro	56%	13%	Medicare, 1964	Pro	50%	25%
	Con	10%	21%		Con	16%	9%
		Q = .80				Q = .08	

Sources: Senatorial data—*Congressional Quarterly;* and public opinion—Survey Research Center.

haps the people who feel most in need of social welfare activities are also those who feel the tax bite most.

Among the most politically alert strata of society, there is strong consistency of viewpoints even when one crosses from one issue domain to another. For example, Table 3-6 shows that one could have fairly good success in predicting a U.S. senator's vote on passage of the Medicare bill from how he voted on passage of the 1964 foreign aid bill, or vice versa. Nothing approaching this general consistency is found for the general public, however, as Table 3-6 shows Medicare attitudes of the general public in 1964 to have been almost totally unrelated to opinions expressed on foreign aid.

Similarly, opinions on other pairs of issues that differ in their subject matter generally are only weakly correlated. Some examples are shown in the bottom row of Table 3-5. Table 3-5(d) shows that one cannot predict a person's opinion on marijuana legalization from his opinion on a guaranteed standard of living. To take another example, Table 3-5(e), one cannot predict a person's opinion on tax reform from his opinion on how far the government should go to protect the rights of accused criminals. One even finds that the public's opinions on domestic spending are uncorrelated with its opinions on military spending, unlike political elites who tend to show either a conservative tendency to favor military spending over domestic spending or a liberal tendency to favor domestic spending over military spending. Among the public, most appear favorably disposed toward both military and domestic spending and in such a pattern that the people most favorable to one kind of spending are not disproportionately unfavorable toward the other. See Table 3-5(f).[27]

The full pattern of relationships between opinions on 10 issues are summarized in Table 3-7. The more positive the correlation coefficient shown, the more consistent the opinions on the two issues. The maximum possible correlation (which is not approached) would be 1.00, indicating that all the liberals on one issue are liberals on the other, or that all the conservatives on one issue give conservative responses on the other. The opposite

Table 3-7. Correlations (Qs) Between Opinions, 1976

	Tax Reform	Domestic Spending	Medical Care	Standard of Living	Minority Aid	Busing	Rights of Accused	Mari-juana	Women's Rights	Military Spending
Tax Reform	—	.11	.30	.28	.26	.30	.14	.11	.11	.16
Domestic Spending	.11	—	.53	.63	.41	.46	.35	.15	.11	.00
Medical Care	.30	.53	—	.70	.55	.53	.42	.31	.18	.31
Standard of Living	.28	.63	.70	—	.77	.69	.39	.10	.23	.20
Aid to Minorities	.26	.41	.55	.77	—	.85	.58	.44	.26	.37
Busing	.30	.46	.53	.69	.85	—	.66	.52	.35	.46
Rights of Accused	.14	.35	.42	.39	.58	.66	—	.45	.38	.32
Marijuana Legalization	.11	.15	.31	.10	.44	.52	.45	—	.77	.64
Women's Rights	.11	.11	.18	.23	.26	.35	.38	.77	—	.35
Military Spending	.16	.00	.31	.20	.37	.46	.32	.34	.35	—

Source: Center for Political Studies, 1976 election data. For the full texts of the opinion questions see the Appendix. Correlation coefficients are Yules Q's, based on the dichotomized items.

extreme is a correlation of -1.00, which would occur if liberalism on one issue were perfectly correlated with conservatism on the other. In between, the .00 benchmark indicates the perfect absence of a statistical relationship—when liberals and conservatives on one issue respond in identical patterns on the second. The correlation coefficients (Qs) shown for the patterns in Table 3-5 may also be a useful reference for interpreting the correlations in Table 3-7.[28]

Is Ideological Constraint Increasing?

We have seen that ideological constraint or consistency is often quite weak, especially when we compare people's viewpoints on issues that are linked by little more than the fact that each has alternatives that are often labeled "liberal" and "conservative." For example, support of Medicare does not logically demand support for trading with Communist nations, even though someone with a general liberal philosophy would be expected to support both. The low correlation between opinions on these two issues suggests that few people approach these two questions from the standpoint of their position on a general liberal-conservative spectrum. Yet earlier we noted an increase in the frequency with which people employ references of liberalism and conservatism to describe party differences, at least over the period from 1956 through 1964. Could this trend be an indicator of an increase in ideological constraint as well, so that correlations between opinions are increasing to become more consistent with conventional ideological expectations? If we follow the trend over time of how opinions on different issues are correlated with each other, correlations do seem to be increasing, with the greatest jump around the turn of the 1964 "ideological" election.[29] Some scholars, however, believe the reported increase in the public's issue consistency has been greatly exaggerated.[30] Their argument is that the observed change is largely illusory—the result of better opinion questions asked by survey researchers since the mid-1960s. This disagreement over the actual amount of growth of opinion consistency is one of the most interesting controversies in current public opinion research.

Opinion on Vietnam as an Example

Between the mid-1960s and the early 1970s, the Vietnam War was a dominant issue in American politics. The intrusion of the Vietnam issue provides an example of what not to expect in the way of ideological consistency on the part of the American public. Although elites such as the highly visible members of the U.S. Senate reacted to the war in a way consistent with their general ideology (the liberals were the first to oppose the war), no clear tendency of this sort was found in public surveys. Consequently, one cannot argue that liberal political orientations led people to oppose the war while conservative orientations compelled people to support it. Both doves and hawks were found within the ranks of people who were liberal or conservative on nonwar related issues. Even attitudes toward other foreign policy questions (e.g., trading with Communist nations) and toward war protesters were unrelated to attitudes toward war policy.[31]

One reason why it was so difficult to predict how people would respond to the war from their other attitudes is that opposition to the war was a liberal yet isolationist position, whereas other isolationist foreign policy views were generally regarded as conservative. Many people evidently reacted to Vietnam according to their isolationist versus internationalist perspective, which makes trading with Communist nations and fighting wars of anticommunism compatible with internationalist viewpoints and their opposite pair of attitudes the logical extension of the old isolationist perspective that the United States should avoid foreign entanglements of any kind. The simple isolationist-internationalist dimension regarding foreign policy appears to be more salient for older voters than the liberal-conservative dimension of international cooperation versus aggression. Table 3-8 illustrates this. In 1968, older voters were more likely to oppose Vietnam involvement if they opposed trade with Communist nations. Younger people, however, followed the opposite pattern, consistent with notions of liberalism-conservatism: those who favored the war also tended to be those who opposed trading with Communist nations. Both tendencies are rather weak, however.[32]

Non-Liberal-Conservative Orderings

The complication of the isolationist-internationalist dimension when one tries to predict Vietnam attitudes suggests that, in other instances as well, portions of the public may operate in some sort of loose ideological fashion that is at variance with conventional notions of liberalism-conservatism. Robert

Table 3-8.　Relationship Between Opinions on Trading with Communist Nations and Opinion on Vietnam Involvement, by Age, 1968 (in Percent)

Opinion on U.S. Involvement in Vietnam	Born before 1915		Born 1915-1928		Born after 1928	
	Pro-trade	Anti-trade	Pro-trade	Anti-trade	Pro-trade	Anti-trade
Oppose	68	74	56	54	56	48
Favor	32	26	44	46	44	52
	100	100	100	100	100	100
N=	[149]	[152]	[150]	[175]	[128]	[166]
$Q =$	$-.14$		.06		.12	

Source:　Survey Research Center 1968 election data.

Axelrod has discovered that an interesting, though weak, tendency of this sort applies to the patterns of attitudes held by very uninformed people.[33] Within the less politically involved strata (for example, nonvoters and the less educated), Axelrod found that a weak "populism" scale best describes their attitudes, with support for social welfare, resistance to taxes, opposition to civil liberties, and foreign policy isolationism correlated with each other. The least informed tend either to support or to oppose the cluster of populist positions more so than they tend to be liberal or conservative in the conventional sense. Other research shows these populist positions, and segregationist sentiments as well, are most typical among people who are also politically alienated.[34] At the same time, Axelrod found that opinions become increasingly correlated in the way one would ordinarily predict if one isolates the relatively informed segment of the public. Thus, although the most politically alert people approach some attitudinal consistency that can be predicted from their liberal versus conservative orientations, their contribution to the overall pattern gets canceled out to some extent by that of the less alert segment of the public who may be responding to an entirely different set of ideological constraints.

One further qualification on the general lack of opinion consistency can be made: in a study of opinion patterns in two Oregon communities, Luttbeg found considerable structure to local-issue opinion patterns, although with opinions again ordered along several separate dimensions rather than the simple liberal-conservative pattern.[35] The major dimension of local-issue opinion involved issues related to a good "community environment" for children (for example, public kindergartens, special education programs, water fluoridation), with people falling into consistent patterns of either supporting or opposing these programs. Other dimensions involved the general issues of taxation, community growth, improving the city core, and increased recreational facilities. A somewhat different set of issue dimensions (once again, not liberalism-conservatism) was found for community leaders. Contrary to this evidence regarding local issues, little constraint is found among people's attitudes toward state-level issues.[36]

Summary

While the American public displays some familiarity with the terminology of liberalism and conservatism, most people cannot be said to order their political viewpoints by means of a general ideological anchor. Many people can describe their position on a liberal-conservative continuum accurately, in the sense that they can sum up the tendency of their viewpoints on various issues to describe their net position. Yet the fact that there is little consistency among people's viewpoints—especially when the opinions cut across issue areas—demonstrates that few people use their ideological position as a cueing device to arrange their responses to the political world. The kind of attitudinal constraint that motivates people toward consistently liberal or moderate viewpoints on issues that are not related in obvious fashion is reserved for a small politically active segment of the American public. Yet to the extent there is any historical trend, it is toward an increase in the ideological consistency of people's viewpoints.

Of course, the failure of the average citizen to arrange his opinions in predictable liberal or conservative clusters does not necessarily mean that his opinions are logically inconsistent with one another. Instead of viewing the mass public as somehow incapable of consistency when thinking about politics, it may be more accurate to view each individual as bringing to bear his own unique ideology toward the political world.

3-3 PARTISANSHIP AND THE ORGANIZATION OF OPINION

So far, our discussion of opinion consistency has ignored the role of partisanship in creating opinion change. In the previous chapter, we saw that compared with people's opinions on policy issues, the party identification a person holds is quite stable over time. As will be elaborated in Chapter 5, the source of one's party identification is often the political values that were transmitted in the family during childhood. At the other end of the causal chain, party identification is the best predictor of how people vote. Following the sequence through, we find that people vote for the party with which their parents had identified.

Since party identification appears to be the central element in most people's political belief systems (except, perhaps, for consensual opinions on which almost all Americans agree), one might suspect that people use their party identification as a cue to order the remainder of their political beliefs. An alert Republican, for example, would eventually learn that a good Republican is supposed to subscribe to conservative opinions on certain issues and would begin to respond accordingly. At the same time, one might suspect that the few people who change their party identification often do so out of awareness of the fact that their views on issues are out of alignment with their partisan heritage. These causal processes could not occur, however, unless people were aware of Democratic and Republican partisan differences on the issues of the day.

Perceptions of Party Differences on Issues

Although prominent political figures may argue that there is "not a dime's worth of difference" between the two major American political parties, people commonly assume that political leaders within the Republican party often subscribe to conservative viewpoints and most Democratic leaders, except perhaps in the South, subscribe to liberal ideas. As we will discuss in

Chapter 9, there is much truth to these assumptions. Here we may ask the question: To what extent does the public perceive these partisan differences on issues?

In its periodic election surveys, the CPS employed various questions that allow the explanation of public perceptions of policy differences between the parties. Results from the 1976 poll are shown in Table 3-9. On each of the selected issues, less than a majority saw the Democratic party as the one more favorable to the policy in question (the liberal alternative). On the other hand, very few guessed "incorrectly" on each issue—that the Republicans would do more. Thus, among people who do see party differences, the direction of the perception is almost always that the Democrats would follow what are regarded as liberal policies and the Republicans the opposite.

Interestingly, although many argue that the relevance of partisanship has been decreasing, the public's perception of partisan difference on issues has been decidedly increasing. Figure 3-3 shows this trend for three issues monitored by the SRC at several times. Particularly striking is the fact that prior to 1964, no public consensus existed regarding which party was most in favor of school integration and of foreign aid (or other civil rights and foreign policy issues either). Before 1964, the public saw the parties only as having opposite policies on social welfare issues. This tendency goes back to the New Deal era of the 1930s when the parties began to develop opposite philosophies toward the role of the federal government in the economy. The then less-salient civil rights and foreign policy issues had been a frequent source of sharp partisan division in Congress, but apparently the people

Table 3–9. Public Perceptions of Party Differences on Issues, 1976

Perceptions of Which Party is More in Favor of . . .	Democrats	Republicans	No Difference, Don't Know, No Interest
Making Rich Pay more Taxes	32%	8%	60%
Government Health Insurance	35	5	60
Guaranteed Good Standard of Living	42	8	50
Aid to Minorities	34	9	57
Busing	28	15	58
Protecting Rights of Accused Criminals	25	10	65
Legalizing Marijuana	17	6	77
Women's Rights	20	5	75

Source: Center for Political Studies, 1976 elections data. The measures of perceived party differences are based on the differences between respondents' ratings of the two parties on seven-point scales.

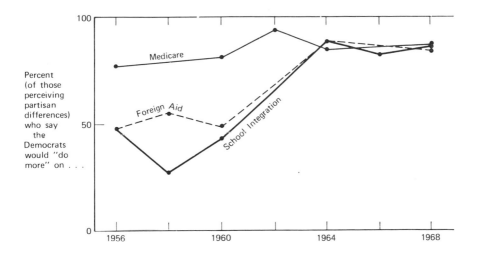

Figure 3-3. Changing perceptions of partisan differences on selected issues, 1956–1968. (*Source.* SRC/CPS elections data.)

failed to notice. The spur to the increased public awareness of party differences, as to so many other changes, appears to have been the ideological Goldwater election of 1964.[37]

Party Identification and Policy Preferences

On most political issues the views of Democratic and Republican identifiers will diverge in predictable ways, although the amount of difference is often slight and varies from issue to issue. Some examples from 1972 data are shown in Table 3-10. Although the views of "weak Democrats," "Independents," and "weak Republicans" are often indistinguishable from one another, the differences between "strong Democrats" and "strong Republicans" are often rather sharp. Clearly, strong Democrats and strong Republicans are most divided on social welfare issues, which is understandable given that the public has only recently begun to perceive that the parties are different on other kinds of issues as well.

The trend in how Republicans and Democrats are divided on issues follows the trend in perceptions of partisan differences. While Democratic members of the electorate have been somewhat more liberal than Republicans on social welfare issues since the 1930s, it is only recently that Democratic identifiers have been more liberal than Republican identifiers on nonsocial welfare issues. Figure 3-4 shows example on two issues that have been monitored continuously since 1956: medical care and school integration. On the social welfare issue of government involvement in medical care,

Table 3-10. Relationship Between Party Identification and Policy Opinions, 1976

| | Percent Liberal of Opinion Holders | | | | |
Issue	Strong Democrat	Weak Democrat	Independent	Weak Republican	Strong Republican	Correlation (Gamma)
Tax Reform	61	53	46	43	31	.228
Domestic Spending	85	85	78	73	60	.278
Medical Care	63	59	52	36	27	.309
Standard of Living	61	49	33	27	12	.434
Aid to Minorities	51	52	45	32	33	.208
Busing	17	16	9	6	4	.344
Rights of Accused	51	43	43	34	29	.174
Marijuana Legalization	24	35	42	23	22	.044
Women's Rights	70	68	74	62	63	.056
Military Spending	20	21	22	13	7	.162

Source: Center for Political Studies, 1976 election data. For full texts of the opinion questions, see Appendix B.

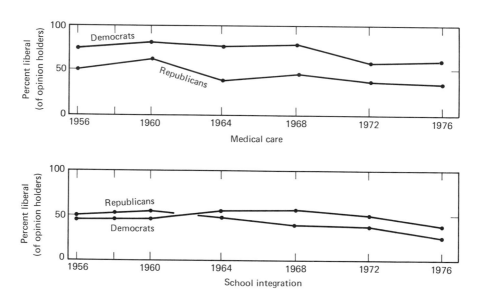

Figure 3-4. Changing partisan differences in opinion, 1956–1976. (*Source.* SRC/CPS election data.)

people who identify with the Democratic party were more liberal than Republican identifiers throughout the 1956–1976 period. But on the issue of school integration, as Figure 3-4 shows, Republicans were once slightly more liberal than their Democratic counterparts. This trend has been reversed since 1964 with Democrats now showing up as the more liberal partisan group on the issue of school integration. Only when the public began to perceive party differences on issues outside the social welfare sphere in the early sixties, did Democrats become noticeably more liberal than Republicans on nonsocial welfare issues.

What causes the consistency between political opinions and party identification? Do people learn their political opinions from their party identification or are political opinons shaped by party identification? For instance, is a liberal Republican more likely to change to a conservative Republican or a liberal Democrat? Undoubtedly, both causal processes are at work, but their relative contributions to consistency between party identification and political opinions can only be roughly estimated. Because one's party identification is often a strongly held attitude, while stands on issues are typically casual at best, most writers on the subject assume that partisanship normally shapes policy opinions rather than the reverse, even though the rare partisan convert often is reacting to issues when he makes his change.[38] William Flanigan concludes:[39]

> "It is relatively unusual in American politics for an issue to become so important that it disrupts party loyalties for large numbers of people. But in rare cases where individuals feel important issues are at stake, it is most unlikely that partisan loyalty . . . will overcome strongly felt interests."

Let us consider the usual case first. When President Nixon instituted a thaw in the U.S. relationship with mainland China, which culminated in his 1972 visit to China, it represented something of an upset of partisan stereotypes. Previously liberal Democrats in Congress had most visibly urged such a change of policy and Republican congressmen and leaders (Nixon included) were most insistent on a hard-line policy. Before Nixon's presidency, Gallup Polls usually showed the identical partisan pattern in the casual attitudes expressed by public samples—for example, Democrats were somewhat more in favor of admitting China to the United Nations than Republicans were. But Nixon's policy change apparently had a greater effect on the China attitudes of Republicans than Democrats, so that by 1972, Republicans had become more in favor of admitting China to the U.N. than Democrats were.[40] Naturally, it was easier for "anti-China" Republicans to change their attitudes toward China than to change their partisan identification.

A slightly different kind of example is provided by changes in the relationship between partisanship and Vietnam opinion. When Lyndon Johnson was President, more Republicans than Democrats viewed the war as a mistake. But when a Republican administration took over, it became easier for Democratic identifiers to oppose war policy and more difficult for Republicans not to justify it. And for this reason, the partisan transition of the Presidency following the 1968 election saw Democratic identifiers beginning to emerge in the Gallup Polls as the partisan group more consistently viewing the war as a mistake.[41]

These limited foreign policy examples suggest that the typical explanation for correlations between party identification and issue stances is that party identification causes the issue response rather than the reverse. Yet not every instance when the issue stances of Democrats and Republicans diverge can be accounted for in this way. Although people are normally stable in their partisan preferences, an unusual amount of shifting may occur when the political parties make major changes in their policy orientations. When this happens, the electorate is said to undergo "partisan realignment."[42] To a certain extent, realignment goes on all time, as each change in a party's policy emphasis is likely to produce a response on the part of the segment of the electorate that has the most vital stake in the issue. For example, World War I and World War II, both fought under Democratic administrations, cost the Democrats the allegiance of some of their German-American adherents.[43] As our previous discussion indicates, the emergence of civil rights as a partisan issue in the 1960s and 1970s has caused some partisan realignment, although it has not yet been as extensive as at crucial times in America's past.

Two crucial realignment periods were around the time of the 1896 presidential election and later, from the late 1920s into the 1930s. The 1896 realignment is evident from the fact that geographic voting patterns that had been stable for decades suddenly became disrupted. This first appeared as a short-term response to the 1893 Depression, and was then compounded by the unusual issue-polarization of the 1896 presidential elections. In its 1896 convention, the Democratic party accepted much of the platform of the Populists, a rising third party of economic protest, and nominated William Jennings Bryan who campaign for the inflationary program of "free silver." This new issue division attracted adherents to the Democratic cause but panicked a greater number into leaving. Consequently, the Republicans became the dominant party until the 1930s.[44]

The more recent major realignment came in two stages. First, the decision of a badly divided Democratic party to oppose Prohibition caused the Democrats to gain urban support but lose rural support in the 1928 election. More importantly, President Roosevelt's "New Deal" policies, which expanded the role of the federal government in the economy to cope with the hardships of the Great Depression, caused voters to realign further in the 1930s.[45] Trace evidence of the issue base of this realignment can be found

Table 3-11 Policy Opinions and Partisan Shifts, 1960–1964

| | Reported Change in Party Identification, 1960–1964 | |
Opinion, 1964	Away from Democrats	Away from Republicans
Percent Pro School Integration	38% (47)	62% (55)
Percent Pro Medicare	44 (45)	57 (51)

Source. CPS/SRC 1964 Presidential Election Study.

even in recent surveys, as older voters who claimed to have left the Republican party in the 1930s are decidedly liberal in their social welfare orientation, while those who shifted their party identification in the opposite direction are quite conservative in these views.[46]

A major cause of contemporary partisan shifting appears to be the public's increasing awareness of partisan differences on the highly salient issue of civil rights. For example, the data of Table 3-11 show that people who in 1964 reported a recent shift away from the Democratic party were decidedly more conservative on the civil rights issue of school integration than their counterparts making the reverse shift away from the Republicans. By comparison, the difference between the Medicare opinions of the two groups of shifters was rather mild, suggesting that social welfare opinions did not spur much switching.

To date, the contemporary currents of partisan realignment appear mild in comparison with major realignments of the past. Although the number of people who call themselves political independents has been increasing, with the biggest jump from 23 percent in 1964 to 29 percent in 1966 (according to CPS data), no basic change has yet occurred in the ratio of Republican to Democratic identifiers or in the frequency with which people report a recent change in their party identification. Moreover, the issues that divide Republican and Democratic identifiers the most are still the issues on the social welfare dimension, as a result of the partisan realignment of the 1930s.

At the same time, the increasing public perception of significant partisan differences on nonsocial-welfare issues is the major source of the partisan shifting that has been occurring. Given this increased awareness, a lack of clear-cut partisan differences on issues does not appear to be a sound explanation for the increase in the number of independents. Instead, many of the new group of Independents (who, as we shall see in Chapter 6, come mainly from the core of young voters) may be rejecting their party affiliation because the partisan issue differences are being more clearly defined. Also, increased awareness of party differences appears to be one cause of the electorate's trend toward increasing liberal-conservative polarization on issues. As perceived party differences expand beyond the social welfare realm to include differences within other policy domains, the public may be becoming more ideologically polarized by simply following the lead of their parties.

FOOTNOTES FOR CHAPTER 3

1. For one inventory of definitions of "ideology," see Robert Lane, *Political Ideology* (New York: The Free Press of Glencoe, 1962), pp. 13—16.

2. For an interesting account of how the John Birch Society dealt with this ideological trap, see Stephen Earl Bennett, "Modes of Resolution of a 'Belief Dilemma' in the Ideology of the John Birch Society," *Journal of Politics*, 33 (August, 1971), pp. 735—772.

3. For a demonstration that the most liberal convention delegates are the most internationalist in their foreign policy views, see Herbert McClosky, "Personality and Attitude Correlates of Foreign Policy Orientation," in James N. Rosenau (ed.), *Domestic Sources of Foreign Policy* (New York: The Free Press, 1967), pp. 82—86.

4. Philip E. Converse, "The Nature of Belief Systems in Mass Publics," in David E. Apter (ed.), *Ideology and Discontent* (New York: The Free Press, 1966), pp. 227—231.

5. For one inventory of the philosophical distinctions between liberalism and conservatism, see Herbert McClosky, *"Conservatism and Personality,"* *American Political Science Review*, 52 (March, 1958), pp. 27—45.

6. This finding is based on an evaluation of CPS data. Most people respond either "warm" or "neutral" toward both liberals and conservatives.

7. Louis Harris, "Political Labels Depend on Who Applies Them," *St. Petersburg Times* (January 18, 1971), p. A10.

8. Hadley Cantril, *Public Opinion 1935—1946* (Princeton: Princeton University Press, 1951), pp. 577—578.

9. Converse, pp. 219—227.

10. Ibid., p. 222.

11. Ibid., p. 223.

12. " 'The New Right.' What It Means," *CBS News*/New York Times *Poll, Press Release*, January 21, 1978.

13. There is ample evidence that people who are most sophisticated about politics are most able to accurately describe their beliefs as liberal or conservative. See James A. Stimson, "Belief Systems: Constraint, Complexity, and the 1972 Election," *American Journal of Political Science*, 19 (1975), pp. 393—417; George F. Bishop, "The Effect of Education on Ideological Consistency," *Public Opinion Quarterly*, 40 (Fall 1976), pp. 337—348.

14. Alfred O. Hero, Jr., "Liberalism-Conservatism Revisited: Foreign vs. Domestic Federal Policies, 1937—1967," *Public Opinion Quarterly*, 33 (Fall 1969), p. 400.

15. Ibid.

16. Ibid., pp. 400—401.

17. Angus Campbell, Philip E. Converse, Warren E. Miller, and Donald E. Stokes, *The American Voter* (New York: John Wiley and Sons, 1960), pp. 216—249.

18. Ibid., p. 232.

19. Ibid., p. 236.

20. Ibid., p. 244.

21. Ibid., p. 246.

22. Ibid., p. 253.

23. John O. Field and Ronald E. Anderson, "Ideology in the Public's Conceptualization of the 1964 Election," *Public Opinion Quarterly*, 33 (Fall 1969), pp. 380–398; John C. Pierce, "Party Identification and the Changing Role of Ideology in American Politics," *Midwest Journal of Political Science*, 14 (February 1970), pp. 25–42.

24. Norman H. Nie, Sidney Verba, and John R. Petrocik, *The Changing American Voter* (Cambridge: Harvard University Press, 1976), pp. 110–122.

25. Arthur H. Miller and Warren E. Miller, "Partisanship and Performance: 'Rational Choice' in the 1976 Presidential Election," paper presented to the 1977 Convention of the American Political Science Association.

26. Campbell et al., pp. 194–197.

27. Robert Weissberg, *Public Opinion and Popular Government* (Englewood Cliffs: Prentice-Hall, 1976).

28. Similar tables of correlations between opinions are found in various sources: for 1956 data, see Robert Axelrod, "The Structure of Public Opinion on Policy Issues," *Public Opinion Quarterly*, 31 (Spring 1967), pp. 51–60; for 1958 data, see Converse, op cit.: for 1968 data, see Robert G. Lehnen, "Assessing Reliability in Sample Surveys," *Public Opinion Quarterly*, 35 (Winter 1971–72), pp. 578–592; for 1972 data, see Arthur H. Miller, Warren E. Miller, Alden S. Raine, and Thad A. Brown, "A Majority Party in Disarray: Policy Polarization in the 1972 Election," *American Political Science Review*, 70 (September 1976), pp. 753–778. Comparisons of inter-opinion correlations for different years are found in Nie et al., pp. 124–155 and Norman Nie and Kristi Anderson, "Mass Belief Systems Revisted: Political Change and Attitude Structure," *Journal of Politics*, 36 (1974), pp. 540–591. The reader should be cautioned that different studies employ somewhat different measures of correlation, so that it is not always appropriate to compare the magnitudes of correlations of different studies.

29. Nie et al., *The Changing American Voter*, pp. 124–155; Nie and Anderson, op. cit.

30. John L. Sullivan, James E. Pierson, and George E. Marcus, "Ideological Constraint in the Mass Public: A Methodological Critique and Some New Findings," *American Journal of Political Science*, 22 (May 1978), pp. 233–249; George F. Bishop, Alfred J. Tuchfarber, and Robert W. Oldendick, "Change in the Structure of American Political Attitudes: The Nagging Question of Question Wording," *American Journal of Political Science*, 22 (May 1978), pp. 250–269. For a response and further comment see Norman Nie and James Rabjohn, "Revisiting Mass Belief Systems Revisited: Or, Doing Research is Like Watching a Tennis Match," *American Journal of Political Science*, 23 (February 1979), pp. 139–175; John L. Sullivan, James E. Piereson, George E. Marcus and Stanley Feldman. "The More Things Change, The More they Stay the Same: The Stability of Mass Belief Systems," *American Journal of Political Science*, 23 (February 1979), pp. 176–186; George F. Bishop, Alfred J. Tuchfarber, Robert W. Oldendick, and Stephen E. Bennett, "Questions about Question Wording: A Rejoinder to Revisiting Mass Belief Systems Revisted," *American Journal of Political* Science, 23 (February 1979), pp. 187–192.

31. Philip E. Converse et al., "Continuation and Change in American Politics: Parties and Issues in the 1968 Election," *American Political Science Review*, 63 (December 1969), p. 1087.

32. The most thorough examination of the dimensions of foreign policy opinion is William R. Caspary, "Dimensions of Attitudes on International Conflict: Internationalism and Military Offensive Action," *Peace Research Society Papers, 12 (1970), pp. 1–10.*

33. Robert Axelrod, op cit.

34. Marian E. Olson, "Alienation and Political Opinions," *Public Opinion Quarterly*, 29 (Summer 1965), pp. 200–212.

35. Norman R. Luttbeg, "The Structure of Beliefs Among Leaders and the Public," *Public Opinion Quarterly*, 32 (Fall 1968), pp. 388–409.

36. Norman R. Luttbeg, "The Structure of Public Beliefs on State Government Policies: A Comparison with Local and National Findings," *Public Opinion Quarterly,* 38 (Spring 1971), pp. 114—116.

37. Although the public has become more aware of party differences, the significance of this change is open to dispute, particularly since many people—in fact most—apparently do not see party differences on topical issues even today. For differing interpretations, compare Gerald L. Pomper, "From Confusion to Clarity: Issues and American Voters, 1956—1968," *American Political Science Review,* 66 (June 1972), pp. 415—428 with Michael Margolis, "From Confusion to Confusion: Issues and the American Voter (1956—1972)," *American Political Science Review* 71 (March 1977), pp. 31—43.

38. Angus Campbell et al., pp. 212—215.

39. William H. Flanigan, *Political Behavior of the American Electorate,* 2nd ed. (Boston: Allyn and Bacon, 1972), p. 98.

40. Between 1966 and 1971, the percentage of Democratic opinion holders who told Gallup they favored UN admission for China rose from one-third to nearly half. Meanwhile Republican support rose from one in four to a clear plurality in favor of admission.

41. The following table illustrates the partisan shifting on the war. Question: "Do you think the United States made a mistake sending troops to fight in Vietnam?" Figures are percentages responding "yes."

	March 1966	Feb. 1968	July 1971
Democrats	24	41	64
Republicans	27	53	56

Source. Gallup Opinion Index

42. On the concept of partisan realignment, see Campbell et al., pp. 531—538; James L. Sundquist, *Dynamics of the Party System* (Washington: The Brookings Institution, 1973).

43. Samuel Lubell, *The Future of American Politics,* 2nd ed. (Garden City: Doubleday and Co., 1956), pp. 143—159.

44. On the 1896 realignment, see Walter Dean Burnham, *Critical Elections and the Mainsprings of American Politics* (New York: W.W. Norton and Co., 1970), pp. 119—120; Sundquist, pp. 120—154.

45. On the New Deal realignment see Everett Carll Ladd, *American Political Parties: Social Change and Political Responses* (New York: W.W. Norton and Co., 1970), pp. 207—228; Sundquist, pp. 183—217.

46. For example, people in SRC's 1964 sample who reported that they shifted from Republican to Democratic in the 1930s favored Medicare by an overwhelming margin of seventeen to two. Respondents who reported making a reverse Democrat to Republican shift in the 1930s opposed Medicare two to eight.

CHAPTER 4

Public Opinion and Democratic Stability

In a democracy public opinion is important because it can influence the decisions that political leaders make. In previous chapters we have discussed the state of public opinon on questions of public policy. Certain other types of political orientations are particularly important because the extent of their existence may influence the functioning of democratic government. In this chapter we shall examine the attitudes and predispositions that are considered to be necessary to maintain a democracy and the degree to which Americans appear to hold them. Ideas about what is vital for democratic stability can be divided into four groups.

First, there should be widespread support for the rules of democracy. An analogy here is the rules of the road for driving an automobile. If most people did not accept the rule that one must stop when the light is red, chaos would ensue. The rules of democracy involve guarantees that the civil liberties of all shall be protected—that majorities rule, but minorities have rights.

Second, democracy's stability may rest on a social consensus regarding values and goals. Disagreement cannot be so fundamental that resolution or compromise cannot be gained by institutionalized procedures. Too great a division may overtax even the best procedures for resolving conflict. Contemporary examples include the Protestant-Catholic division in Northern Ireland, the Christian-Moslem division in Lebanon, and possibly the French-English conflict in Canada's Quebec province.

Third, if people are to accept government decisions, they must believe that their political actions can be effective and that they can trust the government to respond to their interests. If political alienation becomes sufficiently intense and widespread, it may pose a threat to democratic stability.

Fourth, in coping with personal anxieties and needs, certain personality types find comfort in blaming others. Alternatively (or simultaneously), some seek a solution to their problems in a strong political leader. When such personalities are common, minority rights become very fragile and the stability of democracy can be threatened.

4-1 SUPPORT FOR DEMOCRATIC VALUES

By the term "democratic values" we are referring to procedural norms. These norms do not refer to the substance of legitimate political conflict, such as the desirable trade off between inflation and unemployment, but to the "rules of the game" in which that conflict takes place. One important set of procedural norms is found in the Bill of rights. Here Americans are guaranteed the right to criticize government (free expression), freedom from unreasonable search and seizure, protection from self-incrimination, a speedy and public trial, free exercise of religion, etc. Two related democratic values of great importance are majority rule and minority rights. At regular intervals the population is mobilized into opposing camps. Each camp proclaims its own virtue and criticizes the opposition. An election is then held and the winners take control of the government. The losers remain free to arouse popular hostility toward the new leaders in the hopes of embarassing them and ultimately replacing them in office. This is normally the way decision makers are chosen in the United States. One therefore expects to find an understanding that these are the methods which should be employed to select public officials, and that nearly all Americans would agree with the following statements:

> Democracy is the best form of government.
>
> Public officials should be chosen by majority vote.
>
> Every citizen should have an equal chance to influence public policy.
>
> The minority should be free to criticize majority decisions.
>
> People in the minority should be free to try to win majority support for their opinions.[1]

Empirical research in fact shows an overwhelming positive consensus on these statements.[2] But note that these assertions are very abstract; there is no reference to any specific person or group. They basically constitute official American political ideology—the sort of lessons that are taught in a variety of both political and nonpolitical contexts by the family and school, and reinforced by the mass media. As statements concerning the rules of the game become more specific, support for these rules declines. Relevant evidence from a number of surveys is presented in Table 4-1. Clearly public support for these procedural rights can at best be described as mixed. On certain questions regarding majority rights and the rights of the accused, support is quite high. Conversely, on any question that smacks of extremism, protests, or demonstrations, support for democratic values declines considerably. Observe that while these statements are more specific than the "consensus" statements just presented, there is still no reference of their

Table 4-1. Support for Democratic Values in the Abstract, By Item

Item	Democratic Response	Undecided	Undemocratic Response
Do you think people should be allowed to circulate petitions and ask the government to act on some issue? (NORC: 1971)	59%	36%	5%
As long as there appears to be no danger of violence, do you think any group, no matter how extreme, should be allowed to organize protest against the government? (CBS: 1970)	21	3	76
If the government makes a decision that most people think is a good one, do you think other people ought to be allowed to criticize it? (NORC: 1971)	48	40	10
Do you think that people should be allowed to hold a peaceful demonstration to ask the government to act on some issue? (NORC: 1971)	47	36	17
. . . Suppose all other methods have failed and a person decides to try to stop the government from going about its usual activities with sit-ins, mass meetings, demonstrations, and the like. Would you approve? (SRC: 1974)	8	40	52
In most criminal cases, the judge conducts the trial and a jury decides guilt or innocence. Instead of a jury, would it be better if the judge alone decided guilt or innocence? (CBS: 1970)	82	4	14
If the police suspect that drugs, guns, or other criminal evidence is hidden in someone's house, should they be allowed to enter the house without first obtaining a search warrant? (CBS: 1970)	66	2	32
At their trials, do you think suspected criminals should have the right to refuse to answer questions if they feel their answers may be used against them? (CBS: 1970)	54	4	42

Table 4-1. Continued

Item	Democratic Response	Undecided	Undemocratic Response
The majority has the right to abolish minorities if it wants to. (McClosky: 1958)	72	N/A	28
People ought to be allowed to vote even if they can't do it intelligently. (McClosky: 1958)	48	N/A	52
If a man is found innocent of a serious crime but new evidence is uncovered, do you think he should be tried for the same crime again? (CBS: 1970)	32	4	58
If a person is suspected of a serious crime, do you think the police should be allowed to hold him in jail until they can get enough evidence to officially charge him? (CBS: 1970)	38	3	58

Sources. NORC: National Opinion Research Center Study, 4119, 1971; CBS: Robert Chandler, *Public Opinion* (New York: R.R. Bowker, 1972), pp. 19-35; CPS: Center for Political Studies Presidential Election Study, 1974; Herbert McClosky, "Consensus and Ideology in American Politics", *APSR,* 58 (June 1964).

application to specific unpopular minority groups such as atheists, Nazis, or Communists. We would expect the endorsement of constitutional rights for these individuals would be even lower. In addition to nonsupport from the generally intolerant, some of the generally tolerant would withdraw support because of their dislike of the persons in question. Presented in Table 4-2 is the support for procedural norms when the statements refer to specific individuals or groups. Fortunately, we have information from differing years so we may also investigate changes in these data over time. Two points immediately attract one's attention, First, there has been a substantial improvement over a 23 year period in the tolerance of the public for the democratic rights of unpopular groups. Second, large segments of the public still remain very unsympathetic to the rights of certain individuals. Forty-three percent believe that books written by admitted communists should not be allowed in a public library. Sixty-one percent would oppose having an atheist teach at a college or university. Thirty-six percent would not let an admitted homosexual make a speech. Many find a situation where a large percentage of the public is uncommitted to democratic values to be discouraging—if not dangerous.

A question that has received considerable attention among academic students of politics is how democracy survives when rejection of democratic

Table 4-2 Public Tolerance for Advocates of Unpopular Ideas: 1954 - 1977

	Person Should Be Allowed to Make a Speech		Person Should Be Allowed to Teach in a College		Person's Book Should Remain in the Library	
	1954	1977	1954	1977	1954	1977
An admitted Communist	28%	57%	6%	40%	29%	57%
Someone against all churches and religion	38	63	12	39	37	60
Someone who favored government ownership of all the railroads and all large industries	65	78[a]	38	61[a]	60	73[a]
Someone who believes that blacks are genetically inferior	b	58	b	42	b	62
A person who advocates doing away with elections and letting the military run the country	b	51	b	40	b	59
An admitted homosexual	b	64	b	51	b	57

Sources. 1954 data is from Samuel Stouffer, *Communism, Conformity and Civil Liberties* (New York: Wiley, 1954); 1977 data is from NORC, General Social Survey 1977.
[a]1974 NORC Survey.
[b]Question not asked in 1954.

87

norms—the procedural rules of the game—is so widespread. Several studies conducted in the 1950s, in addition to the one reported in Table 4-2, demonstrated that sizable majorities were often opposed to democratic rights when these rights were stated in specific terms.[3] Tolerance has since increased, but democratic government and protection for civil liberties was not qualitatively different in the 1950s than it is today. An influential theory was advanced to account for these findings. It is commonly referred to as "the theory of democratic elitism."[4] The theory was spawned by the observation that support for democratic values is not evenly spread throughout the population. Three groups are regarded as being particularly relevant: the politically uninterested, the educated and politically alert, and professional politicians.[5] These groups differ in their levels of commitment to democratic values, with the uninterested group being the least committed and the practicing politicians the most committed. Several investigators have presented data to show that the better educated tended to give more support to democratic procedures.[6] In addition, some argue that even within categories of education political elites are more tolerant than the public. For example, one author inferred from the Stouffer data (part of which is presented in Table 4-2) that the "difference between leaders and the community at large does not seem due simply to education, since 79 percent of the college educated leaders are among the more tolerant as compared to 66 percent for the general college educated population."[7] According to the theory, political leaders are more tolerant than their education alone would predict because of their exposure to the democratic values which permeate the American elite political culture.[8] The system works, therefore, because those who are least attached to democratic values are very unlikely to be active or influential in politics. On the other hand, those most committed to democratic tolerance are the ones who have the most influence on actual political outcomes because of their high interest and high levels of political participation. In the words of one of the more influential writers on the subject: "Democratic viability is . . . saved by the fact that those who are the most confused about democratic ideas are also most likely to be politically apathetic."[9] Thus for democratic stability to exist, a near consensus on support for the rules of the game need only exist among the political influentials.

Reanalysis of the Stouffer data by Robert Jackman casts considerable doubt on the claim that political influentials are more supportive of democratic values than are others who share their education, sex, region of origin, and other distinguishing characteristics.[10] However, most political activists and office holders are highly educated, and there can be little doubt that education is a strong determinant of at least verbal support for democratic norms. Presented in Table 4-3 are questions measuring tolerance of specific groups for respondents with a grade school, high school, and college education. It is quite clear that as education increases, support for democratic norms also increases. The college educated, in particular, tend to be quite

Table 4-3. Support for Democratic Values by Education

Belief	Grade School	High School	College Graduate
Allow atheist to speak	30%	68%	82%
Allow atheist to teach in college	18	39	61
Allow atheist's book to remain in libraries	32	63	81
Allow racist to speak	44	61	73
Allow racist to teach in college	37	38	55
Allow racist's book to remain in libraries	15	39	45
Allow homosexual to speak	34	70	81
Allow homosexual to teach in college	21	55	71
Allow homosexual's book to remain in libraries	26	61	76

Source. NORC General Social Survey: 1977.

tolerant when rights are stated in both the abstract and stated in reference to unpopular groups.

The educated are also more likely to translate their agreement with the abstract principles of democracy into support for the rights of specific groups. The failure of those with low education to endorse the rights of unpopular groups is thus both a function of nonsupport for abstract democratic norms and a failure, among those who *are committed* to those abstract principles, to apply the principles in specific cases. For example, in a national survey analyzed by David Lawrence, respondents were asked if petitioning should be allowed "always," "sometimes," or "never." Seventy-nine percent of the college educated sample compared to 40 percent of those with a grade school education responded "always." In addition, the educated who responded "always" very consistently applied the principle in specific situations. Ninety-one percent of this group felt that "radical students" ought to be allowed to petition. But among those with a grade school education who responded "always" to the abstract principle, only 61 percent felt that "radical students" ought to be allowed to petition.[11] Thus the educated elite is both more supportive of general democratic norms and more consistent in applying them in specific instances. Proponents of democratic elitism can point to countries like Argentina, where government has been very unstable, and find confirmation for their theory in that educated political activists there are very *low* in support for democratic values.[12] That American political elites score very high on these values is then interpreted as an explanation for democratic stability in the United States.

Considerable criticism has been directed at the theory we have just discussed. Any explanation of democratic stability which portrays political activists and office holders as saviors and common people as villains will be found immediately suspect by many. One very obvious assumption that needs to be questioned is the relationship between anti-democratic *attitudes* and anti-democratic *behavior*. Empirical research has shown that statements of intent and the ability to put them into action depend on a variety of situational factors.[13] For example, a person would probably look for group support before attempting to prevent an atheist from speaking or removing books by a communist from the public library. The perceived likelihood that one's actions might be challenged also influences whether or not persons will act on their beliefs. Thus translating anti-democratic beliefs into behavior may be considerably more difficult than translating preference for some political candidate into the behavior of casting a vote. One factor that may make it difficult is the perception of reasonably widespread support for the democratic rights.[14]

Critics also point out that elites themselves are far from perfectly committed to democratic values. For example, 23 percent of the college educated would not allow a communist to speak and 28 percent would not allow a homosexual to teach in a college or university (see Table 4-3). Despite the survey evidence, the actual record of tolerance for democratic rights by the mass public has not, in the view of most people, been unduly alarming. On the other hand, one can point to certain elite behaviors which many find to be dangerously undemocratic. Among the examples are the internment of Japanese-Americans during World War II, the failure of political elites to critically respond to violations by Senator Joseph McCarthy of traditional norms of free speech and due process, and the events surrounding the break-in at the Watergate by persons in the employ of the president of the United States. Such anti-democratic behavior on the part of elites may constitute the real threat to democracy since mass behavior is often responsive to the actions and proposals of political leaders. V. O. Key has observed that the masses do not corrupt themselves, but rather if corrupted, blame must rest with their political leaders.[15]

A very different type of critique holds that the survey evidence which supports the elitist theory is itself invalid. Mary Jackman argues that any question employing an "agree-disagree" format (or its equivalent) is substantively of little meaning.[16] She argues that in responses to survey questions, the less educated tend to be "yea-sayers"—to agree with survey statements. The better educated display the reverse tendency; they are "nay-sayers." Unless a statement is very carefully qualified they will disagree with it. Since a preponderant number of these questions tend to be positively stated, differences between educational groups is artificially inflated by these response sets.[17] A more fundamental criticism (since questions can and have been improved) made in another paper by Mary Jackman is that the better educated learn what are socially desirable and "appropriate" answers to questions about democratic tolerance. Evidence for this claim can be seen in Table 4-3. Note that 45 percent of the college educated would not allow a racist to teach. They may have learned that it is now socially *chic* to condemn racists, even though their rights of free expression are no different than those of communists or any other group. In other words, the groups that were unpopular in the 1950s may no longer be as unpopular today. It is not support for democratic rights which has changed, but the unpopularity of certain groups. This point is supported in a paper by Sullivan, Piereson, and Markus which demonstrates that when individuals are allowed to define their own unpopular group, support for the rights of that group are lower than the just-cited literature would suggest.[18] Furthermore, the college educated are more adept at moving back and forth between general and specific statements. They can recognize logical contradictions. But this learning is of a very superficial sort. Jackman argues that in truly demanding *applied* situations (like racial integration), the well educated are no more likely to be tolerant than the poorly educated.

This debate may, however, soon turn out to be of only passing interest. As can be seen from Table 4-2, there has been a very substantial increase in support for democratic values. Changes of over 20 percentage points are not common in survey data. Furthermore, many students of democratic tolerance predict an even greater change in the tolerant direction.[19] At the very least, the need for an "elitist defense" of these values does not seem as pressing now as it did in 1954.

The most convincing explanation for this change is that increases in exposure to social and cultural diversity lead to an increase in support for democratic norms. The two changes of the most consequence in this process are probably rising levels of education and the move from rural to urban areas. The proportion of people who have been to college and who have college degrees has more than doubled since the middle 1950s. Currently, almost 50 percent of the nation's high school graduates go on to college.[20] Educated people are more likely to understand the importance of protecting democratic liberties, if only in their own self-interest. They realize that a free society cannot exist unless one is tolerant of unfamiliar attitudes and behaviors. Also, social and cultural diversity, such as that found in the city, brings individuals into contact with people who are not like them. They learn that those who are different are not always dangerous.[21]

The single most important factor accounting for the rise in tolerance is cohort replacement.[22] The older generation dies and is replaced by a new one. Two aspects are involved. First, the younger age groups are better educated, and education is an important determinant of tolerance. However, even with education controlled, older people tend to be less tolerant than those who are younger. This is probably due to a generation effect; older people were socialized to politics in a less tolerant era. Many of those over 60 in 1954 (the most intolerant age group) had died by 1977 and were replaced by younger age groups which are considerably more supportive of democratic values.

Interestingly, there is an increase in tolerance beyond what one would predict as simply due to the factors we have just mentioned. For example, within categories of education (like high school graduates) people are more tolerant today than they were in 1954.[23] There is an unexplained residual increase in support for democratic norms that cannot be accounted for by standard variables such as education and occupation. So far there has been no convincing explanation as to why, but in the words of one writer: "I'll be damned if I know what I think about it myself. But I'm sure glad about it."[24]

4-2 POLITICAL CONSENSUS

Clearly, a democracy will be more stable if citizens agree, or are in consensus over basic values and goals. Some conflict over issues is inevitable in a democracy, because public policies generally cannot benefit or penalize all persons or groups equally. Intense or severe political conflict, however, is undesirable because it may threaten the stability of democracy. Robert Dahl defines intensity of conflict as a function of the extent to which each side sees the other as enemies to be destroyed by whatever means necessary.[25] As issues become more intensely debated, the language of conflict becomes harsher; opponents are accused of acting out of less than honorable motives, and tactics that were once regarded as illegitimate are given serious consideration. The Protestant-Catholic split in Northern Ireland is a classic example of a political division that makes democratic government and protection of civil liberties virtually impossible.

The United States has clearly experienced political conflict, but unlike many countries there has not been significant controversy over a number of fundamental issues. Evidence from several surveys indicates that (1) the broad elements of the constitutional order are widely endorsed; (2) there is a consensus that defects should be remedied by legal processes of change; (3) most people are satisfied with the economic order; few want the nationalization of large corporations; big business is widely accepted; labor unions are less popular, but few would like to see them eliminated; (4) Americans believe that opportunity exists for personal achievement; the doors of success are open for those willing to work; and (5) most people are content with their lot; Americans believe the United States is the best place in the world to live. Almost no one wants to emigrate.[26]

Traditional sources of cleavages that have posed problems in other countries have, for the most part, been moderate in the United States. Among the most important of these are class, regionalism, and religion. Particularly important is the fact that political attitudes and actions are only weakly related to these divisions.

Identification with social class is moderate. In most surveys, about one out of three respondents refuse to identify with either the working class or the middle class. Even among those who do identify with one of these classes, sentiments do not seem to be very strong.[27] As we discuss in detail in Chapter 6, the working class tends to be somewhat more conservative on noneconomic questions. However, these differences are at best modest, and there is considerable diversity *within* these classes. Regional differences also tend not to be intense. The American public is very mobile. Beginning in the 1950s, about one family in four moved each year, often to considerable distance. Even the South, on the question of race, is beginning to lose some of its uniqueness.[28] Religious antagonisms, too, do not lead to severe issue conflicts. One reason is that religious preference is only slightly related to social class. One's religion does not determine one's opportunities or economic well-being. The low salience of these conflicts is evidenced in that only 8 percent of the public (in 1969) said they *would not* vote for a Jew for President. An identical 8 percent said they would not vote for a Catholic.[29]

Two contemporary issues, however, have proved to be very divisive— race and (until its termination) the Vietnam war. Violence and anti-democratic behavior have accompanied attempts to resolve each. The race issue, of course, has existed since the beginning of the Republic, and has been the principal threat to the survival of democratic rights in the United States. The most recent violent manifestation of this cleavage was the urban riots that existed in virtually every American city between 1965 and 1968. Although the violence has subsided, there still exists a very wide gap between the opinions of whites and blacks on a wide range of issues. These differences are most pronounced on questions of racial integration (see Chapter 6), but exist in other domains as well. For example, in 1972, 66 percent of black Americans leaned toward Vietnam withdrawal compared with 40 percent of whites.[30] The possibility for conflict between the races is intensified by the fact that socioeconomic differences reinforce issue disagreements. Most blacks are working class, while a considerably greater proportion of whites belong to the more affluent sections of American society.

Unlike the race issue, which threatens to polarize along racial lines, the Vietnam war polarized along ideological lines. The disagreement was so intense that it resulted in a number of actions at the fringe of legality and some that went considerably beyond. Readers are no doubt familiar with most of these: demonstrations, riots, occupying buildings, violence (police, hardhats versus hippies), and shooting down unarmed demonstrators. As a counter to the perceived threat of the radical left, the government engaged in a number of illegal practices such as wiretapping, surveillance and subversion.

The Vietnam war caused many of the traits that are characteristic of intense political conflict to be displayed. The stakes were high, there were substantial numbers on both sides with strongly held beliefs, and there was no compromise acceptable to competing sides. While relatively few were directly affected by the war, a very vocal minority was outraged over the notion of American boys being required to fight and sometimes die in someone else's civil war. Another sizable minority saw the war resisters as traitors. They wanted to employ maximum military power to terminate the war. Compromise was extremely difficult; both sides were committed. In addition, the North Vietnamese would accept only one solution—total American withdrawal.

While attitudes about the war posed a very serious cleavage, there were two factors that served to diminish its polarizing effect. First, the entire population was not divided into two extreme camps. Rather, after 1968, the majority tended toward a middle position. They viewed the war as a mistake, but did not want it ended by an immediate withdrawal or an all out military attack.[31] There also existed "cross cutting cleavages." Extreme conflict becomes most threatening when an individual's attitudes and group memberships reinforce each other. An example would be a very high proportion of "doves" that are college educated, under 30, white, Democrats, pro-affirmative action, pro-abortion, anti-business, and religious agnostics. However, attitudes toward the Vietnam war were not highly associated with other attitudes or with group membership. Doves were not necessarily pro-abortion, college educated, under thirty, or religious nonbelievers. Rather, views on the War cut across these divisions. The existence of crosscutting cleavages served to mute the intensity of the conflict.[32]

4-3 POLITICAL SUPPORT: TRUST AND EFFICACY

A common assumption is that the political system works better when citizens give it their support than when they are "alienated," or estranged from government. The two most prominent dimensions of political support are political trust and efficacy. Trust is the affective component of support. Those high in trust are satisfied with the procedures and products of government. The opposite of trust is political cynicism, or the evaluation that government is not producing policies according to expectations. Efficacy is the cognitive or belief component of support. It is the extent to which a person believes his political activities will influence government. Trust relates to an assessment of government output, and efficacy relates to the consequences of one's input.

Political Trust and Democratic Stability

No government has the complete trust of all its citizens. However, many argue that it is important for democratic government to maintain some minimal (usually unspecified) level of trust among its citizens. One argument is pitched at the normative level. If the distinctive characteristic of democracy is the substitution of voluntary consent for coercion, it is no small moral shortcoming when citizens withdraw trust out of a conviction that government is not acting in their best interests.[33] Others make claims of a more practical bent. Levels of trust are thought to affect the leadership strategies available to political-decision makers. Leaders must be able to make decisions and commit resources without first consulting those persons who will be affected by the decisions and called upon to supply the resource material. According to William Gamson, when trust in government is high, "the authorities are able to make new commitments on the basis of it and, if successful, increase such support even more. When it is low and declining, authorities may find it difficult to meet existing commitments and govern effectively."[34] Thus, in 1964, the government could draw on its "credit rating" with the electorate and send troops to fight an overseas police action with little public debate. That sort of freedom to act will likely be constrained considerably in the near future. If trust drops sufficiently low, some contend, it can lead to social disruption. Disruption may serve as an impetus to needed reform, or it may threaten the stability of the existing regime. At the very least, a portion of state resources will have to be diverted to cope with the disturbances. Almond and Verba write that insufficient trust is particularly dangerous when the system is not performing in an adequate fashion, for example, during an economic depression.[35] Lipset provides evidence that in the 1930s, when many democratic governments ceased to be effective, those which had induced a sense of trust among their citizens were able to withstand the strain, while those not so advantaged (Austria, Germany, Spain) succumbed to anti-democratic movements.[36] More recently, Arthur Miller has flatly asserted, "A democratic political system cannot survive for long without the support of a majority of its citizens."[37]

Levels of political trust may serve as a barometer indicating how well government is performing. It is, therefore, no surprise that scholars have paid considerable attention to the fluctuations in trust over time.[38] As can be seen from Table 4-4, recently there has been a rather dramatic decline in the trust Americans feel for the political order.

Table 4-4. Trends in Political Trust By Item: 1958 - 1976

Item[c]	1958	1964	1966	1968	1970	1972	1974	1976	Change[b]
Government use of tax money									
Distrust	45.1	48.1	a	60.6	69.7	67.0	75.7	76.4	−31.3
Trust	54.9	51.9	a	39.4	30.3	33.0	24.3	23.6	
Trust government to do right									
Distrust	24.2	22.3	32.1	37.2	45.3	45.8	63.2	68.2	−44.0
Trust	75.8	77.7	67.9	62.8	54.7	54.2	36.8	31.8	
Government run for big interests									
Distrust	a	27.8	38.5	43.6	55.1	58.6	72.5	73.5	−44.8
Trust	a	72.2	61.5	56.4	44.9	47.4	27.5	26.5	
Are government leaders capable									
Distrust	37.7	30.9	a	39.2	46.2	42.2	49.1	53.1	−15.4
Trust	61.3	69.1	a	60.8	53.8	57.8	51.9	46.9	
Are government officials crooked									
Distrust	25.5	30.1	a	26.4	32.7	37.7	46.8	44.1	−18.6
Trust	74.5	69.9	a	73.6	67.3	62.3	53.2	55.9	

Source. SRC/CPS American National Election Studies: 1958-1976.
[a]Question not asked.
[b]Percent change in the direction of less trust.
[c]The percentage in the distrust row should be interpreted to mean the percentage of the population giving a response to the question indicating distrust.

The data for 1958 reflect the tranquillity of the Eisenhower years. After 1964, trust began to decrease at a steady pace up until 1972. Common explanations normally include the government's handling of the civil rights movement, the economy, and the Vietnam war. Arthur Miller has shown the decrease comes about equally from the dissatisfied left and the dissatisfied right.[39] For example, cynics on the left tend to think the government has moved too slowly on civil rights; cynics on the right feel it has moved too rapidly. Miller concludes that disenchantment of this sort with government policies (outputs) is the primary reason for the decline in trust between 1964 and 1970. Between 1972 and 1974 there was another very sharp decline in trust, particulary on the questions concerning beliefs that "the government will do right" and that the "government is run for a few big interests." The most plausible expanation is Watergate. Daily accusations of break-ins, slush funds, wiretapping, extortion, coverups, etc. are not designed to encourage enthusiasm for government. But note there is no recovery between 1974 and 1976. In fact, despite the claim by President Ford that he had restored faith in government and the campaign pledge by Jimmy Carter that he would restore trust and confidence if elected, levels of trust declined even further. The only exception was a slight improvement on the question of whether or not government officials are crooked.

There is general agreement that dissatisfaction with government performance is the source of the increase in cynicism. There is considerable disagreement, however, over what it all means.[40] First, does the decline in trust indicate a withdrawal of allegiance from the political system as a whole, or is it simply dissatisfaction with the performance of incumbent office holders? Obviously, the former is considerably more serious than the latter. Loyalty to the political order does not necessarily preclude cynicism about the policies and procedures of those currently holding public office. One can trust the government as an institution, but greatly dislike those responsible for its management in the recent past. This interpretation is supported by evidence from the 1976 SRC/CPS election study. Respondents were asked in a straight-forward fashion whether they thought the lack of trust in government was due to the individuals in office or if there was something more seriously wrong with government in general. Sixty-eight percent thought the problem resided with incumbent political officials.[41] To borrow an analogy from Jack Citrin, "political systems, like baseball teams, have slumps and winning streaks. Having recently endured a succession of losing seasons, Americans boo the home team when it takes the field. But fans are often fickle; victories quickly elicit cheers. And to most fans what matters is whether the home team wins or loses, not how it plays the game."[42] According to this analysis, a few wins and perhaps a few new faces in the lineup may once again elicit the accolades of political trust from the mass public.

A second issue concerns the effects of low political trust on the day-to-day operation of government. How far must it decline before it makes a difference? One obvious observation is that the process of government does not currently seem to operate in a manner fundamentally different from the late 1950s. The weapons of war are still being built, pensions are paid, and the garbage is collected. On some of the items reported in Table 4-4 the level of trust is below 30 percent. One author speculates that the support of 10 to 15 percent of the population is enough.[43] But the social location of that group is important. In the United States, support is highest among the white, nonSouthern, nonJewish, middle-aged, upper middle class. The trust of this group may be a key to democratic stability.[44] A final argument is that low trust, when combined with high efficacy, can lead to regime threatening actions by the public. We shall discuss this possibility below.

Political Efficacy and Democratic Stability

The concept political efficacy was originally developed in the early 1950s to explain variations in voting turnout. The four-item scale used to measure it has been repeated frequently and over a longer time span than almost any other social indicator of a survey sort. Efficacy can best be described as a belief that one can influence the political process; a feeling that an active citizen can play a part in bringing about social and political change; and that one's input counts.[45] Since it was first developed, the concept has been generalized to account for a wide variety of political activities. In the most comprehensive study of political participation to date, Sidney Verba and Norman Nie found a strong association between efficacy and their overall index of political participation (16 items).[46] The study, in addition, generally shows that the higher the sense of political efficacy the greater the likelihood that one will participate in political activities of a relatively demanding sort. Conversely, a low sense of efficacy is one of the factors normally associated with political apathy.[47]

One would expect an increase in political efficacy over time. In surveys, people with the most education score highest on measures of political efficacy.[48] Since the education of the American population has been increasing, levels of efficacy should be rising as well. This relationship corresponds with common sense. The educated are usually more politically knowledgeable, interested, and self-confident.

Presented in Table 4-5 are the trends in the four items which comprise the efficacy scale. One immediately notes that the first two items have changed in a fashion quite different from the last two. For the NO SAY and DON'T CARE items the population has become *less* efficacious since 1952. For COMPLEX there has been little change. In the case of VOTING there has been a dramatic increase in the proportion of the population giving an efficacious response. It seems quite apparent that the individual questions are not measuring the same phenomenon. This suspicion is supported by a number of studies investigating the validity and reliability of the items.[49] The first two items (NO SAY and DON'T CARE) seem contaminated in that they also measure trust. It seems quite plausible that cynics would believe that people have no say in government and that public officials care little about them. The latter two items (COMPLEX and VOTING) are more clearly indicators of efficacy.[50] This is particularly true of VOTING, which more visibly taps the norm that participation in politics can be effective.[51] The item also behaves as theory predicts. The upward change over time is greatest among the better educated.[52] Note also the large increase between 1964 and 1968. Converse argues this reflects an expansion in political activity brought about by the Civil Rights movement and protest against the Vietnam war.[53] During this period, activities beyond voting, such as demonstrations, marches, sit-ins, and the like became common methods for expressing dissent.

Given the difficulties with the efficacy scale, why continue to use it? The basic reason is that the questions have been asked at least every four years since 1952. They are therefore invaluable for trend analysis. But given the importance of the concept, it would seem incumbent upon us to develop a better measure. One recent attempt by Joe Aberbach is an index he calls "power consciousness."[54] It is measured by the question: "Do you think people like you have too little political power or just about the right amount?" If the respondent answers "too little" he or she is then asked why. The reasons are basically classed (we are simplifying) into individual or group deficiencies and political system-level problems. Those who were dissatisfied and blamed the system were generally the most politically active.[55] Unfortunately, the technique seems rather insensitive as a measure of positive political efficacy.

Aside from its association with participation, political efficacy plays an important role in theories of democratic stability. Theorists of "participatory democracy" are concerned with the effect political participation has on individual character development. They see an elevated sense of efficacy as a desirable consequence of political activity; a belief that one can and should be self-governing is an important aspect of a meaningful existence.[56] A related perspective can be found in the five-nation study by Gabriel Almond and Sidney Verba, *The Civic Culture.*[57] They see a strong sense of political efficacy as a key element in forming the ideal political culture in a stable democracy. Almond and Verba view the ideal citizen as believing in the success of his political actions (efficacy), believing that he is obligated to participate (citizen duty), but as being rather inactive politically in actual practice. While they concede that "unless there is some control of government elites by nonelites, it is hard to consider a political system democrat-

Table 4-5. Trends in Political Efficacy by Item: 1952 - 1976

Item		1952	1956	1960	1964	1968	1972	1976	Change
					Year				
NO SAY: People like me don't have any say about what the government does.	Agree	31.4	28.4	27.4	29.6	41.2	40.5	42.1	−10.7
	Disagree	68.6	71.6	72.6	70.4	58.8	59.5	57.9	
DON'T CARE: I don't think officials care much what people like me think	Agree	36.3	27.0	25.0	36.9	43.7	50.1	53.7	−17.1
	Disagree	63.7	73.0	75.0	63.1	56.3	49.9	46.3	
COMPLEX: Sometimes politics and government seem so complicated that a person like me can't understand what's going on.	Agree	71.3	63.9	58.8	67.9	71.2	73.9	72.7	−1.5
	Disagree	28.6	36.1	41.2	32.1	28.8	26.1	27.3	
VOTING: Voting is the only way that people like me can have any say about how the government runs things.	Agree	82.7	74.4	74.3	74.0	57.5	62.3	56.4	+26.3
	Disagree	17.3	25.6	25.7	26.0	42.5	37.7	43.6	

Source. University of Michigan SRC/CPS Presidential Election Studies, 1952-1976.

ic;" the authors also argue that elites must have the power to initiate and carry out policies, adjust to new situations, meet internal and external challenges," and generally make authoritative decisions.[58] Thus, low participation gives government room to operate, but people's strong confidence in the potential effectiveness of their participation assures that political leaders will act in a responsible fashion.

Almond and Verba believe that the best manifestations of the desired political culture are in the United States and Great Britain. They argue that the citizens of these countries have a strong sense of civic duty to participate and great confidence that participation would be effective. Yet they view the American and British public as relatively politically apathetic in practice. The authors base their conclusions on an ambitious survey of opinion in the United States, Great Britain, West Germany, Italy, and Mexico. The major findings are presented in Table 4-6.

The first six differences among the countries shown in the table support Almond and Verba's conclusion. Americans and Britons are more likely to sense a responsibility to be actively involved in their community and to feel they can do something about local and national unjust or harmful regulations. But, like their fellow citizens in the other countries, they show little actual participation, at least as judged by a lack of attempts to influence local government and a failure to regularly follow politics and governmental affairs. However, whether citizens can and do influence government matters little. What counts is the belief. According to the authors:

> The citizen's . . . role, as an active and influential enforcer of the responsiveness of elites, is maintained by his strong commitment to the norm of active citizenship, as well as by his perception that he can be an influential citizen. This may in part be a myth, for it involves a set of norms of participation and perceptions of ability to influence that are not quite matched by actual political behavior. Yet the very fact that citizens hold to this myth—that they see themselves as influential and as obligated to take an active role—creates a potentiality of citizen influence and activity. . . . A citizen within the civic culture has, then, a reserve of influence. He is not constantly involved in politics; he does not actively oversee the behavior of political decision makers. But he does have the potential to act if there is need.[39]

If, however, we identify the actual percentage in each country showing the three attributes of the ideal citizen identified in *The Civic Culture,* the conclusion that the United States and Britain come closest to satisfying the model political culture receives only modest support. These attributes are that citizens (1) believe they should be active, (2) are optimistic that they would be successful if active, and (3) are not very politically active. The percentage of the population in each country showing all three properties is:

United States   22%
United Kingdom   17
Germany   9
Italy   3
Mexico   10.[60]

Table 4-6. Evidence of Civic Cultures in Five Democracies

	United States	United Kingdom	Germany	Italy	Mexico
Percent believing the ordinary man should be active in his community	51	39	22	10	26
Percent who say they can do something about an unjust national regulation	75	62	38	28	38
Percent who say they can do something about an unjust local regulation	77	78	62	51	52
Percent reporting they regularly or occasionally discuss politics	76	70	60	32	38
Percent saying they would likely have success if they tried to change harmful local regulation	52	36	32	22	37
Percent saying they would likely have success if they tried to change harmful national regulation	41	25	13	11	29
Percent who follow accounts of political and governmental affairs regularly	27	23	34	11	15
Percent who say they have attempted to influence local government	28	15	14	9	6

Source. Gabriel A. Almond and Sidney Verba, *The Civic Culture.* Pages respective to items above: p. 169, p. 185, p. 89, p. 116. The last two items are taken from the Inter-University Consortium For Political Research Codebook, *The Five Nation Study* (Ann Arbor: ICPR, 1968), pp. 29 and 83.

These minorities would hardly seem to be an adequate base on which to build stable democracies, assuming stability does indeed rest on such beliefs.

Citizen Roles: Combinations of Trust and Efficacy

It should come as no surprise that political efficacy and trust are related to one another; that those who feel they can influence government also tend to trust it.[61] Presented below are four possible linkages between efficacy and trust.

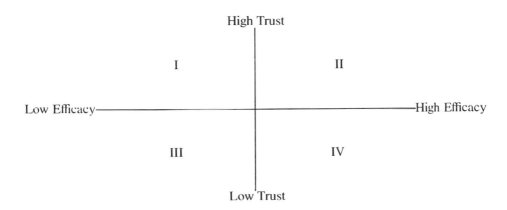

Our principal interest is in persons characterized by quadrant IV, because of their potential for violence and anti-democratic behavior. But first we shall briefly discuss the other three types. Type I is the loyal subject, high on trust but low on efficacy. These individuals are strongly attached to the symbols of the American political community. The slogan "my country right or wrong" so permeates their political outlook that it stifles any desire to become politically active or politically involved. Type II is the combination many would consider to be the ideal democratic citizen. A person with a very positive outlook on the political order, politically attentive and involved—but involved within the limits of accepted social convention. Type III individuals, cynical and without hope, are classic examples of the politically alienated. They are hostile, suspicious, and mistrustful of government, but they lack the self-confidence to take action. Individuals from quadrant IV, cynical and efficacious, can be mobilized for political activity, but are often of a volatile and unconventional sort. It is often argued that the numbers of these persons must be minimized to maintain democratic stability.

Considerable research has been conducted into the behavior patterns of those low on trust but high on efficacy. This research has been of two sorts.

One approach has been to look at the "predisposition" to engaged in unconventional or violent behavior. Abravanel and Busch find, for a sample of college students, that type IV respondents are likely to employ "nontraditional" forms of exerting political influence.[62] Muller's Waterloo, Iowa study demonstrates a "readiness to engage in acts of unconventional dissent against the state."[63] Schwartz reports a repudiation of "conformist" modes of political participation among both students and urban blacks.[64] Another approach is to analyze the orientations of persons who have actually engaged in violent or anti-democratic behavior. Two studies of riot participants are relevant. Jeffery Paige found those involved in the 1967 Newark, New Jersey riot were highly efficacious, but very mistrustful of local government.[65] Sears and Maconahay find a similar attitudinal syndrome among participants in the 1965 Watts riot.[66]

Although there is little doubt about the reliability of these relationships, there is considerable uncertainty about the links between these attitudes and behavior. Those studies which investigate "predispositions" are subject to the criticism we made earlier (see Section 4-1) about the linkage between statements of intent and political action. The studies of riot participants raise the question of the direction of causation. The respondents were interviewed after the riots were over. Did the attitudes cause the behavior, or did participating in the riot lead to a change in attitude? One could well imagine someone feeling considerably more efficacious after than before a violent outburst. Also, there is the possibility that riot behavior may be motivated by narrow or local grievances (for example, refusal of a supermarket chain to cash a check), but later justified by indicting the entire political order. The linkages between efficacy, trust, and political action are provocative, but have yet to be firmly established.

4-4 PERSONALITY AND PUBLIC OPINION

Individual political opinions can have their roots in the entire spectrum of human existence. Why many physicians and dentists oppose further extension of Medicare seems fairly obvious. They do not think Medicare is in their best personal interest or in the best interest of the medical profession. It is not as easy to understand why some people are adamantly opposed to the fluoridation of drinking water, while others accept it as a desirable form of preventive medicine. One explanation that has received considerable attention is that certain attitudes and behaviors are possibly influenced by personality.

Although there is no agreed-upon definition, we shall follow Eysenck and define personality as "the more or less stable and enduring organization of a person's character, temperament, intellect, and physique which determines his unique adjustment to his environment."[67] The basic element is the enduring, abstract perspective that a person uses to order the world and meet personal needs, for example, constructing a self-image in which one is an attractive and socially useful individual.

While trait psychologists have tried to associate personalities with specific attitudes and behavior, most researchers interested in personality dismiss such efforts as simplistic and naive. Rather, they pursue investigations across a very wide range of attitudes and beliefs. As might be expected, such extensive and time-consuming assessments for each individual result in few persons being evaluated. The most frequently cited studies of personality and political behavior examine no more than 24 individuals. Such groups can in no way be considered a meaningful sample of any segment of the population. If the dynamics of personality and behavior noted in those limited groups were universal or identical to those of other people, as is sometimes claimed, these works would be more definitive. But their primary contribution is insight into the psyches of people other than ourselves, and the comfortable feeling that we know them personally, as opposed to the formality of a tabular presentation of 1000 or so faceless survey respondents. One study, however, that combines both a clinical perspective and a survey perspective is *The Authoritarian Personality.*

The Authoritarian Personality

Influenced by events in Germany during Hitler's rule, a group of psychologists from the University of California at Berkeley began a systematic investigation into the personality structure of individuals particularly susceptible to anti-Semetic and Fascist political appeals.[68] The study was completed in 1950 and has had a profound influence on all branches of the social sciences.[69]

The thesis of the book is straightforward. Prejudice, suspicion, distrust, and hostility are manifestations of attempts to resolve deep-seated psychological conflicts. At the heart of these conflicts is a highly ambivalent and *intense* orientation toward authority. Authoritarians are very submissive to those above them in the social order and very condescending toward those below. As depicted in German folklore, they are like a person on a bicycle—above they bow, below they kick.[70] While such persons are outwardly very deferential, they in fact harbor considerable hostility toward authority. This hostility, however, is mostly unconscious, and authoritarians are only intermittently aware of the hate side of this love-hate amalgam. Rather, negative feelings are repressed by primitive ego defensive mechanisms. They are extremely servile toward authority, driving from consciousness the malice they feel toward those above them. But repression has its costs, and the tensions created seek some alternate outlet. To compensate for feelings of personal weakness authoritarians present a very tough façade. They are very critical of those they see as beneath them, particularly those who are different (such as members of minority groups).[71] Other characteristics of the authoritarian syndrome include (1) conventionalism, a rigid adherence to conventional middle class values, (2) anti-intraception; opposition to the tenderhearted, subjective, and imaginative, (3) superstition, a belief in mystical determinants influencing one's fate, (4) cynicism, a generalized hostility toward people and (5) projectivity, a belief that wild and dangerous things are going on; that conspiracies are being carried out in secret places.[72]

Authoritarianism is thought to primarily originate with childhood family relationships. Persons displaying the syndrome often describe parent affection as being given only as a reward for good behavior. Their parents employed rigid, punishment-oriented disciplinary practices, as opposed to discipline based on love withdrawal. Family roles were clearly defined in terms of dominance and submission. According to Adorno and his colleagues: "Forced into surface submission to parental authority, the child develops hostility and aggression which are poorly channelized. The displacement of a repressed antagonism toward authority may be one of the sources, and perhaps the principal source, of his antagonism toward outgroups."[73]

The implications of *The Authoritarian Personality* for public opinion and democratic stability became obvious to students of politics soon after its publication. One of the first tasks investigators set for themselves was to determine the political correlates of authoritarianism (are authoritarians prejudiced toward minorities; do they hold anti-democratic political beliefs, etc.?). This undertaking was greatly aided by the fact that *The Authoritarian Personality,* unlike other such studies, provided a ready-made paper and pencil test to measure the extent to which the syndrome exists. This instrument, the California F- (for fascism) scale, has become virtually synonomous with authoritarianism. Typical agree/disagree items from the F-scale are:[74]

> What young people need most of all is strict discipline by their parents.
>
> Most people who don't get ahead just don't have enough will power.
>
> Sex criminals deserve more than prison; they should be whipped in public or worse.

Investigators soon discovered that there were some very severe methodological problems with the F-scale. Among the most difficult to resolve has been response set. All 20 items in the original F-scale were worded in a positive direction (to agree was authoritarian). As we indicated earlier, people with low education tend to be "yea-sayers." It is very difficult to separate the effects of education from the effects of personality. One solution is to reverse some of the items so that disagreeing with the question is the authoritarian response. While this strategy has merit, it is something less than a completely satisfactory solution.[75] Also, one essential requirement of a personality measure is that it not be contaminated by political content. It is charged that the F-scale is biased in the direction of right-wing authoritarianism. For example, one item from the F-scale states: "Homosexuals are hardly better than criminals and ought to be severely punished." Such a question may tap both personality traits and right-wing political outlooks. Consequently, the F-scale might not be sensitive to authoritarians of the left (such as American Communists). In an attempt to deal with this problem, Milton Rokeach has developed a "Dogmatism" scale which he claims is able to tap authoritarianism of both the right and the left (but all the questions are still worded positively).[76]

As a result of these criticisms, research on authoritarianism is now looked upon with suspicion. Due to the ease of administering the F-scale (and similar instruments),[77] there have been literally thousands of published pieces which employ authoritarianism as a variable. Many of these have been poorly done or are little more than "crass empiricism." The field is poorly integrated since many studies are contradictory or noncomparable. Despite these problems, the question of the relationship between authoritarianism and political opinion has merit. It is slippery, elusive, and hard to measure, but the circle of association between authoritarianism and prejudice, intolerance, use of stereotypes, attraction to extremist movements, and sensitivity to authority relationships is simply too wide to be easily dismissed.[78]

Furthermore, there *are* studies indicating an authoritarian effect which meet commonly accepted standards for scientific inquiry. For example, in one investigation a persuasive message was presented in several different forms to a number of different groups. Those scoring high on the F-scale were particularly likely to change their attitude when the message was delivered by a high status source. The effectiveness of the message increased further when its content suggested change in a prejudiced direction.[79] One particularly interesting inquiry involved the classic experiment developed by Stanley Milgram to measure obedience to authority.[80] In this experiment a naive subject ("the teacher") is required by the study director ("the authority figure") to administer an electrical shock each time "the learner" fails to satisfactorily perform a rote memorization task. The teacher is not aware that the learner is in league with the person running the experiment, and is in fact receiving no shock at all. However, each time the learner fails the task, the authority figure (the experimenter) orders the teacher to shock the learner at an even higher level of voltage. As the shocks presumably become stronger, the learner cries out in pain. The object is to see how long the teacher will obey the authority figure and continue to administer the shocks. One disturbing feature of this study is that many subjects will continue to administer the shocks until the learner is in an apparent state of unconsciousness. Alan Elms administered the "teachers" the California F-test before conducting the Milgram experiment. He found that those who scored high on authoritarianism were highly reluctant (as predicted) to disobey the authority and terminate the experiment. Elms explains:

... The relationship between obedience and some elements of authoritarianism seems fairly strong; and it should be remembered that the measure of obedience is a measure of actual submission to authority, not just what a person says he's likely to do. Too much of the research on authoritarianism ... has been on the level of paper and pencil responses, which don't necessarily get translated into behavior. But here we have a realistic and highly disturbing situation.... So it does look as if those researchers in the late 40s had something, something which can be translated from abstract tendencies into actual authoritarian behavior: submitting to the man in command, punishing the weaker subordinate.[81]

Is There A Democratic Personality?

Considerably less attention has been paid to the possibility that there might exist certain personality traits which promote support for democratic principles. Much of what has been written is either speculative or consists of inferences based on intensive interviews with small samples. Writers like Lasswell, Lane, and Inkeles talk about the democratic character as being warm, outgoing, high in self-esteem and ego strength, flexible, and tolerant of ambiguity.[82] One characteristic of this literature is a rather cavalier tendency to portray the democratic personality as the "healthy" personality and the nondemocratic personality as having psychological maladjustments.

It is misleading to talk about a democratic personality as if it were a distinct psychological type. But there may be certain personality traits which illicit support for democratic values as these values interact with particular environmental situations. The emphasis on environment is important because personality traits which encourage support for democratic principles (the accepted norm) among citizens of the United States would probably encourage support for totalitarian communism (the accepted norm) among citizens of the Soviet Union. In a study of self-esteem and support for democracy, Paul Sniderman makes the important point that personality may affect political attitudes both in terms of *motivation* and *learning.*[82] The motivational effect is the more familiar and is the theme of books like *The Authoritarian Personality.* For example, certain psychic tensions motivate individuals to be prejudiced. Sniderman claims that, in addition to motivation, one personality trait, self-esteem, affects support for democratic values through the mechanism of social learning. Low self-esteem seems to discourage social interaction and block political learning. Those high on this personality trait tend to be in the social mainstream and exposed to political information. They are in a position to learn the values of the political order. The rhetoric of American culture celebrates democracy. Those with high self-esteem will more frequently be exposed to this rhetoric and are better able to comprehend its meaning. Because of the worth society places on the ideal of democratic tolerance, understanding it encourages its acceptance.[84]

4-5 CONCLUSION

There seem to be two fundamental prerequisites for the existence and maintenance of democratic rights and freedoms. One is economic and the other is psychological. In the case of the former, considerable research indicates that some minimal level of economic development is necessary before a democracy can successfully operate. The most relevant factor associated with economic development is communication networks. Without sufficiently developed channels of communication, interests cannot be articulated and aggregated; conflicting groups cannot exchange information on goals and desires.[85]

But once a minimal level of economic development has occurred, psychological factors become important. As Deane Neubauer has demonstrated, after a certain "threshold" the most economically advanced nations are not necessarily the most democratic.[86] We have analyzed a number of political attitudes commonly thought to affect the stability of democracy. All may be of consequence, but none alone, or even in combination provides a total explanation for the continued protection of democratic values in the United States. America has perhaps been most fortunate in that there have been few intense group or issue cleavages dividing the population. As long as some modest consensus exists, and most of the population has a minimal degree of economic security, the system seems able to tolerate a wide variety of personality types, a relatively low level of trust for government, and considerable lack of enthusiasm (although perhaps not outright hostility) for procedural democratic norms.

FOOTNOTES FOR CHAPTER 4

1. These statements are from James W. Prothro and Charles M. Grigg, "Fundamental Principles of Democracy: Bases of Agreement and Disagreement," *Journal of Politics*, 22 (Spring 1960), p. 281.

2. Ibid., pp. 276–294.

3. Samuel A. Stouffer, *Communism, Conformity and Civil Liberties* (New York: John Wiley and Sons, 1955); Herbert McClosky, "Consensus and Ideology in American Politics," *American Political Science Review*, 58 (June 1964); A. M. Rose, 'Alienation and Participation," *American Sociological Review*, 27 (December 1964), pp. 831–842.

4. The aspect of theory we are concerned with is most associated with V. O. Key, Jr., *Public Opinion and American Democracy* (New York: Alfred A. Knopf, 1961), and Robert Dahl, *Who Governs* (New Haven: Yale University Press, 1961).

5. Ian Budge, *Agreement and the Stability of Democracy* (Chicago: Markham Publishing, 1970), p. 24.

6. Stouffer; McClosky; Rose.

7. William Kornhauser, *The Politics of Mass Society* (New York: Free Press, 1959), p. 67.

8. McCloskey, p. 365.

9. Ibid., p. 376.

10. Robert W. Jackman, "Political Elites, Mass Publics, and Support for Democratic Principles," *Journal of Politics*, 34 (August 1972), pp. 753–773.

11. David G. Lawrence, "Procedural Norms and Tolerance: A Reassessment," *American Political Science Review,* 70 (March 1976), pp. 90—95.

12. Robert A. Dahl, *Polyarchy* (New Haven: Yale University Press, 1971), p. 139.

13. See Irwin Deutscher, *What we Say/What we Do* (Glenview, Illinois: Scott, Foresman, 1973).

14. Budge, pp. 21—25.

15. Key, p. 558.

16. Mary Jackman, "Education and Prejudice or Education and Response Set?" *American Sociological Review,* 38 (June 1973), pp. 327—339.

17. For example, see McClosky; and Prothro and Grigg.

18. Mary Jackman, "General and Applied Tolerance: Does Education Increase Commitment to Racial Integration?," *American Journal of Political Science,* 22 (May 1978), pp. 302—324; John L. Sullivan, James E. Piereson, and George E. Marcus, "A Reconceptualization of Political Tolerance: Illusory Increases 1950s—1970s (unpublished manuscript).

19. J. Allen Williams, Jr., Clyde Z. Nunn, and Louis St. Peter, "Origins of Tolerance: Findings from a Replication of Stouffer's Communism, Conformity and Civil Liberties," *Social Forces,* 44 (December 1976), pp. 394—408; James A. Davis, "Communism, Conformity, Cohorts, and Categories: American Tolerance in 1954 and 1972—73," *American Journal of Sociology,* 81 (November 1975); see also Clyde Z. Nunn, Harry J. Crockett and J. Allen Williams, *Tolerance for Nonconformity* (San Francisco: Jossey-Bass, 1978).

20. See Chapter 5, The Political Implications of Higher Education.

21. Williams et al., p. 395.

22. Davis.

23. Stephen J. Cutler and Robert L. Kaufman, "Cohort Changes in Political Attitudes: Tolerance of Ideological Nonconformity," *Public Opinion Quarterly,* 39 (Spring 1975), pp. 63—81, and Davis.

24. Quoted in Davis, p. 510.

25. Robert A. Dahl, *Democracy in the United States* (Chicago: Rand McNally, 1976), p. 335.

26. Robert A. Dahl, "The American Oppositions: Affirmation and Denial," in Robert A. Dahl (ed.), *Political Oppositions in Western Democracies* (New Haven: Yale University Press, 1966), pp. 40—41.

27. Dahl, *Democracy in the United States,* p. 358.

28. Ibid., p. 349.

29. George Gallup, *The Gallup Poll* (New York: Random House, 1972), p. 1290.

30. Gerald Pomper, *Voter's Choice* (New York: Dodd, Mead and Company, 1975), p. 132.

31. Dahl, *Democracy in the United States,* p. 407.

32. Much of our discussion of the Vietnam war draws on Dahl, *Democracy in the United States,* Chapter 26.

33. Joseph Tussman, *Obligation and the Body Politic* (New York: Oxford University Press, 1960); George Sabine, "The Two Democratic Traditions," *The Philosophic Review,* 61 (August 1952); William Gamson, *Power and Discontent* (Homewood, Illinois: The Dorsey Press, 1968).

34. Gamson, pp. 45—46.

35. Gabriel Almond and Sidney Verba, *The Civic Culture* (Boston: Little, Brown and Company, 1965) p. 354.

36. Seymour M. Lipset, *Political Man* (Garden City: Doubleday, 1960), p. 69.

37. Arthur H. Miller, "Political Issues and Trust in Government: 1960—1970," *American Political Science Review,* 68 (September 1974), p. 951.

38. The literature on political support is voluminous. Among the better studies are: Edward N. Muller and Thomas O. Jukam, "On the Meaning of Political Support," *American Political Science Review,* 71 (December 1977), pp. 1561–1595; Gamson; Almond and Verba; Joel Aberbach and Jack L. Walker, "Political Trust and Racial Ideology," *American Political Science Review,* 64 (December 1970), pp. 1199–1219; Jeffery Paige, "Political Orientation and Riot Participation," *American Sociological Review,* 36 (October 1971), pp. 810–820; Edward N. Muller, "A Test of a Partial Theory of Potential for Political Violence," *American Political Science Review,* 66 (September 1972), pp. 928–959; Miller.

39. Miller.

40. A good discussion can be found in Jack Citrin, "The Political Relevance of Trust in Government," *American Political Science Review,* 68 (September 1974), pp. 973–1001.

41. Inter-University Consortium for Political and Social Research, 1976 Presidential Election Codebook, variable 3366.

42. Citrin, p. 987.

43. James D. Wright, *The Dissent of the Governed* (New York: Academic Press, 1976), p. 269.

44. Ibid.; see also Robert S. Gilmour and Robert B. Lamb, *Political Alienation in Contemporary America* (New York: St. Martin's Press, 1975).

45. Angus Campbell, Gerald Gurin, and Warren Miller, *The Voter Decides* (Evanston, Illinois: Row, Peterson, 1954), p. 187.

46. Sidney Verba and Norman Nie, *Political Participation in the United States* (New York: Harper and Row, 1972), p. 88.

47. Ibid., p. 133.

48. Philip E. Converse, "Change in the American Electorate," in Angus Campbell and Philip Converse (eds.), *The Human Meaning of Social Change* (New York: Sage, 1972), p. 326.

49. George I. Balch, "Multiple Indicators in Survey Research: The Concept 'Sense of Political Efficacy'" *Political Methodology,* 1 (Spring 1974), pp. 1–44; Herbert Asher, "The Reliability of the Political Efficacy," *Political Methodology,* (Spring 1974), pp. 45–72; J. Miller McPherson, Susan Welch, and Cal Clark, "The Stability and Reliability of Political Efficacy: Using Path Analysis to Test Alternative Models," *American Political Science Review,* 71 (June 1977), pp. 509–521.

50. Balch, "Multiple Indicators."

51. However, the VOTING also has problems with ambiguity. The question is supposed to be interpreted to mean there is no way *other* than voting to influence politicians. Some respondents interpret the question in a way that even voting cannot be used to influence politics. This latter interpretation makes the nonefficacious appear to in fact be efficacious.

52. Converse, pp. 328–329.

53. Ibid.

54. Joel Aberbach, "Power Consciousness: A Comparative Analysis," *American Political Science Review,* 71 (December 1977), pp. 1561–1598.

55. Ibid., p. 1158.

56. Carole Pateman, *Participation and Democratic Theory* (Cambridge: Cambridge University Press, 1970), pp. 45–46.

57. Almond and Verba, *The Civic Culture.*

58. Ibid., p. 476.

59. Ibid., pp. 346–347.

60. Recomputed from data supplied from the Inter-University Consortium for Political and Social Research.

61. Walker and Aberbach; Martin B. Abravanel and Ronald J. Busch, "Political Competence, Political Trust, and the Action Orientation of University Students," *Journal of Politics*, 37 (February 1975), p. 73.

62. Abravanel and Busch.

63. Muller, "A Partial Test of a Theory of Potential for Political Violence."

64. David Schwartz, *Political Alienation and Political Behavior* (Chicago: Aldine, 1973), Chapter 8.

65. Paige, "Political Orientation."

66. David O. Sears and John Maconahay, *The Politics of Violence* (Boston: Houghton Mifflin, 1973).

67. Cited in Paul Sniderman, *Personality and Democratic Politics* (Berkeley: University of California Press, 1975), p. 13.

68. Nevitt Sanford, "Authoritarian Personality in Contemporary Perspective," in Jeanne N. Knutson (ed.), *Handbook of Political Psychology* (San Francisco: Jossey-Bass, 1973), p. 141.

69. Theodore Adorno, et. al., *The Authoritarian Personality* (New York: Harper and Row, 1950).

70. Theodore W. Adorno, "Freudian Theory and the Pattern of Fascist Propaganda," in Geza Goheim (ed.), *Psychoanalysis and the Social Sciences* (New York: International Universities Press, 1951), p. 291n.

71. Fred I. Greenstein, *Personality and Politics* (Chicago: Markham, 1969), pp. 106–107.

72. John P. Kirscht and Ronald C. Dillehay, *Dimensions of Authoritarianism: A Review of Research and Theory* (Lexington: University of Kentucky Press, 1967), pp. 5–6.

73. Adorno et al., p. 482.

74. Ibid., p. 167.

75. For a further elaboration see Fred Herzon, "A Review of Acquiescence Response Set in the California F Scale," *Social Science Quarterly*, 53 (June 1972), pp. 66–78.

76. Milton Rokeach, *The Open and Closed Mind* (New York: Basic Books, 1960).

77. For a review of many of these studies see Kirscht and Dillehay, *Dimensions of Authoritarianism*.

78. Ibid.

79. O. J. Harvey and G. Berverly, "Some Personality Correlates of Concept Change Through Role Playing," *Journal of Abnormal and Social Psychology*, 27 (March 1961), pp. 125–130.

80. Stanley Milgram, *Obedience to Authority* (New York: Harper and Row, 1969).

81. Alan Elms, *Social Psychology and Social Relevance* (Boston: Little, Brown and Company, 1972), p. 133.

82. Harold Lasswell, "Democratic Character," in H. D. Lasswell, *The Political Writings of Harold D. Lasswell* (Glencoe, Ill: The Free Press, 1951), pp. 464–525; Alex Inkeles, "National Character and the Modern Political Systems," in Francis L. K. Hsu (ed.), *Psychological Anthropology: Approaches to Culture and Personality* (Homewood, Ill: Dorsey Press, 1961), pp. 178–200; Robert Lane, *Political Ideology* (New York: The Free Press, 1962), pp. 400–412.

83. Sniderman, Chapter 5.

84. Ibid., pp. 185–186.

85. The thesis was first developed in Seymour Martin Lipset, "Some Social Requisite of Democracy: Economic Development and Political Legitimacy," *American Political Science Review*, 53 (March 1959), pp. 69–105.

86. Deane E. Neubauer, "Some Conditions of Democracy," *American Political Science Review*, 61 (December 1967), pp. 1002–1009.

CHAPTER **5**

The Agents of Political Socialization

Individuals do not react to political events in an unbiased fashion. Throughout one's life a variety of agents are exerting influence on a person's political outlooks. Just as one learns to read and to write and what is fashionable in clothing, one learns about politics. A considerable portion of this learning occurs before the individual is old enough to enter the voting booth. It is a common observation, for example, that children tend to share the same partisan preference as their parents. However, the process continues throughout the life cycle. Candidate choice in a presidential election may be influenced by inherited partisanship or by a news story heard the night before the balloting. This chapter focuses on the forces that shape the way an individual acquires knowledge, feelings, and evaluations of the political world—what political scientists call the process of "political socialization."

5-1 THE PREADULT YEARS

Students of childhood political socialization approach their subject from a variety of perspectives.[1] Dawson, Prewitt, and Dawson present perhaps the most inclusive conceptualization of the field in their argument that "adult political behavior is the logical extension of values, knowledge, and identification formed during childhood and youth."[2] Freud's basic premise that variations in human behavior originate in early childhood experiences underlies this perception of the field.[3] Others see the planting of ideas and values in youth as part of a continuing social process that is essential to the society's stability and survival.[4] Societies, they argue, must see to the training of each new generation of citizens; they must insure generational continuity and prevent sharp breaks with the past which may endanger the smooth functioning of government. Of course, if this training results in a total commitment to socially acceptable beliefs, the forces for change and improvement in society would be greatly diminished. Indeed, one view is that the public school provides an authoritarian and overly conservative environment that (perhaps unintentionally) does not properly train young citizens for an activist role in democracy.

To analyze the development of preadult political orientations we shall divide the childhood years into four periods: (1) preschool (ages three to five), (2) early childhood (ages six to nine), (3) late childhood (ages ten to twelve), and adolescence (ages thirteen to eighteen). These are approximate categories, for just as children differ in their physical development they differ in their political development. Nevertheless, these categories basically fit with what we know about the stages of childhood political development. We shall use them to describe how children relate to the political world and how they change as they become older.

Preschool

The dawnings of political recognition begin before the child ever commences his or her formal education. Political impressions are often vague and inaccurate, but early awareness may lay the foundations for later political development. The most important public figures for children under the age of ten are the president and the policeman. Both these officials (as we shall see) play a major role in shaping the child's attachment to the political order. But it is the policeman, not the president, that first becomes visible to the preschooler. Schwartz found that 90 percent of her preschool sample were able to recognize the "man in the picture" as being a policeman, and 75 percent were able to correctly answer the question, "What does the policeman do?"

The responses most frequently given concerned regulating traffic, helping lost children, and "catching bad people." The children, for the most part, saw the policeman as a benevolent authority figure. Less visible is his punitive and prohibitive role. Compared to the policeman, the president is a shadowy figure. Less than 10 percent of the preschool sample recognized a picture of (then) President Nixon. When asked, "what does the president do?" only a few could give an accurate or specifically political characterization. The president is not viewed by these young children as being particularly benevolent, especially when compared to the policeman.[5] This may be due simply to the president's lower visibility—a situation which along with perceived benevolence changes dramatically at the next stage of political development.

Public servants are not the only political symbols visible to the preschool child. Even at this early age children manifest a sense of political community. When presented with a picture showing nine different flags, the vast majority of the children were able to identify the American flag. When asked "which flag is your favorite?" 60 percent identified the American flag and another 19 percent identified the Liberian flag, which closely resembles the American flag.[6] Thus preschool children both know and identify with the symbol of the American political community.

Early Childhood

With the onset of early childhood the content of the young person's political world begins to rapidly expand. However, the increase in content is almost entirely in terms of feelings and affect. Political understanding and critical thought have yet to emerge. The young child now becomes very aware of the existence of the President. Government is personalized; that is, the child becomes aware of political authority by becoming aware of certain individuals—notably the President and the policeman. The young person sees these figures possessing great power, and is aware that they stand above the family in the obedience hierarchy. Unlike adults who often tend to be quite cynical about politics, the young child sees the President and the policeman (and political authority) as trustworthy, helpful, and benevolent. This outlook is illustrated by the following excerpt from an interview with a third-grade boy.

Q: What does the president do?

A: He runs the country, he decides the decisions that we should try to get out of, and he goes to meetings and tries to make peace and things like that.

Q: When you say he runs the country, what do you mean?

A: Well, he's just about the boss of everything. . . ."

Q: And what kind of person do you think he is?

A: Well, usually he's an honest one.

Q: Anything else?

A: Well, loyal and usually is pretty smart.

Q: Who pays him?

A: Well, gee, I don't know if anybody pays him; he probably doesn't get too much money for the job—I don't know if he gets any money.

Q: Why would he take the job?

A: Well, he loves his country and he wants this country to live in peace.[7]

To a surprising extent young children believe that the policeman and especially the President "would always want to help me if I needed it," that "they almost never make mistakes," and that "they know more than anyone."[8] Students of political socialization attach considerable importance to the idealization of authority by young children. First, it is commonly believed that orientations learned early are of the most lasting consequence. Second, it is thought that the image of the president formed in early childhood has a direct effect on the formation of attitudes and beliefs about other political figures and institutions. There is a "spillover effect" from this early view of the president to later perceptions of other political authorities. Therefore, it is believed to be very significant that the child's introduction to politics is a very positive one. Later in life when the individual is able to make critical judgments about politics this early idealization, the "benevolent leader syndrome," builds what Easton and Dennis refer to as "diffuse support." It is a reservoir of good will toward the political system that is independent of any benefit the individual might receive. It helps legitimize the political order, and in times of political stress the residue of this early idealization helps maintain a positive attitude toward government.[9]

The individual also learns another very important political orientation during early childhood—party identification. By the second grade 36 percent of the children in a study by Robert Hess and Judith Torney claimed an identification with one of the two major political parties. By the fifth grade the figure was 55 percent. The levels of identification through grade eight and for teachers are presented in Table 5.1. While children often identify with a party at an early age they have little understanding of what partisan politics are all about. Greenstein finds that not until the eighth grade can children give any meaningful response to the question of how the political parties differ.[10] It would seem party identification is learned in a fashion similar to religious identification. Children know they are Republicans or Democrats in much the same way they know they are Catholics, Anglicans, Methodists, etc. They are told by their parents. But they have little idea

Table 5-1.   Children's Party Preferences by Grade in School

Grade Level	N	Republican	Demo-crat	Some-times Democrat, Some-times Republican	Don't Know Which	Don't Know What Demo-crat and Republican Mean
2	1639	22.4%	13.4%	9.4%	21.1%	33.7%
3	1668	24.8	17.2	10.2	19.8	28.1
4	1738	30.1	19.0	15.0	16.9	19.0
5	1794	30.0	25.2	21.5	14.5	8.8
6	1744	28.2	28.8	26.0	12.6	4.5
7	1715	24.5	31.9	28.6	12.5	2.6
8	1685	20.5	32.5	31.6	13.8	1.6
Teachers	383	19.8	23.8	55.4	1.0	[a]

Source. Robert D. Hess and Judith V. Torney, *The Development of Political Attitudes in Children* (Chicago: Aldine, 1967), p. 90.
Note.—Item: If you could vote what would you be? Choose one.
[a]No DK alternative.

what the labels mean. Once the choice is made, however, it usually does not change. That choice will have important consequences for the way the individual sees the political world in later adult life.

Late Childhood

Beginning about the age of ten or eleven children start moving away from a personalized view of government to one based on a more sophisticated understanding. During this period the child learns the "civics book" norm of not always voting for the same political party, but rather for the "best man." Forty-nine percent of Hess and Torney's fourth graders say a good citizen would join a political party and vote for its candidates instead of voting for the best man. But by the eighth grade only 26 percent still endorse this strategy. It is favored by even fewer teachers (13 percent). The evidence indicates the strong consensus in civics education against the practice of party voting. Views of what constitute "good citizenship" also undergo change.[11] Young children tend to see the good citizen as someone who is "helpful to others" and "always obeys the laws." By late childhood, however, good citizenship is defined more in terms of adult conceptions—political interest, voting, and getting others to vote.[12] Also at this stage political knowledge increases at a rapid rate. Greenstein reports that only 23 percent of the fourth graders in his sample could give a "reasonably accurate" account of the president's duties, while 65 percent of the seventh graders could do so.[13] Roberta Sigel and Marilyn Brookes investigated conceptions of democracy among fourth graders. They found only 17 percent answered "yes" to the question, "Is a democracy where the people rule?" ("I don't know" was the most frequent response.) She reinterviewed the same students two years later (then in the sixth grade) and found that 44 percent could respond correctly.[14] However, definitions of democracy in late childhood and even through adolescence seldom include the right to criticize government. Only 54 percent of the eighth graders in Hess and Torney's sample checked the option "you can say things against the government" as one possible definition of democracy. And fully 84 percent of the eighth graders agree that "the government usually knows what is best for the people."[15] As we noted in Chapter 4, many theorists see such open acceptance of government and intolerance for dissent as dangerous to political stability. Perhaps people who continue to hold such attitudes into adulthood are incompletely socialized.

It is in late childhood that the young people begin to separate individual from institutional roles. They begin to understand the difference between the office and the man or woman who holds the office. The presidency and the president are no longer seen as the same. Children also display the beginnings of critical judgment; they are sensitive to partisan and policy considerations. Children who identify with the Republican party are more critical of a Democratic president than those who identify themselves as Democrats. The president also becomes associated with certain policy positions.[16] Still, political understanding is basically immature. Children will often revert back to personalization if asked about something they cannot comprehend.

Adolescence

The major spurt in a child's political learning usually comes during early adolescence. An important aspect of this growth is the ability to comprehend the abstraction of community interest apart from self-interest. Ideas such as community and society are usually beyond the grasp of eleven-year-olds, but not beyond those who are fifteen. When asked about the purpose of vaccinations, income tax, and public education the younger children see only individual or personal implications. For example, 70 percent of the eleven-year-olds in one study saw the purpose of vaccination to be the avoidance of illness and only 23 percent mentioned the community interest in avoiding epidemics. Fifteen-year-olds, however, saw exclusively the community purpose. The biggest change came between the ages of eleven and thirteen.[17]

By mid-adolescence the individual is in many ways politically beginning to resemble an adult. By the ninth grade, adolescents possess reasonably coherent policy conceptions. That is, they have some ability to think along liberal-conservative dimensions. This ability continues to increase through grade twelve.[18] Adult levels of political efficacy are also reached by the ninth grade.[19] One orientation which shows surprisingly little growth between the sixth and twelfth grades (and sometimes surprisingly little endorsement) is support for democratic values (free speech, minority rights, rules of the game, etc.). Merelman asserts that "conclusions about the extent of shifts in pro-democratic attitudes between the sixth and twelfth grades should be considered with care . . . but with few exceptions (they) do not indicate major pro-democratic changes during this period."[20] An orientation that begins in early childhood and, for the most part, continues unchanged through to adolescence is the positive belief most preadults have in the political system. Despite "de-idealization" and increased sophistication about most political topics during adolescence, American youth retain a generally positive view of the political order.[21] However, not all adolescents have an overwhelmingly warm feeling for the government. Roberta Sigel and Marilyn Brookes Hoskin investigated the relationship between satisfaction with specific governmental policies and general affect for the political system. While most adolescents were positive in their feelings for "the United States," "the Flag," and "the Constitution" the dissatisfied adolescents were unwilling to describe their feelings as "extremely warm."[22] It would seem that wide ranging dissatisfaction with immediate government performance during adolescence has the potential to erode the benevolent image of government learned during preschool and early childhood.

The Impact of Events

Much of the research into the development of preadult political orientations was conducted during the late 1950s and early 1960s. The political climate of the late 1960s and 1970s is obviously quite different. First the Civil Rights Movement and then the Vietnam war undermined public confidence in government. By the late 1960s trust in government and faith in American political institutions was dropping rapidly among the adult population. Americans were becoming cynical about politics.[23] The culmination of these events came with the break-in at the Watergate by individuals in the employ of the Committee to Re-elect the President. For almost two years the event dominated the news media and was a frequent topic of conversation among adults. The President of the United States was accused of being a common criminal and was ultimately forced to leave office. What effect might Watergate have on the socialization of children to politics? Recall, the young child is introduced to politics primarily through the personalization of the president—the president and the political order are seen as one. Furthermore, the president of the 1950s and early 1960s was seen as being very benevolent. How might the Nixon presidency during Watergate impact upon political socialization? Children might be affected quite differently than adults by crisis events. Adult political orientations are already shaped; defenses exist. The young child, on the other hand, is exposed to the crisis event *tabula rasa*—a blank slate.

The available evidence indicates that Watergate at its height had a substantial impact on childhood and adolescent political orientations, but that after 1975 learning about politics began to return (but not all the way) to normal. There is, however, disagreement on the exact magnitude of the effect. One group of investigators report a "dramatic decline" in the positive image of the president,[24] while another group sees a much less severe decline.[25] There are a number of differences between these studies which make them difficult to compare—samples taken at different times, dissimilar questions, open- versus closed-ended items. But one plausible explanation is that those reporting the *sharp* decline tended to have conducted their studies outside the South. In the case of two major studies, one was done in Boston[26] (the only state to go for McGovern in 1972) while the other was done in Florida[27] (a basically conservative, southern state where Mr. Nixon was more popular). Both may be accurately gauging the effect of Watergate in their respective regions; it was simply more intense in Boston than in Florida.

In the Boston sample Christopher Arterton found that attitudes toward the President in the fall of 1973 "could only be described as wholly negative."[28] The benevolent leader was transformed by Watergate into a "malevolent" leader. Presented in Table 5-2 are a series of questions that were first asked in 1962 and were then asked again in 1973 (it should be noted that the 1962 and 1973 studies were done in different cities). The percentages for 1962 and 1973 appear to be mirror images of each other. Even the youngest children, in 1973, have a highly negative impression of the president. In 1962, depending on grade, anywhere from 50 to 66 percent of the children indicated that the president was either their "favorite of all" or "of almost all." By 1973 the range was 5 to 23 percent, with the older children (fifth graders) being less positive. Turning to negatively worded questions, in 1962 only 11 percent of the fifth graders responded that the president is "not one of my favorites;" in 1973 the figures were 63 percent of the third grade, 82 percent of the fourth grade, and 75 percent of the fifth grade. Children in 1962 and 1973 were also asked to compare politicians "those who try to get elected to political office" with "most people" in terms of power, selfishness, intelligence, honesty and trustworthiness. The "spillover effect" of the president's image to other political authorities, which was positive in 1962, is negative in 1973. Particularly large differences between 1962 and 1973 exist on selfishness and trustworthiness. Fifty-four percent of the fifth graders in 1962 thought that politicians were less selfish than other people; only 19 percent thought so in 1973. In 1962, 52 percent felt that politicians were more trustworthy than most people; in 1973 the figure was 24 percent. Arterton replicated this study in 1975 and found an improvement in the president's image, but the attitudes expressed remained on the whole negative. Furthermore, *affect* for politicans declined even further than it had in 1973.[29] In the Florida study the impact of Watergate was less severe. Most young children had a highly positive image of the president. It was not until the sixth grade that it began to decline. But interestingly, young children who thought Watergate was important saw the president as considerably less benevolent (much like those in the Boston sample) than those who were unconcerned about Watergate.[30] Thus the difference between the Boston and Florida studies may simply be that in Boston Watergate was more publicized and feelings toward the president were more hostile. As a consequence, children were more likely to be aware.

Will children politically socialized during Watergate differ as adults from those who were not? One interpretation holds that Watergate children will grow into adulthood with ambivalent feelings about the legitimacy of their government. Others argue that the pattern in the Florida data is more typical of Watergate's impact. The decline in perceived benevolence was only moderate, and took place only during late childhood when the individual could distinguish between the man (Mr. Nixon) and the institution of the presidency. We won't really know, however, until the generation socialized during Watergate reaches adulthood.

Table 5-2. Comparison of 1962 and 1973 Ratings of the President for "Is the President your favorite?" (Percent of Children Responding)

		1 He is my favorite of all	2 He is almost my favorite of all	3 He is more a favorite of mine than most	4 He is more a favorite of mine than many	5 He is more a favorite of mine than a few	6 He is not one of my favorites	
3rd	1962	39%	27%	14%	8%	7%	6%	100%
3rd	1973	8	15	11	4	15	47	100%
4th	1962	28	30	17	11	7	7	100%
4th	1973	2	5	2	8	13	70	100%
5th	1962	21	29	21	13	9	8	100%
5th	1973	2	3	8	13	11	64	100%

Source. F. Christopher Arterton, "The Impact of Watergate of Children's Attitudes toward Authority," *Political Science Quarterly*, 89 (June 1974).

If events do influence political socialization one might expect that membership in certain disadvantaged subgroups might have a negative effect on political outlooks. One would hardly expect a ghetto black to be as positively oriented to government as a middle class white. However, during early childhood there are hardly any differences in the way whites, blacks, or chicanos view political authority. It is universally positive.[31] Also there is very little difference through adolescence in the way various subgroups react to the political community. For example, one study shows only a 6-percent difference between ninth grade blacks and whites in response to the statement, "Sometime I'm not very proud to be an American."[32] However, the attitudes toward the government and toward political leaders of black and chicano preadults become increasingly less positive as they pass through late childhood and adolescence. More than whites they are inclined to not trust government, to be politically alienated, and to be suspicious of authority (as in the case of the police).[33] The best explanations for these differences seems to be simple political reality. By early adolescence many blacks and chicanos believe that they do not receive equal treatment and they adjust their political orientations accordingly.[34]

The Agents of Childhood Socialization

Having traced the development of political attitudes through the preadult years we shall now attempt to sort out the agents most responsible for this development. The family seems the most influential source of preadult attitudes, but it is certainly not the only source. Schools make an effort to indoctrinate children, and it seems unlikely that the effort is totally unsuccessful. Other possible agents of early political socialization include childhood friends and the mass media, although these have received less attention from scholars.

The Family. Political influence is a function of two factors, communication and receptivity. Parents score high on both these dimensions. Children, particularly young children, spend a large amount of time with their parents. The opportunities for children to learn parental attitudes and for parents to exert influence on children are considerable. Also, in terms of receptivity, few bonds are as strong as the affective ties between parents and children. The stronger this tie and the more personal the relationship the greater the ability to exert influence.

A common assumption is that the political attitudes of family members are highly similar. Since most family members appear to share the same party preference it seemed logical to many investigators that the same pattern would hold for other political orientations. Evidence to support this belief came from a number of studies conducted prior to 1960 (although some are still being done) in which parents and children were not independently interviewed.[35] Children (normally students) would be interviewed and then asked to report the political attitudes of their parents. The parents were not interviewed. We know now that this methodology grossly overestimates the amount of parent-child similarity on most political issues. In reporting parent attitudes children tend to "project" their own attitudes on to parents, artificially inflating attitude correspondence.[36] In actuality, the similarity in political attitudes between parents and their offspring since World War II could at most be described as only moderate. Table 5-3, taken from a study by Kent Jennings and Richard Niemi, displays the relationships between a national sample of high school seniors and their parents on four public policy issues.

The correlation between student and parent attitudes on school integration and school prayers is moderate in strength. Reading across the rows in the table we can see that the students are much more likely to be pro-school integration and pro-school prayer when their parents favor these positions. For example, of the pro-integration parents 83 percent have children that also favor integration, but when parents oppose integration the percentage of children favoring integration drops to forty-five—a difference of 38 percent. The relationship weakens considerably for the question of an elected communist being allowed to hold office and virtually disappears on the question of allowing speeches against churches. In the case of the latter, knowing the parent's attitude is of no use in predicting the student's attitude. Most students favor allowing speeches against churches regardless of what their parents think. One can infer that parents have little influence on these latter two issues. Also, parents seem to have little influence on more diffuse orientations like political efficacy and political trust. Relationships are very similar to those for the "legally elected communist" and "speech against churches" issues.[37]

In sharp contrast to the situation for issues is the case of party identification. Table 5-4 documents the widespread agreement between parents and children on the question of party preference. Again reading across the rows of the table, when we move from parents who are Democratic to those who are Independent to those who are Republican the percentages of Democratic children drop dramatically. The reverse holds for the case of Republican parents. Analyzing the data from a slightly different perspective we find that 59 percent of the adolescents share the same partisan orientation as their parents. When parents agree between themselves on partisanship (74 percent do agree), 76 percent of the adolescents follow the preferences of their parents. It is quite obvious that parents exercise considerable influence over the partisan choice of their children.[38] This generational continuity is important because it helps maintain the ascendancy of the dominant political party. Since the New Deal the Democratic party has been preferred by a majority of Americans. As long as parents continue to successfully socialize children

Table 5-3. Relationship between Student and Parent Opinions on Four Policy Issues

Students	Federal Role in School Integration[a] Parents			Prayers in Public Schools[a] Parents			Elected Communist Can Hold Office Parents			Allow Speeches against Churches Parents		
	Pro	Depends	Con	Pro	Depends	Con	Pro	Depends[b]	Con	Pro	Depends[b]	Con
Pro	83%	64%	45%	74%	62%	34%	45%	—	32%	88%	—	82%
Depends	7	17	14	3	8	7	1	—	0	0	—	0
Con	10	18	41	23	30	59	53	—	67	12	—	18
Total	100%	99%	100%	100%	100%	100%	99%	—	99%	100%	—	100%
	(961)	(202)	(453)	(1253)	(68)	(238)	(528)	—	(1337)	(1376)	—	(523)
	tau = .34			tau = .29			tau = .13			tau = .08		

Source: M. Kent Jennings and Richard G. Niemi, *The Political Character of Adolescence* (Princeton, N.J.: Princeton University Press, 1974), p. 78.
[a]Based on pairs in which both the parent and student were "interested enough" to give a pro or con response.
[b]Ten or fewer cases.

Table 5-4. Student Party Identification by Parent Party Identification

	Parents			
Students	Democratic	Independent	Republican	
Democrat	66%	29%	13%	(43%)
Independent	27	55	36	(36%)
Republican	7	17	51	(21%)
Total	100%	100%	100%	
Marginals[a]	(49%)	(24%)	(27%)	100%

Source. M. Kent Jennings and Richard G. Niemi, *The Political Character of Adolescence* (Princeton, N.J.: Princeton University Press, 1974), p. 41.

[a]The marginal totals present the proportion of parents and students that hold a particular party preference. For example, looking at the column marginals we can see 49 percent of the parents are Democratic. Looking at the row marginals we can see that 43 percent of the students in the sample are Democratic.

to their own party preference the Democratic party seems to be in a strong position to continue its favored position with the electorate (barring a "re-aligning election," see Chapter 3). As can be seen from Table 5-4, 43 percent of the new voters entering the electorate in 1965 were Democrats as compared to only 21 percent who were Republicans, a clear advantage for the Democrats. These same 18-year-olds (in 1965) were reinterviewed in 1974. While there had been a considerable amount of shifting from Independence to partisanship and vice versa (almost 40 percent), only 9 percent switched party allegiance (moving from Democratic to Republican and the reverse). Interestingly, the Democratic Party, already dominant among the electorate, was the principal beneficiary of this movement.[39]

Why is it that party identification is passed on from parent to child with so much more success than other political orientations? The best explanation seems to be that most political questions are remote from the day-to-day concerns of the family. Few parents hold their political opinions strongly, and few children have an accurate perception of those opinions. In this regard party identification is unique. It is one attitude that is normally of some consequence to parents and is highly visible to children. At election time young children will often ask if "we" are Democrats or Republicans. One study showed high school seniors to be much more aware of the party identification of their parents than they were of parent attitudes toward any one issue. Kent Tedin found that while 72 percent of the seniors in a midwestern city knew the partisanship of their parents, only 36 percent had an accurate perception of parent attitudes toward any one issue. These data suggest that the reason parental influence is weak on political issues may simple be that adolescents are unaware of their parents' views. When parent attitudes, including party identification, are unknown to students there exists no relationship between the two generations. But when students have an accurate perception of parent attitudes the relationship between adolescent-parent attitudes on the issues is as high as for party identification. Much the same sort of phenomenon exists in the case of issue salience. When issues (or partisanship) are important to parents, parents exert considerable influence on adolescent attitudes.[40] But while there are a sizable number of "strong partisans," few political issues are highly salient to most of the adult population. Thus parents seem to have the potential to exert more influence than they currently do. Perhaps in an era like the Depression of the 1930s, when politics were polarized and certain issues were seen by many as being highly important, parents would use considerably more of their available resources to politically socialize their young.

The Peer Group. Like parents the peer group enjoys considerable opportunity to influence attitudes and behavior. There are strong affective ties involved, and young people normally spend a substantial part of their time with friends. Parents and peers differ, however, at the point in the preadult's life when influence is greatest. Parents dominate the lives of their offspring until adolescence, then peers become increasingly important.[41] Despite the considerable attention *paid to* peer groups in the Unites States there is relatively little research and (perhaps as a logical consequence) little agreement on the role of peers as an agent of political socialization. Some students argue that peer groups are the most important of all adolescent socialization agencies,[42] while others assert that the influence of peers is largely redundant.[43] Peers are seen as simply reinforcing the lessons learned in the family and school. It is clear, however, that adolescent peers can be influential in areas involving the individual's status in the group. But in the contemporary era these areas have not usually involved politics, but rather matters of taste in music, clothing, and hair styles.

In the Jennings-Niemi national study of parents and students a subset of the students were asked to indicate their best friend of the same sex, who was then included in the sample. Presented in Table 5-5 are the correlations between the attitudes of the students and parents and students and their best friends. Observe in the case of the 18-year-old vote that the correlation with peers exceeds that with parents. On the other hand, for party identification the correlation with parents far exceeds that with peers. This is the pattern one would expect. Partisanship is learned during early childhood and is not a particularly "youth oriented" issue. On the other hand, preadults are more likely to become aware of the 18-year-old vote issue during adolescence, and the issue is particularly relevant to high school seniors. We would, therefore, expect more peer influence in the latter instance. In situations where parents and peers disagree on partisanship, the student is more likely to follow the parent. But when parent and peer disagree on the 18-year-old vote,

Table 5-5. Relationships on Political Values Between Students and Parents and
Students and Friends

	Student-Parent[a]	Student-Friend
Partisanship	.66	.26
Vote Preference	.44	.34
Political Trust	.31	.28
Political Efficacy	.17	.28
18-year-old Vote	.08	.29

Source. M. Kent Jennings and Richard G. Niemi, *The Political Character of Adolescence*
(Princeton, N.J.: Princeton University Press, 1974), p. 243.
[a]The relationships are product/moment correlations.

the student is more likely to follow the peer.[44] Thus peer-versus-parent influence seems to be issue specific.

To what extent are parent and peer attitudes redundant? Parents and
peers tend to agree with one another, but not to the extent that was once
thought. For the sample under discussion, 63 percent of the parents and
peers agree on party identification and 53 percent agree on the attitude toward the 18-year-old vote.[45] When parents and peers agree it is not clear
who is exerting influence. Inferences about peers are particularly trouble-
some. Unlike membership in the family, over which one has no control,
friendships are a matter of choice. While politics is usually not an important
basis for this choice, friendships are normally made between persons of similar social class and with whom there is an agreement on general social outlook. These friends may be simply reinforcing the values already learned
from parents.

It is difficult to make any absolute assessment of peer influence, but it
seems certain that even in adolescence peers are not as important as parents. When politics are remote from one's day-to-day concerns, and when
family social harmony as well as one's status in the peer group are only
slightly affected by politics, parents probably have an advantage over peers
in the socialization process. We have noted that one important precondition
for influence is communication. Politics are more important to the 35- to 50-
year-old group (the common age of parents with adolescent children) than to
those under the age of twenty-one.[46] If one assumes all other things are
equal, adolescents are more likely to be aware of and receptive to parent
attitudes simply because most contemporary political issues are more important to parents.[47] But there can be exceptions, as in the case of the 18-year-
old vote.

The School. A very large number of political theorists, practical politicians,
political reformers, and political revolutionaries believe or have believed that
the school is an instrumental agent in the political training of the young.

Examples abound. After the Soviet revolution children were removed from the family (presumably still attached to the old order and to anti-state values like religion) and required to spend long periods of time in school for political retraining. The Allied Powers followed a similar policy after the defeat of the Nazis in World War II. The schools were "de-Nazified," and German youth were instructed in the principles of democratic government as defined by the West.

It is a popular assumption that some nations spend an inordinate amount of time politically "indoctrinating" their young. Usually singled out are communist states, notably the Soviet Union. One study, however, showed that American schools expend even more time on "political education" that do those in the USSR.[48] Regardless, it is important to understand that virtually all states require the schools to devote considerable attention to building support for the political order and teaching obedience to political authority. This practice is certainly widespread, and from the standpoint of maintaining political stability and continuity it is a necessity. One need only observe the difficulties encountered by nations where primary loyalties do not reside with the national government. For example, in many new African States tribal loyalty comes before national loyalty. In the case of Nigeria, the result has been a bloody civil war. Political stability is highly dependent upon the ability of the agents of socialization to produce in children feelings as to the rightness, the oughtness, the legitimacy of the political order. In virtually all nations this task is assigned to the schools. They are the one agent of political socialization over which the government has considerable control.

There can be little doubt, as we noted in the section on childhood political development, that preadults in the United States generally learn the lessons of patriotism and obedience. What is not clear is the relative role of the family and the school in teaching these orientations. The extent to which the school makes a unique contribution in this area or simply reinforces the lessons taught by the family is open to question. What is not open to question is the time and attention the school gives to socializing loyal citizens. In one of the major studies of the public schools, Robert Hess and Judith Torney conclude that "[c]ompliance to roles and authority is the major focus of education in elementary schools."[49] Most readers are undoubtedly aware of the patriotic rituals which characterize most classrooms—voluminous pictures of American heroes, the display of the American flag and proclaiming one's allegiance, singing of patriotic songs, "young citizen's leagues," and the emphasis upon obedience to authority.

However, students of political education agree that teaching loyalty and obedience is only one aspect of political education. There are other goals that are equally important, such as teaching political knowledge, political participation skills, democratic orientations, and politically relevant intellectual skills. On these goals there is a consensus that political education in the public schools does not fare well. In fact, many specialists argue that the emphasis on compliance and conformity is so inflexible that political education actually inhibits the development of other political skills.[50] For example, in the case of high school seniors a recent Gallup survey showed that 61 percent said they were "not very" or "not at all" interested in politics, and only 52 percent could give the name of the current vice-president.[51] Other dimensions of political learning are equally bleak. Support for democratic values tends to be low. One study of seniors found that 60 percent favored allowing the police and other groups to censor books and movies,[52] and another reported that only 36 percent were in favor of allowing a legally elected communist to assume office.[53] On participation, only 25 percent of a sample of 17-year-olds could list four or more ways to exert political influence.[54] In terms of sophisticated political thinking 50 percent of a sample of high school juniors thought the assertion "The American form of government may not be perfect, but its the best type of government yet divised by man" was a factual statement (as opposed to being a value statement).[55]

In the field of civics education the public school seems to have a very modest impact except perhaps in the area of political indoctrination. Critics advance many reasons, almost all of which derive from the school's overriding concern with obedience. Textbooks are criticized for being simplistic, chauvinist, ethnocentric, and manifesting a "we are the greatest" philosophy. A widely used twelfth-grade text contains the following passage:

> We are proud of the fact that it is a system in which "we, the People" are all-powerful and in which government exists only to do our bidding. We are proud too, that our system of government is, and has been for generations, the envy of other peoples the world over.[56]

Many would claim that this statement is little more than propaganda. Part of the blame for the shortcomings of civics education is also focused on the teacher. Few civics teachers are undergraduate government majors or even social science majors.[57] Studies show that teachers normally do not discuss social issues during class time, particularly those which are controversial. Byron Massialas further concludes that most teachers simply are not intellectually prepared to effectively handle discussion of issues in the classroom.[58] For example, one investigation demonstrated that teachers were not very much more adept than students in distinguishing between factual statements and value statements.[59] It therefore comes as little surprise that there is virtually no relationship between the number of civics courses taken in high school and most political predispositions.

A national study of high school seniors by Kenneth Langton and Kent Jennings showed that whether or not students had taken any civics courses was largely irrelevant to their levels of political knowledge, political interest,

interest in political media, political discussion, political efficacy, civic tolerance, political trust and participation orientation. However, taking civics courses did have a modest effect on some political orientations of blacks. It increased their political knowledge, sense of efficacy, and support for democratic values. The authors argue that while the civics curriculum is redundant for most whites, it contains new information for many blacks.[60]

5-2 THE POLITICAL IMPACT OF HIGHER EDUCATION

Today almost one of every two high school graduates goes on to college. At the turn of the century most young people did not even graduate from high school, let alone contemplate attaining a college degree. Consequently, the proportion of the adult population with college experience has been rising steadily. For example, over the short span of time from 1948 to 1976 the proportion with at least some college rose from 15 percent to 32 percent; the proportion with actual college degrees from 7 percent to 16 percent.[61] The trend will undoubtedly accelerate, as a lagged result of the post-World-War-II education boom, so that "the electorate of 1970 should look positively uninstructed by comparison with that of the year 2000."[62]

What are the political implications of the growth of the college-educated public? Although college students today are decidedly more liberal than the general population, this has not always been the case. As recently as 1960, Republican presidential candidates generally ran better in campus straw polls than in the actual elections. Despite such indicators, the college experience was generally regarded as liberalizing even before the upsurge in campus political activism of the 1960s. Evidence in support of this view can be found in studies going back to the 1920s. College seniors were consistently found to be less conservative than entering freshman.[63] Data indicating that students move further to the left as college exposure increases are in Table 5-6. For comparative purposes, information for both 1971 and 1975 is presented, as some commentators see contemporary college students as being

Table 5-6.   Ideological Self-Placement of College Students by Year in School, 1971 and 1975

	Far Left, Left		Middle of theRoad		Far Right, Right		Don't Know	
	1971	1975	1971	1975	1971	1975	1971	1975
Freshmen	28%	30%	56%	44%	14%	24%	2%	2%
Sophomores	31	40	52	38	15	20	2	2
Juniors	41	47	43	29	14	22	2	2
Seniors	40	53	46	24	9	20	5	3
All Students	35	40	49	36	13	22	3	2

Source. Gallup Opinion Index, February 1972, p. 7 and September 1975, p. 19.

more conservative than those during the Vietnam War era. Clearly for both years students are more inclined to call themselves liberals as they progress through college. However, in 1975 there is an increasing polarization with the left and the right gaining adherents at the expense of the middle. There also exists a clear gap between college students and their noncollege age-group peers, with the former being considerably more liberal, at least on noneconomic issues such as civil rights and civil liberties. Data illustrating this point, taken from a 1970 survey, are presented in Table 5-7.

Why does progressing through college tend to make students increasingly liberal? There seem to be two factors involved—awareness and enlightenment. Two of the stronger correlates of education are political knowledge and use of the political media. Being informed about innovations and current events is directly related to education. One scholar advances the hypothesis that "thanks largely to wider personal contacts and greater exposure to the media of opinion, the better educated are the first to sense changes in the climate of opinion and quickly respond to new fashions in social thought."[64] For example, in a study of support for the civil rights of women and blacks, one investigator found a large increase in support for women's rights occurring among the educated shortly after the media began devoting considerable attention to the issue. No parallel increase was found in support for black civil rights, indicating the increased liberalism on the women's issue was due to an awareness factor.[65] It is also claimed that education leads to "enlightenment" which in turn leads to liberalism. According to William Stephens and C. Stephen Long:

> Students learn in school. They become more sophisticated, knowledgeable, broadened, attuned to the world outside, and this is why they become more liberal and more politically aware. . . Education promotes enlightenment; enlightenment promotes liberalism and political interest and participation.[66]

The impact of the college experience cannot, however, account for all the differences between the college educated and the rest of the public. Individuals who choose to go to college are already somewhat more liberal than their non-college age-group peers before they ever set foot on campus.[67] Also there is considerable variation within the college student population. As Table 5-7 indicates, 20 percent of the students considered themselves on the political right in 1975. Left-leaning students are not found to be randomly distributed among colleges and universities. Rather, they tend to be concentrated in "prestige" schools. While part of this phenomenon may be due to self-selection, David Knoke and Larry Isaac argue that there is a genuine causative effect operating, as these schools have disproportionately liberal faculties and diverse student bodies.[68] Finally, the political stance a student takes is partially influenced by predispositions learned in the family. For example, Kenneth Keniston offers the interesting conclusion that where the

Table 5-7. Values of Youth Attending College and Political Values of Youth Not Attending College

Values	Percent Who Agree	
	College	Non-College
There is too much concern with equality and too little with law and order	17%	42%
There should be more respect for authority	59	86
Money is very important	18	40
Patriotism is very important	35	60
Having an abortion is morally wrong	36	64
Containing the Communists is worth fighting for	43	69
The right to private property is sacred	75	87
Religion is very important	38	64

Source. Robert Chandler, Public Opinion (New York: R.R. Bowker Company, 1972), pp. 6-13.

father is supportive of the student's leftist leaning (presumably it works for rightest leanings as well), the probability that the student will engage in radical behavior is enhanced. When this parental support is missing, students with radical political orientations are more likely to become alienated and apathetic rather than politically active.[69]

At present, we cannot say for sure whether the relatively leftist political climate on college campuses will increase, or even that it will not be replaced by a genuine mood of political quiescence and conservatism. Whatever the case, a relevant question is whether or not current college students will lose their left-of-center views once they leave college. The long-run implications of this question are obvious. If students become more conservative as they grow older, the liberalizing impact of higher education will be temporary and limited to the generation in college at the moment. But if liberal students retain their views in later life, then each graduating class will add to the cumulative totals of educated "liberals" within the general population. Relevant to this inquiry is the persistent finding that differences in attitudes among education levels decline with age.[70] One might interpret this pattern to mean that college-educated people gradually drift toward the conservatism of the rest of the population as the effects of their education wear off. But there is a case for a much different explanation that does not depend on a drift toward conservatism in the latter stages of life. The greater conservatism of older well-educated people may have resulted from the greater conservatism of their campus environment when they obtained their education. In other words, each successive college generation may be more liberal than those before it. There is indirect support for this view from the sketchy findings from the few panel studies that have followed college graduates in later life: over time, college graduates do not express more conservative views and may actually tend to drift in a liberal direction. Although far from a sufficient amount of evidence, it appears that an increase in the "liberalizing" effect of higher education plus the increase in the number of young people who go to college may portend an acceleration of the rate at which public opinion moves to the left.[71]

5-3 THE IMPACT OF THE MASS MEDIA

For some people who are disturbed by the course of certain political trends the mass media and the people who run them are a convenient set of scapegoats. Certain perceived faults in the publics thinking would disappear if the media would stop "biasing" the news, and public preoccupation with annoying governmental and societal problems would change in the desired direction if the news media would only give them different emphasis. These kinds of charges have come from both the political right and left. For example, an occasional book is published charging that the television networks are biased in a liberal direction or that they favor Democratic candidates, or alternately, that the network bias is in the conservative or Republican direction.[72] Newspapers are often criticized because of the obvious Republican leanings of their editorial pages, but in 1964 the Republican presidential candidate complained that he was not given a fair shake by the American press. This charge has been made again in reference to Watergate by many of the supporters of former President Nixon. Similarly, the content of what the media cover is often under fire from both ideological directions. For example, liberals often charge that television gives only limited news coverage to controversial topics of the type they would like to see. Yet hard-hitting television documentaries, such as CBS's "The Selling of the Pentagon," often draw objection from conservative critics.

There are many ways that bias can slip into the presentation of public events by the media. However, people in the communications industry feel a certain responsibility to report the news with reasonable objectivity. They also fear governmental intervention in terms of increasing regulation—a possibility that former Vice President Agnew occasionally called for in his attacks upon the news media. It is one of the tasks of the social sciences to understand the nature of the media, its biases, and its impact on American political behavior.

Newspapers and Public Opinion

The newspaper business in America has changed considerably over the years. In the nineteenth century, a town big enough to have a daily newspaper usually had more than one—including at least one highly partisan Republican paper and one with an equally partisan Democratic leaning.[73] This situation allowed the newspaper consumer to choose from among a diverse but hardly objective array of information sources. Over time, however, the number of publishing newspapers has dwindled, so that today no more than 3 percent of American cities publishing newspapers have more than one newspaper under separate ownership.[74] With this consolidation and with increased reliance upon wire services for newspaper copy, the bias to newspaper coverage—particularly of national and world events—has declined. Thus the number of choices open to the newspaper consumer has decreased, while the "objectivity" of the product has increased. Beyond its local news coverage, the content of the typical reader's home town paper is much like that of the newspaper in the next town down the road. Of course unique and important exceptions exist—certain "prestige" newspapers with reputations for unusually good coverage of national and world events. National political and business leaders pay close attention to the prestige papers (most notably the *New York Times* and the *Washington Post*). People in the lower echelons of newspaper journalism also pay close attention to the prestige papers as a source of cues.

Recent research has uncovered surprisingly strong effects of newspapers on political information and voter choice. In a panel study of the 1972 election Patterson and McClure claimed individuals who regularly read newspapers gained almost twice as much knowledge about political issues as those who read them infrequently. Regular readers displayed a 35 percent increase in issue awareness during the campaign compared to an 18 percent increase for the less diligent readers.[75] The quality of the newspaper also makes a difference. Peter Clarke and Eric Fredin find that readers of newspapers with strong reputations for excellence are more politically informed than readers of less notable newspapers—a difference that persists with standard controls for social background factors.[76]

There has been much speculation about the impact of the conservative and pro-Republican newspaper editorials on public opinion. An indicator of the ideological and partisan bias of newspapers is that in most presidential elections of modern times, American newspapers have endorsed the Republican candidate over his Democratic opponent by margins of greater than 3 to 1. In 1972, 93 percent of the newspapers making endorsements supported Richard Nixon.[77] The normal Republican tendency of the editorial page should not be surprising, since the publishers who determine editorial policy are wealthy businessmen who tend to reflect the ideology of their local business community. Also, major advertisers can influence editorial content by threatening to withdraw their ads and the money they bring in if editorial policy does not suit them. A side benefit of the growth of local newspaper monopolies has been the decline of this form of pressure, since advertisers are reluctant to withdraw their ads from the only newspaper in town.

Does a newspaper's editorial stance influence the political opinions of its readers? Although editorials are not the most widely read sections of newspapers, John Robinson has shown that many voters are aware of the presidential endorsements of their favorite newspaper.[78] Although the tendency is declining, newspapers usually magnify the extent of their editorial "bias" by presenting the reader with the writings of syndicated columnists who share the publisher's editorial stance.[79] The publisher's bias can extend even to the selection of the correspondence selected in the "letters to the editor" section and sometimes to the news content itself. One study showed presidential candidate endorsement was a strong predictor of the dominant political tone in newspapers' published letters.[80] Although not all studies of the subject show the same thing, a newspaper's partisan leanings sometimes spill over (in moderate amounts) from the editorial page into the supposedly neutral news columns.[81] For example, there is some evidence that during the 1972 campaign, newspapers gave less coverage to the growing Watergate story if they supported Nixon for President.[82] Editors' attempts to guide news coverage into alignment with editorial policy, however, are less frequent than they once were. For example, from the late 1930s to the early 1960s, there was a decline in the rate at which Washington correspondents reported their home newspapers killed or modified their stories for political reasons.[83]

To some extent, the effect of conservative editorial opinion is counteracted by the liberal tendency among working newspaper journalists. One study of Washington correspondents found that 55 percent considered themselves liberal compared to 27 percent who considered themselves conservative.[84] Limited evidence also suggests that the editorial "gatekeepers" who make the day-to-day decisions regarding what news gets in their paper share the same ideological tendency.[85]

The failure of many Republican papers to endorse Barry Goldwater in 1964 provides a rather unusual opportunity to estimate the impact of newspaper presidential endorsements. (Only 35 percent of American newspapers endorsed Senator Goldwater, while 42 percent endorsed President Lyndon Johnson, with the remaining 23 percent neutral.)[86] The very number of such papers allows us to compare the voting responses of their communities with the responses where the local paper did stick to their partisan tradition and support Goldwater. Table 5-8 shows the results of such an analysis. Counties with Johnson-endorsing papers (but previously Republican) and counties with Goldwater-endorsing papers were matched by geographic proximity and similar voting in the 1960 presidential election. In 17 out of 18 cases (the details are not shown for lack of space), the 1960—1964 Democratic vote gain was greatest in the county where the paper endorsed Johnson, with an average difference of 6 percent of the two-party vote.[87] Apparently, a publisher's decision to support Johnson over Goldwater added, on the average, about

Table 5-8. Relationship between the 1964 Presidential Endorsement of Normally Republican Newspapers and the 1960-1964 Vote Shift in the County of Publication: Based on a Matching of Counties According to their 1960 Vote and Geographic Proximity[a]

Mean	Percent Democratic, of Two-Party Presidential Vote			
	1960	1964	Change	Number of Cases
Johnson endorsement	43.2%	61.8%	+18.6%	(18)
Goldwater endorsement	44.3	56.7	+12.4	(18)
Difference	− 1.1	+ 5.1	+ 6.2	

[a]For details of the county selection, see footnote 87.

six percentage points to Johnson's local vote total. Inferentially, it would seem that the normal Republican trend of the press is worth at least a couple of percentage points to the Republican party nationwide. Humphrey might have defeated Nixon in 1968 for example, with a more equitable division of newspaper endorsements between the two major party candidates. More elaborate statistical analysis than can be shown here confirms that newspaper endorsements are an important influence on presidential elections.[88] For lower offices, the impact of newspaper endorsements is unclear, although one might expect that a newspaper would be more not less influential below the presidential level. Regarding local elections and issues, the content of newspaper coverage is often deemed crucial, although face-to-face communications are sometimes thought to neutralize the media impact on the most controversial issues.[89] Especially when the election is nonpartisan or involves an extremely long ballot, the newspaper's decision regarding what to report and who to endorse can be very important. As one newsperson reportedly once said, "you can't tell the players without a scorecard, and we sell the scorecards."[90] Studies seem to show that newspapers have good success in endorsing local candidates who win.[91] But this can be partially attributable to newspapers' endorsements of candidates who look like winners rather than to any influence of the paper on the electoral decision. However, statistical analyses of long-ballot elections suggest that in the kind of election where voter confusion is maximum, newspaper support is the major key to victory.[92]

Beyond charges of liberal or conservative bias, the media have been accused of fermenting the increasing levels of cynicism, distrust, and general political malaise which have characterized American politics since the late 1960s (see Chapter 4). While it is not possible to establish a clear-cut cause and effect, Doris Graber demonstrates that the tone of newspaper discussion of presidential qualities (professional image, personality traits, style, capacities, relations with public, philosophy and organizational politics) was decidedly negative in 1968 and even more negative in 1972. Candidates were found to be lacking in certain desirable qualities, or it was implied that the existence of such qualities could not be ascertained. In 1968, 41 percent of the qualities mentioned in newsprint had negative overtones. In 1972, the figure was 51 percent.[93] At the very least, one can conclude that newspapers do little to encourage a positive or happy beat to American politics. But then, some might argue, why blame the messenger?

Television and Public Opinion

According to self-reported behavior, more people depend on television for news of public events than on any other medium.[94] It thus comes as no surprise that many people are concerned about the influence television may have on the political opinions of the mass public. Although it is generally assumed that television reporters are more politically liberal than the general public, TV coverage is attacked in about equal amounts by people to the political right and by those to the political left.[95] In recent years, a number of polemics have been written accusing the visual media of a wide variety of biases in political reporting. We shall see, however, that most of these are greatly exaggerated. Nevertheless, television is of consequence to mass political outlooks. Given the controversy that surrounds the uses to which it is put, it is important that the exact nature of television's impact be understood.

Television as a Disseminator of Political Information. Most research on television as a source of political information has concerned presidential elections. One of the more interesting discoveries is that the network nightly news has almost no value as a source of information about either issues or candidate qualifications. It should first be realized that only 20 percent of the voting-age public watch the evening news on a regular basis.[96] But even this small group is not appreciably informed. The reason is quite straightforward. As can be seen in Table 5-9, the network news devotes most of its campaign coverage to candidate "events" which have a strong visual impact—the candidate shaking hands in a crowd, the candidate in a motorcade, the candidate being heckled. Considerably less attention is paid to campaign issues and candidate abilities. The same authors who discovered an information gain from newspaper reading in the 1972 campaign did not find a comparable gain for watchers of TV news. Over the course of the campaign those individuals who paid little or no attention to the network news showed a 25 percent increase in political information, while those who watched the evening news on a regular basis were only slightly more informed—showing a 28 percent increase.[97] Individuals do, however, get political information from television, although some may be surprised by the source. Political advertisements contain substantial information about candidates and issues. These

Table 5-9. How the Networks Distribute Their News Minutes (1972 Election)

Event	ABC	CBS	NBC
Time given to campaign activity (e.g., rallies, motorcades, polls, strategies, big labor)	140:58[a]	121:34	120:20
Time given to the candidates' key personal and leadership qualifications for office	19:30	16:24	8:05
Time given to candidates' stands on key issues of the election	35:19	46:20	26:14

Source. Thomas E. Patterson and Robert D. McClure, *The Unseeing Eye* (New York: G. P. Putnam and Sons, 1976), p. 41.
[a]Time in news minutes.

messages are more than simply attempts to build an image, they also relate the candidate to particular issue positions. Patterson and McClure found that 74 percent of viewer reaction to presidential commercials in the 1972 campaign centered on the political information contained in the advertising message.[98]

Knowledge about issues increased 36 percent among those regularly exposed to political ads during the campaign as opposed to 25 percent for those with minimum exposure. The authors conclude that "the contribution of advertising campaigns to voter knowledge is truly impressive."[99] The televised Carter-Ford debates also proved to be a source of candiate information. Several studies demonstrated that following the debates voters had a heightened political awareness and a perception of greater issue differences between candidates and parties.

Does TV "Bias" Public Opinion? Does television coverage of the news favor the liberals or the conservatives? A large amount of research has been done which shows that television's handling of political events favors neither liberals nor conservatives, Democrats nor Republicans. These investigations have been conducted at two levels. One is an analysis of the partisan content of the news, and the other is an inquiry into the effects of watching television on candidate and issue preferences. C. Richard Hofstetter conducted a meticulous content analysis of every news broadcast by the three networks, beginning in early July of 1972 and ending just after the election. He found the networks devoted close to equal time to both candidates. McGovern received slightly more exposure, but this can be explained by the fact that President Nixon chose a strategy of presenting himself as "the working President" and did not spend much time on the campaign trail.[100] Approximately 77 percent of the stories treated the candidates in a neutral fashion, and those which were critical or laudatory did not appreciably favor either the Republicans or the Democrats (Mr. Nixon had a slight advantage).[101] Research at the individual level demonstrates that viewing the nightly news had virtually no effect on either candidate image or the ultimate vote decision in November.[102] These findings strongly challenge accusations that journalistic bias toward one candidate or the other is present in the coverage of the news.

Television and Political Malaise. While television coverage of political events is handled in a reasonably even-handed fashion in that no partisan faction is favored over another, some researchers have made the controversial claim that television has contributed to the decline in political efficacy and trust by taking a critical and highly negative approach to political events. While reporters are expected to be nonpartisan, they are also expected to be watchdogs of the public interest. This has often led to very energetic attacks on government, regardless of the political party in power. Commonly cited are the coverage of student demonstrations, the Vietnam war, and documentaries such as "Hunger in America" and "The Selling of the Pentagon." Some commentators argue that heavy criticism of government officials, procedures, and agencies over a long period of time will undermine the legitimacy of the regime. There is considerable controversy over this thesis. Two studies on the way television handled the Vietnam war came to very different conclusions—one found the majority of journalistic comment was critical of administration policy and the other found even-handed neutrality.[103] A study of TV's coverage of the student demonstrations of the late 1960s did not find any disproportionate negative portrayal of authority.[104] On the other hand, Michael Robinson, in an experimental study, found that persons who viewed the CBS documentary "The Selling of the Pentagon" became not only more cynical about the military but also less politically efficacious.[105] Robinson and others have also demonstrated that watching great amounts of television is correlated with such presumably undesirable attitudes as social distrust, misanthropy, and cynicism.[106] However, the cause-effect relationship between these attitudes and television use has yet to be settled.

Public Perceptions of Media Bias. On November 13, 1969 in a speech in Des Moines carried by all three television networks at prime time, Vice President Agnew charged that the networks had been misusing their "vast power" by their "querulous criticism" of the Nixon administration. "Perhaps it is time," he said (and to some appeared to threaten), "that the networks were made more responsive to the views of the nation."[107] Shortly thereafter, Agnew extended his criticism to the printed media as well. A poll conducted for ABC shortly after the Des Moines speech found 51 percent agreeing with Agnew that the networks had been biasing the news, and only 33 percent disagreeing.[108] Lou Harris found the public to vote 2 to 1 that Agnew "was right to criticize the way TV networks cover the news."[109] Pluralities in the Gallup Poll agreed that both television and newspapers "tend to favor one side" rather than "deal fairly with both sides."[110] Mail streaming into the networks and their affiliates was even more one-sided, although the volume of mail to NBC was less than they received after the cancellation of "Star Trek."[111]

Were these responses valid indicators of public dissatisfaction with the way its news media presented the news? Apparently the pro-Agnew response was a combination of strong enthusiasm from a vocal minority and superficial acquiescence on the part of poll respondents, who, everything else being equal, like to support a Vice President. Two years after Agnew's intitial broadside against the media, anti media responses in polls returned to their previous low levels, as a 1971 Roper survey disclosed when it asked its national sample the question, "Do you think television is fair or is not fair about showing different points of view?"[112]

Fair	69%
Not fair, too much to the left	7
Not fair, too much to the right	2
Not fair, too much conventional middle of the road opinion	6
Not fair, other or no elaboration	6
Don't know or no answer	10
	100%

Depending on one's view of media objectivity, figures such as these can be interpreted either as reassurance or as an indication that the public is being fooled.

Political Advertising

With the advent of television came a major change in the way political campaigns were conducted. Many believe that television has made candidate "image" a more important electoral consideration than in the past. And in fact campaign strategists now devote considerable time to the development of their candidate's TV image. The technological sophistication demanded to run a television oriented campaign has spawned an entire new industry of campaign managers who specialize in hiring themselves out to political clients. Their work includes polling research and evaluation, advising (or telling) the candidate what changes he or she should make in appearance or issue stands, calculation of the proper mix of media exposure, and the creation of media advertisements.[113]

The effects of this change—to which some apply the ambiguous "new politics" label—are several. First, it has taken campaigning out of the hands of the party professionals and put it into the hands of television image makers. Second, greater emphasis than before is placed on the image potential of possible candidates when party leaders make their selection. Third, and perhaps most important, the costs of campaign spending (for all offices) have increased by more than 350 million dollars between 1952 and 1972.

The most frequently discussed danger of the new politics is the potential for the artificial creation of political leaders who meet the needs of candidate imagery rather than the needs of the offices they must fill. However, this danger seems to be greatly overstated. Political candidates cannot be sold over television like a box of soap. It has long been recognized that highly interested partisan voters cannot be reached through campaign ads. Their candidate commitments are too intense and their defenses against dissonant information too well developed.[114] Through the psychological mechanism of "selective perception" people tend to "tune out" messages that not accord with the choices they have already made and concentrate on messages that support these choices. Committed voters tend to see in political commercials pretty much what they want to see, which greatly reduces the persuasive impact of a political ad.[115] It now appears that even voters with low involvement and low interest are relatively unpersuaded by political ads. Their amount of information increases (which may ultimately affect their vote decision), but the ads do not affect their candidate image. Patterson and McClure analyzed seven traits of candidate image associated with personality and leadership. Over the course of the 1972 campaign, Nixon's image improved by 35 percent and McGovern's suffered a 28 percent decline. But exposure to political ads, for any group, was only slightly related to these changes. Those not exposed to political ads changed as often and in the same direction as those who were exposed.[116] In the case of undecided voters, it was only after they had made a decision that there was any change in candidate image.[117] Patterson and McClure estimate that at best political advertising may account for one or two percent of the vote.[118]

Several cautions need to be raised at this point. First, the research just cited is based on a subjective report by the respondent of the number of political ads viewed. This is a very crude measure which ignores the intensity of the attention level. This intensity is likely to vary considerably, and there may indeed be an effect among those who pay particularly close attention to the ads. Second, the research addresses itself only to the question of change. Political advertising may play an important role in reinforcing opinions already held and minimize potential defection of supporters to the opposing candidate. Also, it may be that if one candidate did not advertise heavily, his opponent's advertising would work. The political ads of the respective candidates may simply be canceling each other out. Finally, even if campaigns have little *direct* effect on an individual, they may affect his candidate image and vote decision *indirectly,* through conservations with others who are attentive to the media. Those other persons, designated opinion leaders," are often attentive to political media. This influence process is known as the "two step flow of communication."[119] The fact that opinion leaders are more politically informed than average suggests that their conversations generally magnify the net impact of the media's political messages.[120] The possibilities are limited, however, since people tend to talk about politics with people of similar political persuasion. Yet, the more a person talks about politics, the more likely he is to talk to people with opposite beliefs. Of particular importance is the finding that opinion leaders are highly represented among the electorally crucial "split ticket voters" (at least at mid-term elections),[121] while advice-takers tend to be late deciders. Because of the two step flow of political communications from generally informed opinion leaders to followers, the influence of the informed public on the flow of public opinion may be greater than their numbers would indicate.

Agenda Setting and Reality Definitions by the Media

There is little evidence that the media change opinions about political issues, but a more important aspect of media influence may be defining what issues are important. As one author notes, the media "may not be successful much of the time in telling people what to think, but it is stunningly successful in telling (people) what to think about."[122] This media function is known as agenda setting. Television may be particularly important in this regard. First, it is the most widely used of the news media. Second, the typical news program is only thirty minutes. If set to print it would take no more than a single page of the *New York Times.*[123] Thus television news editors have tremendous discretion in determining what stories are "newsworthy." Table 5-10 presents a comparison of how Americans ranked certain problems in importance in 1965 with how they rated them in 1970. The most obvious change is a sharp increase in concern about pollution. One might wonder whether this change would have happened if the networks had not begun to publicize the urgent pleas of environmentalists. Conversely, would the con-

Table 5-10. Changing Issue Priorities of the American Public, 1965-1970

Problem (in Order of Change in Concern)	1965	1970	Change
Reducing pollution of air and water	17%	53%	+36%
Reducing the amount of crime	41	56	+15
Improving housing, clearing slums	21	27	+ 6
Beautifying America	3	5	+ 2
Helping people in poor areas	32	30	− 2
Reducing racial discrimination	29	25	− 4
Improving highway safety	18	13	− 5
Conquering "killer diseases"	37	29	− 8
Reducing unemployment	35	25	−10
Improving public education	45	31	−14

Source. Gallup Opinion Index, June 1970, p. 8.

Question: Which three of these national problems would you like to see the government devote most of its attention to in the next year or two?

cern be even greater if more news about environmental conditions had been presented?

Because people in the communications industry must be trend conscious, they naturally accelerate the pace of the acceptance of new ideas and new terminology, even if the process is an unwitting one. For example, television (and the other media) were responsible for the quick substitution of the word "black" for "Negro"—a shift that occurred even though polls from as recently as 1970 showed that most blacks preferred the word "Negro" or even "colored." Leo Bogard explains how the media fostered the change.

> To the militant minority, the word "Negro" carried a bitter historical burden which had to be cast off in the search for a proud new identity. This minority was concentrated within the spirited elements of urban youth who were not only more assertive and visible than their elders in contacts with authority, but also more likely to supply the Negro newsmen big city newspapers, television networks, and magazines were belatedly eager to recruit. White media practioners in many instances fell in line with the terminology preferred by their own young Negro reporters, either in ignorance of what the Negro majority preferred or out of indifference to the whole matter. And since the term "black" was daily reiterated by white reporters in the newscasts and in the press, it was also adopted by Negro publications, and entered the consciousness and usage of those to whom the term applied.[124]

Agenda setting is usually measured by comparing issues the media emphasize with issues that are seen by the mass public as being the most important. Most research indicates a correlation between the two, but once again there is uncertainty over causal connections.[125]

Not only do the media set the agenda, they often set standards by which to judge certain events. The most criticized instances of this practice have occurred during presidential primaries. For example, two months before the New Hampshire Democratic primary in 1972, columnist David Broder wrote. "As the acknowledged front-runner and a resident of the neighboring state, Muskie will have to win the support of at least half the New Hampshire Democrats in order to claim a victory." The 50 percent figure gradually emerged as a media consensus as the election approached. When Muskie ultimately got 46 percent as compared to 37 percent for George McGovern, it was widely interpreted as a McGovern victory and a defeat for Muskie. Media coverage of the New Hampshire primary probably hastened the end of the Muskie candidacy.[126]

5-4 PRESIDENTIAL LEADERSHIP

Because of the prestige of his office, the president has, potentially, more power to lead public opinion than any other individual or institution. Simply by taking his case to the people, a popular president could conceivably command broad support for his legislative program. One such incident apparently was President Johnson's appeal for the new Civil Rights Law enacted in 1964 to give Americans of all races equal access to public accommodations such as hotels and restaurants. Between June 1963 (during Kennedy's administration) and January 1964, public support for the proposed law rose from a slim plurality (49 to 42) to a commanding majority of 61 to 31—a shift far greater than normally occurs over a seven month period on a controversial, emotional issue.[127] If Johnson's plea was responsible for this opinion shift, it was reinforced by the special circumstances of a new president pleading for enactment of the program of a martyred president. Other than this example, there is little evidence that public support for domestic policy proposals rises and falls with the momentary public enthusiasm of the president. Although the absence of sufficient poll data relevant to this question may be partially responsible for this conclusion, another reason is that in domestic policy the president is viewed as a partisan figure representing unique constituencies rather than the public at large. In one well-documented instance, a well-publicized presidential proposal was followed by decreasing public support and congressional rejection. This was Roosevelt's short-lived effort in 1938 to expand the size of the Supreme Court in order to dilute the power of its then conservative majority.[128]

Presidential leadership in shaping the political opinions of Americans is greatest on matters of foreign policy—an area of limited public knowledge and interest. Insufficiently informed to guide foreign policy decisions, the public puts its faith in presidential leadership, on the seemingly sensible grounds that the president is better equipped than the people to make rational foreign policy decisions. As Seymour Lipset put it, "the opinion data indicate that national policymakers, particularly the president, have an almost free hand to pursue any policy they think correct and get public support for it," for the reason that the public agrees on "certain larger objectives . . . and find it necessary to trust the judgment of national leaders as to what is possible given these purposes."[129]

Evidence offers strong support for this general rule. In polls taken in the mid-1960s, the proportion favoring mainland China's admission to the UN substantially increases when respondents are asked what they would think if "the president suggested" it, or if, "it would improve U.S.-China relations."[130] The fact that public attitudes toward China softened considerably once the President decided the time had come for a thaw confirms the role of presidential leadership in shaping the public's opinion toward China. If President Nixon had followed the public opinion polls in strict fashion he would never have tried to open relations with China, and his popularity would not have increased the way it did following his China trip. Of course, the public's previous response of verbal belligerence toward China was also a result of official policy at the time.

Public acquiescence to presidential decisions can be seen from simple comparisons of opinion before and after presidential decisions. Vietnam episodes provide several examples. Immediately prior to President Nixon's decision to send troops to Cambodia, only 7 percent favored sending troops while 59 percent rejected such a step. After President Nixon's speech explaining the new committment to enter Cambodia, 50 percent told the Harris poll that the President was right to send troops and only 43 percent said "no."[131] Each time Nixon stepped down the military action, public support for the particular policy in question increased. For example, support for a bombing halt increased from 40 percent to 64 percent once President Johnson announced such a policy in 1968.[132] Related to this problem, in repeated 1953-1954 surveys, national samples voted almost 2 to 1 for sending ground troops to Indochina, if it appeared the French would lose control to the Communists.[133] President Eisenhower's failure to follow this expression of public opinion by sending troops did not hurt his popularity in the slightest.

Foreign policy crises are followed by upsurges in the public's rate of approval of the President's performance. By this index, Truman gained 9 points when he decided to resist the Communist invasion in South Korea; Eisenhower gained 8 points following the 1956 Suez crisis; and Kennedy gained 13 points following the 1962 Cuban missile crisis. More recent examples show boosts in popularity for Johnson after the Dominican Republic crisis (1965), for Nixon after the Cambodia invasion (1970), for Ford after the Mayaguez affair (1975), and for Carter after the Camp David summit (1978). Even crisis events that seem to reflect badly on the President's decision-making prowess normally produce upsurges of presidential popularity. Eisenhower gained following the U-2 incident and summit collapse in 1960 as did Kennedy after the Bay of Pigs invasion of 1961.[134]

As the case of Vietnam suggests, there are obvious limits to the President's ability to mobilize popular support for his foreign policy actions. What are these limits? The public reactions to both the Korean and the Vietnam Wars suggest that, whatever the short-term public reaction to presidential actions, the public becomes increasingly unwilling to support land wars fought to ambiguous conclusions over the long run. At the beginning of both the Korean and Vietnam adventures, the public did give the President broad latitude to act within the broad guidelines of combating Communist aggression while avoiding a larger war. But as the wars went on, presidents got boxed in by what they saw, perhaps incorrectly, as the possibility of even greater public opposition to their stepping outside the apparent limits of decision-making latitude—either by stepping up the war drastically or ending it in apparent defeat, Johnson and Truman both suffered marked declines in popularity as the wars in Korea and Vietnam went on under their administrations. (Nixon avoided as great a decline in approval only because his stated goal was the withdrawal of troops—but at a slower rate than the majority was willing to support.) In Truman's case, the greatest decline in his popularity occurred following his firing of the popular battlefield leader, General Douglas MacArthur. The vast majority of Americans sided with MacArthur over Truman, and consequently registered disapproval of Truman's administration for the remainder of his term.[135] Johnson's greatest descent in the popularity polls was a seven point drop after the Viet Cong's Tet offensive in the winter of 1968 provided the necessary feedback to the public to belie the official optimism. Both turning points illustrate sources of the limits of presidential ability to command support in the foreign policy sphere. Truman's case illustrated that a president who is already low in the popularity polls cannot gain support by decisions as unpopular as the firing of a popular general. Johnson's decline shows that a president cannot register support indefinitely for a war effort that the overwhelming evidence from news reports shows to be going badly. In each case, the loss of public confidence limited the president's options severely, so that new changes in policy could not have induced the normal public acceptance. For example, that Truman could not have gotten away with ending the Korean War on the same terms that Eisenhower did shortly after taking over the presidency is generally assumed. Similarly, if he had wanted to, Nixon could have ended the Vietnam war on almost any terms immediately upon his takeover of the presidency.

FOOTNOTES FOR CHAPTER 5

1. For a discussion see Stanley A. Renshon, "Models of Man and Temporal Frameworks in Political Socialization Theory," *Youth and Society,* 8 (March 1977), pp. 245-276.

2. Richard Dawson, Kenneth Prewitt, and Karen Dawson, *Political Socialization,* 2nd ed. (Boston: Little, Brown, 1977), p. 48.

3. Richard M. Merelman, "The Adolescence of Political Socialization," *Sociology of Education,* 45 (Spring 1972), p. 135

4. David Easton and Jack Dennis, *Children and the Political System: Origins of Political Legitimacy* (New York: McGraw-Hill, 1968), p. 9.

5. Sandra K. Schwartz, "Preschoolers and Politics," in David C. Schwartz and Sandra K. Schwartz (eds.), *New Directions in Political Socialization* (New York: The Free Press, 1975), pp. 236-237.

6. *Ibid.,* pp. 242-243.

7. Robert D. Hess and Judith V. Torney, *The Development of Political Attitudes in Children* (Chicago: Aldine, 1967), p. 42.

8. Richard G. Niemi, "Political Socialization," in Jeanne N. Knutson (ed.), *Handbook of Political Psychology* (San Francisco: Jossey-Bass, Inc., 1973), p. 123.

9. Easton and Dennis, *Children and the Political System,* Chapter 1.

10. Fred Greenstein, *Children and Politics* (New Haven: Yale University Press, 1965), p. 68.

11. Hess and Torney, p. 96.

12. *Ibid.,* p. 37.

13. Fred Greenstein, "The Benevolent Leader: Children's Images of Political Authority," *American Political Science Review*, 54 (December 1960), p. 937.

14. Roberta Sigel and Marilyn Brookes, "Becoming Critical about Politics," in Richard G. Niemi (ed.), *The Politics of Future Citizens* (San Francisco: Jossey-Bass, 1974), p. 110.

15. Hess and Torney, p. 75.

16. Robert Weissberg, *Political Learning, Political Choice and Democratic Citizenship* (Englewood Cliffs, N.J.: Prentice-Hall, 1974), p. 54.

17. Joseph Adelson and Robert P. O'Neil, "Growth of Political Ideas in Adolescence: The Sense of Community," *Journal of Personality and Social Psychology*, 4 (July 1966), pp. 295–306.

18. Richard Merelman, *Political Socialization and Educational Climates* (New York: Holt, Rinehart and Winston, 1971), p. 71.

19. Ibid., pp. 69–70; see also Hess and Torney, p. 220.

20. Merelman, p. 79.

21. M. Kent Jennings and Richard G. Niemi, *The Political Character of Adolescence* (Princeton, N.J.: Princeton University Press, 1974, p. 140–144.

22. Roberta S. Sigel and Marilyn Brookes Hoskin, "Affect for Government and its Relation to Policy Output among Adolescents," *American Journal of Political Science*, 21 (February 1977), pp. 111-134.

23. Arthur Miller, "Partisanship Reinstated? A Comparison of the 1972 and 1976 Presidential Elections," *British Journal of Political Science*, 8 (July 1978), p. 138.

24. F. Christopher Arterton, "The Impact of Watergate on Children's Attitudes Toward Political Authority," *Political Science Quarterly* 89 (June 1974), pp. 269-288; Frederick Hartwig and Charles Tidmarch, "Children and Political Reality: Changing Images of the President," (paper presented at the 1974 annual meeting of the Southern Political Science Association); Jack Dennis and Carol Webster, "Children's Images of the President and of Government in 1962 and 1974," *American Politics Quarterly* 4 (October 1975), pp. 386-405; Robert P. Hawkins, Suzanne Pingree, and Donald Roberts, "Watergate and Political Socialization," *American Politics Quarterly* 4 (October 1975), pp. 406-436; Harrell R. Rodgers and Edward B. Lewis, "Student Attitudes Toward Mr. Nixon," *American Politics Quarterly* 4 (October 1975), pp. 423-436.

25. Marjorie Randon Hershey and David B. Hill, "Watergate and Preadults' Attitudes Toward the President," *American Journal of Political Science* 19 (November 1975), pp. 703-726; Bruce Campbell, "Racial Differences in the Reaction to Watergate," *Youth and Society* 7 (June 1976), pp. 439-460; Michael Lupfer and Charles Kenny, "Children's Reactions to the President: Pre- and Post-Watergate findings," (paper presented at the 1974 Annual Meeting of the American Political Science Association).

26. Arterton, "The Impact of Watergate."

27. Hershey and Hill, "Watergate and Preadults' Attitudes."

28. Arterton, p. 273.

29. F. Christopher Arterton, "Watergate and Children's Attitudes toward Political Authority Revisited," *Political Science Quarterly*, 91 (Fall 1975), pp. 475-497.

30. Hershey and Hill, p. 716.

31. Edward Greenberg, "Orientations of Black and White Children to Political Authority," *Social Science Quarterly*, 51 (1970), pp. 934-943; F. Chris Garcia, *Political Socialization of Chicano Children* (New York: Praeger, 1973).

32. Edward Greenberg, "Black Children and the Political System," *Public Opinion Quarterly*, 34 (Summer 1970), p. 341.

33. Harrell Rodgers, "Toward Explanation of the Policy Efficacy and Political Cynicism of Black Adolescents: An Exploratory Study," *American Journal of Political Science*, 18 (May 1974), pp. 257-282; Garcia, *Political Socialization of Chicano Children*.

34. Paul R. Abramson, *The Political Socialization of Black Americans* (New York: The Free Press, 1977).

35. Many of these studies are discussed in Herbert Hyman, *Political Socialization* (Glencoe, Illinois: The Free Press, 1959).

36. Kent L. Tedin, "The Reliability of Reported Political Attitudes," *American Journal of Political Science,* 17 (February 1976), pp. 117—123.

37. Jennings and Niemi, pp. 127—132, 146—147.

38. It is interesting to note that, contrary to conventional wisdom, mothers exert more influence on the political attitudes of their children than do fathers. See Jennings and Niemi, Chapter 6. Following conventional wisdom, the evidence indicates that when husbands and wives disagree on party preference, wives are more likely to change in the direction of the party preference of their husband than vice versa. See Terry S. Weiner, "Homogeneity of Political Party Preferences Between Spouses," *Journal of Politics* 40 (Febraury 1978), pp. 208—211.

39. M. Kent Jennings and Richard G. Niemi, "The Persistence of Political Orientations: An Over-Time Analysis of Two Generations," *British Journal of Political Science,* 8 (July 1978), p. 349.

40. Kent L. Tedin, "The Influence of Parents on the Political Attitudes of Adolescents," *American Political Science Review,* 68 (December 1974), pp. 1579—1592.

41. Paul Allen Beck, "The Role of Agents in Political Socialization," in Stanley A. Renshon (ed.), *Handbook of Political Socialization* (New York: The Free Press, 1977), p. 117.

42. Ted G. Harvey, "Computer Simulation of Peer Group Influence on Adolescent Political Behavior" *American Journal of Political Science,* 66 (November 1972), p. 601.

43. Sara L. Silbiger, "Peers and Political Socialization," in Renshon, p. 174.

44. Suzanne K. Sebert, M. Kent Jennings, and Richard G. Niemi, "The Political Texture of Peer Groups," in M. Kent Jennings and Richard Niemi, *The Political Character of Adolescence,* p. 243.

45. Computed from Table 9.3 in Sebert, Jennings, and Niemi, p. 246.

46. Lester W. Milbrath and M.L. Goel, *Political Participation,* 2nd edition, (Chicago: Rand McNally, 1977), pp. 114-116.

47. Kent Tedin, "Measuring Parent and Peer Influence on Adolescent Political Attitudes," *American Journal of Political Science,* 24 (February 1980), forthcoming.

48. George Z. F. Bereday and Bonnie B. Stretch, "Political Education in the USA and USSR," *Comparative Education Review* 7 (June 1963), pp. 9—16.

49. Hess and Torney, p. 126.

50. See Robert Hess and Judith Torney, "The Family and School as Agents of Socialization," in Norman Adler and Charles Harrington (eds.), *The Learning of Political Behavior* (Glenview, Illinois: Scott, Foresman, 1970); Michael Riccards, *The Making of American Citizenry* (New York: Chandler Publishing Company, 1973); Joseph Decaroio, "What Research Says to the Classroom Teacher," *Social Education* 36 (January 1972), pp. 92-93; John Patrick, "Implications of Political Socailization Research for the Reform of Civil Education," *Social Education,* 33 January 1969), pp. 14-21; Robert Clearly, *Political Education in the American Democracy* (Scranton: Intext, 1971).

51. Gallup Survey "Six of Ten Teenagers Show Little Interest in Politics, Politicians," *Houston Post,* October 19, 1977.

52. H. H. Remmers and Richard D. Franklin, "Sweet Land of Liberty," in H.H. Remmers, (ed.), *Anti-Democratic Attitudes in American Schools* (Evanston: Northwestern University Press, 1963), p. 62.

53. Jennings and Niemi, *The Political Character of Adolescence,* p. 65.

54. Ellen Shantz, "Sideline Citizens," in Byron G. Massialas (ed.), *Political Youth, Traditional Schools* (Englewood Cliffs, New Jersey: Prentice-Hall, 1972), pp. 69–70.

55. Ibid., p. 74.

56. William A. McClenaghan, *Magruder's American Government* (Boston: Allyn and Bacon, 1972), p. 5.

57. M. Kent Jennings, Lee H. Ehman, and Richard G. Niemi, "Social Studies Teachers and Their Pupils," in Jennings and Niemi, *The Political Character of Adolescence*, p. 210.

58. Byron Massialas, *Education and the Political System* (Reading, Massachusetts: Addison-Wesley, 1969), p. 170.

59. Ibid., p. 177.

60. Kenneth P. Langton and M. Kent Jennings, "Political Socialization and the High School Civics Curriculum in the United States," *American Political Science Review*, 62 (September 1968), pp. 852–877.

61. Extrapolated from Figure 4 in Philip E. Converse, "Change in the American Electorate," in Angus Campbell and Philip E. Converse (eds.), *The Human Meaning of Social Change* (New York: Russell Sage Foundation, 1972), p. 324; Warren E. Miller and Arthur H. Miller, *The CPS 1976 American National Election Study* (Ann Arbor: ISPCR, 1976).

62. Ibid., p. 323.

63. See the summary of the extensive literature on this point in Kenneth Feldman and Theodore M. Newcomb, *The Impact of College on Students*, Vol. 2, (San Francisco: Jossey-Bass, 1969), pp. 16–24 and 49–56.

64. Charles H. Stember, *Education and Attitude Change: The Effect of Schooling on Prejudice Against Minority Groups* (New York: Institute of Human Relations Press, 1961), p. 172.

65. E. M. Schreiber, "Education and Change, in American Opinions on a Woman for President," *Public Opinion Quarterly*, 42 (Summer 1978), pp. 171–182.

66. William N. Stephens and C. Stephen Long, "Education and Political Behavior," in James A. Robinson (ed.), *Political Science Annual: An International Review*, Volume 2, (Indianapolis: Bobbs-Merrill, 1970), p. 17.

67. M. Kent Jennings, *The Student-Parent Socialization Study* (Ann Arbor: ISPCR, 1971). Students were asked if they planned to go to college (V228). Those who said yes were more liberal than the rest of the sample.

68. David Knoke and Larry Isaac, "Quality of Higher Education and Sociopolitical Attitudes," *Social Forces* 54 (March 1976), pp. 525–529.

69. Kenneth Keniston, "Notes on Young Radicals," *Change,* 1 (November-December, 1969), pp. 32–32.

70. Norval D. Glenn. "The Trend in Differences in Attitude and Behavior by Education Level." *Sociology of Education*, 39 (Summer 1966), pp. 255–275; Samuel Stouffer, *Communism, Conformity, and Civil Liberties* (New York: Doubleday, 1955); John L. Spaeth, "Public Reactions to College Student Protests," *Sociology of Education*, 42 (Spring 1969), pp. 199–206.

71. Erland Nelson, "Persistence of Attitudes of College Students Fourteen Years Later," *Psychological Monographs*, 68 (1954); Andrew M. Greeley and Joe L. Spaeth. "Political Change Among College Alumni," *Sociology of Education*, 43 (1970), pp. 106–113. This movement to the left seems, however, basically limited to social issues rather than economic issues.

72. Two recent examples are (from the left), Robert Cirino, *Don't Blame the People* (Los Angeles: Diversity Press, 1971), and (from the right) Edith Efron, *The News Twisters* (Los Angeles: Nash Publishers, 1971).

73. Ben H. Bagdikian, *The Information Machine* (New York: Harper and Row, 1971), p. 137.

74. Raymond B. Nixon and Jean Ward, "Trends in Newspaper Ownership," *Journalism Quarterly*, 38 (Winter 1961), pp. 3—12.

75. Thomas E. Patterson and Robert D. McClure, *The Unseeing Eye* (New York: G. P. Putnam's Sons), pp. 51—53.

76. Peter Clarke and Eric Fredin, "Newspapers, Television and Political Reasoning," *Public Opinion Quarterly* 42 (Summer 1978), pp. 143-160. The inference about the quality of the newspapers in this article is ours and is not made by Clarke and Fredin.

77. John P. Robinson, "The Press as Kingmaker: What Surveys Show from the Last Five Campaigns," *Journalism Quarterly* 51 (Winter 1974), p. 592.

78. John P. Robinson, "Perceived Media Bias and the 1968 Vote: Can the Media Affect Behavior After All?" *Journalism Quarterly* 49 (Summer 1972), pp. 239—246.

79. Ben H. Bagdikian, "How Editors Pick Columnists," *Columbia Journalism Review,* 5 (1966), p. 41.

80. Jae-Wan Lee, "Editorial Support and Campaign News: Content Analysis by Q Method," *Journalism Quarterly* 49 (Winter 1972), p. 710.

81. According to one review of studies of "biased" news coverage, the reported bias was in the direction of the newspaper's partisan leanings in 78 out of 81 cases. See Ben H. Bagdikian, "The Politics of American Newspapers," *Columbia Journalism Review,* 10 (March/April 1972), pp. 9—10.

82. Ben H. Bagdikian, "The Fruits of Agnewism," *Columbia Journalism Review* 11 (January/February 1973), pp. 9—23.

83. Ibid., 81.

84. William Rivers, "The Correspondents after 25 Years," *Columbia Journalism Review* 1 (Spring 1962), pp. 4-10; see also Edward M. Glick, *The Federal Government Daily Press Relationship* (Washington: The American Institute for Political Communication, 1967).

85. Bagdikian, *The Information Machine,* p. 108.

86. Robinson, "The Press as Kingmaker." p. 592.

87. The matched counties were drawn from a pool of northern counties where newspapers published in the major city accounted for at least two-thirds of the county's newspaper circulation and reached at least two-thirds of the county households. Newspaper endorsement data were obtained from *Editor and Publishers* polls, supplemented by results of a postcard questionnaire sent to editors who did not respond. Where the 1960 endorsement of a Goldwater-endorsing paper is unknown, it is assumed to be Republican. The matched counties were within the same state and within at least eight percentage points of each other in their 1960 presidential two-party vote. No counties were matched if the largest city in one was more than three times as populous as the largest city in the other. For further evidence regarding the effect of newspaper endorsements of presidential candidates, see Robert S. Erikson, "The Influence of Newspaper Endorsements in Presidential Elections: The Case of 1964," *American Journal of Political Science,* 20 (May, 1976), pp. 207—234.

88. Robinson, "The Press as Kingmaker."

89. Ibid., 87.

90. Edward C. Banfield and James Q. Wilson, *City Politics* (New York: Vintage Books, 1963), p. 159.

91. James E. Gregg, "Newspaper Editorial Endorsements and California Elections, 1948—1962," *Journalism Quarterly,* 62 (1965), pp. 534—536; Reo M. Christenson, "The Power of the Press: The Case of the *Toledo Blade,*" *Midwest Journal of Political Science,* 3 (1959), pp. 230—239.

92. John E. Mueller, "Choosing Among 133 Candidates," *Public Opinion Quarterly*, 34 (Fall 1970), pp. 395-402; Michael Hooper, "Party and Newspaper Endorsement as Predictors of Voter Choice," *Journalism Quarterly*, 43 (Summer 1969), pp. 302–305.

93. Doris A. Graber, "Press and TV as Opinion Resources in Presidential Campaigns," *Public Opinion Quarterly*, 40 (Fall 1976), pp. 285–303.

94. "An Extended View of Public Attitudes Toward Television and Other Mass Media, 1959–1971," a report by the Roper Organization to Television Information Office, pp. 2–3.

95. Rivers.

96. John P. Robinson, "The Audience for National TV News Programs," *Public Opinion Quarterly*, 35 (Fall 1971), pp. 403–405.

97. Patterson and McClure, p. 53.

98. Ibid., p. 110.

99. Ibid., p. 116.

100. C. Richard Hofstetter, *Bias in the News* (Columbus: Ohio State University Press, 1976), p. 44.

101. Ibid., p. 74.

102. Patterson and McClure, pp. 59–73.

103. Edith Efron, *The News Twisters* (Los Angeles: Nash, 1971); Frank D. Russo, "A Study of Bias in TV Coverage of the Vietnam War: 1969–1970," *Public Opinion Quarterly* 35 (Winter, 1971–1972), pp. 539–543.

104. Richard A. Pride and Barbara Richards, "Denigration of Authority? Television News Coverage of the Student Movement," *Journal of Politics*, 36 (August, 1974), pp. 637–660.

105. Michael J. Robinson, "Public Affairs Television and Growth of Political Malaise: The Case of 'The Selling of the Pentagon' ", *American Political Science Review*, 70 (June 1976), pp. 409–432.

106. Ibid.; George Gerbner and Larry Gross, "The Social Reality of Television Drama," (Annenberg School of Communication, University of Pennsylvania, unpublished mimeo, 1973); *idem*, "Television as Enculturation," (Annenberg School of Communications, University of Pennsylvania, unpublished mimeo, 1975).

107. Marvin Barrett (ed.), *Survey of Broadcast Journalism 1969–1970* (New York: Grossett and Dunlap, 1970), pp. 31–32.

108. Ibid., p. 33.

109. Hazel Gaudet Erskine, "The Polls: Opinion of the News Media," *Public Opinion Quarterly*, 34 (Winter, 1970–1971), p. 638.

110. Ibid., pp. 636–637.

111. Barrett, p. 32.

112. "An Extended View of Public Attitudes Toward Television and Other Mass Media, 1959–1971," A Report by The Roper Organization to Television Information Office, pp. 13–14.

113. Dan Nimmo, *The Political Persuaders* (Englewood Cliffs: Prentice-Hall, 1970), pp. 134–162.

114. Philip Converse, "Information Flow and the Stability of Partisan Attitudes" in Angus Campbell, et al., *Elections and the Political Order* (New York: Wiley, 1966), pp. 136–158.

115. David Sears and J. L. Freedman, "Selective Exposure to Information: A Critical Review," *Public Opinion Quarterly*, 31 (Summer 1967), pp. 194–213.

116. Patterson and McClure, pp. 115–116.

117. Ibid., p. 115.

118. Ibid., p. 138.

119. The two step flow was originally formulated in Paul Lazarsfeld, Bernard Berelson, and Hazel Gaudet, *The People's Choice* (New York: Columbia University Press, 1948); for a summary of the current state of the evidence see John P. Robinson, "Interpersonal Influence in Election Campaigns: Two Step-flow Hypotheses," *Public Opinion Quarterly*, 40 (Fall 1976), pp. 304−319.

120. The role of opinion leaders in elections has received the most extensive treatment in the earliest voting studies. See Chapter 12 of Paul Lazarsfeld, Bernard Berelson, and Hazel Gaudet, *The People's Choice* (New York: Duell, Sloan and Smith, 1944); Bernard Berelson, Paul Lazarsfeld, and Chapter 6 of William N. McPhee, *Voting* (Chicago: University of Chicago Press, 1954). Opinion leadership is most thoroughtly studied in nonpolitical realms.

121. John W. Kingdon, "Opinion Leaders in the Electorate," *Public Opinion Quarterly*, 34 (Summer 1970), pp. 256−261.

122. Bernard Cohen, *The Press and Foreign Policy* (Princeton: Princeton University Press, 1963), p. 13.

123. Robert MacNeil, *The People Machine* (New York: Harper and Row, 1968), p. 40.

124. Leo Bogart, *Silent Politics* (New York: Wiley, 1972), p. 69.

125. Maxwell McCombs and Donald Shaw, "The Agenda-Setting Function of Mass Media," *Public Opinion Quarterly*, 36 (Summer 1972), pp. 176−187; Ray Frankhauser, "The Issues of the Sixties: An Exploratory Study in the Dynamics of Public Opinion," *Public Opinion Quarterly* 37 (Spring 1973), pp. 62−75; David H. Weaver, Maxwell E. McCombs, and Charles Spellman, "Watergate and the Media," *American Politics Quarterly*, 4 (October 1975), pp. 458−472.

126. Herbert B. Asher, "The Media and the Presidential Selection Process," in Louis Maisel and Cooper (eds.), *The Impact of the Electoral Process* (Beverly Hills: Sage Publications, 1977), p. 214.

127. AIPO news release, February 2, 1964. The exact question was, "How would you feel about a law that would give all persons—Negro as well as white—the right to be served in public places such as hotels, restaurants, theaters, and similar establishments? Would you like to see Congress pass such a law, or not?"

128. Frank V. Cantwell, "Public Opinion and the Legislative Process," *American Political Science Reivew*, 55 (1946), pp. 924−935.

129. Seymour Martin Lipset, "Doves, Hawks, and the Polls," *Encounter*, 27 (October 1966), p. 39.

130. John E. Mueller, "Presidential Popularity From Truman to Johnson," *American Political Science Review*, 64 (March 1970), p. 29.

131. Milton J. Rosenberg, Sidney Verba, and Philip E. Converse, *Vietnam and the Silent Majority* (New York: Harper and Row, 1970), pp. 26−27.

132. Gallup Poll, as reported in Mark V. Nadel, "Public Opinion and Public Policy" in Robert Weissberg and Mark V. Nadel (eds.), *American Democracy: Theory and Reality* (New York: Wiley 1972), p. 539.

133. NORC polls, as reported in Kenneth N. Walz, "Electoral Punishment in Foreign Policy Crisis," in James Rosenau (ed.), *Domestic Sources of Foreign Policy* (New York: The Free Press, 1967), p. 286.

134. Ibid., pp. 272−273; Fred I. Greenstein, "Popular Images of the President," *American Journal of Psychiatry*, 122 (November 1965), pp. 523−529; *Gallup Opinion Index*.

135. John E. Mueller, "Presidential Popularity from Truman to Johnson," *American Political Science Review*, 64 (March 1970), p. 29. See also Samuel Kernell, "Explaining Presidential Popularity," *American Political Science Review*, 72 (June 1978), pp. 506−522.

CHAPTER 6

Group Differences in Political Opinions

People often think of differences in political opinion and voting behavior in terms of group stereotypes. Everyone is aware of the polarization between blacks and whites. In addition other group characteristics are often thought to be predictors of attitudes and voting. For example, we often hear that the young are more liberal than the old, or that Catholics and Jews are more Democratic than Protestant voters. Geography is also often assumed to make a difference: that is, the "liberal" Northeast and the "conservative" South, the "liberal" big cities versus the "conservative" small towns and rural areas. Social class is often thought to make a difference too, with working class people more Democratic and more liberal on economic issues than their middle-class counterparts. But on noneconomic issues, this polarity often seems reversed, with working class "hard hats" the group most opposed to change.

In this chapter we will explore the validity of generalizations that are frequently made about group differences in attitudes and voting. Most of these generalizations we will find to be correct—but only to a degree. Knowing a person's group characteristics increases our ability to predict his political responses: but the exceptions make political predictions on the basis of group characteristics far from perfect.

6-1 ECONOMIC STATUS AND POLITICAL OPINIONS

An obvious source of political polarization is alignment along lines of economic class, with the poor or "have nots" disagreeing politically with the more wealthy. In most European countries the major political battle lines are drawn in this fashion, with a working class "socialist" party (and sometimes a significant Communist party) in opposition to one or more "middle class" parties. As indicated by the fact that the United States has never had an appreciable socialist movement, America has escaped the more extreme forms of class conflict. Even so, divisions on the basis of economic status are often found when the political attitudes and behavior of the American public are examined.

Class Differences on Social Welfare Issues

Typically, poorer people rather than the well-to-do are more favorably inclined toward government social welfare programs that are designed to raise living standards. To take an initial example, back in 1949, Gallup found there was a strong relationship between living conditions and opinion when he asked a national sample whether they thought "that the government should do more to improve the conditions of the poor people; that the government is doing just about the right amount of things now; or that the government has already done more for the poor people that is good for them:"[1]

	Do More	Right Amount	Too Much	No Opinion	Total
Prosperous	28%	42%	23%	7%	100%
Upper middle	35	38	20	7	100
Lower middle	44	36	12	8	100
Poor	57	27	7	9	100

The tendency for poorer people to be the most sympathetic to social welfare legislation persists today. Thus, when in 1968 a national sample of white voters was asked whether they would "favor more government programs to help the poor in things like medical care, education, or housing," 54 percent of the respondents in the manual or "blue collar" occupational category gave the affirmative response, whereas only 45 percent of the nonmanual or "white collar" people did so.[2]

Figure 6-1 shows how family income is related to opinions on the issues of medical care, guaranteed job, and good standard of living among white respondents in the CPS 1976 survey. Each of the five income groups compared contain approximately the same number of respondents. The figure shows that support for the belief that "there should be a government insurance plan which would cover all medical and hospital expenses" is negatively related to income since support for this "liberal" belief decreases gradually from 66 percent of the opinion holders in the lowest income group to 35 percent in the highest income group. Similarly, on the question of whether the government should "see to it that everyone who wants to work has a job and a good standard of living," the percentage favoring this government guarantee declines from 51 percent among the poorest fifth to only 21 percent among the most prosperous. Nonwhites are not included in the sample upon which Figure 6-1 is based, because we wish to show the effect wealth has on social welfare attitudes independent of race. With nonwhites included, the opinion disparity between the least prosperous income category and the others would loom even larger, since prosocial-welfare racial minorities tend to cluster toward the bottom of the income scale.

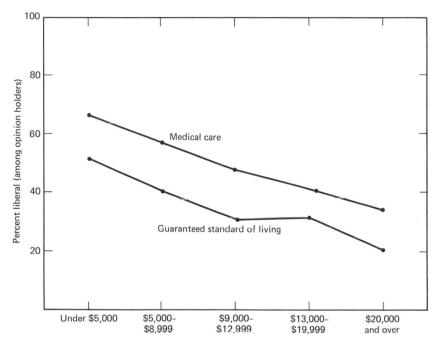

Figure 6-1. Family income and opinions on two social welfare issues, 1976 (nonwhites excluded). (*Source.* SRC/CPS, 1976 election data.)

Because income standards vary with the community, the occupation of the head of the respondent's household is generally preferred over income as a status indicator when a national sample is employed. Figure 6-2 compares the opinions on medical care, guaranteed job, and good standard of living among whites in five occupational categories from unskilled manual workers at the lowest income level to professionals (lawyers, teachers, and accountants, for example) at the top.[3] This figure shows that attitudinal difference among occupational groups on the two social welfare issues are similar to the attitudinal differences among income groups: unskilled workers at the bottom of the status ladder are most in favor of government help to pay medical bills and provide a good standard of living; while business and professional people at the other end of the status ladder are least supportive.

Programs of government assistance for medical care or a guaranteed job and good standard of living presumably give greatest benefit to the poor. Therefore, it is not surprising that support for these two programs generally decreases as one goes up the economic ladder. There are, however, more wealthy economic liberals and poor economic conservatives than one might expect if political attitudes were formed largely on the basis of economic self-interest. When the issue is a spending program that would presumably

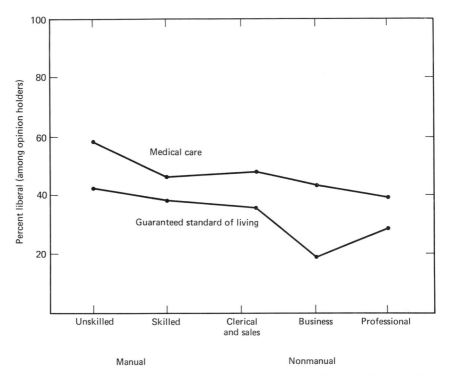

Figure 6-2. Occupational status and opinions on two social welfare issues, 1976 (nonwhites excluded). *(Source.* SRC/CPS, 1976 election data.)

benefit all economic classes equally—such as the space program—it is usually the lower-income groups who are the least enthusiastic. For example, when in 1969, following the first successful landing of men on the moon, Gallup asked people whether they favored a proposal to "set aside money" for a project to "land a man on the planet Mars," the following distribution resulted:[4]

Income	Favor Mars Project	Oppose Mars Project	No Opinion
$7000 and over	46%	48%	6%
$5000-$6999	36	53	11
$3000-$4999	26	61	13
Under $3000	25	66	9

Similarly, it is usually people of relatively high economic status who are most in support of spending for foreign aid, national defense, or pollution control. It might be speculated that the greater opposition to these nonclass-

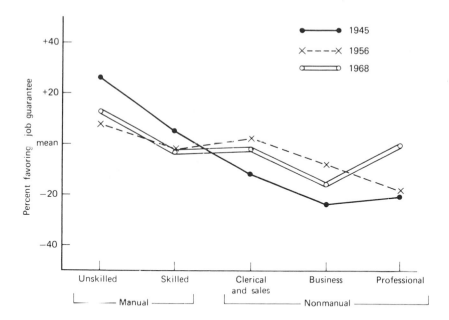

Figure 6-3. The changing relationship between occupation and opinion on a "guaranteed job," 1945-1968 (white male samples). [*Sources.* Richard Centers, *The Psychology of Social Classes* (Princeton. Princeton University Press, 1949), p. 62; Survey Research Center, 1956 and 1968 election data.]

related spending programs on the part of the lower economic groups may be indication that poor people feel strongly that priority should be placed on programs designed to raise the living standards of those who are less economically well-off.[5]

There is some indication that class differences in social-welfare attitudes are not as great today as they have been in the past. Evidence of such a decline is shown in Figure 6-3. This figure displays the relationship between occupation and opinions toward a "guaranteed job" as measured by three surveys—in 1945, 1956, and 1968.[6] Since the line representing the relationship is much steeper for 1945 than for 1956 or 1968, the relative difference in economic liberalism between people of high and low status occupations appears to have declined during the post-World-War-II era. Apparently the change from the poverty of the Depression era to postwar prosperity was the cause of this shift. It should be noted, however, that the response to the increase in prosperity was not a noticeable net shift in social welfare attitudes on the part of the population as a whole. Instead, the change has been that the lower economic strata (among whites) has become less demanding of social welfare legislation while the more prosperous have become less resistant.[7]

Class Differences On Noneconomic Domestic Issues

For reasons we shall explore shortly, on noneconomic issues liberalism tends to increase rather than decrease as one goes up the status ladder. Typical are the relationships between occupational status and opinions on women's rights and on rights for accused criminals, shown in Figure 6-4. Support for an equal role for women rises sharply as one moves up the status ladder. In less regular fashion, support for the liberal position that every effort should be made to protect the rights of the accused is mildly correlated with occupational status.

Similar relationships between status indicators and opinion can be found on many other social issue questions. Table 6-1 shows how income and education (among whites) are related to scores on a composite scale of "cultural intolerance" or "antimodernism" derived from survey data by Lipset and Raab. The table clearly shows that people with the least education and the lowest incomes tend to have the highest scores on "cultural intolerance."

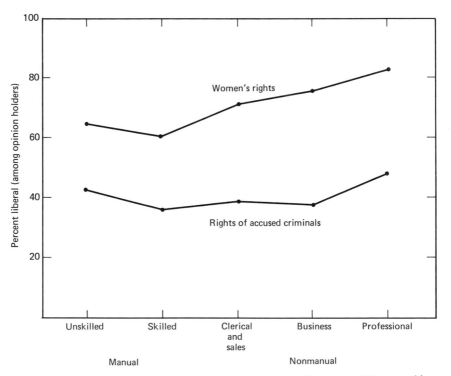

Figure 6-4. Occupational status and opinions on two noneconomic issues, 1976 (nonwhites excluded). *(Source.* SRC/CPS, 1976 election data.)

Table 6-1. Income, Education, and "Cultural Intolerance"

	Percent "High" on Cultural Intolerance	Number of Cases
Education		
8th grade	52	(435)
High school	39	(836)
Some college	28	(204)
College graduate	12	(179)
Income		
Under $5000	47	(603)
$5000 to $9999	35	(649)
$10,000 to $14,999	29	(259)
$15,000 and over	27	(71)

Source: Seymour Martin Lipset and Earl Rabb, *The Politics of Unreason* (New York: Harper and Row, 1970), Table 78, p. 447. 1965 national sample, nonwhites excluded.

Intolerance of minority viewpoints has continually been found to be most frequent among people in low-status categories—particularly among those with little education. This pattern has been found, for example, when people are asked whether Communists, Socialists, atheists, and other advocates of dissenting positions should be allowed to speak in their community.[8] Similarly, people of higher status or higher education were the most tolerant of antiwar protesters and campus radicals during the turbulent Vietnam war era.[9]

Regarding white attitudes toward government programs to help blacks and other minorities, liberalism tends to increase with status. The correlations, however, are far from strong. Typical are those correlations shown in Figure 6-5 between occupational status and opinions on federal programs to give social and economic aid to blacks and other minorities and between occupational status and opinions on school busing to achieve racial balance. Although in each case liberalism increases somewhat with status, the correlations are rather ragged.[10]

When intolerant or "nonliberal" attitudes on noneconomic issues tend to be found most frequent among people in the lower economic strata, they are often attributed to a syndrome of "working class authoritarianism." Many writers have suggested that the working class's more rigid family upbringing promotes an authoritarian, intolerant, and perhaps even undemocratic tendency in political beliefs.[11] There is evidence, however, that it is education rather than class upbringing that is the critical variable here.[12] If we examine the separate effects of income and education we find high education but *not* high income is associated with liberalism on *noneconomic*

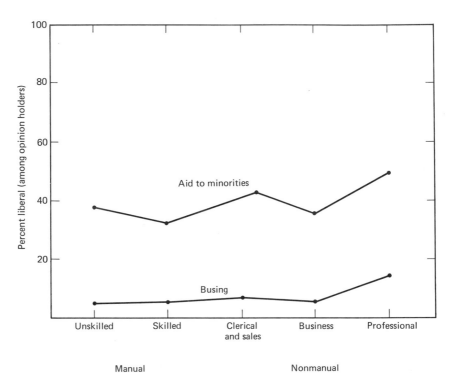

Figure 6-5. Occupational status and opinions on two civil rights issues, 1976 (nonwhites excluded). (*Source.* SRC/CPS, 1976 election data.)

issues. On the other hand, high income is negatively related to *economic* liberalism while education is not. Table 6-2 shows some relevant examples. This table indicates that within each of three income categories liberal opinions on the noneconomic issue of marijuana legalization increases with educational attainment, but for people with the same education the differences in income have virtually no effect on attitudes toward the marijuana issue. The reverse pattern can be seen for the economic issue of medical care. As family income goes up, individuals become more conservative on the medicare issue. But for people who have the same income, differences in education have little impact on their medicare attitude. The third issue—minority aid—taps both the economic dimension of financial aid and the noneconomic dimension of attitudes toward minorities. On this issue one can see the joint liberal effect of high education (which affects the noneconomic part of the issue) and the conservative effect of high income (which affects the economic part of the issue).[13]

Clearly, education has an independent effect on noneconomic issues; liberalism increases with each increase in educational attainment. In turn,

Table 6-2.   Joint Effects of Income and Education on Opinions on Selected Issues

Percent Liberal (of Opinion Holders) on Marijuana Legalization			
Family Income	Not High School Graduate	High School Graduate	Some College
Low	13% (283)	29% (124)	49% (115)
Medium	16% (125)	27% (232)	53% (163)
High	24% (70)	29% (227)	53% (277)

Percent Liberal (of Opinion Holders) on Medical Care			
Family Income	Not High School Graduate	High School Graduate	Some College
Low	67% (305)	65% (156)	64% (105)
Medium	56% (129)	47% (250)	47% (186)
High	51% (81)	37% (270)	40% (354)

Percent Liberal (of Opinion Holders) on Aid to Minorities			
Family Income	Not High School Graduate	High School Graduate	Some College
Low	51% (271)	49% (161)	67% (104)
Medium	38% (117)	49% (238)	50% (180)
High	26% (80)	27% (244)	50% (315)

Source. CPS, 1976 election data. For the full texts of the opinion questions, see Appendix B. Nonwhites excluded. Numbers in percentages are the (weighted) numbers of cases on which the percentages are based.

the impact of education largely accounts for the apparent conservatism of lower status individuals on noneconomic issues. Working class people often show up as conservatives on such issues not because of their class position but because of their lesser education.

Class Differences on Foreign Policy Issues

The major class difference in foreign policy attitudes is that people in the lower economic strata are continually more ready to take "isolationist" positions than the more "internationally minded" higher status groups. For example, people of higher status and education are most in favor of such internationalist policies as foreign aid, trading with Communist nations, and admitting Red China to the United Nations.

   Since internationalism on such issues has often been equated with a liberal outlook, the isolationist tendency among the lower occupational groups has often been cited as another example of working-class authoritarianism.

But complications arise with this interpretation, for if the working class people are authoritarian in their foreign policy attitudes, they ought to have a relatively aggressive and warlike attitude toward other nations. Actually, the accumulation of survey evidence indicates that economic status has virtually no impact on the aggressiveness of one's foreign policy stance.[14]

The lack of relationship between education and foreign policy aggressiveness was clearly shown in polls on the Vietnam war. Comparing people with different educational attainment most polls, like the one shown in Table 6-3 demonstrate that nonhigh-school-graduates tended to be slightly more opposed to the war than people with a college background. This regularity was most clear in response to the question of whether the United States did the right thing in getting involved in Vietnam. For example, among white opinion holders in the 1968 SRC sample, the percentage saying that U.S. involvement was wrong ranged from 68 percent among nonhigh-school-graduates to 58 percent among people with a college background. This may seem surprising since the most visible war opponents were found on college campuses. Only if we refine the education index to isolate the small segment of voters with graduate degrees or four-year degrees from the more prestigious universities do we find disproportionate antiwar sentiment at the top of the education ladder.[15]

One cannot extract too much significance from class difference in foreign policy attitudes because the nonopinion rate on foreign policy questions increases dramatically as one goes down the status ladder.[16] Apparently people in the lower-status categories find little time to devote to questions of foreign policy. This makes the answers they do offer on foreign policy questions somewhat suspect. We may particularly suspect that poor people and people with little education often grope for what they perceive to be the "official" policy when asked to give their foreign policy views.[17] For example, such a tendency may at least be the partial reason why, according to surveys, the less educated had been the most opposed to letting Red China in the United Nations. The better educated had the advantage of knowing that the idea of China's admission was gaining respectability. As the Viet-

Table 6-3.   Education and Vietnam Policy Preference, 1968

	Not High School Graduate	High School Graduate	Some College
Withdraw	24%	17%	20%
Stay, but try to end fighting	38	43	39
Expand war	39	40	41
	100%	100%	100%
Number of cases	(441)	(426)	(368)

Source. CPS/SRC 1968 election Study.

nam example shows, the more educated also have a propensity to support the official foreign policy position. Better educated people are more able to accurately identify the official or government position. Thus, when the government position on a nuclear test ban flip-flopped in the early 1960s, the poll responses of the more educated respondents changed accordingly, while those of the less educated remained stable.[18] Such a pattern may only occur if considerable sophistication is demanded in order to follow changes in the official line or in main currents of thought. The "dovish" trend on the war, for example, developed among people in all education categories.

Economic Status and "Liberalism-Conservatism"

We have seen that the direction of the relationship between status and political liberalism depends on the issue. On domestic issues, people of higher status tend to be the most conservative if the issue taps the social welfare dimension but are often the most liberal on civil rights and, especially, social issue questions. On many foreign policy questions, higher-status people are the most internationalist—a position that is generally associated with liberalism except when foreign policy belligerence is involved.

These tendencies are shown schematically in Table 6-4. Suppose we try now to extract a relationship between status and a summary measure of liberalism, based on a composite of the opinions of each status group on a variety of issues. The relationship between occupational status and the average percentage of opinion holders who give the liberal response to the six issue questions we have examined in the preceding graphs is as follows.

	Unskilled	Skilled	Clerical and Sales	Business	Pro-fessional
Average percent liberal	44%	39%	32%	30%	36%

There were two social welfare issues (guaranteed standard of living and medical care), two civil rights issues (minority aid and busing), and two "social issues" (rights of accused criminals and women's rights). There is no consistent relationship between occupational status and this measure of overall liberalism.

Of course our method of constructing the summary index of the liberalism of each occupational group was entirely arbitrary. Let us instead examine the relationship between a person's status and his self-ranking as a liberal or a conservative. This relationship has undergone an interesting change in recent years. The change is most apparent using education as the status indicator, as in Table 6-5. In 1964 the higher a person's educational attainment the more likely he was to call himself a conservative. But between

Table 6-4. Typical Relationships Between Status and Opinions

Type of Issue	Lower Status (Low Income, Education and Occupational Status)	Higher Status (High Income, Education and Occupational Status)
Social welfare (Medical care, guaranteed job)	more liberal	more conservative
Civil rights (racial integration)[a]	more conservative	more liberal
"Social issues" (dissent, civil liberties)	more conservative	more liberal
Foreign policy	more isolationist (conservative)	more internationalist (liberal)

[a]Tendency shown is greater in South than North.

1964 and 1972 noncollege people became more inclined to call themselves conservative while the college educated became more liberal in their self-identifications. As a result by 1970 the college trained had suddenly become the most liberal of the three categories.

In Chapter 3, we had suggested that in popular usage, the terms "liberal" and "conservative" had once referred mainly to differences in social welfare policy preference; whereas today the terms are more often applied to noneconomic issues. This interpretation explains why the college educated were the most conservative group in 1964: they were relatively wealthy and therefore relatively conservative on economic issues. Today the college trained are the most likely to call themselves liberals because they are more liberal than the average on most noneconomic issues. As mentioned earlier,

Table 6-5. Education and Self-Identification as a Liberal or a Conservative

Education	Percentage of Liberal and Conservative Identifiers Who Call Themselves Liberals[a]		
	1964	1977	Change
Grade School	51	36	−15
High School	46	37	− 9
College	45	49	+ 4

Sources. Lloyd A. Free and Hadley Cantril, *The Political Beliefs of Americans* (New York: Simon and Schuster, 1968), p. 223; Gallup Opinion Index, May 1972, p. 10; May 1977, pp. 28, 29.

[a]Percentage may be in error by about 1 percent, since they were recalculated from original tables in which middle-of-the-roaders and nonopinion-holders were included in the percentage base. The exact question wordings in 1964 and 1977 are slightly different.

the change in the popular meaning of the liberal-conservative terminology appears to indicate a change in the kinds of issues to which people give top priority. Since people are giving decreasing weight to economic issues, we are now more likely to find self-declared "liberals" among people of high economic status and education, whereas the reverse was true only a short while ago.

Class Differences in Party Preferences

Especially since the years of Franklin Roosevelt's presidency, the relationship between economic class and party preference has reflected class differences on economic issues, with preference for the Democratic party decreasing as one goes up the status ladder. In the 1930s, Roosevelt's efforts to expand the federal government's role in order to combat the economic effects of the Great Depression caused a "partisan realignment" of the American electorate. During this realignment of the New Deal era the increased salience of economic issues pushed the relatively poor toward increasing loyalty to the Democratic party and the smaller group of relatively prosperous voters toward the Republicans. This basic partisan division of the American electorate, of course, remains today, largely because party identifications formed during the Depression era remain stable and are transmitted across generations.

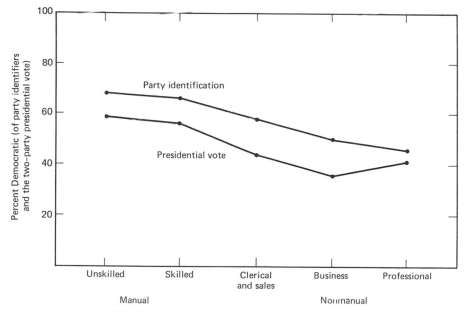

Figure 6-6. Party identification and presidential voting, 1976, by occupational status (nonwhites excluded). (*Source.* SRC/CPS, 1976 election data.)

Class differences in party identification and in presidential voting in 1968 are shown in Figure 6-6. To remove the impact of racial differences in party preference and voting, the sample excludes nonwhites. First, looking at the relationship between occupational status and party identification, we see that the percentage of party identifiers who call themselves Democrats rather than Republicans decreases as one goes up the status ladder, from 68 percent among unskilled workers to 46 percent among professionals. Similarly, Democratic voting for president in 1976 decreases with increasing status.

Figure 6-7 traces the relationships between class and presidential voting going back to 1936. For simplicity, the voters are split into only two occupational categories—manual and nonmanual—for this comparison. The gap between the two classes in their frequency of Democratic voting is a useful indicator of "class voting."[19] No pattern stands out from this graph except for the fact that the voting gap between classes was highest in 1948. The reader may be surprised to notice that class voting in the Roosevelt elections shown here—1936 to 1944—was not unusually high. However, the Depression did have considerable impact on the era's young voters whose party identification had not yet crystallized. Consequently, during the 1930s and into the 1940s, young voters—who might be called the "Depression generation"—developed voting habits that were generally consistent with their class interests. It was the tendency of older voters to retain their predepression party identification that prevented the overall degree of class voting during the Depression era from being unusually high.[20]

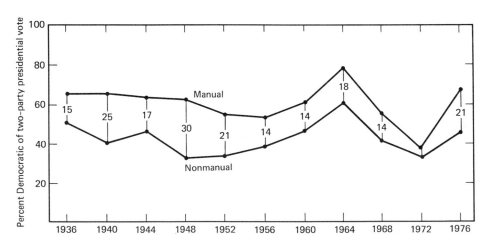

Figure 6-7. Occupational status and presidential voting, 1936–1976 [*Sources.* 1936–1960: Robert R. Alford, Party and Society (Chicago: Rand McNally, 1963), pp. 352–353, Table B-3. Alford has reported the results of more than one survey for each year. We have averaged the results together. 1964–1976: SRC/CPS election data.]

Figure 6-7 shows that after reaching a peak in 1948, class voting declined steadily since that date. Because of this change, many observers have suggested that the New Deal partisan alignment along class lines is rapidly eroding and being replaced by a newer partisan alignment along noneconomic issues. Certainly in at least one recent presidential election — the 1972 race between Nixon and McGovern—the traditional New Deal issues were replaced by others in determining voter choices. But following trend lines does not always make good forecasts, as the figures for class voting in 1976 show. In the 1976 Carter-Ford contest, class voting was at its highest point since 1948, as people in the manual (blue collar) occupation category were 21 percentage points more Democratic in their presidential voting than were voters in the nonmanual (white collar) occupation category. As we will see in Chapter 7, economic issues played a major role in 1976, much like in earlier elections.

Despite the fluctuations in the degree of class voting over the years, class differences in party identification have remained stable. Examples from two widely separated years of the relationship between occupational status and party identification are shown in Figure 6-8. In 1939 and 1968 the relative Democratic tendencies (in party identification) among occupational groups was about the same. The only change over time has been an increase in Democratic identification across all five occupational categories. This is a

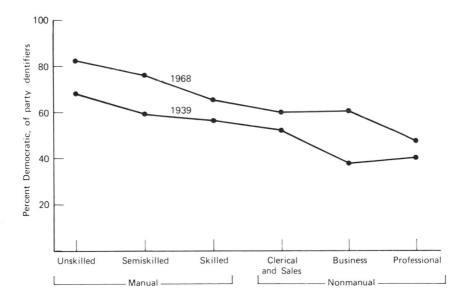

Figure 6-8. Continuity in the relationship between occupation and party identification, 1939–1968. [*Sources.* Hadley Cantril, *Public Opinion 1935–1946* (Princeton: Princeton University Press, 1951), p. 576; Survey Research Center, 1968 Election data.]

sign that as Americans have moved up the status ladder from the dark days of the Depression era they have not become more Republican in partisanship.[21]

If, in fact, economic classes of this country are becoming decreasingly polarized against one another in their voting behavior and party preference, this would not necessarily be a sign of increasing political stability. Great Britain, for example, is often cited as a model of stability; yet there are few other democratic nations where economic class is as important a determinant of electoral choice. British voters in the manual strata prefer the Labour party to the Conservatives by a ratio of about 3 to 1; whereas the reverse ratio holds for nonmanuals.[22] France and Italy have less class voting but a more volatile brand of politics.[23] The major determinant of a nation's degree of class voting is the extent to which noneconomic issues play a role in shaping electoral decisions. In Great Britain, for example, no major noneconomic set of issues—either regional, racial, or religious—cuts across class lines. As a consequence, an Englishman's class interest substantially determines how he will vote. Even though France and Italy have sizeable Communist and Socialist parties, these countries have major divisions on noneconomic issues—particularly over the role of the Catholic Church. Thus, in these countries we find many lower status supporters of conservative parties (particularly among women) and many middle-class "leftists." The fact that class conflict has never dominated American partisan politics to the extent it has in Europe may have been one long-term source of stability of the American political system. But a possible further decline in the political importance of the traditional class-related issues may augur something quite different from a period of political tranquility, for the increasingly important racial, and social issues obviously could intensify political conflict in the years to come.

6-2 RACE AND POLITICAL OPINIONS

It is often said that Americans are becoming increasingly polarized on the basis of race. In this section we will examine one aspect of this racial division—differences between whites and blacks in their opinions on standard political issues and in voting behavior. In 1976 when the SRC's national sample was asked whether they favored "strict segregation" of the races, "desegregation," or "something in between" the difference between the responses of whites and blacks were as follows:

	Whites	Blacks
Desegregation	39%	75%
Something in between	52	24
Strict segregation	9	1
	100%	100%

Unlike what either a white racist or a black nationalist might prefer to believe, blacks are almost unanimous in rejecting racial segregation. Of course no such consensus exists among whites. The polarization of the races might be seen even more clearly by comparing the responses of whites and blacks on the issue of whether civil rights leaders are trying to "push too fast," "too slowly," or "at about the right speed:"

	Whites	Blacks
Not fast enough	4%	45%
About right	52	46
Too fast	44	7
	100%	100%

Similarly, 77 percent of the black opinion holders in a 1972 survey said the civil rights movement was "peaceful," while a majority of whites (51 percent) said it was "violent." Also 88 percent of the blacks but only 47 percent of the whites said the civil rights movement "helped" the black cause. Clearly whites and blacks see the civil rights movement quite differently.

Even on issues that are tangential to civil rights, blacks are much more likely than whites to take the liberal position. Some examples are shown in Table 6-6. On social welfare issues such as a guaranteed job and good standard of living, black opinion holders are nearly unanimous in supporting government action. More so than whites, blacks support specific aspects of civil liberties. Even on foreign policy questions such as trading with Communist nations, blacks are more liberal than whites.

Table 6-6. Race and Opinion on Selected Noncivil Rights Issues

Opinion	Percent Support Among Opinion Holders	
	Whites	Blacks
The government in Washington should see to it that every person has a job and a good standard of living (CPS, 1976)	33	80
Favor a government insurance plan which would cover all medical and hospital expenses (CPS, 1976)	47	75
Oppose the death penalty for persons convicted of murder (Gallup, 1976)	26	57
Our farmers and businessmen should be allowed to do business with Communist Countries (SRC, 1968)	43	65

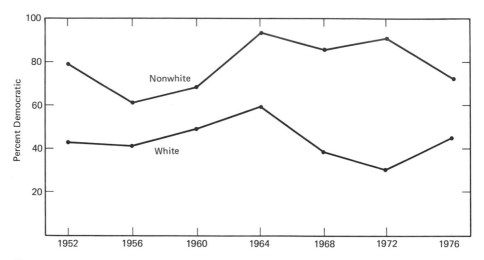

Figure 6-9. Race and presidential voting, 1952–1976. (*Source.* Gallup Poll.)

In partisan preference American blacks have undergone a longterm reversal in allegiance. Between the Civil War and Franklin Roosevelt's presidency, most blacks who could vote opted for the Republican Party because it was the party of Lincoln. From the 1930s to the present, however, most black voters have supported the Democratic Party. Initially, this shift was a response to economic issues rather than any greater attempt on the part of the Democratic Party to remove racial barriers. Only in recent years could the Democratic Party be identified as the party with clearly greater sympathy for the civil rights cause. But, as a consequence of the Democrats' increasing image as the more "pro-civil rights" party (beginning in the 1960s), the Democratic tendency in black voting at the presidential level has changed from only a tendency to near unanimity. This change is shown in Figure 6-9. Clearly the Democratic voting of blacks is a pivotal factor in presidential elections. In state and local elections, black voters will often vote for a Republican if he is the more liberal candidate on civil rights.[25] Thus the black voters' allegiance to the Democratic Party is contingent upon the Democrats giving at least somewhat more support than the Republicans do to the civil rights cause.

6-3 AGE AND POLITICAL OPINIONS

From the recent talk about the "generation gap," one might suspect that American public opinion is strongly polarized on the basis of age, with older people much more conservative than the young. Comparisons of young and old voters in samples of the adult electorate do reveal that opinions on most issues vary somewhat with age, but not always by wide margins and some-times not even in the predicted direction.

On most standard poll questions older people are found to be somewhat more conservative than young adults. Typical patterns are shown in Table 6-7 in which the political opinions of the under-30 generation are compared

Table 6-7. **Age and Opinion on Selected Political Issues**

	Percent Support Among Opinion Holders		
Opinion	21-29 Years Old	50 Years or Older	Difference
The use of marijuana should be made legal. (Gallup, 1977)	52	11	−41
Oppose stricter community standards regarding sale of sexually explicit materials. (Gallup, 1977)	67	32	−35
Red China should be admitted to the United Nations. (Gallup, 1970)	60	34	−26
Do not disapprove all protest marches that are permitted by the local authorities. (SRE, 1968)	59	34	−25
The government in Washington should make every possible effort to improve the social and economic position of blacks and other minority groups. (CPS, 1976)	56	35	−21
Women should have an equal role with men in running business, industry, and government. (CPS, 1976)	79	58	−21
The government in Washington is paying too much for national defense. (Gallup, 1977)	37	18	−19
Oppose the death penalty for persons convicted of murder. (Gallup, 1976)	37	27	−10
The government in Washington should see to it that every person has a job and a good standard of living. (CPS, 1976)	43	37	− 6
Favor a government insurance plan which would cover all medical and hospital expenses. (CPS, 1976)	53	51	− 2

Note. For Gallup data, percentages may be in error by about one percent, since they were recalculated from original tables in which nonopinion holders were included in the percentage base.

with those of people 50 years of age or older. The questions, taken from SRC and Gallup surveys, are ordered according to the percentage difference in the responses of the two generations.

On all ten issues, the younger generation is the more liberal, by margins of from 2 to 41 percentage points. The widest gap is on marijuana legislation. This is understandable, as is the fact that the lowest gap is on the medical care issue. With their higher medical costs, older people have an understandable reason for supporting government help in paying medical bills.

The reader may expect that the relationships between age and attitudes toward the war in Vietnam was similar to the strongest relationships shown in Table 6-7. However, despite the fact that active opposition to the war quite obviously was most prevalent among the young, it was older people, on the whole, who appeared more dovish on the war issue. Although this statement may seem surprising, there can be little doubt of its accuracy. For example, virtually every Gallup Poll taken on the issue shows agreement on the statement that getting into the war was a "mistake," to be more frequent among voters 50 years of age or older than among young voters in their twenties.[26] Much of the seeming antiwar sentiment of older people stems from their retention of the old isolationist belief that all foreign entanglements should be avoided instead of the humanitarian grounds offered by the more vocal opponents of the war. The isolationism of much of the older generation may explain, for example, why they are the age group that was both most opposed to a war against communism in Vietnam and also the most opposed to the seating of Communist China in the United Nations. Certainly the antiwar sentiment of the older generation should not be taken to mean that they were the age group most sympathetic to antiwar protesters. Polls clearly show the opposite is true.

With interesting exceptions on certain issues, young adults do hold more liberal opinions than their elders. Has this generation gap in opinions always been with us, or is it a new phenomenon? On most issues, the opinion differences between age groups are about the same as they had been in earlier surveys. But on youth-related issues, the gap between the opinions of the young and the old has been widening. For example, until the late 1960s, young adults—and even 18 to 20-year-olds—had been no more in favor lowering the voting age than had the 50-and-older generation of the time. As recently as 1965, the 20 to 29 age group were only two percentage points more favorable than the 50-and-older people toward a lowered voting age. By 1971, the gap had widened to a 22 percentage point difference.[27]

Young and old voters are also becoming more polarized in their self-identification with liberal or conservative labels. As Table 6-8 shows, in 1964 young voters were only slightly more liberal than their elders in self-identification. By 1976, the gap had widened considerably.

Why is it that older voters are generally more conservative than the

Table 6-8.   Age and Self-Identification as a Liberal or a Conservative

Age	Percent of Liberal and Conservative Identifiers Who Call Themselves Liberals[a]		
	1964	1977	Change
18-29	50[b]	56	+ 6
30-49	50	36	−14
50 and older	44	34	−10

Sources. Lloyd A. Free and Hadley Cantril, *The Political Beliefs of Americans* (New York: Simon and Schuster, 1968), p. 223; *Gallup Opinion Index,* December 1977, pp. 28-9.
[a]Percentages may be in error by about one percent, since they were recalculated from original tables in which "middle-of-the-roaders and nonopinion holders were included in the percentage base. The exact question wordings in 1964 and 1977 are slightly different.
[b]21-29 years old.

young? One possibility—an "aging" explanation—is simply that people may become more and more conservative as they grow older. There is also another possible explanation that does not demand that people change their political attitudes as they age: the reason why older people are the most conservative may be that each generation entering the electorate is socialized to more liberal values than the generations before them. To fully understand the relationship between age and conservatism, we need to monitor generations at several points in time to see if they become more conservative. For example, if people in a given generation—say those born between 1930 and 1935—give increasingly conservative responses to the same poll question year after year, then the "aging" explanation would be accepted. But if their answers remain constant over time, then a explanation in terms of generational differences would be proper. The evidence generally tends to support the generational interpretation. People do not become more politically conservative as they grow older. Nor do they become more Republican. One question that has continually been asked over the years is the party identification of the respondent. Consequently we may take party identification as a rough measure of liberalism-conservatism and find out whether the party identification of various generations changes over time. If a trend toward increasing Republicanism on the part of each generation can be identified, we could infer that people become more conservative with age. Figure 6-10 shows the distribution of party identification for different generations in 1960 and in 1976. The figure shows that each of the two generations surveyed in both years (those born between 1908 and 1923 and those born between 1924 and 1939) maintained a remarkably stable party identification over the sixteen-year period from 1960 to 1976. Numerous other studies that follow the party identification of different generations over time, show a similar pattern of stable partisanship rather than growing Republicanism as people go through the life cycle. Thus, if Republicanism equals conservatism, people do not become more conservative as they advance in years.[28]

Older voters are somewhat more Republican than younger voters, but for the reason that older generations entered the electorate with a more Republican orientation rather than because voters get more Republican as they age. Figure 6-10 shows that the chief relationship between partisanship and age is that people born after the early part of this century tend to be more Democratic than those born before. The apparent reason for this pattern is that the earlier generation entered the electorate and developed its party identification before the impact of the Depression-based realignment of the 1930s that tipped the partisan balance somewhat in favor of the Democratic party.[29] Because the pre-Depression generation is a decreasing portion of the American electorate, the percentage who call themselves Democrats has been increasing at a glacial pace over the years. This slight trend is stopping, however, since mortality has been reducing the pre-Depression generation to insignificant size. As the pre-Depression generation dies off, the relationship between age and party choice is also disappearing, since among voters born after the first part of this century there is virtually no relationship between age and party identification.[30]

If the American electorate is now undergoing a new partisan realignment, it would probably be more evident among younger voters. Although today's younger voters have not tilted in an unusually Republican or Democratic direction, a clear change in the party choice of young voters is the surprising degree to which they reject identification with either party. As

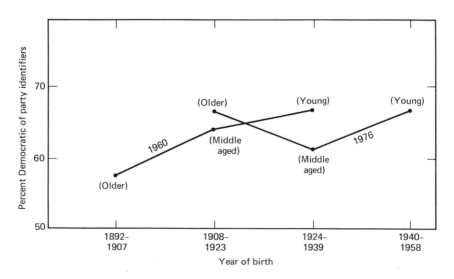

Figure 6-10. Age and party identification, 1960 and 1976. (*Source.* SRC/CPS election data.)

Figure 6-11 shows, about half of the younger voters in 1976 called themselves Independents rather than Republicans or Democrats. In fact since the
mix-sixties, about half of the younger voters defined as those who entered
the electorate *since* the mid-sixties have called themselves Independent. Although young voters have been the most Independent in earlier years, such
as shown in the graph for 1960, the trend had never been as strong as in
recent years. Indeed it is the rejection of the parties by young voters that
explains the recent upsurge of Independent self-classification rather than a
large-scale switching to Independent classification by older partisans.[31] The
disinclination to identify with either party is a generation effect—largely a
characteristic of youthful voters alone. If one of the two major parties eventually captures most of the support of young voters, it could establish itself
as the dominant party for future decades.

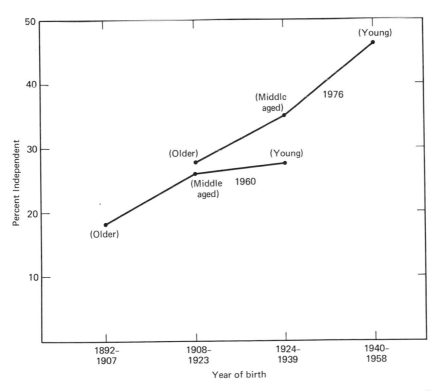

Figure 6-11. Age and frequency of "Independent" self-classification, 1960 and 1976. (*Source.*
SRC/CPS election data.)

6-4 RELIGION AND POLITICAL OPINIONS

In religion, Americans are divided into a Protestant majority, a Catholic minority of about 25 percent, and a still smaller but significant minority of about 3 percent who are Jewish. The partisan tendencies of the three major faiths are well known. Protestants are the most Republican group, Catholics tend to vote Democratic, and Jewish voters vote Democratic also, to an even greater extent than Catholics. Religious divisions were at their clearest in the 1960 presidential election when the Democrats broke tradition and nominated a Catholic, John F. Kennedy, for president. Among northern whites, the breakdown of the 1960 presidential vote by religion was as follows:[32]

	Protestant	Catholic	Jewish
Percent Democratic (Kennedy)	28%	83%	93%
Percent Republican (Nixon)	72	17	7
	100%	100%	100%

Almost three-fourths of the Protestant vote among northern whites were for Nixon, the Republican candidate, while over 80 percent of the Catholic and Jewish vote was Democratic. In more typical elections, without a Catholic candidate, the religious division is smaller, but still there. For example, the religious division in the presidential election of 1976—again among a northern white sample was the following:[33]

	Protestant	Catholic	Jewish
Percent Democratic (Carter)	39%	54%	71%
Percent Republican (Ford)	61	45	29
	100%	100%	100%

The temporal stability of the partisan differences between Protestants, Catholics, and Jews is shown in Figure 6-12. The figure shows, for each of five presidential years, the percentage of the party identifiers within each religious denomination (among northern whites only) who call themselves Democrats. Typically, the Democratic percentage (in terms of party identification) is about 90 percent among Jews, 70 percent among Catholics, but slightly less than 50 percent among Protestants. Since these differences are fairly constant from year to year, there is little reason to suspect that the fairly wide partisan divisions between religious denominations are eroding.

There are several possible explanations for the differences in the partisan tendencies of Catholics and Protestants. A small part of the explanation

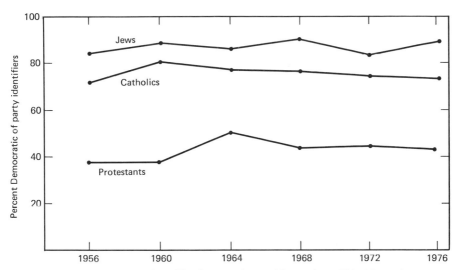

Figure 6-12. Religion and party identification (northern whites only), 1956–1976. (*Source.* SRC/CPS election data.)

may involve differences in Protestant and Catholic theological emphasis: Protestant churches have placed somewhat greater stress on "individualism," which is indirectly linked with the conservative philosophy of the Republican party. More important, the Democratic party has from its time of origin made a greater effort than the Republicans and their forerunners to woo the immigrant voters, most of whom were Catholic. The payoff of this policy for the Democratic party has been the allegiance of most members of Catholic ethnic groups—especially the Irish, Italians, and Polish—many of whom are now several generations removed from immigrant status. The exceptions tend to prove the rule: in localities where the Republican party made a successful effort long ago to win over certain Catholic ethnic groups (such as the Italians in New Haven), the Republican adherence persists today.[34] Still

a simpler explanation for the Democratic voting of Catholics is that at one time American Catholics were much less affluent than their Protestant neighbors—a condition that would naturally cause them to gravitate to the Democratic party for economic reasons. But this explanation may be inadequate for the reason that Catholics have now caught up to and even surpassed Protestants in average economic status. Also, in surveys going back to 1940, when most Catholics were poorer than Protestants, the more frequent Democratic voting by Catholics persisted even when economic status was held constant.[35] Certainly an economic explanation for the overwhelmingly Democratic tendencies of Jewish voters would certainly be ill-founded since of the three major denominations Jews are clearly the wealthiest. Probably the

Jewish allegiance to the Democratic party is partially a response to their status as an often persecuted minority; as with blacks, and perhaps even Catholics, their minority status moves them toward the generally more liberal Democratic party. Additionally, the explanation for the liberal and Democratic tendencies of Jewish votes may involve the unique Jewish cultural heritage.[36]

Perhaps the best explanation for the Democratic allegiance of Catholics is simply that their minority status attracts them to the more "left-leaning" Democratic Party. As evidence, in countries where the Catholic Church is the major religion its adherents are usually identified with the more conservative political parties. Some political observers have been predicting that the Catholic ethnic groups are ripe for massive conversions to Republicanism because of their supposed political conservatism. But the premise of a unique Catholic conservatism is false since the partisan difference between Protestants and Catholics is also reflected in their political opinions.[37] Possibly the reason Catholics are more liberal than Protestants on most political issues is that they have learned to identify with the liberal policy positions of their favored Democratic Party.

Table 6-9 shows a pattern of increasing political liberalism as one goes from Protestants to Catholics to Jews among northern whites in the CPS's 1976 sample. On all but one of the ten issues shown, the Jewish respondents are the most liberal. Catholics follow, since they are more liberal than the Protestants in the sample on seven of the ten issues.

A further, but somewhat less fruitful, exploration of the relationship between religion and political opinion can be made by comparing the opinion tendencies of different Protestant denominations. Theological distinctions

Table 6-9. Religion and Political Opinions (Northern Whites Only) Percent Liberal Among Opinion Holders

Issue	Protestant	Catholic	Jewish
Tax Reform	46	52	48
Domestic Spending	73	82	94
Medical Care	40	60	77
Guaranteed Standard of Living	28	35	47
Aid to Minorities	40	38	56
Busing	9	6	13
Rights of Accused	44	37	50
Marijuana Legalization	28	34	74
Women's Rights	66	71	86
Military Spending	17	19	43
Mean Percent Liberal	*39*	*43*	*59*

Source. Center for Political Studies, 1976 election data. For full text of the opinion questions, see Appendix B.

between Protestant denominations are often thought to have political implications; the emphasis on personal salvation in the Baptist church and other "fundamentalist" groups seemingly should make members of the more fundamentalist denominations relatively conservative, while the more "worldly" involvement in social problems on the part of many leaders of nonfundamentalist groups (Presbyterians and Episcopalians, for example) ought to make their members relatively liberal. Very sharp differences of this sort have been found between the political attitudes of Protestant clergymen of fundamentalist and nonfundamentalist churches and among church members who are very politically involved. For example, membership in anti-feminist groups tends to be heavily drawn from fundamentalist religions.[38] However, differences between the mass memberships of Protestant denominations are usually slight, and when they are found, they often reflect the strong economic and educational differences between denominations. For example, Table 6-10 shows that Baptist and other fundamentalists are actually more liberal than members of less fundamentalist Protestant groups on the economic issue of guaranteed standard of living. This is because fundamentalists are relatively low on the economic ladder. On some noneconomic issues members of the most fundamentalist churches display the most conservative views. This tendency can be explained, however, by the lower education and socioeconomic status of fundamentalist churchgoers.

When comparisons of members of different Protestant churches have included added controls for differences in economic status or education, opinion differences have not been strong enough to provide adequate evidence of a denominational effect. This is true for interdenominational differences in party preference and voting as well as for differences in political issues. Among Protestants, religious fundamentalism is normally related to support for the Democratic Party because members of fundamentalist churches are drawn heavily from among the poor. A seeming exception occurred in 1968 when the "conservative" presidential candidacy of George Wallace received disproportionate support from Baptists and other religious fundamentalists.[39] Yet it is not clear that their religious affiliation was the cause of the fundamentalists' attraction to Wallace. Instead it may have been a function of the low education, low status, and Southern origin of fundamentalist churchgoers.[40]

6-5 GEOGRAPHY AND POLITICAL OPINIONS

People commonly think of American political opinion as being somewhat polarized along lines of geographic region. The South stands out particularly for its political conservatism—especially on civil rights issues. Among the nonSouthern regions, the East is often thought to stand out for its political liberalism. There have also been other regional stereotypes that once may have been valid but do not seem to be today. The South, for example, was

Table 6-10. Protestant Denomination and Political Opinions

| | Percent Liberal Among Opinion Holders | | | | | |
| | Least Fundamentalist | | | Most Fundamentalist | | |
Opinion	Episcopal	Presbyterian	Methodist	Lutheran	Baptist	Fundamentalist Sects
Guaranteed Standard of Living	19	13	24	28	38	41
Aid to Minorities	35	37	30	41	32	30
Rights of Accused Criminals	41	44	31	46	37	42
Women's Rights	89	75	67	64	58	43
Military Spending	25	18	12	17	11	12

Source. CPS, 1976 election data. For the full texts of the opinion questions, see the Appendix. Nonwhites are excluded. Denominations are arrayed in the order of increasing frequency of belief (among CPS respondents) that "the Bible is God's word and all it says is true." The fundamentalist sect category includes all denominations listed as "neofundamentalist" in the 1976 CPS codebook, except Southern Baptists who are grouped with their Northern brethren. Not all Protestant denominations are included in this table.

once perhaps the most internationally-minded region in foreign policy, largely because of the cotton growers' interest in unrestrained trade with other nations. The Midwest at one time had the reputation, seemingly deserved on the basis of poll results, of being the most isolationist (or least internationalist) region of the country.[41] Most regional differences in political opinion have been washing away, however, even to the extent that North-South differences on civil rights issues are less acute now than in the 1950s.

The basic similarity of opinion distributions in the four regions is shown in Table 6-11, from the CPS's 1976 survey data. For the most part, regional differences shown in this table are so slight that they could be attributable to sampling error. Remembering the basic regional similarities, we can cautiously assign liberalism scores to the four regional groups by averaging their responses to the 10 issue questions. When this is done, the East barely exceeds the West as the most liberal region. Except for the fact that the South often shows up as the most conservative region, especially on civil rights, this relative ordering is typical of most regional breakdowns of opinion.

Some people hypothesize that regional differences in opinion reflect important differences in the political cultures of the various regions, with residents of different regions learning from their political environment to adapt to different sets of political beliefs.[42] But except for the resistance of white Southerners to racial integration, no clear cultural differences emerge when we examine regional opinion differences on standard political questions. Even the small differences that appear between regional groups are for the most part simply a function of the different group compositions of the regions. For example, if the East is truly the most liberal region, it is because Easterners are more likely than residents of other regions to be a member of a liberal ethnic or religious minority group—either black, Catho-

Table 6-11. Regional Differences in Political Opinions

Issue	Percent Liberal Among Opinion Holders			
	East	Midwest	South	West
Tax Reform	50	48	47	48
Domestic Spending	83	76	78	77
Medical Care	64	41	48	51
Guaranteed Standard of Living	44	32	45	30
Aid to Minorities	50	42	40	48
Busing	11	10	11	14
Right of Accused	41	42	37	50
Marijuana	38	30	24	45
Women's Rights	73	67	65	76
Military Spending	23	16	15	26
Mean Percent Liberal	*48*	*40*	*41*	*47*

Source: Center for Political Studies, 1976 election data.

lic, or Jewish. If we limit our regional comparison to only the relatively conservative white Protestant majority, opinion differences between Easterners, Midwesterners, and Westerners wash away almost all together, as Table 6-12 shows. Comparison of only white Protestants, however, does accentuate the difference between the North and the South. Table 6-12 shows that white Protestants in the South are much more opposed to busing and to minority aid than their Northern counterparts. The Southerners in the white Protestant sample are also the most conservative on other noneconomic issues—rights of accused criminals, marijuana, women's rights, and military spending. But on domestic economic issues—tax reform, domestic spending, medical care, and a guaranteed standard of living—even white Protestants living in the South give opinions that are much like those of their counterparts in the rest of the country.[43]

Regional differences are much more apparent on matters of partisan preference and voting than in opinions on national issues. Ever since the Civil War, the South has been the most Democratic region. Table 6-13 shows that this tendency still exists in party identification; whereas only slight majorities of party identifiers in the North call themselves Democrats, the ratio of Democrats to Republicans in the South is 4 to 1. Examining the party identification of white Protestants alone, we still find Southerners to be the most Democratic group in terms of party identification. Restricting analysis to white Protestants also reveals partisan differences among Northern regions. White Protestants in the "liberal" East are considerably less likely than their Midwestern and Western counterparts to call themselves Democrats. This difference up to 1976 reflects the historical tendency of the East to be the most Republican region of the country.

Table 6-12.   **Regional Differences in Political Opinions of White Protestants**

Issue	Percent Liberal Among Opinion Holders			
	East	Midwest	South	West
Tax Reform	45	47	44	44
Domestic Spending	75	72	73	74
Medical Care	49	34	39	43
Guaranteed Standard of Living	35	28	33	24
Aid to Minorities	50	35	27	40
Busing	10	7	2	11
Rights of Accused	40	41	32	51
Marijuana Legalization	27	26	17	32
Women's Rights	64	64	58	72
Military Spending	17	15	12	19
Mean Percent Liberal	*41*	*37*	*34*	*41*

Source. Center for Political Studies, 1976 election data.

In recent presidential elections, the regions have gone against their historical partisan tendencies. In 1964, 1968, and 1972, the Democratic South was the least Democratic region in terms of presidential voting. (This trend was arrested in 1976, when a southerner headed the Democratic ticket.) The liberal but historically Republican East, on the other hand, has been the most Democratic region in recent presidential voting, including 1976. This Democratic tendency in the presidential voting of Easterners is attributable to the disproportionate black, Jewish, and Catholic vote in the East. As the data in Table 6-13 show, when only white Protestants are compared, it was Easterners who were the least Democratic group in presidential voting and party identification.

A somewhat better predictor of a person's political opinions than the region he lives in, is whether he resides in a city, a suburb, or the country. Most big cities are, relatively speaking, centers of political liberalism and Democratic politics. Somewhat more conservative and Republican than the cities are the suburbs that surround them. Residents of small towns and rural areas are also relatively conservative and outside the South, relatively Republican in their politics. These tendencies among the general adult population are shown in Table 6-14.

As with region, most difference of opinion tendencies by city size can be explained in terms of the differences in the kinds of people who live in the different places. City residents show up as relatively liberal in surveys, for example, because people with relatively liberal group characteristics—blacks, Catholics, and Jews—are more likely than others to live in the city. A major reason why suburbs are more conservative than their central cities is that blacks comprise a much smaller proportion of the suburban population. Small town and rural areas are conservative because normally they are predominantly Protestant and outside the South, contain few blacks. Also,

Table 6-13. Regional Differences in Political Partisanship

	East	Midwest	South	West
Percent Democratic of Party Identifiers				
All respondents	54	55	73	56
White Protestants only	35	42	63	41
Percent Democratic 1976 presidential vote				
All respondents	55	48	54	47
White Protestants only	40	42	42	36

Source. CPS, 1976 election data.

Table 6-14. Urbanism and Political Opinions

| | Percent Liberal Among Opinion Holders | | |
	City	Suburbs	Small Town and Rural
Domestic Spending	80	78	77
Tax Reform	54	46	46
Medical Care	61	48	45
Standard of Living	48	33	36
Aid to Minorities	54	43	38
Busing	18	8	9
Rights of Accused	45	43	37
Marijuana Legalization	41	41	18
Women's Rights	75	74	58
Military Spending	24	20	14
Mean percent liberal	*50*	*43*	*38*
Percent Democratic			
1976 presidential vote	59	48	49
of party identifiers	74	58	59

Source. Center for Political Studies, 1976 election data.

since the South is a relatively rural region, conservative Southerners are more likely than Northerners to be small town or rural residents.

In other words, if we hold constant the group characteristics of people by comparing only those with similar group characteristics, differences of opinion by area size tend to wash away. This is shown in Table 6-15, which compares Northern white Protestants in different places of residence. When comparing only northern white Protestants, small town and rural residents are still noticeably less liberal than their urban and suburban counterparts, especially on noneconomic issues. But suburban residents seem just as liberal as city residents when the comparison is limited to northern white Protestants. (While suburbanites are slightly less liberal on most issues, this tendency is balanced out by the fact that they are much more liberal than city residents on issues of marijuana and women's rights.) Partisan differences by size-of-place are also slight when only Northern white Protestants are compared. For example, suburbanites in the sample are the most Democratic groups in terms of presidential voting but less Democratic than even small town and rural residents in terms of party identification.[44]

In terms of population trends, big cities have been losing people while their suburbs have been gaining rapidly. In some popular discussions of voting trends the suburban movement has been heralded as a sign of increasing voter conservatism and growing Republicanism.[45] As people move to the conservative suburbs, so the argument goes, they conform politically by adapting the more conservative opinions and Republican voting habits of their

Table 6-15. Political Opinions by Size of Place, Northern White Protestants Only

	Percent Liberal Among Opinion Holders		
	City	Suburbs	Small Town and Rural
Domestic Spending	69	73	75
Tax Reform	55	52	39
Medical Care	42	41	37
Standard of Living	32	27	27
Aid to Minorities	47	41	34
Busing	11	7	9
Rights of Accused	48	46	39
Marijuana Legalization	27	42	17
Women's Rights	68	77	54
Military Spending	25	18	12
Mean percent liberal	*42*	*42*	*34*
Percent Democratic			
1976 Presidential vote	41	42	38
of party identifiers	47	36	41

Source. Center for Political Studies, 1976 election data.

new neighbors. There are several flaws, however, in this argument. We have seen that people with similar group characteristics, but in different places of residence, are pretty much alike politically. Second, even if suburbanites are slightly more conservative than their city counterparts with similar characteristics whom they left behind, the explanation could be that the most conservative city dwellers flee to the suburbs instead of becoming more conservative once they get there. Finally, even if it were true that people who move from city to suburb become more conservative as an adaption to suburban living, the reverse would also be true; the influx of allegedly liberal city folk would make the political norms of the suburbs more liberal.

Although the population movement to the suburbs may have little impact in terms of a national trend of opinion or partisanship, the flight to the suburbs continues; most major cities will have black majorities in a few years, which may lead to a greater racial polarization of local politics than we have already. Also, since it is the more affluent who move to the suburbs, the financial base of the cities is becoming severely weakened at a time when their need to spend money for urban problems is becoming more acute. In the coming decades this growing urban crisis will become even more of a political focal point than it has in the past. As the cities demand more money from suburbanites who work in the city, from their often unsympathetic state legislatures, and from Congress, a heightened urban-rural conflict over spending priorities may develop.

6-6 SEX AND POLITICAL OPINIONS

Differences in the political attitudes of men and women are so slight that they deserve only brief mention. When female suffrage was implemented in the United States with the ratification of the 19th Amendment in 1920, some observers voiced the apprehension that extension of the franchise to women would somehow transform the nature of American politics in a less desirable direction. Of course, no such fear was justified. For a while, women were less likely to exercise their right to vote than were men; yet this gap has decreased along with the disappearance of the cultural belief that political activity is incompatible with the feminine role.[46] In political attitudes and voting, people are seldom different because of their sex.

With the recent advent of the women's rights movement, one might expect a growing polarization between men and women on issues dealing with women's rights. However, no such tendency has occurred. In fact, most of the numerous polls on the issues of abortion and the Equal Rights Amendment show more men than women in favor of liberal abortion laws or the ERA. Although differences between men and women on political issues is generally nonexistent, there are some exceptions as shown in Table 6-16. One apparent pattern shown is that women react to some political issues in what might be called a more "tender minded" fashion than men. For example, women were more opposed to the war in Vietnam and capital punishment, but more in favor of a guaranteed job and gun control legislation. On "social issues" women show what apparently is a more "puritanical" streak; they are more opposed to the legalization of marijuana and liberalization of divorce laws, and more in favor of a crackdown on pornography. Even these differences, however, can hardly be called significant.

6-7 CONCLUSION

Although the divisions we have discussed in this chapter do not exhaust all the possibilities for consideration, we have examined those that politicians and students of politics think are most important. Group characteristics do make some difference in a person's opinions and voting behavior. For example, the more affluent one is, the more likely one is to resist government aid to the less advantaged and to vote Republican. Blacks and whites are politically divided over even nonracial issues. Perhaps because of their minority status, Jews and Catholics support the Democratic party and its programs more than Protestants. But some group characteristics do not appear to exert much influence on political opinions or voting behavior. Although Southern whites are rather conservative on civil rights and will vote accordingly, they are hardly different from their Northern brethren on other kinds of political issues. Living in the cities, suburbs, or country does not seem to influence people's political attitudes either. It is important to keep in mind that

Table 6-16.   Opinion Differences Between Women and Men on Selected Issues

Opinion	Percent Support Among Opinion Holders		
	Women	Men	Difference
The laws governing the sale of handguns should be made more strict. (Gallup, 1976)	79	66	−13
We should have stayed out of Vietnam. (SRC, 1968)	69	57	−12
The government in Washington should see to it that every person has a job and a good standard of living. (CPS, 1976)	44	32	−12
The government in Washington should make every possible effort to improve the social and economic position of blacks and other minority groups. (CPS, 1976)	47	42	− 5
Oppose the death penalty for persons convicted of murder. (Gallup, 1976)	32	27	− 5
The use of marijuana should be made legal. (Gallup, 1977)	24	35	+ 9
Divorce in this country should be easier to obtain. (Gallup, 1969)	15	24	+ 9
Oppose stricter community standards regarding sale of sexually explicit material. (Gallup, 1977)	38	50	+12

Note. For Gallup data, percentages may be in error by about one percent, since they were recalculated from original tables in which nonopinion holders were included on the percentage base.

even when a group distinction has some political importance, the identified social group will be far from uniform in its political opinions and voting behavior. Moreover, rarely does any group make a dramatic shift in its voting pattern that is different from the movement of the rest of the population.

Over time, certain group distinctions may increase or decrease in importance. For example, the distinction between farmers and nonfarmers has receded in relevance with the decline in the farm population. Group distinctions that may increase in importance are between young and old, the highly educated and the less educated, and perhaps men and women. Although the women's movement has yet to result in a male-female division in political polls, evidence of issue polarization along lines of age and education are beginning to emerge. Although it has not happened yet, these aditional sources of polarization of issues may also become more powerful as sources of voting alignments as well, replacing or joining the usual partisan distinctions between rich and poor, Northerner and Southerner, Protestant and nonProtestant, and white and black.

FOOTNOTES FOR CHAPTER 6

1. "The Polls," *Public Opinion Quarterly*, 12 (1948), p. 781.

2. These figures are recomputed from Table 63 in Seymour Martin Lipset and Earl Raab, *The Politics of Unreason* (New York: Harper and Row, 1970), pp. 402–403.

3. Because farmers as a group cannot be meaningfully placed either high or low on the status hierarchy, they are excluded from our analysis of the relationship between occupational status and political attitudes. The dwindling number of farm owners and managers are more politically conservative than the national average. In terms of partisan politics farmers often vote for Republicans or Democrats according to the economic conditions they face and which party is in power at the time. On agrarian political behavior in the modern era, see Angus Campbell, et al, *The American Voter* (New York: Wiley 1960), Chapter 15; and Michael S. Lewis-Beck, "Agrarian Political Behavior in the United States," *American Journal of Political Science*, 21 (August 1977), pp. 543–566.

4. Gallup Opinion Index, August 1969, p. 20.

5. There is evidence that on local referendums concerning proposals that if passed would raise property taxes to pay for various local projects, richer homeowners vote "yes" more frequently than do low-income property owners. See Edward Banfield and James Q. Wilson, "Public Regardingness as a Value Premise in Voting Behavior," *American Political Science Review*, 58 (December 1964), pp. 876–887; Dennis S. Ippolito and Martin L. Levin, "Public Regardingness, Race, and Social Class: The Case of a Rapid Transit Referendum" *Social Science Quarterly*, 51 (December 1970), pp. 628–633. Banfield and Wilson offer the provocative but controversial interpretation that upper-income groups are more "public regarding" than the "private regarding" poor taxpayers. By "public regarding," they mean that the affluent place the greater priority on the value of spending for "the public interest" or the "welfare of the community," as opposed to narrowly conceived "self-interest."

6. The "job guarantee" questions employed in the three surveys are slightly different. In 1945 respondents were asked: "Which of these statements do you most agree with? (1) The most important job for the government is to make it certain that there are good opportunities for each person to get ahead on his own. (2) The most important job for the government is to guarantee every person a decent and steady job and standard of living." In 1956 people were asked whether they agreed or disagreed with the statement that "the government in Washington ought to see to it that everybody who wants to work can find a job." The 1968 question was whether "the government in Washington should see to it that every person has a job and a good standard of living" or whether "the government should just let each person get ahead on his own." Because the 1945 sample contained only white males, the analysis of the latter surveys is limited to white males also. The decline in the relationship between economic status and "job guarantee" opinion was first demonstrated by Philip E. Converse, "The Shifting Role of Class in Political Attitudes and Behavior," in Eleanor E. Maccoby et al. (eds.), *Readings in Social Psychology*, 3rd ed. (New York: Holt, Rinehart, and Winston, 1958), pp. 388–399.

7. Detailed empirical assessment of the declining role of economic class in the shaping of social welfare attitudes is difficult because of the frequent changes in the questions pollsters ask. The most complete evidence of the shifting importance of economic class is found in Philip E. Converse, "The Shifting Role of Class."

8. Samuel A. Stouffer, *Communism, Conformity, and Civil Liberties* (Garden City, N.Y.: Doubleday, 1955); James W. Prothro and Charles Grigg, "Fundamental Principles of Democracy: Bases of Agreement and Disagreement," *Journal of Politics*, 22 (May, 1960), pp. 276−294.

9. John P. Robinson, "Public Reaction to Political Protest," *Public Opinion Quarterly*, 34 (Spring 1970), pp. 1−9.

10. For further evidence concerning the relationship between status and civil rights attitudes see Paul B. Sheatsley, "White Attitudes Toward the Negro," *Daedalus* (Winter 1966), pp. 217−238; Charles H. Stember, *Education and Attitude Change* (New York: Institution of Human Relations Press, 1961); Harlan Hahn, "Northern Referenda on Fair Housing." *Western Political Quarterly*, 21 (September 1968), pp. 483−495; Howard D. Hamilton, "Voting Behavior in Open Housing Referenda," *Social Science Quarterly*, 51 (December 1970), pp. 715−729; Angus Campbell, *White Attitudes Toward Black People* (Ann Arbor: Institute for Social Research, 1971); and Richard Hamilton, *Restraining Myths: Critical Studies of U.S. Social Structure and Politics* (New York: Halsted Press, 1975), pp. 147−182.

One subtlety in the relationship between status (or, at least, education) and social attitudes is that although the most educated whites are the most tolerant of black rights *in principle* (they are, for example, the least likely to call themselves "segregationists"), it is not clear that the most educated favor specific government programs to promote integration or to help blacks. One interpretation of this pattern is that while education promotes awareness of democratic principles, education does not "instill a deeper commitment to the democratic norm of tolerance." For an elaboration of this view see Mary Jackman, "General and Applied Tolerance: Does Education Increase Commitment to Racial Integration?" *American Journal of Political Science*, 22 (May 1978), pp. 302−324.

11. Seymour Martin Lipset, *Political Man* (Garden City, N.Y.: Doubleday, 1960), Chapter 4.

12. Stember, *Education;* Lewis Lipsitz, "Working Class Authoritarianism: A Re-Evaluation," *American Sociological Review*, 30 (1965), pp. 103−109.

13. As we saw in the previous chapter, the gap between the political opinions of the more- and less-educated decrease with age.

14. For evidence that high status is associated with foreign policy belligerence, see Richard Hamilton, "Voting Behavior," pp. 183−217 and Martin Patchen, "Social Class and Dimensions of Foreign Policy Attitudes," *Social Science Quarterly*, 51 (December 1970), pp. 649−667. Also, a careful analysis of voting in local referendums on the Vietnam issue has shown that the lower status voting precincts were the ones with the greatest sentiment for withdrawal. See Harlan Hahn, "Correlates of Public Sentiments about War: Local Referenda on the Vietnam Issue," *American Political Science Review*, 64 (December 1970) pp. 1186−1198.

15. Milton J. Rosenberg et al, *Vietnam and the Silent Majority* (New York: Harper and Row, 1970), pp. 54−65.

16. V. O. Key, Jr., *Public Opinion and American Democracy* (New York: Alfred A. Knopf, 1961), p. 134; see also, the data reported in Richard Hamilton, "Voting Behavior," and Patchen, "Social Class."

17. For a discussion on interpreting polls on foreign policy, see Milton J. Rosenberg, "Images in Relation to the Policy Process: American Public Opinion on Cold-War Issues," Chapter 8 in Herbert C. Kelman (ed.), *International Behavior: A Social-Psychological Analysis* (New York: Holt, Rinehart, and Winston, 1965), pp. 290−291, 317−318.

18. Eugene J. Rossi, "Mass and Attentive Opinion on Nuclear Weapons Tests and Fallout," *Public Opinion Quarterly*, 29 (1965), pp. 280−297.

19. This simple measure of "class voting" was first employed by Robert R. Alford in *Party and Society* (Chicago: Rand McNally, 1963).

20. On the Depression's impact upon the relationship between class and voting among the "Depression generation," see Campbell, et al, *The American Voter*, pp. 356−361.

21. For a discussion of this point, see Everett C. Ladd, Jr., *American Political Parties: Social Change and Political Response* (New York: W. W. Norton, 1970), pp. 243−311.

22. Computed from Tables 4.3 and 4.8 in David Butler and Donald Stokes, *Political Change in Great Britain* (New York: St. Martin's Press, 1969), pp. 70, 77.

23. In 1956, 70 percent of France's industrial workers and 42 percent of its nonfarm nonmanuals voted Socialist or Communist. The comparable figures for Italy in 1953 were 68 percent and 31 percent. (Recomputed from Lipset, *Political Man*, tables on pp. 225−227.) On international differences in class voting within other nations, see Alford, *Party and Society*; and Seymour M. Lipset and Stein Rokkan (eds.), *Party Systems, and Voter Alignments* (New York: The Free Press, 1967).

24. Even blacks in higher status occupations are nearly unanimous in supporting social welfare programs. The black-white differences in social welfare opinion may be thought of as one form of class polarization—that is, the dominant white majority versus the black "underclass." Black-white differences are especially acute on the question of solving the problems of the urban ghetto.

25. An example of high black voting for a Republican candidate occurred in the 1966 gubernatorial election in Maryland. The Democratic primary winner campaigned on the single issue of opposition to open housing legislation. As a consequence, the black wards of Baltimore voted overwhelmingly for the successful Republican candidate—Spiro T. Agnew. For an analysis of the election statistics of this contest, see Walter Dean Burnham, *Critical Elections and the Mainsprings of American Politics* (New York: W. W. Norton, 1970), pp. 152−159.

26. Hazel Erskine, "The Polls: Is War a Mistake?" *Public Opinion Quarterly*, 34 (Spring 1970), pp. 66−69.

27. Hazel Erskine, "The Polls: The Politics of Age," *Public Opinion Quarterly*, 35 (Fall 1971) pp. 482, 486−497. The evidence also indicates that the age group differences are not due to the differing social composition of the generations— for example, that younger age groups are better educated than older groups. See Kent Tedin, "Age vs. Social Composition Factors in Explaining Generational Political Differences," *Aging and Human Development*, 9 (4, 1978−1979), forthcoming.

28. The evidence that age cohorts do not become more Republican with time is quite convincing. See Neal E. Cutler, "Generation, Maturation, and Party Affiliation," *Public Opinion Quarterly*, 33 (Winter 1969−1970), pp. 583−588; and Norval Glenn and Ted Hefner, "Further Evidence on Aging and Party Identification," *Public Opinion Quarterly*, 36 (Spring 1972), pp. 31−47. For evidence on age and conservative political attitudes see Chapter 5 of Gerald Pomper, *Voter's Choice* (New York: Dodd, Mean and Company, 1975), Noval D. Glenn, "Aging and Conservatism," *Annals of the American Academy of Political and Social Science* (September 1974); and Stephen J. Cutler and Robert L. Kaufman, "Cohort Changes in Political Attitudes: Tolerance of Ideological Nonconformity," *Public Opinion Quarterly* (Spring 1975).

29. According to Campbell, et al., *The American Voter*, the sharpest cutting point in the relationship between age and party identification is between voters who came of political age before the Roosevelt era and those who entered the electorate during the earlier Thirties or later. pp. 153−159.

30. Thus, although age is apparently becoming a good predictor of people's issue attitudes it is declining as a predictor of presidential voting or party identification. See the Gallup data reported in Erskine, "The Polls: The Politicis of Age," pp. 491—494.

31. In addition to the very noticeable recent partisanship decline in young voters a much smaller partisanship decline in older generations can also be discerned. This tendency is stronger for older generations in the South than in the North. See Carol A. Cassel, "Cohort Analysis of Party Identification Among Southern Whites: 1952—1972," *Public Opinion Quarterly*, 41 (Spring 1977), pp. 28—33; and Paul Allan Beck, "Partisan Dealignment in the Postwar South," *American Political Science Reivew*, 71 (June 1977), pp. 477—496. Many new Independents in the South may be conservative, former Democrats who have rejected the party of their heritage in response to the national Democratic party's liberal policy on civil rights.

The slight decline in partisanship by older generations since the mid 1960s may be an abnormal situation. There is evidence that during times when partisanship is not declining (pre1964), people become stronger partisans as they age. See Philip E. Converse, *The Dynamics of Party Support* (Beverly Hills: Sage, 1976). For a different interpretation, see Paul R. Abramson, "Generation Differences and the Decline of Party Identification in America," *American Political Science Review*, 70 (June 1976), pp. 469—478.

32. *Source:* Survey Research Center, 1960 Election data. In this table and the following comparisons of Protestants, Catholics, and Jews, only Northern whites are compared in order to control for regional and racial differences. Almost all Southerners and blacks are Protestants. In party preference they are predominantly Democratic. Consequently, inclusion of Southerners and blacks would mask the importance of religion as a determinant of party preference.

33. Center for Political Studies, 1976 election data.

34. Raymond E. Wolfinger, "The Development and Persistence of Ethnic Voting," Lawrence H. Fuchs (ed.), *American Ethnic Politics* (New York: Harper and Row, 1968), pp. 163—193.

35. Bernard R. Berelson, et al. *Voting* (Chicago: University of Chicago Press, 1954) pp. 64—66.

36. Lawrence H. Fuchs, "American Jews and the Presidential Vote," in Fuchs, ed., *American Ethnic Politics*, pp. 144—162.

37. For the most complete examination of what surveys show to be the political attitudes of Catholic ethnic groups, see Andrew M. Greeley, "Political Attitudes among American White Ethnics," *Public Opinion Quarterly*, 36 (Summer 1972), pp. 213—221.

38. Harold E. Quinley, "The Protestant Clergy and the War in Vietnam," *Public Opinion Quarterly*, 34 (Spring 1970), pp. 43—52. On religion and the feminist/anti-feminist movement see David W. Brady and Kent L. Tedin, "Ladies in Pink: Religion and Political Ideology in the Anti-ERA Movement," *Social Science Quarterly*, 56 (March 1976); Kent L. Tedin, David W. Brady, Mary E. Buxton, Barbara M. Gorman, and Judy L. Thompson, "Social Background and Political Differences between Pro- and Anti-ERA Activists," *American Politicis Quarterly*, 5 (July 1977); and Kent L. Tedin, "Religious Preference and Pro/Anti Activism on the Equal Rights Amendment Issue," *Pacific Sociological Review* 21, (January 1978).

39. Lipset and Raab, *The Politics of Unreason*, Chapter 10.

40. However, one study of white Atlantans found evidence suggesting that even with education held constant, Baptists were more likely to vote for Wallace than were Protestants of less fundamentalist denominations. See Anthony M. Orum, "Religion and the Rise of the Radical White : The Case of Southern Wallace Support in 1968," *Social Science Quarterly*, 51 (December 1970), pp. 674—688. Studies based on local samples of limited size suggest some support for a novel hypothesis regarding the relationship between fundamentalism and politics: the more frequently fundamentalists attend church, the more politically conservative they are. But the

more frequently nonfundamentalist Protestants attend church, the more liberal they are. See Benton H. Johnson, "Ascetic Protestantism and Political Preference," *Public Opinion Quarterly*, 26 (Spring 1962), pp. 35–46; Benton H. Johnson, "Ascetic Protestanism and Political Preference in the Deep South." *American Journal of Sociology*, 69 (January 1964), pp. 359–366.

41. To take but one instance of one-time regional differences in foreign policy "isolationism," Southerners when asked in 1945 whether the United States and Russia "should make a permanent military alliance," responded favorably by a ratio of greater than 2 to 1. At the other extreme, a slight majority of Midwesterners opposed such an alliance. See Hadley Cantril, *Public Opinion 1935–1946* (Princeton: Princeton University Press, 1951), p. 961. By the late 1950s, such disparities had largely disappeared. See Key, *Public Opinion and American Democracy*, pp. 106–107.

42. Samuel C. Patterson, "The Political Cultures of the American States," in Norman R. Luttbeg (ed.), *Public Opinion and Public Policy* (Homewood, Ill.: Dorsey Press, 1968), pp. 275–292.

43. The most politically relevant way of dividing states into regions may not be the customary division into East, Midwest, South, and West. For example, one study divided states on the basis of similarity of political characteristics with the result that three major regions emerged, labeled "Industrial," "Southern," and "Northwestern" states. See Norman R. Luttbeg, "Classifying the American States: An Empirical Attempt to Identify Internal Variations." *Midwest Journal of Political Science*, 15 (November 1971), pp. 703–721. Even using this new classification, there is little regional variation in mass political opinion, once we control for race and religion.

44. Among the many studies of the political impact of suburban living are Campbell, et. al., *The American Voter*, pp. 119–126; and Joseph Zikmund, "Suburban Voting in Presidential Elections: 1948–1964," *Midwest Journal of Political Science*, 12 (May 1968), pp. 239–258.

45. Kevin P. Phillips, *The Emerging Republican Majority* (New Rochelle, N.Y.: Arlington House, 1969).

46. The gap between male and female voting rates decreased only recently in the South. See Carol A. Cassel, "Change in Electoral Participation in the South," *Journal of Politics*, 41, (August 1979).

CHAPTER 7

Elections as Instruments of Popular Control

In a democracy, the public supposedly controls the behavior of its public officials by exercising its influence at the ballot box in a rational fashion. We call this the Rational Activist Model. But the democratic institution of free elections is not in itself sufficient guarantee of public influence over governmental decisions. An example would be if none of the candidates the public can choose from offer what the public wants. Or, through some combination of misguidance, ignorance, and indifference, the voters may behave "irrationally" when given a meaningful choice by failing to vote into office the candidates who would best represent their interests. Also, if officeholders perceive that the public is not watching, or that it does not care, they may feel free to make policy decisions without consideration of public opinion.

Looking at the matter in a positive rather than negative fashion, we can state the conditions that do allow elections to be an effective instrument for inducing policy decisions that are responsive to public opinion. First, the candidates should offer a meaningful choice of policy options for the voters to choose from and once elected, the winner should try to carry out his campaign pledges and also respond to changes in public opinion and new policy demands. Second, the voters should be informed about the issues that separate the candidates and vote for those who best represent their own views. Clearly, the fulfillment of each of these two sets of conditions are interdependent. For example, political leaders will pay greatest attention to public opinion when they believe that the public is alert enough to throw them out of office if they do not. Similarly, voters have the greatest opportunity to vote intelligently on the basis of policy issues when the politicians act from the assumption that they are going to do so.

In the present chapter we examine the behavior of the electorate when it carries out its assigned responsibility. Then in the following chapters we examine the responsiveness of political elites to public opinion.

7-1 POLITICAL CAMPAIGNS AND THE VOTER

Prior to each election, voters are bombarded by news and propaganda about the candidates who seek their favor. The amount of money that politicians spend on political campaigns is staggering. Listed below are approximate estimates of all political spending in presidential years since 1952.[1]

$140 million in 1952
155 million in 1956
175 million in 1960
200 million in 1964
300 million in 1968
425 million in 1972
500 million in 1976

Judging by this attention that politicians give to the voters at election time, one might conclude that the voter reacts to campaign stimuli in the fluid manner that he does as a consumer, reacting to advertising stimuli in the mass media. Just as the person about to purchase a product such as a detergent might vacillate in his choice of brands until the moment of purchase, so might the voter waver between the candidates until his entry into the voting booth forces him to make a final decision. But this image of the voting process exaggerates the number of voters available for seduction by political campaign appeals, since it ignores the typical voter's reliance on "brand loyalty" to one political party or the other.

As we have already discussed in Chapter 3, most American voters have a more or less permanent attachment to either the Republican or Democratic party. It is through the filter of party identification that most voters view the partisan aspects of the political world. The anchor of party identification prevents most voters from wavering in their candidate choice during a campaign, and they do not change in the party they vote from one election year to the next. For example, the Survey Research Center's panel study of the American electorate over the 1956–1960 period disclosed that of all the people who voted for president in both 1956 and 1960, 78 percent voted for the same party both times.[2] Similarly, most voters decide who they will support for president as early as convention time and stick to this choice over the course of the campaign. Panel studies of voter choices over the 1960 and 1964 presidential campaigns revealed that about 80 percent of the voters in each November election had voted for the same candidate as had been their preference in August.[3] When partisans change their candidate choice during the campaign, it is usually due to an initial attraction to the opposition's candidate and is followed by a return to the fold by election day. The percentage of the voters who stick with their party's choice is even higher in elections below the presidential level because the lesser amount of information that reaches voters is often too slight to give them any reason to go against their party. Only in nonpartisan elections and primary contests (in which party identification cannot be a criterion of choice) do voters vacillate in an erratic manner. In fact, voter preferences in *primary* contests are so fluid that pollsters have great difficulty predicting outcomes even when they monitor opinion as late as a day or two before the election.[4]

Of course, if party identification were the sole determinant of how people vote, election results would simply reflect the balance of Democratic and Republican identifiers. And since the ratio of Democratic to Republican identifiers is essentially stable over time, election results would be almost identical from one election to the next. This is the pattern in some multiparty democracies (for example, in Scandinavia and Holland) where party loyalties are hardened even more than in the United States because parties concentrate their appeal on specific blocs of voters. But in America, as in other democracies like Britain and Canada, where the parties make broad appeals to the electorate as a whole, election results often depart considerably from the voter division that would occur with a strict party line vote.

When an election is decided essentially on a party line basis, the result is called the "normal vote." Assuming a 50−50 split by Independents and only a minimum partisan defection rate that is equal on both sides, the normal vote in a national election would result in a victory for the Democrats who would obtain about 54 percent of the two-party vote.[5] This calculation reflects the Democrats' edge in party identification (approximately three Democrats for every two Republicans) that more than counterbalances the effect of a higher turnout rate among Republicans than Democrats. The normal vote is approximated by the nationwide returns of midterm elections in which national issues are seldom important, while Republican and Democratic trends generated by various state and local contests cancel themselves out. The breakdown of the 1970 vote for the House of Representatives, by party, is shown in Table 7-1 and represents the typical midterm pattern. The low frequency of Democratic voting on the part of Republican identifiers is balanced by an equally low defection rate on the part of Democratic identifiers. The Independents (whose turnout rate is particularly low in midterm elections) split their votes about evenly between the two parties.

Table 7-1. Party Identification and the Congressional Vote, 1970

Vote for House of Representatives	Party Identification			
	Democrat	Independent	Republican	Total
Democrat	83%	55%	12%	54%
Republican	17	45	88	46
	100%	100%	100%	100%
N =	(304)	(168)	(209)	(681)

Source. Survey Research Center, 1970 election data.

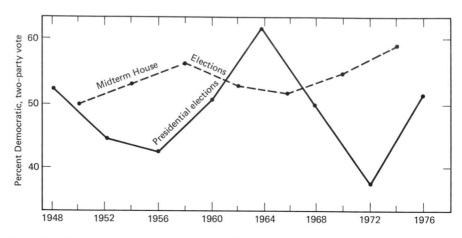

Figure 7-1. Voting trends in presidential and midterm House elections.

When election results depart appreciably from the normal vote expectations, the "short-term partisan forces" of the campaign favor one party more than the other. Unlike the national midterm pattern, strong short-term forces are often generated by the highly visible presidential campaigns, and push the election results away from the normal vote baseline. This tendency is shown in Figure 7-1, which contrasts the variability of the vote for president with the stability of the normal vote pattern of midterm House election results. In four presidential elections shown (1948, 1960, 1968, and 1976), the results were close to normal. But the short-term forces greatly favored the Republicans in 1952 and 1956, when the popular General Eisenhower headed the Republican ticket, and in 1972 when Richard Nixon led the Republicans. In the 1964 Johnson-Goldwater contest, the short-term forces swung heavily in favor of the Democrats.[6] Actually, departures from normal voting in presidential races are due not only to public reaction to events over the short campaign period between the summer nominating conventions and the November election, but also to the public's accumulated four-year response to the incumbent administration and their images of the candidate once the major-party nominees are known. Generally the eventual victor's support peaks quite early in the campaign and declines somewhat thereafter, as the loser regains some support from the return to the fold of many of his party's usual followers once the campaign heats up. For example, the victories of Johnson in 1964 and Nixon in 1968 were both by smaller margins than predicted by pre-election polls from a few months earlier. One notorious exception more or less proves the rule: In 1948 polls during the campaign indicated a Republican victory, but a last-minute surge toward Truman on the part of wayward Democrats who had been temporarily attracted to his opponent

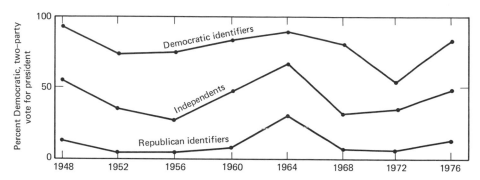

Figure 7-2. Party identification and the vote for president, 1948–1976. (*Source.* SRC/CPS election data.

allowed the final vote and result to be a normal Democratic victory. Since "normal" elections at the national level are won by the Democrats, the Republican party needs strong short-term forces in its favor to win national elections. In fact, even when the Democrats win the presidency with less than 54 percent of the vote (the normal outcome), as in 1976, the Republicans actually have the edge in short-term forces.

The departure of election results from the normal vote does not signify that the usual role of party identification in shaping electoral choices has broken down. Instead, one finds that the party favored by the short-term forces is the beneficiary of most of the short-term partisan defections and wins most of the Independent votes. Figure 7-2 shows this pattern over the eight presidential elections from 1948 through 1976. When the short-term forces favor the Republicans, Democrats "defect" beyond their normal rate; Republicans are even more loyal to their party than usual; and Independents vote overwhelmingly Republican. With pro-democratic short-term forces, the pattern is the reverse—with unusually frequent Republican defections and a Democratic trend among Independents.

Short-term Forces Below the Presidential Level

Relative to the excitement of presidential contests, campaigns for office below the presidential level attract little voter interest. For this reason people often assume that campaigns waged for lower office have little impact on election outcomes, with the results rarely deviating far from a simple reflection of normal voting strengths in the area, except for a possible adjustment in presidential years for the residual "coattail" impact of presidential contests. However, this extreme view that candidates and campaign issues are unimportant in nonpresidential elections exaggerates the importance of party identification. For example, it ignores the fact that in some postelection polls as many as half the respondents report that they split their ticket rather than vote for one party's candidates for all offices. Because of this ticket-splitting behavior, the same constituency often will vote the Democrats into one office and the Republicans into another—a practice that has been increasing over the years.[7]

Figure 7-3 offers one illustration of short-term forces operating in non-presidential campaigns. For states that elected both a governor and a U.S. senator in 1974, it shows the relationship between the statewide vote divisions for the two offices. If there had been no short-term forces generated by the separate campaigns for the different offices, all the observations shown in the graph would fall along the diagonal line—with the same vote division for each office. Instead, the states scatter on the graph without a pattern, so that one could not predict how a state was going to vote for governor from knowledge of the outcome of the race for senator, or vice versa.

Even the relatively invisible campaigns for the U.S. House of Representatives often have a sizeable impact on the outcomes of these congressional contests. Figure 7-4 shows the distribution of the 1972–1974 shifts in the congressional vote for two types of districts—those in which each major

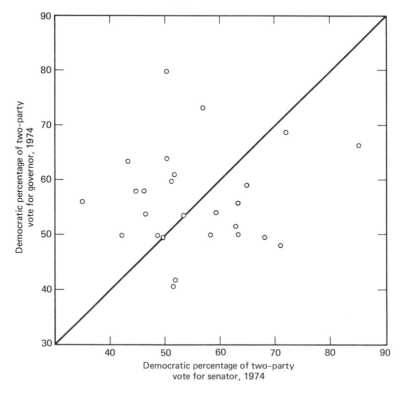

Figure 7-3. Relationship between vote for governor and vote for senator, by state, 1974.

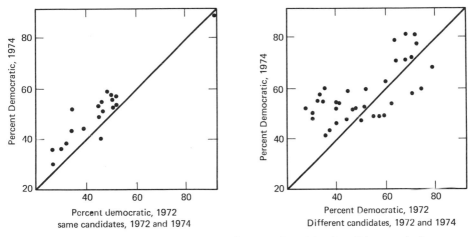

Figure 7-4. Partisan change in U.S. House elections as a function of candidate continuity.

party ran the same candidate in both 1972 and 1974, and those in which both parties ran different candidates in the two elections. Where the 1974 contests were reruns of 1972 races with the same candidates, the vote shifts were uniform with slight shifts to the Democrats due to the 1974 Democratic trend. But where each party fielded a new candidate the vote shifts were quite varied, reflecting the change in the short-term forces produced by changes in the candidates running.

Who Are The "Floating Voters"?

We have seen that the campaign stimuli that are presented to the voters affect elections independent of partisan loyalties, so that election results often depart from the normal party vote. An important question is whether it is the most informed or the least informed voters who respond most to these campaign-generated short-term forces. If the "floating voters" who switch their vote in response to short-term campaign forces are more politically informed than average, we would think that election trends are essentially the response to the most politically alert segment of the public. But if the reverse were true—that floating voters are more politically ignorant than the average—then we might be compelled to support the more dismal conclusion that election trends are largely the result of campaign appeals that successfully reach the voters least capable of evaluating them.

Because of their "neutral" status, the Independents are more responsive to short-term forces than voters who develop party identifications. Since Independents lack the strong rooting interest in election outcomes that partisans often have, Independents vote less frequently than partisans do, and show up relatively low on tests for political involvement in campaigns. Although these indicators would imply that Independents are also less politically informed than partisans, this is not true. Instead, the most accurate portrayal of voters selecting the Independent label appears to be that they are a heterogeneous lot. They include voters too apolitical to articulate a partisan leaning, others who are temporarily disenchanted with the party to which they have previously given their loyalty, and some "model" nonpartisan citizens ready to shift their political weight in response to the issues. Since the least informed Independents fail to attain the involvement "threshold" that would motivate them to vote in elections, the remaining Independents who do vote are actually slightly more informed than voting partisans. For example, Table 7-2 shows such a tendency present for the Survey Research Center's 1964 sample. On four crude measures of "political informedness," Independents show up as more informed than partisans.[8]

Although the least-informed voters are not overly represented among those who gravitate to the Independent label, they do display the greatest tendency to change their partisan leanings when new campaign information reaches them. The highly informed voters are most resistant to the impact of campaign propaganda, because their accumulated storage of political information can bolster their initial views against the intruding information. For example, a Republican who is highly informed about politics is better equipped to discount Democratic propaganda than one who is more politically ignorant. But it does not always follow that the least attentive voters ac-

Table 7-2. **Strength of Party Identification and Political "Informedness" of Voter (1964)**

	"Strong" Partisans	"Not so Strong" Partisans	Independent
Percent know mainland China to be Communist, not in UN	75	72	84
Percent interested in "government and politics"[a]	79	74	82
Percent high in mass media usage[b]	61	57	62
Percent who identify the Republicans as the most "conservative" party	65	63	66
Percent attended college	27	23	32
$N =$	(462-463)	(422-424)	(218-219)

Source. Survey Research Center, 1964 election data.

[a]Voters saying they follow government and politics either "all the time" or "some of the time" are scored as "interested." Other responses are "only now and then" or "hardly at all."

[b]"High" media usage means that the voter reports that he followed the campaign in at least three of the four mass media (newspaper, magazines, radio, TV).

count for most of the voting trends of elections, because the least attentive voters sometimes receive no campaign information at all. Instead, the general rule appears to be that the least attentive voters are most easily persuaded to vote against their initial partisan leanings—but only when the campaign is visible enough to reach them.[9] In a "low stimulus" election, in which the flow of campaign information is minimal, only the most attentive voters have sufficient knowledge to motivate a vote against their party. In contrast, even the least attentive voters usually receive some exposure to "high stimulus" presidential campaigns. Therefore, they respond more to the short-term forces of the campaign than the more attentive voters who follow the campaign closely.

U.S. House elections fit the category of low stimulus elections, since they are so invisible that only about half the voters claim to have read and heard anything about either of their local candidates before casting their ballot.[10] In such contests, only the most politically alert voters are able to respond to short-term forces generated by the campaign, but only a small amount of information reaches even them. As Table 7-3 shows, the least informed voters in House elections are least likely to vote against their party's candidate because they possess virtually no information about the candidates. Consequently, the electorate's response to short-term forces in low stimulus elections appears to be largely the product of the small amount of information obtained by the most attentive voters.

In high stimulus presidential contests, which attract great interest and large voter turnout, almost all voters receive some campaign exposure. For example, awareness of the candidates' names is nearly universal during a presidential campaign.[11] The general increase in the intake of political information during a presidential campaign temporarily loosens a greater number of voters from their partisan moorings—particularly among the least attentive voters. The tiny fraction of presidential voters who manage to avoid the campaign completely maintain stable candidate preferences throughout the

Table 7-3. Party Voting in U.S. House Elections, by Salience of Candidates in Contested Districts, 1958 (in Percent)

	Voter Was Aware of		
Voted for Candidate	Both Candidates ($N = 196$)	One Candidate ($N = 234$)	Neither Candidate ($N = 368$)
Of own party	83	88	92
Of other party	17	12	8
Total	100	100	100

Source. Adapted from Table 4 in Donald E. Stokes and Warren E. Miller, "Party Government and the Salience of Congress," *Public Opinion Quarterly*, 26 (Winter 1962), p. 541.

campaign. But setting these few cases aside, partisan defections and pre-election wavering in candidate choice are most frequent among voters with only slight exposure to the presidential campaign.[12] Similarly, voters who switch their presidential vote from one party to the other in successive presidential elections are on the whole less politically informed than voters who vote for the same party both times. The best demonstration of this rule is provided by the Survey Research Center's panel study of changing voter preferences over the 1956–1960 time period. Table 7-4 shows how the vote patterns of respondents who voted in both 1956 and 1960 varied with their degree of attention to the 1960 presidential campaign. Shifts in presidential voting from one party to the other were less frequent among the highly attentive voters (defined as those who monitored the campaign in three or more mass media—newspapers, radio, TV, magazines) than among the less attentive. Moreover, the shifts of the relatively inattentive were more uniformly in the predominant Republican to Democratic direction than were the less frequent shifts of the more attentive voters. Consequently the net Democratic gain between 1956 and 1960 was greatest among voters who were low in campaign attention (from 38 to 56 percent within the sample) than among voters who were high in attention (only from 39 to 45 percent within the sample).[13]

From the kinds of findings just examined, we often say that presidential election trends are largely determined by the behavior of the least informed voters. Converse states it this way: ". . . not only is the electorate as a whole quite uniformed, but it is the least informed members within the electorate who seem to hold the critical 'balance of power' in the sense that alternatives in governing party depend disproportionately on shifts in their sentiment."[14] Indeed, we might even be tempted to conclude that the most effective kind of presidential campaign would be one aimed directly at the voter who is normally inattentive and uninformed about politics. But this interpretation ignores another consideration, that the less malleable attentive voter is at least a more accessible target for campaign messages. Equally important is that the potential contribution of relatively uninformed people to electoral trends is diluted by their low motivation to vote. As Table 7-5 shows (for 1956–1960), with nonvoters taken into account the net interelection vote shifts are not crucially different between information strata. Stated differently, although voters who respond to short-term forces of presidential campaigns tend to be somewhat less informed than the average voter, as a group they are about as informed as the average member of the eligible electorate.[15]

Table 7-4. Presidential Vote Shifts, 1956-1960, by Mass Media Attention[a]

		Low Mass Media Attention, 1960 (N=259)					High Mass Media Attention, 1960 (N=467)		
		1956 Vote					1956 Vote		
		Democrat	Republican	Total			Democrat	Republican	Total
1960 Vote	Democrat	33%	23%	56%	1960 Vote	Democrat	33%	12%	45%
	Republican	5%	39%	44%		Republican	6%	49%	55%
	Total	38%	62%	100%		Total	39%	61%	100%

Source. Survey Research Center, 1956–1960 panel data.

[a]Mass media attention was classified as high if the respondent followed the 1960 campaign in at least three of the four mass media (newspapers, magazines, radio, TV), and low if the respondent followed the campaign in two or fewer.

Table 7-5. Net Vote Shifts, 1956-1960, by Media Attention Level[a]

Low Mass Media Attention, 1960				High Mass Media Attention, 1960			
	1956	1960	Change		1956	1960	Change
Democrat	24%	39%	+15%	Democrat	35%	44%	+9%
Republican	37	32	– 5	Republican	54	51	–3
Nonvote	39	29	–10	Nonvote	11	5	–6
Total	100%	100%		Total	100%	100%	

Source. Survey Research Center, 1956-1960 panel data.

[a]High media users are defined as those who followed the 1960 campaign in at least three mass media (newspapers, magazines, radio, TV). Low media users are the remainder.

7-2 THE ROLE OF ISSUES IN ELECTIONS

The previous section has shown that despite the constraint of fairly constant party loyalties, partisans cross party lines in sufficient numbers to produce considerable fluctuation in the parties' electoral fortunes. If elections cannot be successfully predicted on the basis of the underlying partisan division of the electorate, election issues (or candidates) must influence election outcomes. Although the term "issue" can refer to many different motivating factors, we focus here on policy issues—the candidates' statements of how they will act on important policy questions.

Despite our current knowledge about voting behavior, scholars do not fully agree on the actual role policy issues play in elections. From what we know about the capabilities of the average voter, we are not surprised that many scholars reject the notion that one can interpret election results as the public's response to policy issues discussed during the campaign. For example, the authors of *The American Voter,* undoubtedly the most influential book on voting behavior, offer the following, somewhat cynical, conclusion:

> We have . . . the portrait of an electorate almost wholly without detailed information about decision making in government. A substantial portion of the public is able to respond in a discrete manner to issues that might be the subject of legislative or administrative action. Yet it knows little about what government has done on these issues or what the parties propose to do. It is almost completely unable to judge the rationality of government actions; knowing little of particular policies and what has led to them, the mass electorate is not able to appraise either its goals or the appropriateness of the means chosen to serve these goals.[16]

The American Voter, however, was based on a study of the two Eisenhower elections. Several more recent studies—most notably *The Changing American Voter*— have analyzed later elections and have come to some rather different conclusions about the capabilities of the voter.[17] Beginning with the Johnson-Goldwater election of 1964, political issues and political ideology have become increasingly important as determinants of the vote—the 1972 Nixon-McGovern election is a prime example. But just how important issues have become remains controversial.

The most balanced view is that candidate policy stances are one of many determinants of election outcomes. If voters select the candidates who best represent their policy views, then elections would be decided by the fact that a majority of voters preferred the policy views of the winning candidate to those of the loser. But because policy issues only influence some voters, in conjunction with other motivating forces, the candidate whose policy views are closest to those of the voters (or even to those of the most issue-oriented voters) cannot be sure of winning his election bid. For example, he or she might be threatened by a loss by being less "well known" than the opponent, because of a lack of a favorable "image" in television appearances, or, especially, if his or her party is the minority party in the area. To win, a candidate whose party is in the minority must successfully encourage massive defections from the stronger opposition party, a task made difficult by the importance of party identification.

Are Voters Motivated by Policy Issues?

For voters to be influenced by policy issues when they cast their ballots, two conditions must be met. First, in order to cast a policy-oriented vote effectively, the voter must be aware of the differences between the policy views of the candidates. In addition, the voter who possesses accurate recognition of the candidate stances must vote for the candidate whose views are closest to his or her own. Some understanding of the role policy issues play in motivating voter decisions can be obtained by examining how accurately survey respondents perceive the candidates' policy positions, and how often their reported votes go to the candidates who come closest to sharing their own stated policy views. Naturally, voters are most likely to be influenced by a policy issue when the divergence between candidate stances is strong and the issue is of considerable importance to the electorate. Let us take a close look at evidence of policy voting from surveys conducted during recent presidential elections, starting with the elections of 1972 and 1976.[18]

Voter Perceptions of Candidate Differences: 1972 and 1976. A necessary condition for voters to cast their ballots on the basis of the candidates' policy positions is that voters perceive actual policy differences between the candidates. In its election surveys of both 1972 and 1976, the Center for Political Studies asked respondents to rate the views of the presidential candidates on a series of seven-point scales for each of several issues. These voter assessments of candidate positions provide a gauge of the extent to which voters actually perceive candidate differences. Table 7-6 arranges these data to

Table 7-6.   Voter Perceptions of Candidate Differences, 1972 and 1976

Issue	1972			1976		
	McGovern Left of Nixon	Nixon Left of McGovern	Rate Both the Same	Carter Left of Ford	Ford Left of Carter	Rate Both the Same
Tax Rate	65%	18%	17%	34%	10%	56%
Standard of Living	79	10	11	43	13	44
Medical Care	72	10	17	33	9	57
Minority Aid	69	10	21	31	13	57
Busing	64	18	18	24	32	45
Rights of Accused	57	12	31	17	21	61
Marijuana	67	7	26	13	17	71
Women's Rights	38	12	50	13	14	74

Source. SRC/CPS 1972 and 1976 Election data.

Note: For exact wording of issue questions, see Appendix B. Each percentage is based on *voters* who rated both candidates on the seven-point issue scale.

show how voters in 1972 and 1976 rated the candidates *relative to each other* on these seven-point scales. Individual voters could rate the Democratic candidate to the left of his Republican opponent, rate the Democrat to the right of the Republican, or give the two candidates the same rating. Excluded from Table 7-6 are the voters (generally about 30 percent) who were unable to rate one or both of the candidates, or who declared no interest in the issues.

Table 7-6 shows that voters saw greater policy differences between the presidential candidates in 1972 than in 1976. The obvious reason is that the candidates *were* farther apart in 1972 than in 1976. Thanks to the ideological nature of McGovern's campaign and clever exploitation of McGovern's far-left image by the Nixon campaign, it was relatively easy for a 1972 voter to see McGovern as more liberal than Nixon. This was true even for issues on which the candidates did not take drastically differing campaign positions. For example, although McGovern attempted to avoid marijuana legalization as a presidential issue, an inference many voters made in 1972 was that McGovern would have been more lenient than Nixon on this issue.

While on every issue in 1972 far more voters saw the Democratic candidate to the left of the Republican than the reverse, this was not true in 1976. On the strictly noneconomic issues in 1976 (marijuana, women's rights, rights of accused criminals, busing), those who saw the candidates as being different were just as likely to see Ford as more liberal than Carter as to see Carter as more liberal than Ford. Since on these issues the candidates were not generally perceived as different, these issues could influence few votes in 1976. This situation does not reflect badly on the voters' capacity for policy voting, because even the most informed and objective observer would have difficulty detecting meaningful differences between the campaign stands of Carter and Ford on these noneconomic issues.

On economic issues, however, the candidates in 1976 did take different stands. Compared to Ford, Carter was *in fact* more favorable to national health insurance, guaranteeing full employment, making the rich pay a bigger share of the tax burden, and aiding minorities. This relative difference was correctly perceived by almost all voters who saw candidate differences on these issues. Thus, if we seek evidence of policy voting in 1976, we should turn to the economic issues that have traditionally divided the Republican and the Democratic parties.

Economic Issues in 1972 and 1976. We have seen that in both 1972 and 1976, voters tended to see the Democratic presidential candidate as more willing than the Republican presidential candidate to spend government money to solve social and economic problems. If economic and social welfare issues influenced presidential votes, we would expect economic liberals to give the greatest support to Democratic candidates.

Such a pattern can readily be found for 1972 and 1976, as shown in Table 7-7. For this table, voters are scored on an index of economic liberalism-conservatism based on the three issues of medical insurance, a guaranteed standard of living, and aid to minorities. Scores range from -3 (a liberal response to all three issues) to +3 (a conservative response to all three issues). As Table 7-7 shows, the most liberal voters by this index were most likely to vote for McGovern in 1972 or for Carter in 1976. Similarly, the most conservative voters by this index were the most likely to vote for Nixon in 1972 or Ford in 1976.

Of course, economic liberals tend to be Democrats and economic conservatives tend to be Republicans in party identification. Thus, the relationship between economic liberalism and the vote is at least in part the result of people simply voting according to their long-standing party identifications rather than responding directly to the stimuli of campaign issues. Table 7-8 shows, however, that the relationship between economic liberalism and

Table 7-7. Presidential Vote by Liberalism-Conservatism on Economic Issues, 1972 and 1976

	Most Liberal				Most Conservative		
	−3	−2	−1	0	+1	+2	+3
1972 (% McGovern)	82%	59%	47%	38%	25%	14%	9%
1976 (% Carter)	90%	64%	62%	57%	42%	36%	29%

Source. SRC/CPS 1972 and 1976 Election data.
Note. Respondent scores are the number of conservative responses minus the number of liberal responses on the three issues of medical care, a guaranteed standard of living, and minority aid.

Table 7-8. Relationship Between Presidential Vote and Economic Liberalism-Conservatism, Controlling for Party Identification, 1972 and 1976

Year	Party Identification	Liberal −3, −2	Center −1, 0, +1	Conservative +2, +3
1972	Democrat	83%[a]	59%	23%
	Independent	65%	31%	14%
	Republican	25%	5%	2%
1976	Democrat	92%	82%	72%
	Independent	63%	48%	33%
	Republican	38%	17%	6%

Source: SRC/CPS 1972 and 1976 Election data.
[a]Cell entries are percent voting Democratic for President.

Democratic presidential voting persists even with party identification held constant. The most liberal Republicans and the most conservative Democrats were the ones most likely to defect from their party in their presidential voting. This tendency is clearest for Democrats in 1972, a group who displayed considerably less than the usual loyalty to its party's candidate. Although McGovern obtained 83 percent support from Democrats who were economic liberals in the CPS sample, he obtained a feeble 23 percent support from Democrats who were economic conservatives. Although voting on the basis of economic issues was less prominent in 1976, the process is quite visible: more than one quarter of both conservative Democrats and liberal Republicans defected from their party's presidential candidate. Issue voting in 1976 is clearest among Independents: Independents in 1976 voted about three to two for Carter if they were economic liberals, but only about one in three Independents voted for Carter if they were economic conservatives.

Noneconomic Issues In 1972 and 1976. Can one base an explanation of the 1972 and 1976 vote distribution on people's positions on noneconomic domestic issues? Table 7-9 shows the relationship between noneconomic liberalism-conservatism and presidential voting in these elections. (Noneconomic liberalism-conservatism is measured as a composite across three issues: rights of accused criminals, marijuana legalization, and womens' rights.) With or without the control for party identification (see Table 7-10), noneconomic liberalism-conservatism is more strongly related to the vote in 1972 than in 1976. Although noneconomic conservatives were considerably more likely than noneconomic liberals to prefer Nixon to McGovern in 1972, the difference between these two groups in their relative preferences for Carter or Ford in 1976 were rather slight. Again an obvious reason is that the voters found it more difficult to discern policy differences between the presidential candidates on noneconomic issues in 1976 than in 1972.

Table 7-9. Presidential Vote by Liberalism-Conservatism on Noneconomic Issues, 1972 and 1976

	Most Liberal				Most Conservative		
	−3	−2	−1	0	+1	+2	+3
1972 (% McGovern)	66%	54%	43%	29%	28%	28%	23%
1976 (% Carter)	68%	55%	50%	50%	48%	46%	49%

Source. SRC/CPS 1972, 1976 Election data.
Note. Respondent scores are the number of conservative responses minus the number of liberal responses on the three issues of rights of accused criminals, marijuana legalization, and women's rights.

Table 7-10. Relationship Between Presidential Vote and Noneconomic Liberalism-Conservatism, Controlling for Party Identification, 1972 and 1976

Year	Party Identification	Liberal −3, −2	Center −1, 0, +1	Conservative +2, +3
1972	Democrat	81%[a]	57%	46%
	Independent	61	25	21
	Republican	13	6	5
1976	Democrat	89	81	78
	Independent	49	42	48
	Republican	13	13	14

Source: SRC/CPS 1972, 1976 Election data.
[a]Cell entries are percent voting Democratic for President.

Clear Policy Choices: Vietnam In 1972, Civil Rights In 1964. The opportunity for policy voting is greatest when both candidates explicitly take opposite stands on an issue of intense public concern. Although such opportunities are rare, two examples from recent presidential elections are Vietnam in 1972 and civil rights in 1964. In each case, the presidential candidates articulated opposite views, which were perceived correctly by the vast majority of voters and thus provided the opportunity for a considerable amount of issue voting.

First, we will consider the Vietnam case of 1972. Although we have already seen the importance of domestic issues (both economic and noneconomic) in the 1972 presidential election, the single issue of 1972 that dominated all others was the war in Vietnam. The heart of McGovern's campaign was his promise to immediately withdraw the American soldiers from Vietnam, a position which President Nixon adamantly rejected. As on other issues in 1972, the SRC/CPS asked its respondents to rate the Vietnam stances of each presidential candidate on a seven-point scale. The low end of the scale (a score of 1) represented the "dovish" stand that "we should *withdraw completely* from Vietnam right now, no matter what the results." The high end (a score of 7) represented the opposite viewpoint that "we should do everything to win a *complete military victory,* no matter the results." Thus, the higher the score a voter gave a candidate on this scale, the more "hawkish" he perceived the candidate's views to be.

Almost all voters agreed that McGovern was a "dove" on Vietnam (average score of 2.1), while most saw Nixon as somewhat "hawkish" (average score of 4.5). The average self-placement of voters was at 3.5—or virtually midway between McGovern and Nixon. Among the voters in the CPS sample who rated both candidates on the Vietnam scale, 90 percent correctly saw McGovern as more favorable to a troop withdrawal than Nixon, while only 4 percent had the reverse (mistaken) impression. The remaining 6 percent saw the candidates as tied. The stage was, therefore, set for people to vote for president in 1972 on the basis of their policy views on the Vietnam War.

Table 7-11 compares the 1972 presidential vote of Vietnam doves and hawks, with party identification held constant. Among strong Democrats, McGovern obtained the vote of almost all the doves, but the vote of only slightly more than half of the hawks. Among weak Democrats and Independents, McGovern won almost two-thirds of the dove vote but only a small percentage of the hawk vote. Although few Republicans voted for McGovern, those that did tended to be doves rather than hawks on the war issue. Table 7-11 is unusual in that it shows far greater evidence of issue voting than can normally be found on a single issue.

The 1964 Civil Rights Act provided an almost equally dramatic example of policy voting. The two presidential candidates—President Johnson and Senator Goldwater—took opposite stands on the Civil Rights Act of 1964.

Table 7-11. Opinion on Vietnam and Presidential Voting, 1972

	Percent Democratic, Presidential Vote	
Party Identification	Immediate Withdrawal[a] (*N*=436)	Military Victory[b] (*N*=266)
Strong Democrats	91%	55%
Weak Democrats	70	17
Independents	69	12
Weak Republicans	29	0
Strong Republicans	13	2
All Cases	67%	14%

Source: SRC/CPS 1972 Election data.
[a]Score of 1 or 2 on 7-point Vietnam scale
[b] Score of 6 or 7 on 7-point Vietnam scale

This act guaranteed all races equal access to public accomodations such as hotels and restaurants. President Johnson successfully pushed the bill through Congress; Goldwater, his eventual opponent, voted against it on the alleged grounds of its unconstitutionality. When asked for the candidates' stands on the Civil Rights law, an overwhelming 95 percent of the Survey Research Center's 1964 respondents who had heard of the act (over three quarters of the total sample) correctly stated that Johnson favored it, while 84 percent correctly stated that Goldwater opposed it.

About three quarters of the voters in the Survey Research Center's 1964 sample expressed opinions on the Civil Rights law for that year, and said their minds were "made up" on the matter. The law's supporters and opponents disagreed considerably in their presidential voting. Johnson's share of the vote was only 47 percent among the law's opponents but an overwhelming 82 percent among its supporters.

Table 7-12 shows that many people broke with their party identification in order to achieve this consistency between their views on public accommodations and their candidate choice. For example, a majority of "weak Republicans" who favored the Public Accommodations Act voted Democratic for president while more than one-third of the "weak Democrats" who opposed the act swam against the partisan tide to vote Republican for president. Only "strong" partisans remained reasonably loyal to their party when their views on the Public Accommodations law varied from those of their party's candidate.

Predicting Votes From Policy Stances

One's ability to predict how a voter will act on the basis of his or her policy views increases if the voter's views over a range of many different kinds of

Table 7-12. Opinion on the 1964 Civil Rights Act and Presidential Voting, 1964

	Percent Democratic, Presidential Vote	
Party Identification	Pro Civil Rights Act, Mind "Made Up" (N=477)	Con Civil Rights Act, Mind "Made Up" (N=386)
Strong Democrats	99%	86%
Weak Democrats	94	64
Independents	79	42
Weak Republicans	58	27
Strong Republicans	27	4
All cases	82%	47%

Source: Survey Research Center, 1964 election data. For exact wording of the question on the Public Accommodations Law, see Appendix B.

issues are taken into account. For example, the first part of Table 7-13 shows that voters who gave mainly liberal responses to a composite ten-item scale (see Chapter 3) voted overwhelmingly Democratic in 1976, while their consistently conservative counterparts voted overwhelmingly Republican. Voters' overall ideology can also be measured on the basis of their self-classifications on a liberal-conservative scale. The second part of Table 7-13 shows that these self-ratings correlate well to presidential voting. Moreover, voters' presidential choices correlate increasingly well with voters' policy views if the voters are allowed to choose the issues that concern them most.[19] On balance, as predictors of how people vote, measures of voters' policy stances summed over several issues perform about as well as party identification and measures that tap voters' evaluations of the candidates' personalities and capabilities for leading the country.[20]

The Problems of Causality

Unfortunately, a portion of the consistency between the policy views people express and those of the candidates they vote for might be attributable to voters adopting issues stances to rationalize candidate choices made on other — possible irrational — grounds. Voters have a need to maintain cognitive consistency among their issue stances, their perceptions of the issue stances of the candidates, and their choice of a candidate. Rational policy voting—the selection of a candidate on the basis of his policy stances—is only one source of this consistency.

Consider the possible modes of resolution for the voter whose beliefs are initially out of alignment—for example, he or she might have liberal views but be initially attracted to the candidate who is more conservative. How such a voter would resolve this dilemma depends on which of the three elements—policy views, perceptions of the candidates' policy views, and candidate preference—is the weakest link. If the voter feels strongly about his or her policy views and is certain that the favored candidate opposes them, the voter could resolve the dilemma by reversing the candidate choice. This, of course, would be a pure case of policy voting. But if the candidate's stands are sufficiently vague or only weakly publicized, the easiest way out would be to shift one's estimate of the candidate stances. This process, known as projection, is perhaps the most frequent resolution of the dilemma. In 1976, for example, liberal Republicans often misperceived Ford as more liberal than Carter and conservative Democrats often misperceived Carter as more conservative than Ford.[21] Only when the candidate stances are clearly different and well-publicized (as those of Johnson and Goldwater on the 1964 Civil Rights Act, or those of McGovern and Nixon on Vietnam in 1972) does a sizeable rate of false projection of candidate stances fail to occur.

Table 7-13. Presidential Vote by Two Summary Measures of Liberalism-Conservatism, 1976

	Ten-Item Composite Issue Index[a]						
	Most Liberal						Most Conservative
	−10 to −8	−7 to −5	−4 to −2	−1 to +1	+2 to +4	+5 to +7	+8 to +10
% Carter	91	88	70	43	46	26	24
% Ford	9	12	30	57	54	74	76

	Self-Identification on Ideological Scale						
	Most Liberal						Most Conservative
	1	2	3	4	5	6	7
% Carter	88	84	74	52	27	19	14
% Ford	12	16	26	48	73	81	86

Source. SRC/CPS 1976 Election data.

[a]For construction of the ten-item composite issue index, see Chapter 3.

A third resolution of the dilemma would be for the voter to change a relatively weak policy stance to make it consistent with that of the preferred candidate. We have already examined this process, known as rationalization, in the context of our discussion of the relationship between issue stands and party identification. Although some people switch their party identification to make it consistent with their issue stances (for example, the conservative Democrat who begins to call himself a Republican), probably the most frequent pattern is a switch of issue stances to align them with one's party identification. A similar pattern may work during a political campaign to change the policy stances of voters, including Independents, into alignment with those of the candidates to whom they are initially attracted (for reasons that have nothing to do with their stances on the particular policy). Rationalization is most evident when a sudden or unexpected policy stance taken by a candidate causes the views of his supporters to be more in line with his position and those of his opponents to become more unfavorable. One rare instance when this process was clearly visible occurred during the 1956 presidential campaign when Adlai Stevenson, the Democratic candidate, unexepectedly announced that he was in favor of a cessation of nuclear testing, a stance that provoked strong opposition from President Eisenhower, his Republican opponent. Whereas normally there had been no difference between the views of Republican and Democratic voters on nuclear policy during the 1950s, the polarization of the candidates on this issued produced a temporary inflation of support for a nuclear test ban among Stevenson supporters and a temporary steep drop in support for a nuclear test ban among Eisenhower voters.[22] Since the complicated test-ban issue was not one on which many voters had strongly crystalized opinions, people reacted to Stevenson's introduction of the issue by switching to their candidate's position rather than by shifting their candidate choice to correspond to their initial test-ban views. Although injection of this issue into the campaign did not greatly influence the election outcome, it did serve the function of temporarily rearranging people's thinking on the subject.

The process of rationalization makes it difficult to disentangle fully the causal process which produces a correlation between voters' policy views and their candidate choice. Consider for example, the problem of interpreting the following results of a survey of Wisconsin voters conducted after a hotly contested gubernatorial election fought on the tax issue.[23] In this 1962 election, the Republican candidate for governor favored an increase in the sales tax to increase revenue, while his Democratic opponent favored an increase in the income tax. Two-thirds of the voters who favored the sales tax voted for the Republican candidate, who represented their views, while the same percentage of the income tax proponents voted for the Democratic candidate. At first glance, it would seem that many Wisconsin voters based their gubernatorial vote on some kind of evaluation of which candidate's tax policy would be better for their state. However, when the voters in the sample were asked the main reason for their candidate choice, only a tiny fraction gave tax policy as the reason. Apparently, then, the strong consistency between tax policy preference and candidate preference occurred mainly because many voters chose a stand on the complicated tax issue by adopting the views of their candidate instead of choosing between the candidates by evaluating the merits of their tax stands. (Also, Wisconsin Democrats and Republicans could have been somewhat divided on tax policy before the election campaign.) Here the candidates for governor gave Wisconsin voters a rare opportunity to choose a governor on the basis of clearly divergent tax proposals. Yet voters used other criteria, essentially relying on their party identification.

The alert reader will notice that any example of consistency between voters' policy preferences and those of the candidates they vote for can in part be due to rationalization rather than policy voting. Consider our previous example of the sizeable correlation between opinion on the Public Accommodations Act and presidential voting in 1964. Some voters may have adopted Johnson's views because they had a preference for Johnson on other grounds, and this caused them to shift toward Johnson's favorable opinion of the law. Or, for others, the attraction of Goldwater provoked opposition of the law. Unfortunately, we have no way of directly testing whether this explanation or its rival—that voters shifted their candidate choice to correspond to their civil rights views—contains the greater validity. Undoubtedly both processes were at work, but in unknown proportions. Scholars who are consistently skeptical of the electorate's capabilities for policy voting may subscribe to the former view, while others who prefer to see evidence of rational electoral decisions may subscribe to the latter view. To settle the matter we need to follow shifts in voters' policy stances and candidate choices over the course of a political campaign. The little evidence that exists suggests voters sometimes change their policy views to correspond to those of their favored candidate.[24] On complicated and remote issues that do not attract much mass interest, we can assume that consistency is mostly a product of post hoc rationalizations of voting decisions. But on "gut" issues that attract public attention or visibly affect people's daily lives, a politician or observer would be foolish to predict that the number of voters who pick their candidate according to their policy views would be insignificant.

Issue Voting As Retrospective Judgment

Only a small segment of the public is capable of policy voting in the manner we have described. People whose votes are shaped by the policy views of the candidates undoubtedly come largely from the ranks of "ideologues" and, to a lesser extent, from group-oriented voters, whose judgments about candidates and parties are formed by evaluations of the groups they represent (for example, rich, poor, black, white). Other voters evaluate the political world around them according to the "nature of the times." If times are perceived to be good, the incumbent party is rewarded; if times are bad, the incumbents are punished. As Richard Brody suggests, the typical citizen's "vote more nearly reflects his reaction to a party's past performance on an issue rather than his desire to give a mandate for a new policy direction."[25]

For example, a very good predictor of whether a person would vote for Carter or Ford in 1976 was whether or not the voter had "approved of" President Ford's past performance as president:

	Approve of Ford's Performance	Disapprove of Ford's Performance
Percent who voted for Ford	77%	7%
Percent who voted for Carter	23	93
	100%	100%

The rule that voters react according to their satisfaction with the incumbent's handling of problems has the interesting implication that the voter will sometimes vote against the incumbent even if his only opponent takes policy stands that are even further removed from the voter's own apparent policy preferences. For example, this principle can be applied to voting behavior in the key New Hampshire presidential primary of 1968, in which Senator McCarthy, running on the issue of opposition to the Vietnam war, "upset" President Johnson. Although McCarthy received his strongest support (82 percent) from the state's few "doves," more of his protest votes came from the numerous hawks than from doves. In fact, hawks who also "disapproved" of Johnson's handling of Vietnam rejected Johnson at a greater rate (52 percent) than did the voters who were in between the dove and hawk ends of the Vietnam policy scale (38 percent).[26] What McCarthy's dove and hawk supporters had in common, despite their different policy preferences, was frustration with the status quo war policies of the Johnson administration—a frustration that was channeled into a victory for Richard Nixon that November. A surprising aspect of McCarthy's national constituency was that many of his supporters were also attracted to George Wallace.[27] Since McCarthy (the challenger from the political left) and Wallace (the challenger from the right) both opposed the established politics of the day, many "alienated" voters who were disturbed about the nation's political course could find comfort in dual support for both of the obvious advocates of change.

The voter whose issue voting is limited to retrospective judgments of the incumbent's performance should not necessarily be ridiculed, because given his limited political information, this course of behavior may be the most rational one available. Many voters do not have the political involvement necessary to evaluate policy proposals for future action or to monitor the candidate's policy proposals. But they can take readings of the incumbents' performance to date, and throw the rascals out if the obvious signs indicate that it is time, in Campbell's words, to let "a new bunch of fellows run things" for awhile.[28] Moreover, even informed voters may agree the time for a change has come even though the incumbent's challenger fails to give a meaningful indication of what he would do differently if elected. For example, although Herbert Hoover was denied a second term in 1932 because he was unfortunate enough to serve during the onset of the Great Depression, the public did not know what it was getting when it decided to let Franklin Roosevelt run the country. Judging from Roosevelt's campaign rhetoric or from the difference between the prevailing Republican and Democratic ideologies of the time, one might have thought that Roosevelt would make even less use of the federal government to reverse the economic trend than Hoover was doing during his last days in office.[29] But buoyed by his mandate to try something different, Roosevelt's policies evolved into the New Deal program involving a far greater role of the federal government in American life than had been known before. In 1936, once Roosevelt's policies became crystallized, the American public gave him an even larger mandate to continue the New Deal policies. Although Roosevelt's 1936 landslide victory can partially be interpreted as a simple "nature of the times" reward for valiant leadership, his policies also produced a massive realignment of voters according to their policy views, with social welfare liberals moving toward Roosevelt and the Democrats and conservatives moving away.

7-3 POLICY VOTING AND ELECTION SHIFTS

Since voters are sometimes influenced by policy issues there is a potential for policy issues to play a decisive role in election outcomes. We have already noted that party fortunes in elections often fluctuate considerably from one election to the next. Could these fluctuations be least partially caused by the electorate's response to the alternative policies offered by the candidates? Alternatively, are fluctuations in party fortunes at election time caused by changing evaluations of the party's last performance record rather than their specific proposals for change?

Shifts in the Public "Mood"

The most obvious way in which issues could produce electoral change would be if shifts in voter sentiment on policy issues produced changes in party fortunes. For example, political journalists often will interpret a Democratic victory as the result of a liberal mood on the part of the electorate and a Republican victory as a conservative reaction. But, as we saw in Chapter 2, the public's mood does not swing cyclically from liberal to conservative. Consequently, short-term public mood fluctuations between liberalism and conservatism cannot explain changes in partisan voting tides, because such mood fluctuations do not exist. To be sure, there can be rare but important exceptions, such as the public's change from predominantly hawkish to dovish views on Vietnam. But normally, when a question of public policy persists over a long period of time (for example, school integration, medicare, foreign aid), any changes in the distribution of mass opinion are glacial.

However, the public does often change its evaluations of the relative problem solving capabilities of the Democratic and Republican parties. Polling agencies have periodically asked public samples which party was most likely to bring about peace. These judgments (see Figure 7-5), largely based on retrospective judgments of the recent performance of the incumbent president's party, can operate as a barometer of election results. They follow predictable rules, such as the incumbent party is most likely to be seen as the party of "peace" when the nation is not at war. For example, the Democratic party, which is normally seen as the prosperity party anyway, made strong short-term gains in its image as prosperity-producer during the "Republican" recessions of 1958 and 1974. That the Democrats made their best midterm showings since the 1930s in the elections of these two years is instructive; while the Republicans fondly look back to their 1946 "landslide" during the post-World War II period of relative economic deprivation and Democratic control of the presidency. Elaborate statistical analysis of historical data going back to the prepoll era has shown that economic prosperity usually produces electoral gains for the party controlling the presidency.[30]

Following the course of public perceptions of which party is the party of peace is also instructive. Largely because the "Democrat-produced" Korean War lasted a frustrating three years, only to end in a bewildering

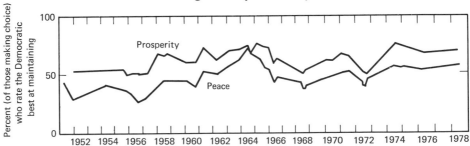

Figure 7-5. Ratings of parties on peace and prosperity. Questions: (prosperity) "Which political party—the Republicans or the Democrats—do you think will keep the country prosperous?". *peace* "Which political party do you think would be more likely to keep the United States out of World War III—the Republican party or the Democratic party?" (*Source.* Gallup Opinion Index.)

stalemate, the public gave the Republicans the overwhelming edge as the peace party during the 1950s. However, the Democrats were able to reverse this trend slightly when they showed that they too could keep the nation out of war in the early 1960s. Then, of course, came the Vietnam war, which by 1968 had given the peace image back to the Republicans, who gradually began to lose it again once the war became theirs.

Which is the more important determinant of presidential election outcomes—the public's shifting evaluations of party capabilities on domestic policy or on foreign policy? Although domestic-policy views compromise the stronger factor in shaping individual voting decisions, in recent times the public's foreign-policy response has caused at least as much electoral *change* at the presidential level. This pattern can be seen from the results of statistical analyses of the forces at work in presidential elections conducted by Donald Stokes and by Michael Kagay and Douglas Caldiera, shown in Figure 7-6.[31] According to these analyses, the Republicans' foreign policy edge declined from a net advantage of about 3.5 percent of the vote in 1952 to a slight net liability in 1964. The peak Republican advantage of 3.5 percentage points returned in 1972, but was reduced to near zero in 1976. Meanwhile, through most of the 1952–1976 period the Democrats held a slight but steady edge on domestic policy, ranging from a peak advantage of 2 percentage points in 1964 to a temporary liability of 1.5 percentage points in 1972.

Responses to foreign policy produce short-term electoral change because the public can respond more readily to sudden international events than to the more gradual changes on the domestic scene. However, drastic changes in the nation's economy, though infrequent, do produce shifts in party fortunes that can be long-lasting. The Great Depression beginning in 1929 did, of course, produce a long-term benefit to the Democratic party. Similarly, the more distant depression of 1893 hurt the Democrats, in power at the time, so badly that they became the minority party for years thereafter.[32] Both of these post-depression political changes were strong enough to be labeled "partisan realignments" of the American electorate.

Shifts In Candidate Issue Stances

Changes in the cast of candidates from one election to another bring about changes in the policy orientations of the candidates from which the voters must choose. If voters do reward and punish candidates on the basis of their policy stances, the fluctuation of candidate policy proposals can be a contributor to electoral change. Part of the popular lore of politics is that in a two-man race the candidate who stakes out the middle ground of the political spectrum will win by virtue of his appeal to the moderate voters. Belief in this principle often causes opposing candidates to gravitate away from the liberal and conservative poles and toward the more moderate range. Follow-

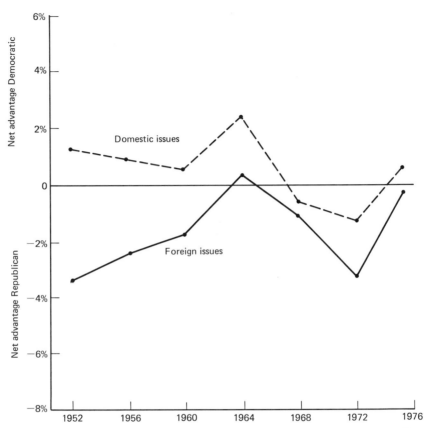

Figure 7-6. Partisan advantage accruing from issues of public policy, 1952–1976. (*Source*, Michael R. Kagay and Greg A. Caldeira, "A Reformed Electorate? Well, at Least a Changed Electorate, 1972–1976." in William J. Crotty (ed.), *Paths to Political Reform* (Lexington, Mass.: D.C. Heath, 1979.)

ing a model developed by Anthony Downs,[33] this situation is depicted in Figure 7-7a. Assuming policy-oriented voters distribute themselves in a bell-shaped curve across the political spectrum, those to the left of center will vote for the candidate slightly to the left of center, while those to the right of center will vote for the candidate slightly to the right. If the candidates are stationed symmetrically (equidistant from the center), neither will have the policy edge. But if one of the candidates veers toward one of the ideological extremes (as does the conservative in Figure 7-7b), then the policy-oriented voters in the middle of the spectrum will vote for the more compatible candidate, only slightly off center, giving him the victory.

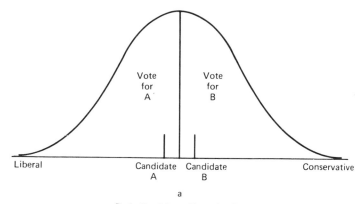

a
Both Candidates Near the Center

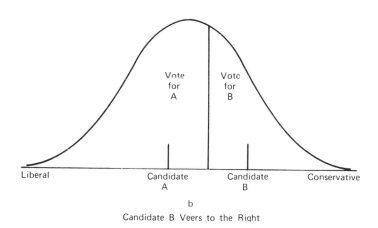

b
Candidate B Veers to the Right

Figure 7-7. Candidate ideology and voter response (hypothetical).

Although only an unknown fraction of the public approaches having the issue sensitivity necessary for this model to work perfectly, the presence of some policy voting by the electorate allows the forces the model describes to have a bearing on election outcomes. If moderate candidates are the best vote-getters, this would normally mean that the least conservative Republicans and the least liberal Democrats make the best candidates.

In U.S. House elections, conservative Republican congressmen are poorer vote-getters than their Republican counterparts who represent the moderate-to-liberal wing of their party.[34] Table 7-14 shows this tendency at work in the 1976 House elections. In 11 of 12 comparisons of relatively

Table 7-14. The Difference in the Vote for Matched Conservative and Liberal Republican Congressmen in 1976

Republican Representative	District		Conservatism Score[a]	Republican Percent Two-Party Vote			
				Pres. Ford	Representative	Republican's Lead Over Ford	Difference
Talcott	CA	16	82	50.4	46.6	-3.8	+17.7
McClosky	CA	12	41	53.4	67.5	+13.9	
Crane	IL	12	96	68.9	72.8	+3.9	+2.2
McClory	IL	13	72	62.7	68.8	+6.1	
Michel	IL	18	88	56.2	57.7	+1.5	+7.7
Anderson	IL	16	40	58.6	67.9	+9.3	
Myers	IN	7	97	52.6	62.7	+10.1	-6.0
Hillis	IN	5	69	57.6	61.7	+4.1	
Emery	ME	1	55	50.6	57.4	+6.8	+22.6
Cohen	ME	2	34	50.1	79.5	+29.4	
McEwen	NY	30	83	58.4	55.7	-2.7	+13.3
Mitchell	NY	31	61	55.9	66.5	+10.6	
Conable	NY	35	77	56.5	64.3	+7.8	+4.0
Horton	NY	34	45	56.7	68.5	+11.8	
Kindness	OH	8	96	54.5	70.5	+16.0	+10.1
Whalen	OH	3	20	48.8	74.9	+26.1	
Ashbrook	OH	17	94	54.2	56.8	+2.6	+13.0
Regula	OH	16	72	51.9	67.5	+15.6	

Johnson	PA	23	85	54.1	43.5	-10.6	
McDade	PA	10	43	51.6	62.6	+11.0	+21.6
Schulze	PA	5	91	61.1	59.5	-1.6	
Coughlin	PA	13	50	57.3	63.4	+6.1	+7.7
Abdnor	SD	2	87	52.3	69.9	+17.6	
Pressler	SD	1	61	49.4	80.2	+30.8	+13.2
Average	Conservative		86	55.8	59.8	+4.0	
	Liberal		61	54.5	69.1	+14.6	+10.6

aConservatism is measured as the average of two ratings by ideological pressure groups-percent support for the positions of the conservative-Americans for Constitutional Action and percent nonsupport for the positions of the liberal Americans for Democratic Action. Republican congressmen are matched if they were at least 20 points apart on this index and represented contiguous districts within the same state.

223

conservative and relatively liberal Republican congressmen from neighboring districts, the more conservative congressman is the poorer vote-getter. This is measured by the difference in their vote leads over Ford's performance in their districts. Although the tendency is far less dramatic for Democrats, moderate Democrats in the House also appear to be somewhat better vote-getters than their more liberal brethren.

Although very few people possess more than a superficial knowledge about their congressman, the tiny minority who are both knowledgeable and seemingly moderate in their preferences shift their political weight in House elections, rewarding moderates and punishing those who by comparison are "extremists." A survey analysis of voting behavior in the 1964 House elections found that the electoral impact of the policy stands of Republican congressmen could be accounted for by the behavior of those Independents and Republicans who voted Democratic for president and were also highly informed about both their congressman and politics in general. Nine such voters who were picked up in the sieve of a national sample had a moderate-to-liberal Republican congressman seeking reelection, and all but one of the nine voted for him. Meanwhile, of the six respondents meeting the outlined criteria who had the choice of voting for the re-election of a conservative Republican congressman, all but one voted Democratic instead.[35]

If even a congressman's electoral margin is affected by his policy stance, certainly the outcome of a presidential contest must also be affected by the policy positions of the candidates. Unlike the case with party identification and issue orientation which are also good predictors of presidential voting, the public's relative attraction to the Republican and Democratic presidential candidate changes dramatically from one election to the next. On the basis of Stokes's and Kagay and Caldiera's statistical analyses of presidential election forces, the public's evaluations of candidate personalities and capabilities comprise the major determinant of presidential voting shifts. Figure 7-8 shows Kagay and Caldiera's estimates of the effects of public evaluations of the candidates' personalities and capabilities for each election from 1952 to 1976. Although most candidates were favorably viewed by the voters, two clear exceptions were Goldwater, the Republican candidate in 1964, and McGovern, the Democratic candidate in 1972. A major reason for Goldwater's negative image may have been his extremely conservative policy orientation. Similarly, a major reason for McGovern's negative image may have been his extremely liberal policy orientation. The most popular candidate in recent years, was Eisenhower in 1952 and 1956, who represented the more moderate wing of the Republican party of his day. Although his great appeal was mostly due to his standing as a military hero and the warmth he projected, it was undoubtedly enhanced by his avoidance of the divisive rhetoric of his party's right wing.

These examples suggest moderate presidential candidates are the most successful. There is additional circumstantial evidence. In the early part of

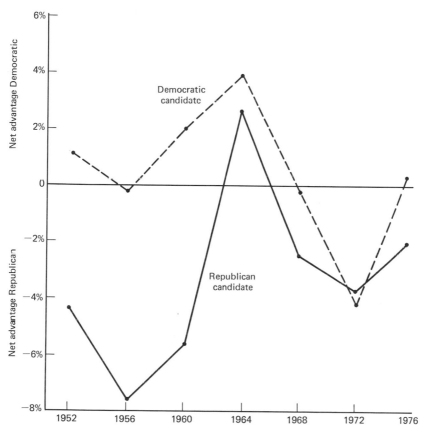

Figure 7-8. Partisan advantage accruing from candidate evaluations 1952–1976. [*Source.* Michael R. Kagay and Greg A. Caldeira, "A Reformed Electorate? Well, at Least a Changed Electorate, 1972–1976," in William J. Crotty (ed.), *Paths to Political Reform* (Lexington, Mass.: D.C. Heath, 1979).

the 1972 campaign, as Senator McGovern became better known by the voters, he was perceived more and more by the public as a liberal. As this perception crystallized, his support in the polls declined. Similarly, in 1976 Carter's image changed from moderate to somewhat liberal as he came into stronger focus.[36] Accompanying this change, Carter lost most of what was at one time a commanding lead in the polls over President Ford. Such evidence, however, is only circumstantial. Even experts disagree, for example, over how much of McGovern's disastrous 1972 performance was due to his liberal image or to such independent factors as his handling of a choice of a running mate.[37]

Whatever were the actual determinants of the 1972 and 1976 election results, the change from Republican landslide in 1972 to close Democratic victory in 1976 was accompanied by a change in how the voters viewed the candidates on issues. At least one reason why Carter won the presidency and McGovern did not was that Carter's views were thought to be closer to those of the voters on the issues. In 1972, voters generally saw McGovern as far to the left, so that average voters saw themselves as closer to Nixon, the Republican, on the issues. In 1976, voters generally saw Carter as more moderate on the issues than McGovern was in 1972, with the result that average voters saw themselves as roughly equidistant between Carter and Ford on the issues.[38] Figure 7-9 shows the voters' average ratings of themselves and the presidential candidates on six of the CPS's seven-point issue scales. Between 1972 and 1976, the issue positions of the average voter moved hardly at all.

Shifts In The Importance Of Issues

Still a third way in which election results could be influenced by policy issues is that the impact of policy issues on voting decisions varies from one election to the next. When issues loom important in campaign debate, voters' reactions to issues might well be different than when issues are muted during a campaign. Although one cannot apply a general rule to predict the consequences of an issue-laden election (such as that either liberal or conservative candidates would usually be favored), some elections are obviously decided more on the basis of policy considerations than others. For example, in neither 1956 nor 1960 did policy issues appear to be responsible for

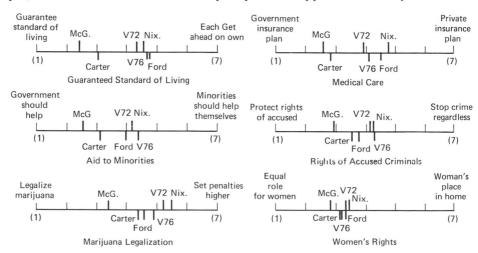

Figure 7-9. Mean ratings by voters of their own positions and candidate positions on six seven-point issues scales, 1972 and 1976. (*Source.* SRC/CPS election data.)

many partisan defections. In 1956, the pervasive popular image of the incumbent president was the predominant force behind the massive Democratic defections. In 1960 most defections in each partisan direction were motivated by the unique "issue" of Kennedy's Catholicism. By comparison, policy issues have played a much greater role in 1964 and thereafter.

Accompanying the trend toward increased policy voting is the recent increase in public perceptions of party differences on policy issues, noted in Chapter 3. Particularly civil rights issues have become an increasingly strong source of Republican and Democratic division. As Figure 7-10 shows, in 1956 and 1960 the presidential-vote divisions among supporters and opponents of federal activity to support school integration were nearly identical. But in 1964 integration supporters began to outdistance opponents of integration activity in their rate of Democratic voting. The same increase in issue voting can be seen, though on a lesser scale, if we examine social-welfare issues. Although presidential voting decisions have been correlated with social-welfare opinions since at least the 1930s, the gap between the Democratic voting rates of social-welfare liberals and conservatives also has widened somewhat, as the figure illustrates for the medical care issue.

Is the strong issue voting found since 1964 a new departure from previous elections? Actually a case can be made that the issue-free 1956 and 1960 campaigns, held during a period of political tranquility, were the deviant cases. Foreign policy and civil rights issues did not exert much influ-

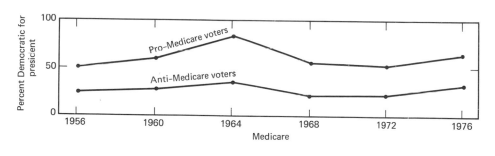

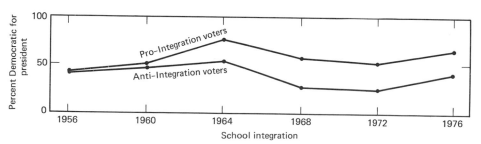

Figure 7-10. The relationship between two issues and the vote for president, 1956–1976. (*Source.* SRC/CPS election data.)

Table 7-15. Social Welfare Issues and the Vote, 1936-1952

1936: "Do you favor the compulsory old-age insurance plan, starting January first, which requires employers and employers to make equal monthly contributions?" (Social Security)

	Yes	No
Percent Roosevelt (Democrat)	69%	35%
Percent Landon (Republican)	31	65
	100%	100%
	(N=2899)	(N=1263)

1940: "During the next four years do you think there should be more or less regulation of business by the Federal government than at present:"

	More Regulation	About Same	Less Regulation
Percent Roosevelt (Democrat)	77%	79%	22%
Percent Willkie (Republican)	23	21	78
	100%	100%	100%
	(N=1204)	(N=958)	(N=2346)

1948: "As things stand today, do you think the laws governing labor unions are too strict or not strict enough:"

	Too Strict	About Right	Not Strict Enough
Percent Truman (Democrat)	77%	58%	36%
Percent Dewey (Republican)	23	42	64
	100%	100%	100%
	(N=460)	(N=693)	(N=637)

1952: "Some people think the national government should do more in trying to deal with such problems as unemployment, education, housing, and so on. Others think the government is already doing too much. On the whole, would you say that what the government has done has been about right, too much, or not enough:"

	Not Enough	About Right	Too Much
Percent Stevenson (Democrat)	56%	46%	11%
Percent Eisenhower (Republican)	44	54	89
	100%	100%	100%
	(N=293)	(N=650)	(N=238)

Sources: 1936, 1940, 1948 percentages recomputed from tables in V. O. Key, Jr., *The Responsible Electorate* (Cambridge: Belknap Press, 1966), pp. 43, 45, 48. 1952 percentages recomputed from Table 1 in Angus Campbell, Gerald Gurin, and Warren E. Miller, "Political Issues and the Vote: November, 1952," *American Political Science Review*, 46 (1953), pp. 359-385.

ence on presidential elections prior to 1956. But from the New Deal era through even 1952—the first Eisenhower election—social welfare liberals and conservatives were rather divided in their voting. Some examples from surveys over the 1936—1952 period are shown in Table 7-15. The major difference between the role that issues play today and 25 years ago is in the increased importance of nonsocial-welfare issues in presidential campaigns.

7-4 THE QUALITY OF ELECTORAL DECISION-MAKING

Because even scholars of voting disagree on how to interpret the data, it is difficult to make an overall assessment of the quality of decisions voters make when they cast their ballots. There is near-universal agreement among scholars that policy voting in presidential elections has increased since the early 1960s. The likely reason is simple: Beginning in 1964, presidential candidates have presented the electorate with clearer policy choices between conservative and liberal alternatives. Interesting evidence that voters are more likely to vote on the basis of issues when the candidates provide a clear choice is provided by an experiment tried by the *Changing American Voter* authors. They asked survey respondents to vote in a mock election for president in which the candidates were Senators Goldwater (an extreme conservative) and McGovern (an extreme liberal). In a close "vote," respondents who were conservative on a summary issue index almost exclusively chose Goldwater, while their liberal counterparts almost exclusively chose McGovern. This mock election between maximally diverse candidates showed more "issue voting" than any real election. When the same respondents were asked to vote in other trial heats between less electorally diverse hypothetical candidates, they displayed considerably less "issue voting."[39]

While there is near agreement that issue voting has increased due to increased candidate divergence, there is less scholarly consensus on the "amount" of issue voting. Although voters tend to vote for the candidate who appears to have views closest to their own views (especially as the voters perceive it), some of this may be due to causal processes other than issue voting. Similarly, although how people vote can be predicted to some extent from their ideological self-identifications as liberals or conservatives, we do not know the extent to which presidential voters search out candidates on the basis of "ideological" compatibility.[40]

Apart from policy issues or ideology, there are additional determinants of the vote. As we have seen, people sometimes vote for or against the incumbent party on the basis of the apparent result of its past performance as well as its proposals for the future. One would find difficulty condemning this behavior as irrational. In addition, two very important predictors of people's votes are their party identifications and their images of the candidates. To the extent people vote on the basis of a party identification that has a policy basis (such as when a staunch conservative is committed to the

Republican party) and to the extent the candidates are typical of their party (see Chapter 9), party voting can be viewed as rational.

But what about voting on the basis of candidate image? One of the best predictors of a person's vote is simply whether the voter likes the personal qualities of the Democratic candidate more or less than the personal qualities of the Republican. We may be tempted to view voting on such a non-issue (or even apolitical) basis to be voting on the basis of irrelevant considerations. But this view may be mistaken. Morris Fiorina puts the question well:[41]

> Considerable misconception surrounds the discussion of the importance of candidate qualities for the voting decision. Various authors have suggested that voting on the basis of candidate qualities is irrational, or at least of a lower order of rationality than voting on the issues . . . Such suggestions apparently stem from the erroneous belief that attitudes toward the candidates reflect no more than Ike's smile, Nixon's beard, or Kennedy's accent. Actually, the bulk of the citizenry's impressions of the candidates focuses on qualities which are of legitimate relevance to the latter's capacity to govern: experience, leadership ability, and so on . . . Why should a candidate's intelligence, administrative ability, etc. be any less a legitimate issue than where he stands on medicare or aid to Israel?

That the voters choose the candidate they find to have the greatest character, competence, or trustworthiness is quite reasonable, even if this candidate is not the one that is closest to the voters on policy issues. Unfortunately, however, voters do not always have the necessary information to make good judgments about a candidate's character until after they have elected him president.

The collective decisions the voter makes at election time contain both elements of stability and of change. That most voting decisions are based on long-standing partisan loyalty adds an element of stability, with election results fluctuating around the baseline figure of the "normal vote." Electoral change is evident from the departures of election results from the normal vote baseline. Although the exact amount cannot be measured with precision, the electorate's response to campaign issues plays some role—even if limited—in producing electoral change.

Electoral shifts are normally only temporary, because voters shifting toward the advantaged party or candidate do not change their party identification in the process. Consequently, they may surge in the opposite partisan direction in a subsequent election, or even do so when voting in another contest held on the same date. Yet it is conceivable that circumstances could be so polarizing as to cause permanent transfers of partisan loyalties, rather than temporary partisan defections. The most recent such realignment period, centered in the 1930s, produced a change from a considerable Republican advantage in national voting loyalties to a long-term Democratic edge in party identification that persists today. This change can be interpreted as at least a partial ratification by the American electorate of President Roosevelt's then unprecedented expansion of federal government services that were applied to cope with the equally unprecedented Great Depression. If another realignment is on the near horizon, it could restore the Republican party to the predominant position, or weaken it further. Or it could change the focus of the issues that separate the two parties without producing a net change in the distribution of partisan loyalties. If any of these possibilities become true, the public will have rearranged its partisan loyalties as a long-term electoral response to the decisive issues of the day.

FOOTNOTES FOR CHAPTER 7

1. These figures as based on the campaign finance scholarship of Herbert Alexander, cited in Milton Cummings and David Wise, *Democracy Under Pressure* (New York: Harcourt, Brace, Jovanovich, 1977), p. 281.

2. Philip E. Converse, "Information Flow and the Stability of Partisan Attitudes," *Public Opinion Quarterly*, 26 (Winter 1962), pp. 578–599.

3. Thomas W. Benham, "Polling for a Presidential Candidate: Some Observations in the 1964 Campaign," *Public Opinion Quarterly*, 29 (Summer 1965), pp. 177–178.

4. Robert P. Abelson, "Computers, Polls, and Public Opinion — Some Puzzles and Paradoxes," *Trans-Action*, 5 (September 1968), pp. 20–27.

5. Philip E. Converse, "The Concept of the Normal Vote," in Angus Campbell, et al, *Elections and the Political Order* (New York: Wiley, 1966), pp. 7–39.

6. On the concept of short-term partisan forces in elections, see Angus Campbell, "Issues and Voters: Past and Present," *Journal of Politics*, 26 (November 1964), pp. 745–757.

7. Walter Dean Burnham, *Critical Election and the Mainsprings of American Politics* (New York: W. W. Norton, 1970), pp. 119–120.

8. The question of the "informedness" of the Independent voter has been subject to some controversy. Apparently the earlier view that Independents are less informed than average was solely inferred from the finding that Independents are less interested in campaigns, care less who wins elections and vote less often than partisans. See, for example, Angus Campbell, et al, *The American Voter* (New York: Wiley, 1960), pp. 142–145. The finding that the Independents are actually not an especially uniformed group is a recent discovery. See William H. Flanigan and Nancy Zingale, *Political Behavior of the American Electorate,* 4th ed. (Boston: Allyn and Bacon, 1979), pp. 61-67.

9. Converse, "Information Flow."

10. Donald E. Stokes and Warren E. Miller, "Party Government and the Saliency of Congress," *Public Opinion Quarterly*, (Winter 1962), pp. 531–546.

11. A Gallup Poll during the 1948 presidential campaign found that 88 percent could recall the name of the Republican presidential candidate (Dewey) and 91 percent could name President Truman as the Democratic candidate. Presidential candidates are not always well-known prior to their nomination. For example, only 34 percent of a sample could identify Adlai Stevenson immediately prior to his Democratic nomination in 1952. Recognition of vice-presidential candidates is, at least according to a 1948 poll, only around the 50 percent mark. For further

details, see Hazel Gaudet Erskine, "The Polls: The Informed Public," *Public Opinion Quarterly*, 26 (Winter 1962) pp. 669–677.

12. Converse has shown that extremely uninformed voters (such as 1960 voters who deliberately avoided the televised debates between the candidates) are almost perfectly stable in their partisan preferences (Converse, "Information Flow"). However, people who vote in presidential elections without any information are too scarce to obscure the general tendency for the most informed to have the most stable partisan preferences. See Edward Dreyer, "Media Use and Electoral Choices: Some Political Consequences of Information Exposure," *Public Opinion Quarterly*, 35 (Winter 1971–1972), pp. 544–553.

13. Table 7-4 shows that in 1956 the informed and uninformed voted alike, while in 1960 the uninformed were more Democratic than were the informed. It is the 1960 pattern that is "normal," since voters in the lower socioeconomic strata tend to be relatively uninformed and relatively Democratic in their voting habits.

14. Converse, "Information Flow," p. 578.

15. Two additional discussions of the floating voter questions are Douglas Dobson and Douglas St. Angelo, "Party Identification and the Floating Vote: Some Dynamics," *American Political Science Review*, 69 (June 1975), pp. 481–490; and Johannes T. Pederson, "Political Involvement and Partisan Change in Presidential Elections," *American Journal of Political Science*, 22 (February 1978), pp. 18–30. Observing partisan defections over several elections, Pederson reports evidence that floating voters (defined as the least politically involved) are most responsive to short-term forces in presidential elections when the incumbent seeks reelection. Apparently, the least involved voters will give disproportionate support to an incumbent president but vote their partisanship when the president does not seek reelection.

16. Campbell, et al, *The American Voter*, p. 543.

17. Norman H. Nie, Sidney Verba, and John R. Petrosik, *The Changing American Voter* (Cambridge; Harvard University Press, 1976). Many other studies have also reported increased issue voting in recent presidential elections. See Mark A. Schulman and Gerald M. Pomper, "Variability in Electoral Behavior: Longitudinal Perspectives from Casual Modeling," *American Journal of Political Science*, 26 (February 1975), pp. 1–18; Eugene Declercq, Thomas L. Hurley, and Norman R. Luttbeg, "Voting in American Presidential Elections, 1956–1972." *American Political Quarterly*, 3 (July 1975), pp. 222–246; and Samuel A. Kirkpatrick, William Lyons, and Michael R. Fitzgerald, "Candidates, Parties, and Issues in the American Electorate: Two Decades of Change," *American Politics Quarterly*, 3 (July 1975), pp. 247–283.

On issue voting in specific elections, see the following. For 1964: Norman Frohlich, et al., "A Test of Downsain Voter Rationality: 1964 Presidential Voting," *American Political Science Review*, (March 1978), pp. 178–187. For 1968: Benjamin I. Page and Richard A. Brody, "Policy Voting and the Electoral Process: The Vietnam War Issue," *American Political Science Review*, (September 1972) pp. 979–995, and Richard W. Boyd, "Popular Control of Public Policy: A Normal Vote Analysis of the 1968 Presidential Election," *American Political Science Review*, 66 (June 1972), pp. 429–449. For 1972: Arthur H. Miller, et al "A Majority Party in Disarray: Party Polarization and the 1972 Election," *American Political Science Review*, 70 (September 1976), pp. 753–778; and Arthur H. Miller and Warren E. Miller, "Issues, Candidates, and Partisan Divisions in the 1972 Presidential Election," *British Journal of Political Science*, 5 (October 1975), pp. 393–434. For 1976: Arthur H. Miller, "Partisanship Reinstated? A Comparison of the 1972 and 1976 U.S. Presidential Elections," *British Journal of Political Science*, 8 (January 1978), pp. 129–152.

18. For analysis of policy voting in 1972 and 1976 similar to ours, see the literature on these elections cited in footnote 17. See also Benjamin I. Page, *Choices and Echoes in Presidential Elections* (Chicago: Chicago University Press, 1978), Chapter 3.

19. David E. Repass, "Issue Salience and Party Choice," *American Political Science Review*, 65 (June 1971), pp. 389–400.

20. Using slightly different methodologies, several authors have attempted to statistically assess the relative effects of issues, party identification, and candidate image on vote decisions in various elections. Examples of the diversity of assessments for 1972 are shown below (from works cited in footnote 17):

	Issues	Party Identification	Candidate Image
		Relative effect (beta weight)	
Miller, Miller, Raine, & Brown	.31	13	.45
Schulman and Pomper	.23	.31	.37
Declercq, Hurley, and Luttbeg	.32	.22	.31

21. Teresa E. Levitan and Warren E. Miller, "Ideological Interpretations of National Elections, Problems in the Analysis of Change," paper presented at the 1978 convention of the American Political Science Association.

22. Eugene J. Rosi, "Mass and Attentive Opinion on Nuclear Weapons Test and Fallout, 1954–1963," *Public Opinion Quarterly*, 29 (Summer, 1965), pp. 280–297.

23. This analysis of a Wisconsin election is drawn from Leon D. Epstein, "Election Decision amd Policy Mandate: An Empirical Example," *Public Opinion Quarterly*, 28 (Winter 1964); and Gerald M. Pomper, *Elections in America* (New York: Dodd, Mead, 1968).

24. Alan I. Abromowitz, "The Impact of a Presidential Debate on Voter Rationality," *American Journal of Political Science*, 22 (August 1978), pp. 680–690. This study presents evidence that voters who learned from the 1976 presidential debates that they disagreed with the unemployment views of their favored candidate became more likely to change their views on the unemployment issue than to change their choice of candidate.

25. Richard A. Brody, "How Vietnam May Affect the Election," *Trans-Action*, 5 (October, 1968), p. 19.

26. Robert E. Craig, "The Protest Coalition: Voting Behavior in the New Hampshire Democratic Presidential Primary, 1968," paper delivered at the 1971 annual meeting of the American Political Science Association, Chicago, Illinois.

27. Philip E. Converse et al, "Continuity and Change in American Politics: Parties and Issues in the 1968 Election," *American Political Science Review*, 63 (December 1969), pp. 1092–1095.

28. Angus Campbell, "Issues and Voters," p. 755.

29. Everett Carll Ladd, *American Political Parties: Social Change and Political Response* (New York: W. W. Norton, 1970), pp. 207–209.

30. Although not all studies of the relationship between economic conditions and the vote find a linkage, two that do are Gerald Kramer, "Short-term Fluctuations in U.S. Voting Behavior, 1897–1964," *American Political Science Review,* 64 (March 1971), pp. 131–143; and Edward Tufte, "Determinants of the Outcomes of Midterm Congressional Elections," *American Political Science Review,* 69 (September 1975), pp. 812–826. These studies find that when appropriate statistical controls are made, certain economic indicators predict the electoral fortunes of the president's party. Seemingly the reason for this is that voters retrospectively punish the "in-party" for their personal hardships and reward it for their personal economic well-being. But the evidence on this point from survey data is unclear (see Morris P. Fiorina, "Economic Retrospective Voting in American National Elections: A Micro-Analysis," *American Journal of Political Science*, 22 (May 1978), pp. 426–443). Moreover, unemployed voters—the group presumably most affected by hard times—display surprisingly little tendency to blame the government for their misfortunes. See Sidney Verba and Kay Lehman Schlozman, "Unemployment,

Class Consciousness, and Radical Politics: What Didn't Happen in the Thirties," *Journal of Politics,* (May 1977), pp. 291–323.

31. Donald E. Stokes, "Some Dynamic Elements of Contests for the Presidency," *American Political Science Review,* 60 (March 1966), pp. 19–28; Michael R. Kagay and Greg A. Caldiera, "A 'Reformed' Electorate? Well, at Least a Changed Electorate, 1971–1976," in William J. Crotty (ed.), *Paths to Political Reform* (New York: Heath Lexington, 1979). Stokes developed the procedure for estimating the relative effects of different variables (such as candidate images) on election results, and applied it to elections from 1952 through 1964. Kagay and Caldiera, along with others, have extended Stokes's analysis to subsequent elections. The procedure is based on a statistical analysis of SRC/CPS respondents' reported likes and dislikes of parties and candidates (see Chapter 3). First the content of the likes and dislikes are divided into six components: the Democratic candidate, the Republican candidate, domestic policy issues, foreign policy issues, group benefits, and party performance. The impact of each component on the election outcome is determined from a statistical analysis of how influential each component is in determining votes, and how one-sided are the evaluations for the particular compoent in the particular election. The most detailed interpretation of the method can be found in Samuel Popkin, et al, "What Have You Done for Me Lately? Toward an Investment Theory of Voting," *American Political Science Review,* 70 (September 1976), pp. 779–805.

32. Burnham (*Critical Elections,* pp. 38–39) traces the 1894–1932 Republican hegemony to the economic crash of 1893. From 1876 through 1892, interparty competition at the national level had been more evenly balanced than during any other period of American history.

33. Anthony Downs, *An Economic Theory of Democracy* (New York: Harper and Row, 1957), Chapter 8.

34. Robert S. Erikson, "The Electoral Impact of Congressional Roll Call Voting," *American Political Science Review,* 65 (December 1971), pp. 1018–1032; Gerald C. Wright, Jr., "Candidates' Policy Positions and Voting in U.S. House Elections," *Legislative Studies Quarterly,* 3 (August 1978), pp. 445–464.

35. Erikson, "The Electoral Impact," pp. 1029–1032.

36. Arthur Miller, "Partisanship Reinstated?"

37. Popkin, et al, "What Have You Done for Me Lately?" and David E. RePass, "Political Methodologies in Disarray: Some Alternative Interpretations of the 1972 Election," *American Political Science Review,* 70 (September 1976), pp. 814–831.

38. For similar analyses of voter proximity to candidates in 1972 and in 1976, see Arthur Miller and Warren Miller, "Issues, Candidates, and Partisan Divisions," and Arthur Miller, "Partisanship Reinstated?"

39. Nie, et al, *The Changing American Voter,* Chapters 17, 18.

40. One reason why it is difficult to sort out the relative importance of different causes of the vote is that the different potential causes are all highly correlated. Voters generally develop a set of attitudes that are consistent (all pro-Democratic or all pro-Republican) with their vote choice. Although this situation makes causal inferences difficult, it paradoxically makes it relatively easy to predict a person's vote choice from his attitudes. For example, over 90 percent of presidential votes can be predicted successfully from the voter's party identification and the partisan balance of his likes and dislikes about parties and candidates alone. See Stanley Kelley, Jr. and Thad W. Mirer, "The Simple Act of Voting." *American Political Science Review,* 68 (June 1974), pp. 572–591.

41. Morris P. Fiorina, "An Outline of a Model Party Choice," *American Journal of Political Science,* 21 (August 1977), p. 618.

CHAPTER 8

The Public and Its Elected Representatives

In the previous chapter, the public showed some ability to utilize elections as a policy expression as prescribed by the Rational Activist Model. While this public competence falls far short of the democratic "ideal," policy-response voters can alter the outcome of a close election. In this chapter, we turn to the political leaders' ability to achieve consistency between public opinion and public policy by way of two additional models of political linkage we discussed in Chapter 1. The Sharing Model considers the agreement between the opinions of leaders and the public that may make policy consistent with public opinion, and the Role Playing Model focuses on the leader's personal concern to represent his constituency as he assesses their preferences.

These three models receive the most extensive evaluation here as they posit characteristics of the representatives that condition their response to the public. The Pressure Group and Political Party Models, positing mediating institutions presumed to encourage political linkage, will be covered in the next chapter.

8-1 OPINION SHARING BETWEEN POLICY MAKERS AND THE PUBLIC

The simplest form of linkage between public opinion and the policy decisions of political leaders would be the simple sharing of common opinions by followers and leaders. Consider, for example, the result if we elected congressmen by lottery. Just as a randomly selected sample of survey respondents is representative of the general population within a certain margin of error, so would be an assembly of 435 randomly selected people acting as a House of Representatives be representative of the population. If such an assembly could act without being distracted by the demands of powerful interest groups or the actual rules of Congress that impede change, then—for better or worse—its decisions would reflect public opinion. In actuality the Congress is less representative than a random sample, if for not other reason than that its members are supposedly chosen for their superior capabilities rather than their typicality.

How then do members of Congress and other political leaders differ from the general population? To answer this question we must find the traits that motivate some but not others to pursue a political career and the traits that favor success in achieving this goal. When people who are active in politics—whether as a local party official or an elected legislator—are interviewed, they often report that a spur to their political career was a very politically active family. The consensus based on several studies is that about 40 percent of the people who are presently politically active grew up in politically active homes. Thus, assuming only 10 percent of the public (at the most) are very active in politics themselves, almost half of our political leaders come from the 10 percent of the nation's families that are most politically active.[1]

Officeholders also differ from the public in that they are often recruited to run for office. Intense political interest alone cannot push a person into a political, leadership role. To contest an election seriously, the would-be political leader must attract the base of support necessary to win. In some cases, the political leader is a "self-starter" who, because of his political interest and ambition, announces his candidacy and then is able to accumulate support. In other cases, the future leader is selected by the local business or party elite for the task of getting elected. Sometimes the community or party leaders can choose from among many active aspirants for the role. But often at the local level, previously nonpolitical people end up as office-holders through the urging of friends or business associates. Kenneth Prewitt finds these "lateral entrants" to politics among members of the nonpartisan city councils he studies.[2] James Barber finds them among members of the highly partisan Connecticut legislature. Many are what he calls "reluctants" — serving not because of their raw ambition or political interest, but because of the insistence of others.[3]

Because the most wealthy and best educated people are most likely to be politically interested and articulate and they have the visibility to be tapped for a leadership role, we are not surprised that these are the people who become some of our political leaders. Put simply, there is an upper-status bias to the political-leadership opportunity structure. For example, as Table 8-1 shows, the congressmen's occupations are predominantly professional or managerial. In society where only 18 percent of the work force is engaged in such occupations. Lawyers and businessmen are particularly overrepresented both in Congress and State legislatures. Additionally, greater percentages of legislators are white, male, Protestant and over 30 years old than are found for the general adult population.[4]

In part, the overrepresentation of the affluent and educated in the councils of government stems from the middle-class leadership structure of the

Table 8-1   Occupations of Congressmen (1979) Compared with Those of the
Public (1970) (in Percent)

Occupation	U.S. Senate	U.S. House	U.S. Labor Force
Agriculture	5	4	2
Business or banking	23	26	8
Clergymen	—a	1	—
Education	6	12	4
Journalism	2	2	—
Labor leaders	—	1	—
Lawyers	52	42	—
Law enforcement	—	1	—
Medicine	—	1	2
Public Service or politics	10	8	1
Scientists	2	—	1
Other occupations	0	0	82

Source. The Congressional Quarterly (Jan. 20, 1979), p. 81; *The U.S. Fact Book, 1976* (New York: Grosset & Dunlap, 1976), pp. 360-365.
afewer than one percent

two major political parties. Even the Democratic Party — supposedly the more representative of the working man—draws its leaders from the middle class. By contrast, in many other democracies, the presence of a Socialist or Labor party draws working-class people into greater political activity. In Norway, for example, political participation is not correlated with affluence as it is in the United States.[5] Although Socialist and Labor parties do not draw their leaders exclusively from the working class that they represent, they do at least open the door for the political recruitment of blue-collar workers that is rather closed in this country.[6]

There is not anything inherently sinister about the status differentiation between political leaders and the general public, since the disproportionate concentration of political leadership skills in the hands of the better educated and prosperous may make it all but inevitable. For example, even the delegates to the "reformed" Democratic National Convention of 1972 were still far better educated and more affluent than the general population, although they were representative on the basis of race, sex, and age.[7] Even movements of economic protest draw their leaders from the most affluent strata within the protest group. For example, Lipset finds this to be the pattern within agricultural protest movements: "The battle for higher prices and a better economic return for their labor has been conducted by the farmers who need it least."[8]

The status "bias" to the leadership structure does not necessarily mean that the political views of political leaders typify their class instead of that of the general public. For example, the 1972 delegates to the Democratic

Convention obviously did not express the prevailing views of the economically comfortable. To be sure, there are potential sources of misrepresentation in the group background of political leaders. For example, one might suspect that state legislatures would be more eager to pass "no fault" insurance laws if they contained fewer lawyers.[9] Or, the city council that is overstocked with local businessmen might well be suspected of reflecting the prevailing norms of the local business community rather than the views of the general population. A more general consideration is that whatever their individual ideologies, the generally affluent leaders might resist wealth-redistribution legislation that would work against their self-interest. For example, a study of the attitudes of national convention delegates (in 1956) found that one of the few issues on which delegates of both parties were clearly more conservative than the public was that of making the rich pay a greater share of the taxes.[10] Of course, one could argue that virtually all political viewpoints found in the general population are also shared by some of the prosperous and better educated—and these might be our leaders. Moreover, even among the affluent, few are sufficiently politically motivated to run for public office, so that political representatives from such backgrounds accurately representing even the opinions of their economic group is unlikely.[11] Thus, one can hope that there is sufficient diversity of viewpoint among the candidates for office from which the people make their selections at the polls. And if not, there is still the possibility that electoral pressure can divert the behavior of political leaders away from unrepresentative personal preferences.

We can also try a direct approach to the question of whether political leaders and the general public share the same opinions by comparing the political attitudes of the two sets of groups. As we saw in Chapter 4, the public gives less support for freedom of speech, including the right of all citizens to strive to implement their positions into public policy. In this instance, the more supportive political leaders aid democracy by *not* sharing public opinion. But the lesser tolerance by the mass public does not negate the importance of representatives sharing their constituents' opinions on specific programs that are being considered by government. No amount of exceptional support for freedom of speech or democratic rules of the game by representatives would make their failure to create a public policy consistent with public opinion more palatable. Like V. O. Key, we see the importance of another standard for democracy," . . . if a democracy is to exist, the belief must be widespread that public opinion, at least in the long-run, affects the course of public action."[12] He is referring here to the opinions on more specific programs and issues before government, and we presume that the belief that public opinion counts rests on its actually having an impact. Our inquiry turns now to the representatives' opinion on specific issues.

Few published data exist from which to assess the correspondence between the policy views of the public and its elected leaders. One instance is a 1973 Harris survey (for a congressional subcommittee) of both the general public and a broad spectrum of elected officials. The results of this comparison are shown in Table 8-2. Each sample was asked which of a series of hypothetical governmental actions they would oppose. Except for the responses to a question about "demonstrators" (leaders were more opposed to government actions against demonstrators), the public and leader responses are very similar.

Table 8-2   Comparison of Public and Leader Opinion on Types of Government Actions Which They Would Oppose

	Public (% opposed)	Leaders (% opposed)
If police said they needed to come into your home without a search warrant to control drug abuse	73	84
If government said price of bread had to go up 5 cents in order to send wheat to Russia and China to keep peace	73	64
If government said people had to keep their gun at a local police station	68	76
If police made spot checks at traffic lights to see if people have safety belts on	64	67
If government required every residence to be inspected for leaks that wasted heat or fuel	60	70
If government required auto owners to bring in their cars every 3 months for inspection	55	61
If government said every family had to pay $50 a year in taxes to clean up air pollution	52	39
If government asked all demonstrations to be called off so government leaders could get their work done	48	77
If government raised taxes for each family to $50 a year to make streets safe	46	44
If government imposed a stiff fine for littering	10	6

Source. U. S. Congress, Subcommittee on Intergovernmental Relations. *Confidence and Concern: Citizens View American Government, Part 1.* 93rd Congress, First Session, December 3, 1973, p. 151.

Another opportunity to access the correspondence between public and leader opinion derives from two polls that have compared public and congressional responses to current political issues: one in 1970 (by CBS) and one in 1978 (by CBS/*New York Times*). Examples for 1978 are shown in Table 8-3. For both 1970 and 1978, the distributions of responses by the public sample and by U.S. House members generally differ by only a few percentage points.[13]

Why are the opinions of congressmen and the general public in even rough correspondence? Possibly, the correspondence is evidence of the Sharing Model at work—congressional candidates are recruited from the same attitudinal milieu as the general population. But also, the similarity could, in part, be the result of elections weeding out the congressional candidates who do not share the public's views. In any case, we should not conclude from this table that policy is also congruent with public opinion. There are forces—such as the inertial drag of congressional rules and norms, the opposition of powerful pressure groups, and the failure of presidential leadership—that can prevent even a representative Congress from doing what the public seems to want.

Table 8-3 Comparison of Public and Congressional Opinion on Selected Policy Issues, 1978

	Public	U. S. House Members
Defense: Percent that say money for natural defense should be decreased	23	26
SALT: Percent in favor of SALT II talks	67	74
Health Insurance: Percent in favor of "National Health Insurance fully paid by the government"	47	45
Tax Cut: Percent opposed to a "large federal income tax cut"	53	51
Abortion: Percent favoring "government paying for abortions for the poor"	41	35

Source: Kathleen A. Frankovic and Laurily K. Epstein, "Congress and its Constituency: The New Machine Politics," paper delivered at American Political Science Association Convention, Washington, D.C., September, 1979. The "public" sample is a nationwide sample of about 9,000 *voters* interviewed as they exited the polling booth in November, 1978. The House members are those elected in 1978. Both the public and House surveys were conducted by the CBS/New York Times poll.

Note: The questions asked the public and congressional samples were not exactly identical in each case, but were sufficiently similar to allow meaningful comparison. Those holding no opinion are excluded from the calculations of percentages.

We might also ask whether, in addition to the correspondence between congressional and public opinion in the aggregate, individual congressmen share the policy of their particular constituencies. As part of an ambitious study (of which more will be said later), Warren Miller and Donald Stokes collected the views of both congressmen and their constituencies following the 1958 election.[14] Although the questions asked congressmen and voters were not identical, they covered the same subjects. Consequently, we can ask whether the congressmen with the most liberal views represented the most liberal House districts. Comparisons were made in three policy domains: civil rights, foreign policy, and social welfare. As Figure 8-1 shows, in each domain the correlation between the congressman's personal attitude and the views of his constituency was positive: + .50 in civil rights, + .32 in foreign policy, and + .26 in domestic welfare. In other words, the most liberal districts tend to elect the congressmen with the most liberal viewpoints. Although the correlations are far from perfect, there would be some correspondence between constituency preferences and the congressman's vote were he to vote solely on the basis of his personal preferences. Here again a major question is, why? In part, it may be the result of simple sharing of personal preferences. For example, at least feeble public-congressional correlations would result if each district's congressman were determined by

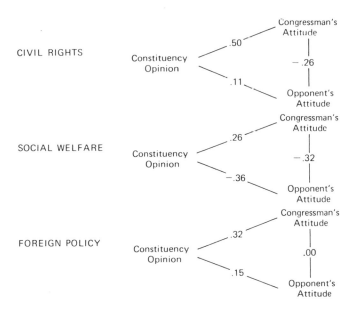

Figure 8-1. Relationship between congressmen's opinions, their opponents' opinions, and constituency opinion. Numbers are correlation coefficients. (*Source.* 1958 Survey Research Study of Representation. From personal correspondence with project director.)

lottery.[15] But, interestingly, the correlations between the views of nonincumbent congressional candidates (who usually lost) and the districts that (usually) rejected them were much weaker than for the winners. Moreover, the more liberal the district on social welfare, the more conservative the losing major-party candidate is likely to be. Although the full reason for this negative correlation defies simple explanation, the filtering process of elections was seemingly at work.[16]

8-2 LEADERSHIP RESPONSIVENESS TO PUBLIC OPINION

We have seen that there is some sharing of political preferences by people and their elected representatives. Thus, if the representatives' preferences guide their behavior in office, there will be at least a modest amount of agreement between public opinion and policy. Agreement would be greater if representatives were to support the choice of the public over their own preference when there is a conflict between the two. For this Role Playing Model to work, two conditions must be met. First, the representative must have some incentive to choose the public's preference over his or her own. This incentive may be the representative's belief that following public opinion is ordinarily the "right" thing to do or that he or she will face electoral reprisals for not going along with public opinion. Second, the representative must know what public opinion is. Below, we will consider the evidence regarding how well these two conditions are met.

Seemingly crucial to the people's having much real control over what their leaders do is a strong desire by public officials to take public opinion into account. But as V. O. Key wrote in 1961, "We have practically no systematic information about what goes on in the minds of public men as they ruminate about the weight to be given to public opinion in governmental decision."[17]

Despite more than two decades since Key's writing, his gloomy statement about the state of our knowledge about the public's direct influence on decision makers could, perhaps, be written today. There do exist bits of evidence, however, that tell us something about leaders' responsiveness to public opinion. Our task, then, is to link these pieces together.

How Legislators See Their Roles

For nearly every circumstance in which one human being interacts with another, such as being a parent, asking a question in the classroom, interviewing for a job, or serving as a representative in a government, people hold beliefs about what the proper behavior would be in those circumstances. These sets of beliefs prescribing behavior for each social situation are normally labeled "roles." Roles vary greatly in their richness, with some encompassing very broad ranges of expected behavior while others give only minimal direction. Our concern here is with the role of the political representative and, more specifically, with that role as perceived by representatives.

Several researchers have explored the various aspects of how legislators see their role—their expected behavior, as they perceive it. Here we consider how legislators see their role vis-a-vis their constituencies. John Wahlke, Heinz Eulau, and their associates, who began the study of legislative roles, identified three types of possible representative roles. They define the "trustee" as the legislator who "sees himself as a free agent in that as a premise of his decision-making behavior, he claims to follow what he considers to be right or just, his convictions and principles, the dictates of his conscience."[18] Moreover, the trustee is fully confident that his constituency expects him to behave in just that manner. At the opposite end of the pole from the trustee is the "delegate" who feels he should follow the wishes of his constituents even if they are contrary to his own. Finally, because the researchers found many representatives who claimed they had to play trustee on some issues and delegate on others, a conditional or mixed role was defined, which they call the "politico." Elaborate questionnaires have been administered to state legislators and congressmen to classify them according to representative roles.

Table 8-4 shows the distribution of the three role types found within several state legislatures and the U.S. House of Representatives. Wisconsin's legislature stands out for its high proportion of delegates, perhaps because of the state's "progressive" political history. The U.S. House of Representatives also contains few trustees, and a high percentage of politicos. If the role orientations of U.S. Senators were measured, given the insolarity of their lengthy six-year term, few would score as delegates.

If legislators do play the role indicated by their questionnaire responses, the public's only coercion on the trustee is its retrospective judgment at the polls regarding his decisions. The delegate and (to a lesser extent) the politico are additionally constrained by their apparently greater desire to work in behalf of constituency desires. Electoral coercion does appear to be a factor here, as delegates face closer elections than trustees.[19] Presumably, the causal connection is that safe seats allow the aloofness of a trustee and not that delegate behavior loses votes.

The sorting of legislators on the basis of their legislative roles is a significant enterprise only if their role designations help us predict their actual behavior. Theoretically, delegates should be more responsive to constituency interests than trustees. Two studies of California legislators suggest this is the case.[20] These studies compare delegates, politicos, and trustees in terms of the extent to which their roll-call voting corresponded to constituency voting on a series of referenda. True to theory, the first of these

Table 8-4 Distribution of Representational Roles (in Percent)

Representational Role Orientation	California N=49	New Jersey N=54	Ohio N=114	Tennessee N=78	Wisconsin N=89	Pennsylvania N=106	Michigan N=77	House of Representatives N=87
Trustee	55	61	56	81	21	33	35	28
Politico	25	22	29	13	4	27	31	46
Delegate	20	17	15	6	66	39	34	23
Not Classified	—	—	—	—	9	1	—	3

Sources. John C. Wahlke et al, *The Legislative System* (New York: Wiley, 1962, p. 281; Frank J. Sorauf, *Party and Representation* (New York: Atherton Press, 1963) p. 124; Malcolm E. Jewell and Samuel C. Patterson, *The Legislative Process in the United States* (New York: Random House, 1966) p. 398; John W. Soule, "Future Political Ambitions and the Behavior of Incumbent State Legislators," *Midwest Journal of Political Science XIII*, No. 3 (August 1969) p. 452; and Roger H. Davidson, *The Role of Congressman* (New York: Pegasus, 1969) p. 117.

studies (by Kuklinski with Elling) found a far higher correlation between constituency liberalism and roll-call liberalism for delegates than for trustees, with politicos in between. The second study (by McCrone and Kuklinski) also reports that among California legislators the delegates are the most responsive to *perceived* constituency opinion and are the most accurate in estimating actual constituency opinion.

This latter study also finds that districts that are consistently liberal or consistently conservative in their referendum voting enjoy the best representation. Even delegates, can represent their districts only if the constituency clearly speaks in its referendum votes. It should be noted that only 19 percent of the districts in this California study did offer such clear indication of their policy preferences. Also California has an exceptionally large number of referenda. We might readily speculate that fewer referenda would leave the representative unsure of district opinion.

As we have seen, the role most conducive to political agreement — that of delegate—appears to be favored by only a minority in most legislatures. To be sure, many legislators would find it too humiliating to admit to being merely the voice of others. Indeed most of us applaud the "courage" of the "statesmanlike" legislator who votes with his independent judgment rather than with the views of his constituency—particularly when we agree with that judgment.

The Fear of Electoral Reprisals

Instead of asking legislators how much they follow public opinion, we can ask them whether they perceive that their re-election chances depend on what they do in office. When asked by political scientists, most legislators will report that they fear electoral reprisals if they stray from satisfying public demands. Eighty-five percent of the congressmen interviewed by Miller and Stokes said their personal record and standing in Congress was either "quite important" or "very important" to their re-election.[21] By comparison, only 46 percent gave ratings of "quite" or "very important" for party loyalties or national issues. How representatives glorify the wisdom of the people and come to believe that they will be carefully judged by them in succeeding elections is easy to see. The representatives uncertainty about why they won causes them to believe that re-election rests with his constituency's reaction to performance in office.

A study of candidates for state and national office in Wisconsin reports that the winners saw the candidates and election issues to be more important than party labels, although losers were more inclined to see the importance of partisanship in determining the outcome.[22] The winners' greater optimism about both public interest and their ability to affect the election results caused John Kingdon to conclude that the difference can be explained by what he labels a "congratulation-rationalization effect."

". . .winners develop complimentary beliefs about voters and losers develop rationalizations for their losses simply by virtue of the outcome of the election. Winners, the argument runs, believe that voters did a good job of choosing. Voters in their view are well informed about politics and vote according to the issues and candidates, rather than blindly following their party. Losers, on the other hand, rationalize defeat by saying that voters are ill informed and vote according to party label rather than the issues or men who are running for office."[23]

Apparently, legislators prefer to believe that they win elections because voters agree with their views rather than because they are successful at catering to public tastes. Many, in fact, resolve perceived disagreements with their constituencies by the psychologically satisfying notion that they are able to educate the voters to accept their views.[24] There is no consensus to the Congressmen's perceptions, regarding the extent to which the public monitors their performance. Many are uncertain of how closely the voters are watching — and perhaps for this reason prefer not to take chances. Generally, they see re-election as largely a matter of maintaining the proper "image" back home. But they do not know how much their behavior in office shapes that image. Perhaps they have room for independence on smaller issues but not on the "big" ones.[25]

Examining what elected representatives do rather than what they say, there is considerable evidence that representatives are quite responsive to the threat of potential electoral defeat. Kuklinski's study of California legislators offers unusually graphic evidence of the responsiveness of legislators to the periodic threat of losing re-election.[26] Kuklinski assesses representation by means of the correlation between constituency liberalism (as expressed in frequent referendum results) and the legislator's roll-call liberalism. Figure 8-2, from Kuklinski's study, indicates that legislators can give substantial representation to their constituencies. California Assemblymen— who face re-election every two years—consistently do so throughout the years examined. For California State Senators, however, who face re-election only every four years, the pattern is more cyclical. The half of the California Senators who faced re-election in 1970 were substantially more responsive in 1970 than in succeeding years when the electoral threat diminished. Completing the pattern, those facing re-election in 1972 sharply improved their representation in 1972 and just as sharply showed a decline thereafter. These examples suggest that representatives do respond to perceived electoral threats by seeking to better reflect their constituents' views as election time approaches.

Like California assemblymen, U.S. House members face re-election every two years. Although we have no exact measure of constituency opinion of U.S. House districts (unlike the case in California, where Kuklinski

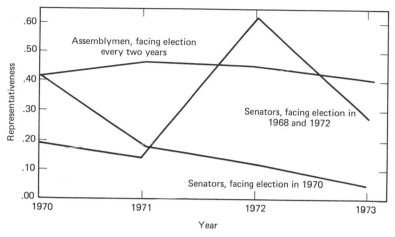

Figure 8-2. Relationship between the temporal proximity of elections and representativeness of California state legislators. [*Source*. James H. Kuklinski, "Representativeness and Elections: A Policy Analysis," *American Political Science Review*, 72 (March, 1978), p. 174.]

had access to referendum results), a serviceable indicator of constituency liberalism-conservatism is the constituency vote in the ideological presidential election of 1972. As shown in Figure 8-3, the constituency vote division in the ideological McGovern-Nixon election is a good predictor of House roll-call voting in 1973. Within each party, the most liberal House members (as measured by the ratings of ideological pressure groups)[27] represent the most liberal districts as measured by the strength of their McGovern vote. Similarly, within each party, the most conservative House members represented the most conservative (pro-Nixon) districts. This apparent responsiveness to constituency opinion is one reason why neither all Democrats nor all Republicans vote alike in Congress. Although Democratic Representatives are generally far more liberal than Republican Representatives *from similar districts,* Democratic Representatives from very conservative districts are generally more conservative than are Republicans from very liberal districts.[28]

A theme than runs through recent studies of congressional behavior is that an overwhelming portion of House Members' behavior is guided by the goal of staying elected. A recent study by Kingdon suggests that the pleasing of constituency interests is a major motivation of House members when they decide how to vote on even routine legislation.[29] David Mayhew suggests that the structural organization of the House of Representatives is best understood as a collective response to the members' needs to stay elected.[30] In contrast to studies of Congressional behavior in Washington, Richard Fenno describes what House members do on their frequent trips to their home districts. Fenno finds that Representatives are often compelled to ex-

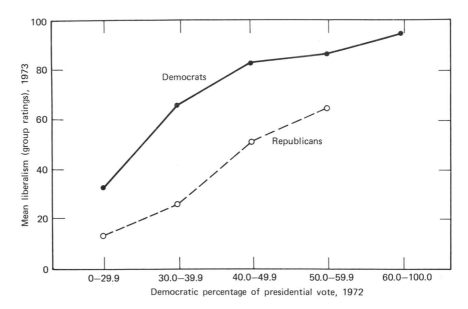

Figure 8-3. Roll-call liberalism of U.S. House members, 1973, as function of their district's presidential vote, 1972.

plain their roll-call votes to the satisfaction of their important constituents, hopefully in a way that inspires trust and confidence.[31] Not all of Representatives' interactions with constituents involve policy issues, however. As Morris Fiorina argues, the growth of Federal programs has resulted in the adaptation by congressmen to being errand boys, ombudsmen, or helpers of individuals frustrated with the bureaucracy.[32] Clearly, by a variety of district-oriented activities, House members enhance their re-election prospects. Paradoxically, although public trust for Congress as an institution has been declining over the years, people appear to respect their *own* congressman more than they used to.[33]

A case can be made, of course, for the position that the continuous preoccupation with staying elected detracts from the congressional policy-making function. It has been proposed, for example, that U.S. House members should be elected every four years rather than every two years.[34] One concern is that when they acknowledge the public's power over them, public officials do not always view it as wisely exercised. As V.O. Key once observed, "public men often act as if they thought the deciding margin in elections was cast by fools; moreover, by fools informed enough and alert enough to bring retribution to those who dare not demonstrate themselves equally foolish."[35]

Political Ambition

The belief that his re-election chances hinge on how well he represents constituency opinion will not influence the officeholder much unless he cares about getting re-elected. As Joseph Schlesinger has described the positive functions of political ambition, "no more irresponsible government is imaginable than one of high-minded men unconcerned for their political futures."[36] Politicians at the top of the political ladder usually try to continue in officer for as long as possible. For example, presidents normally want to stay in office for their constitutional allotment of two full terms. Even Truman and Johnson, who both opted for retirement in the spring of their re-election years, did so only after the results of the first presidential primaries indicated that even renomination by their party would have been a difficult hurdle. Most governors also seek re-election when constitutionally able—for example, 72 percent of 25 cases in 1974. Ambition for continuation is also rather high in the case of congressmen. For example, of the 34 senators up for re-election in 1974, only seven did not seek re-election. The same year, only 15 of the 435 U.S. House members voluntarily retired from public life. (Thirteen others gave up their House careers to try for the higher offices of U.S. senator or governor.)[37]

Interestingly, the inclination of congressmen to hang onto their office for several terms is a relatively recent phenomenon. In the 19th century, House and Senate members quite frequently returned to private life after only a term or two.[38] This situation persists in the career pattern of lower-level office holders. Prewitt's study of Bay Area councilmen disclosed that almost one-fifth did not (at the time of their interview) plan to seek re-election.[39] Although it is not known how prevalent this pattern is at the local level throughout the nation, the retirement rate of some state legislators appears to be even higher. On the average, however, the retirement rate is about 16 percent in state legislatures.[40]

The rate at which members of a legislative body retire appears to have very delicate effects. Observers of Congress often moan that the institution is handicapped by the presence of too many old men who refuse to give up their seats. Students of state legislatures offer the opposite complaint: that frequent retirements (often to seek higher office as well as to go back home) produce a depletion of experienced personnel. Our chief concern is that the retiring legislator may be relatively indifferent to public opinion.

One should not necessarily infer that the nonambitious office holder's escape from electoral pressure typically frees him or her to pursue worthy goals that are too advanced for public opinion to accept. Surely, many politicians are strongly motivated to advance their conception of the "public interest." But this pursuit of accomplishments only feeds their ambition for further public service, which requires reelection. This reasoning suggests the hypothesis that the political leaders with the strongest policy motivations tends to feel the most electoral pressure to satisfy public opinion—at least on matters that concern them least.

At the other extreme, we may, following Prewitt, identify a different type of policy maker whom Prewitt calls the "volunteer-citizen politician." The volunteer's most frequent habitat is a low-paying post in a nonpartisan setting. Likely to have wandered into politics as a natural extension of participation in civic organizations, they see themselves as performing a duty to serve a term or two. They do not see their role as satisfying constituency demands because, as Prewitt says, voters are not asked to "replace the inept church leader, the misguided little league organizer, or the irresponsible library board members".41 Indeed, the public is not likely to monitor the volunteer leader's performance closely; thus, the Rational Activist Model does not supply political linkage. Having entered politics from the local business establishment, the volunteer leader may not represent the views of the entire community. Thus, the Sharing Model also seems improbable. Only the Role Playing Model seems at all likely to be effective since, like most citizens of a democracy, the volunteer leader feels that what others say should be given consideration. But little additional motivation seems likely and, in any case, the people he or she talks to will be members of his or her own circle. In short, models of political linkage seem ineffective in holding the volunteer accountable. But the number of such volunteers in political positions remains unassessed.

The Leader's Desire to Represent

We have tried to assess how much the politicians' fear of electoral sanctions acts as a motivation for following public opinion. The data suggest politicians give greater credit to the public's monitoring capabilities than the evidence would warrant. Even more difficult to assess in the extent to which political leaders heed public opinion simply because they think it is what they ought to do. We cannot test the validity of this role-playing model directly, for it is impossible to enter politicians' minds and locate their value structures. However, some observers of politics have argued that the wide-spread belief that public opinion should be followed is a major source of the democratic linkage that does exist. V.O. Key, for example, argues that within the subculture of political leaders a value of fundamental importance is a "regard for public opinion, a belief that in some way or another, it should prevail".42

Miller and Stokes' study of congressional representation provides some evidence of how frequently politicians follow their perception of constituency views. As part of this study, correlations were computed between the congressman's roll-call behavior and both personal views and perceptions of what the district wanted. Figure 8-4 shows that in the three policy areas

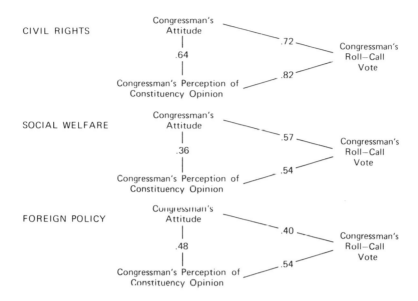

Figure 8-4. Relationship between congressmen's opinions, their perceptions of constituency opinions, and their roll-call votes. (*Source.* See Figure 8-1.)

examined, the representatives' personal preferences and their perceptions of constituency preference were about equally (and positively) correlated with their roll-call behavior. The positive correlation between the congressmans' views and their perceptions of constituency views makes the matter difficult to disentagle beyond the tentative inference that congressmen typically give about equal weight to both considerations

8-3 HOW ELECTED OFFICIALS LEARN PUBLIC OPINION

Even if political decision makers want to follow public opinion, they cannot do so effectively unless they know what the people want. According to political lore, good politicians have acute political antennae that detect the prevailing political mood when they wander among the "grass roots". Of course, the policy maker is also sometimes able to "read" public opinion more directly by examining the results of available opinion polls.

Unlike the president, the lower-level elected officials (such as the state legislator) rarely have the resources to conduct their own polls. But one group of officeholders who do make frequent use of polls are members of U.S. House of Representatives. Thanks to their franking (free mailing) privilege, House members can send questionnaires to each household in their district for only the printing costs. The number of House members who do take constituency polls has been steadily rising—from 11 percent in the early 1950s to 74 percent in 1969–1970.[43] Since these polls are administered by mailed questionnaires, they have a low-return rate (about 14 percent on the average)[44] that can permit the views of a small minority (typically the better educated and more wealthy) to be mistaken for "public opinion". But one might argue that since the minority who take the trouble to respond to congressional polls presumably feel most intensely about the issues, any bias in the poll results would be weighted in favor of the more attentive segment of the public who will vote according to their beliefs.

How accurate are congressional polls, and how much weight do congressmen give them? One study of opinion on the fallout-shelter controversy in the early 1960s compared the results of congressional polls and professionally completed polls and found a high correspondence between them.[45] The study also found that congressmen often altered their votes on the shelter issue as a response to the declining public support for fallout shelters manifested in their own polls. But the increased use of polls notwithstanding, representatives also rely on other means of detecting constituency opinion. Tables 8-5 and 8-6 show that U.S. House members and Wisconsin candidates are more confident in other, more impressionistic ways of judging constituent opinion. Let us examine how precisely the politician can determine the most popular course to take from the techniques available.

Opinion Polls. Perusing the results of opinion polls gives the policy maker additional insight into what his constituency wants. Yet, like everybody else, the politician must read them with caution. Let us examine why the office holder who bases every decision on what the polls show to be the majority preference does not always take the most politically rewarding course. As we saw in Chapter 2, the distribution of opinion on an issue can vary with

Table 8-5   Extent of Reliance upon Various Communication Channels by Congressmen from 116 Districts, 1958 (in Percent)

	Source of Information				
Extent of Reliance	Personal Contact	Mail	News-papers	Party Organi-zation	Opinion Polls
A great deal	62	25	5	8	6
Quite a bit	19	30	27	10	7
Some	8	23	24	15	11
Not much	8	19	29	28	15
None	2	3	15	39	61

Source. Warren E. Miller, "Policy Preferences of Congressional Candidates and Constituents," paper presented at the 1961 Annual Meeting of the American Political Science Association.

Table 8-6   Use and Perceived Reliability of Various Sources of Information among Wisconsin Candidates (in Percent)

Reliability	Source				
	Polls	Party People	Volunteers	Past Statistics	Warmth of reception
Rely without qualification	13	21	19	45	57
Rely with qualification	5	16	19	38	8
Do not rely on source	8	48	29	5	31
No information from source	74	15	33	12	3
Total	100	100	100	100	99
N	61	61	58	60	61

Source. John W. Kingdon, *Candidates for Office: Beliefs and Strategies* (New York: Random House, 1966), p. 91.

the exact question wording. Consequently, the side of the issue on which majority opinion lies may shift with the seemingly innocuous change in the question wording. Given such circumstances, following public opinion as registered by a single reading on the issue may make little political sense.

Actually, the policy option that would yield the political leader the most votes (and satisfy the most people) is not always the majority position anyway. For example, according to unsubstantiated political lore, the minority who are gun enthusiasts have managed to defeat several politicians who advocate strict gun control even though polls show a majority favor strict gun registration laws. Presumably, the average person who, when asked, will favor gun control but not translate these convictions into action at the ballot box; the gun enthusiast will.

Paradoxically, the way to build a winning majority at the polls may sometimes be to create a coalition of intense minorities, suppose, for example, opinion on three issues is divided 80 to 20, with the different minorities on each issue feeling several times more intensely about the matter than those on the other side do. Then if one candidate supports the majority side on all three issues, and the other appeals to the minority side, the candidate of the minorities could win 60 percent of the vote (20 times 3), assuming all vote on the basis of the issues. There would be nothing inherently undemocratic about the majority side losing out on each question, as a majority of voters would have more to gain from their representation on the one question they feel strongly about than they would by representation on the other two issues. A related reason why finding an accurate profile of the entire population's opinion and acting on it may not be the best re-election strategy, is that money contributors and volunteer workers probably hold unrepresentative opinions and may respond unsympathetically to candidates articulating the representative public opinion.

Politicians may sometimes feel free to ignore the polls because they recognize that the public generally expects its political leaders to use their own judgment, acting as trustees rather than delegates. In one Iowa poll, most respondents said state legislators should act according to their conscience rather than according to constituency preferences when there was a conflict between the two.[46] As we saw in Chapter 5, the public normally gives the president even greater latitude to use his own judgment. The public seems to react with displeasure at being asked to do what they think they elect officials to do, namely make decisions. For example, many defeats of fluoridation referenda seem based on public displeasure at their elected officials' failures to take a stand on the issue by passing the buck to the voters.[47]

Indeed, by following majority opinion, the politician may be discounting the potential effects of his own leadership. For example, President Nixon would not have reaped the political benefits of his trip to China if he had followed the opinion polls showing that the public was hostile toward China. Here, the President was able to influence opinion by redefining the situation for the American public. Indeed, one might argue that a reasonably popular president can mobilize majority support for virtually any policy action he takes in the foreign policy sphere. Of course, the leadership potential of the politician depends on the prestige of his office, his popularity, and the nature of the issue. For example, a "lowly" congressman may not create much of a ripple in public thinking by advocating some new foreign policy course. Even a president cannot automatically count on the public following his lead in the domestic sphere.

Another reason why the office holder acting on one's personal policy preferences may yield more electoral benefit in the long run than acting like a delegate is that, at election time, the voters will react more to the apparent success or failure of a representative's performance in office than to their initial impressions of his or her decisions. If the politician expects to be rewarded or punished for the "nature of the times" polls of current public sentiment about what ought to be done are sometimes of little help. Obviously, a president would make economic policy on the basis of expert opinion rather than on what the polls say the public thinks would work best.

The Vietnam war provides one example of a discrepancy between the public's policy preference at the moment and the public's eventual reaction to the consequences of that policy. According to the polls, the public supported the war at the time the crucial steps of escalated involvement were taken. If the high officials in the Kennedy-Johnson administrations had foreknowledge of the extent of the public's eventual opposition to a prolonged war, perhaps they would have made different decisions. Here, politicians, had to make crucial guesses about public reactions to their possible options—for which polls could not give answers.

These considerations undoubtedly comprise some of the reasons why office holders place surprisingly little stock in polls. But other sources of their estimates of public opinion also contain pitfalls. Crowd reactions, obviously, can be misleading indicators given the disproportionately politicized and partisan nature of political audiences. How accurate are other sources of opinion cues—election returns, constituency groupings, the mail, and the people back home to whom the representative talks?

Election Returns. After elections, a popular fad is to analyze the results to determine the new "mood" of the voters. We saw earlier that changes in the voters' partisan preferences are not the result of ideological mood swings: Republican gains do not necessarily mean the public has swung farther to the right, for example. The winning politician who mistakenly interprets his landslide victory to be a mandate for his favorite programs may experience a sudden erosion of his popular support. The urge to decipher meaning from particular issue-oriented election contests can also lead to errors; if the judgment is made without consideration of the general partisan trend. For example, in retrospect, an overinterpretation of election results by concerned political observers may have been the reason why official Washington overestimate the popular support for demagogic Senator Joe McCarthy in the early 1950s. Although, at first, other senators disassociated themselves from McCarthy's unsubstantiated claims that some indefinite number of known Communists were running loose in the State Department and elsewhere in government, the defeat of several of McCarthy's senatorial critics in the 1950 and 1952 elections silenced the remainder.[48] In retrospect, we see that most of the defeated McCarthy opponents would have lost anyway in the anti-Democratic tide.[49] Almost unnoticed, McCarthy trailed his party's ticket when he won re-election from Wisconsin voters in 1952. Actually, McCarthy was never supported by a clear majority of the public; most of his supporters came from predictable sources such as small-town Republicans. If otherwise alert politicians had paid closer attention to the polls than to isolated and misleading election returns, the "climate of opinion" that assumed McCarthy was invincible may never have been created. As it was, McCarthy's downfall—forced by his attack on the U.S. Army—was as sudden as the initial rise of what became known as "McCarthyism."

Although politicians may overinterpret partisan electoral trends or the electoral fate of certain candidates who are linked to particular causes, they may learn something meaningful about the general political preferences of their constituences from how they vote in comparison to others. Earlier (Figure 8-3), we saw that the 1973 rolls call voting of U.S. Representatives was correlated with 1972 presidential election returns in constituencies. Although we do not known whether this relationship resulted because House members consciously tried to adjust their behavior in direct response to the election returns, we can reasonably infer that the district's voting in the ideological 1972 presidential contest was a good gauge of whether it was a relatively conservative or a relatively liberal district. Although the extent to which constituency opinion is related to partisan voting has not been fully explored, one Florida study finds that the 1968 presidential election returns were a good predictor of referendum voting on certain issues in state legislative districts. Moreover, legislators appeared to respond to the cue of past district voting when they were asked to predict the referendum verdicts in their districts.[50]

Group Characteristics. In their interviews with John Kingdon, the Wisconsin candidates claimed to cue off supporting groups, labor for Democrats, and business for Republicans, in judging the policy positions they need to take to insure support at election time.[51] More research is needed regarding the representative's reliance on guessing the social composition of his constituency and attributing opinions to it based on those characteristics. For example, if a politician's district contains an unusually high proportion of elderly voters, is he or she correct in concluding that they support extension of Social Security payments. Such judgments can be quite difficult, especially with a diverse district or an obscure issue. But this type of assessment may be vital to the politician who seeks to know public opinion.

The Mail. Political officeholders place only slight stock in the mail they receive as a source of constituency opinion. Skepticism is highest when a barrage of letters clearly originates from a pressure group campaign.[52] But, setting such cases aside, is there any bias to the mail political leaders receive? Writing a letter to an elected official is not a regular activity for the average person. President Lincoln receive about 44 letters each year per every 10,000 literate adults, or from less than one-half of one percent of the population. Similarly, Wilson received about 47 per 10,000. Roosevelt received 160, meaning that about 2 literate persons in every 100 felt the need to write him.[53] The infrequency of this action causes us to suspect the representativeness of the letter-writing public. V.O. Key notes that the preponderance of letters to the White House are supportive or approving, which might cause the president to have a myopic view of public support for his program.[54]

Only about 15 percent of the public admit to ever having written a public official and about two-thirds of all letters written to officials originate from three percent of the public.[55] The politician who measures public opinion solely from the content of his mail or from "letters to the Editor" would judge public opinion to be more conservative than it is. Figure 8-5 compares

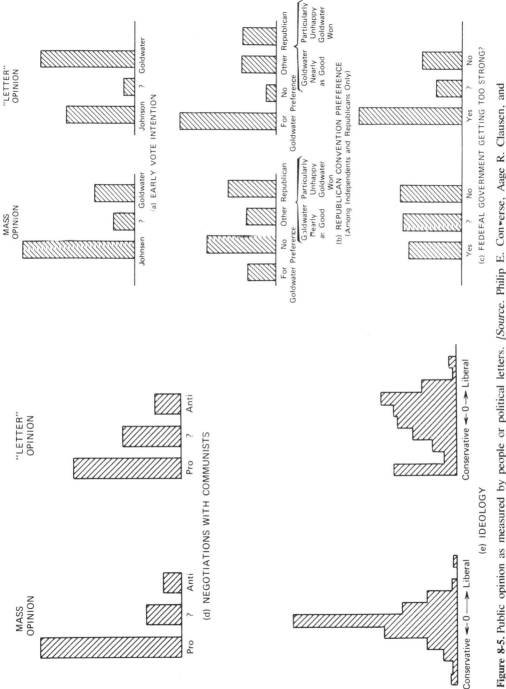

Figure 8-5. Public opinion as measured by people or political letters. [*Source.* Philip E. Converse, Aage R. Clausen, and Warren E. Miller. "Electoral Myth and Reality: The 1964 Election," *American Political Science Review*, 59 (June 1965), p. 334.]

letter opinion (the opinions of those claiming to have written to public officials) with public opinion (the opinions of the total population measured in the sample survey) in 1964. If letter opinion was misperceived as being public opinion, we would conclude that in 1964, Goldwater held an appreciable lead midway in the campaign, that Republicans and Independents toasted his nomination above all other Republican candidates, and that Americans were upset with the growing strength of the Federal Government and were decisively conservative. Goldwater's optimism regarding the public reception of his conservative campaign might well have rested on misplaced confidence that volunteered opinion (rather than poll opinion) best reflected public opinion.

These findings have been replicated by a national survey that assesses public attitudes toward the war in Vietnam. Sidney Verba and Richard Brody found the relationships between various forms of participation and attitudes toward Vietnam shown in Table 8-6. If an official read the state of public attitudes from his mail, he would have found "a little more than one and a half times as many hawks as in the population as a whole."[56] The eight demonstrators in the sample, if proportionate to their number in the total population, would mean that approximately 750,000 people had taken part in a demonstration. Such numbers would, of course, attract considerable attention and might well cause the official to take this activity and its message as public opinion. Naturally, such a conclusion would yield an unrepresentatively dovish perception of public opinion. A third subgroup, the minority who tried to convince others, differed from the general public in still a different way—they clustered more toward both the dove and hawk poles of the Vietnam spectrum.[57]

Attentive Constituents. Little is known about the constituents with whom officeholders do maintain regular contact. As part of one study, Iowa legislators were asked which constituents they would regard as politically knowledgeable and aware and whose advice they might seek on legislative issues or problems.[58] The attentive constituents thus identified were then interviewed. The attentive constituents have many desirable attributes to help achieve accountability in representatives. They are informed about the procedures of the legislature and the people who control it; they are interested in the political process (including recruitment); and have extensive communication with state, local, and national officials and they are strongly supportive of the legislature. But in terms of their socioeconomic standing, these attentive constituents are in an even more high-status group than the legislators. For these influential people also to have contacts with the average citizen, the accurate exchange of opinions and attitudes would have exist despite a very substantial social gap. Consequently, that the constituents to whom officeholders talk are adequate conduits for channeling the opinion of the public at large up to the political leadership is quite unlikely.

Table 8-7 Position on the Hawk-Dove Scale of the Population as a Whole and of Various Activist Populations (in Percent)

Vietnam Preferences	Whole Population	Those Who Have Discussed Vietnam	Those Who Have Tried to Change Opinions of Others	Those Who Have Written Letters	Those Who Have Demon- strated
Hawk	18	20	26	30	1 case
Mild hawk	31	31	28	33	None
Middle	26	26	19	10	1 case
Mild dove	13	12	10	10	None
Dove	12	11	17	17	6 cases
Total	100	100	100	100	
Percent of population	100	68	13	2.5	.5

Source. Sidney Verba and Richard Brody, "Participation, Policy Preferences, and the War in Vietnam," *Public Opinion Quarterly,* 34 (Fall 1970), p. 330.

How Accurately do Officials See Public Opinion?

Given the multiple devices officeholders employ to sense public opinion, how accurate are their perceptions of public opinion? One approach to answering this question is to sample opinion and then see how closely the public's representatives can predict what it is. In their study of congressional representation, Miller and Stokes sampled opinions in congressional districts and then asked the districts' representatives what they thought the opinion of their home constituency would be (see Figure 8-6). On civil rights issues, the correlation between constituency opinion and the congressman's perception of it was a fairly robust +.74—a not surprising indication that representatives of pro-civil-rights black constituencies and anti-civil-rights Deep South districts are aware of their constituencies' views. Correlations are also positive on social welfare issues (+.17) and foreign policy issues (+.25). Although the latter correlations are relatively weak, they are reduced somewhat by sampling error in the estimates of constituency opinion. There is reason to believe that if constituency opinion were measurable without error, the observed correlations between constituency opinion and congressional perceptions of it would be considerably higher.[59]

Perhaps the most difficult test for the representatives' political antennae to pass is correct estimation of constituency opinion on issues that do not attract much public attention. Accordingly, Ronald Hedlund and H. Paul Friesema quizzed Iowa state legislators about their constituencies' majority preference on four statewide referendum questions that were about to be put

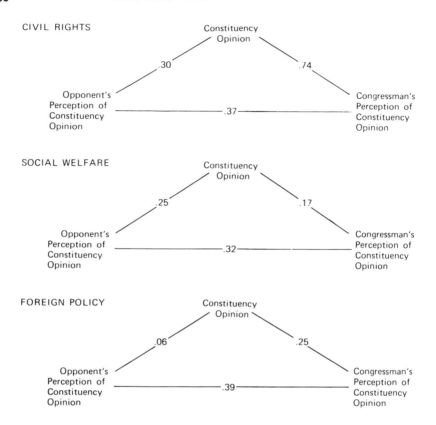

Figure 8-6. Relationship between constituency opinion and the perceptions of constituency opinion held by congressional candidates. (*Source.* See Figure 8-1.)

before the voters.[60] On the four questions, the accuracy of the legislators' predictions varied from 59 to 92 percent. (Simply by guessing randomly, the legislators would have been correct half the time.) The predictions on home rule for cites (92 percent) and reapportionment (82 percent) were reasonably accurate. But the rates of successful prediction on annual legislative sessions (59 percent) and giving the governor the item veto (64 percent) were only slightly beyond the guess range. Hedlund and Friesema argue that the home rule and reapportionment referenda attracted greater public interest than annual legislative sessions and item vetoes. This suggests greater accuracy in representatives' predictions of public opinion in those areas where the public expresses the most interest.

Following up on the Iowa study, in 1972 two of the authors of this book asked Florida legislators to predict the percentage-point breakdown in their district and in the state on three "straw ballot" referendum issues.[61] One of these straw-ballot issues dealt with the volatile question of "forced" school busing to achieve racial balance. Here the legislators' estimates were not far off the mark; for example, the 56 responding House members erred by an average of only 7 percentage points in predicting their district's anti-busing vote. But estimates were less accurate on the less publicized, remaining straw-ballot issues. On the question of allowing prayers in schools, the average error in prediction was 11 percentage points; on the question of rejecting the dual (or segregated) school system, the average was 12 percentage points. Once again, the legislators' awareness of public opinion is weaker when the public focus on the issue is weak.

8-4. DO ELECTED OFFICIALS NEED TO FOLLOW PUBLIC OPINION?

We have seen that although politicians sometimes have difficulty reading public opinion, they apparently do at least try to consider public opinion when making decisions—partly from fear of electoral retribution if they do not. Actually, there are reasons for suspecting that public officials do not need to weigh public opinion very heavily in order to get re-elected. Incumbent office-holders do not lose re-election bids at a rate that should stimulate electoral anxiety. Furthermore, most people do not monitor their leaders' policy decisions with sufficient attention to produce massive voter reactions.

Judging from the re-election rate of congressmen, incumbents are returned to office with astounding regularity. For example, in 1974 the re-election rate for members of Congress was 89 percent in the House and 83 percent in the Senate. Governors, however, are more vulnerable. For example, in 1974 only 72 percent of those who sought re-election were returned to office.[62] Governors appear electorally insecure because, like presidents, they are held accountable for the nature of the times of their administration.[63] Legislators face less electoral difficulty than executives because voters find difficulty in tracing the consequences of legislators' actions or in holding them individually responsible for government outputs, such as the state of the economy.

To what extent do voters react to the content of their leaders' policy decisions and policy proposals for the future? In the previous chapter we saw that, in a presidential race, a sizeable share of the voters will be somewhat aware of major issues and will be influenced by them. But in subpresidential contests, the public's information is usually too low to allow the expectation of much rational voting. The best data in this regard concern public awareness of the U.S. House of Representatives and their particular congressman.

Congress is not a very salient institution to most people. When asked which party has more congressmen, more give the correct answer than the incorrect one. But with an adjustment for correct guessing, the best estimate is that typically less than half the congressional-election voters cast their ballot with firm knowledge of which party is in control.[64] Once, following the

1966 election, a plurality in an SRC poll incorrectly responded that the Republicans controlled Congress—apparently confusing the big Republican gains that were reported in the news media with a Republican majority.[65] When people are asked how good a job Congress is doing, one might suspect that their response would depend on their party identification and the party in power—Democrats would like Congress best when the Democrats control it, for example. But it does not work out this way. A person more frequently rates Congress' performance as good when his party controls the White House but not Congress, than when his party controls Congress but not the White House.[66]   When we turn to voters' knowledge of their individual congressmen and congressional candidates, no improvement is found. First of all, the local news media rarely give much coverage to the congressman's roll-call stands or to the substantive issues of congressional campaigns.[67] Consequently, even if more people had the urge to follow the congressional politics of their district, they would have great difficulty in doing so. Only slightly more than half the public can even name their congressman. Similarly, at election time only about half will claim to have read or heard anything about their representative in Washington or his opponent. When interviewers probe to find out what the voter has read or heard about the congressional candidate, the answer is typically a vague reference such as "he is a good man", or "he knows the problems". Specific references to the representative's legislative actions comprise only a fraction of the responses—"not more than a thirtieth" say Stokes and Miller, based on their 1958 survey. Slim improvement is shown with application of a more generous test: only seven percent of the 1958 sample gave a reason for their candidate choice that "had any discernible issue content".[68] Other studies confirm that voters are not very knowledgeable about congressional candidates, although the impressions they do develop often influence their vote.[69]

On even heatedly debated congressional issues, few people know where their congressman stands. Table 8-8 condenses the results of an interesting survey that asked people how they and their congressman stood on the funding of the Supersonic Transport plan (SST) shortly after Congress rejected it. Most people polled were unable to state how their representative voted on the SST. Those who tried to answer the question were wrong almost as often as they were right—suggesting that even those who tried to answer were mostly guessing. Thus, the voters were almost totally unaware of how their congressman voted on an issue that had commanded a substantial share of newspaper headlines for a period of months. Evidently, congressmen were able to vote on the SST without attracting much public attention back home.[70]

From these survey findings, one might well wonder whether the congressman needs to pay any attention to his constituency's views when he weighs the alternatives of each legislative decision. As Warren Miller and

Table 8-8   Voters' Awareness of Their Congressman's Position on the Supersonic Transport Plane, 1971 (in Percent)

	Congressman Pro-SST		Congressman Anti-SST	
	Constituents' SST Opinion	Constituents' Perceptions of Congressman's SST Stand	Constituents' SST Opinion	Constituents' Perceptions of Congressman's SST Stand
Continue work	24	12	16	3.5
Stop spending	56	14	68.5	27.5
Not sure	19	74	15.5	69
Total	100	100	100	100

Source. John Kraft, Inc., "A Review of Voter Attitudes in Ten Key Congressional Districts," (August 1971), A Report to The American Businessmen's Committee for National Priorities.
Note. Responses are district means. The 10 congressmen whose districts were sampled were: (pro-SST) Albert, Arends, Boggs, Bow, G. Ford, Herbert, Mahon, and Mills; (Anti-SST) J. Byrnes, O'Neil.

Donald Stokes put it: "Congressmen feel that their individual legislative actions may have considerable impact on the electorate, yet some simple facts about the Representative's salience to his constituents imply that this could hardly be true."[71]

Indeed, we may have a major political linkage between mass opinion and leader response that is generally overlooked—although the public is not watching, leaders sometimes do what they think the public wants because they mistakenly believe the public is paying attention! If this is true, then leaders' responsiveness to public opinion would quickly evaporate once somebody points out to them that surveys show the public to be rather indifferent to what they do. On the other hand, maybe the politicians do not exaggerate the importance of their record to their electoral fate as much as the polls seem to suggest. Let us explore the reasons why officeholders do have to tread carefully when they consider violating something called public opinion.

First, the high re-election rate of incumbent office holders does not actually provide much security because the office-holder may want to win not only the next election, but also several thereafter. Consider the case of U.S. House members, who have a success rate of about 90 percent per re-election attempt. Most will survive their *next* election, but in the long run about one-third eventually leave office via an electoral defeat.[72] Such odds on long-term electoral survival can give House members reason to pay special attention to constituency desires.

Second, the easiest way for voters to become aware of their elected leader's record is for it to be exploited by an opponent as a stand against public opinion. Therefore, although name recognition generally wins votes, lack of public knowledge of a political leader's policy stands may sometimes actually be a sign of successful representation. Put another way, if congressmen became more casual in their consideration of constituency views—for example, if representatives of liberal districts started acting like conservatives and vice versa—the polls might show much more evidence of constituency awareness and, on election day, more representatives would be defeated. David Mayhew puts it this way:

> When we say "Congressman Smith is unbeatable," we do not mean there is nothing he could do that would lose him his seat. Rather we mean, 'Congressman Smith is unbeatable as long as he continues to do the things he is doing.' If he stopped answering his mail, or stopped visiting his district, or began voting randomly on roll calls, or shifted his vote record eighty points on the ADA scale, he would bring on primary or November election troubles in a hurry."[73]

Third, one should note that there does exist a sprinkling of informed voters who shift their political weight according to the policy views of the candidates. Even if these alert voters comprise a tiny fraction of the total, their opinion leadership allows them to influence election outcomes to an extent beyond what their numbers would indicate. As information about the congressman diffuses downward from relatively informed opinion leaders to the mass public, many voters may "get simple positive or negative cues about the Congressman which were provoked by his legislative actions but no longer have a recognizable policy content," as Miller and Stokes suggest.[74] By responding to such cues, a significant number of voters may act as if they are relatively informed about their congressman's record. As a result, the collective electoral decisions in congressional contests may be more responsive to roll-call records than our knowledge about individual voters would indicate.

In the previous chapter, we saw that the result of this process is visible in election returns. Congressmen lose votes when they take ideologically extreme public positions. Normally, a congressman's vote loss due to policy stands is not sufficient for defeat, since he or she is often protected by a modest incumbency advantage and a one-party district. But the few who do lose can often blame their own policy stands for their misfortune. The role of issues in determining defeat or victory is clearest for Republicans—those who lose tend to represent the more conservative wing of their party. Consider 1974, when Watergate contributed to an unusually high 22 percent defeat rate for Republican incumbent candidates in the House. Casualties were a heavy 35 percent among the 48 Republicans with voting recores of 90 percent or more conservative by the ACA/ADA index. In contrast, the 47 most moderate Republicans with voting records of less than 75 percent conservative were fairly immune, with a loss rate of only 8.5 percent.[75] Back in 1964, when better than one quarter of the northern Republican House members who sought re-election were rejected by the voters in the anti-Goldwater tide, most of the losers were archconservatives. For example, 41 percent of the 37 northern incumbent candidates who signed a preconvention statement promoting Goldwater's conservative presidential candidacy went down to defeat themselves in November 1964. In contrast, only 12 percent of the 33 northern Republican House members who publicly disassociated themselves from the Goldwater candidacy by accepting the support of the liberal "Committee to Support Modern Republicanism" lost their re-election bids.[76] The public's ideological selectivity when determining which Republican House members it will defeat has, therefore, had a moderating or liberalizing effect on the Republican House membership. If conservative and moderate Republicans lost re-election bids at equal rates, House Republicans would, as a group, be more conservative than they are.

8-5 CONCLUSION

In this chapter we have examined some of the possible factors that could compel the policy maker to make decisions that are congruent with public opinion. Complete understanding of the linkage between public opinion and policy is beyond the present knowledge of political scientists. Here we can report the results of one study that did attempt to measure the overall linkage between policy decisions and constituency preferences. Once more, we are referring to Miller and Stokes' representation study. Figure 8-7 shows the correlations found between constituencies' preferences and the roll-call decisions for their congressmen, in addition to the correlations between the various links in the chains we have already examined. The relationship between constituency attitudes and the roll-call result is moderately high on civil rights ($+.65$), modest on social welfare ($+.38$), and almost non-existent on foreign policy ($+.19$). Given the public's disinterest in foreign policy details, particularly in the pre-Vietnam era when this study was conducted, the latter correlation is hardly surprising.

Since the number of voters whose views were sampled is very low in many of the districts examined, there is reason to believe that constituency opinion is actually more strongly related to roll call behavior than Miller and Stokes' reported correlations would suggest.[77] The strength of Miller and Stokes' analysis is their statistical assessment of the source of the linkage that does exist between constituency preferences and roll-call behavior. Across all three issue domains examined, the congressmen prove as likely to vote their perceptions of constituency attitudes as they are to vote their own attitudes. The next question is whether constituencies influence roll-call be-

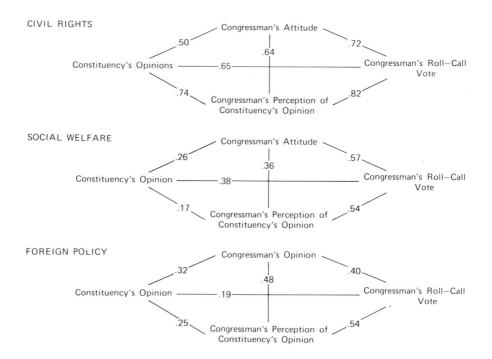

Figure 8-7. The relationship between congressmen's opinions, perception of constituency's opinions, constituency's opinions, and the congressman's vote. (*Source.* 1958 Survey Research Center study of representation. From personal correspondence with project director.)

havior because congressmen accurately perceive constituency positions or because constituency opinion somehow influences congressional attitudes. Using a statistical procedure known as "path analysis," Miller and Stokes report that in the area of civil rights, the major source of linkage is the congressman's responsiveness to correctly perceived constituency opinion. In the area of social welfare, they report the major source of linkage is that congressmen tend to share the same views as their constituents.[78] One reason for the modest linkage between constituency attitudes and congressional attitudes is that candidates tend to share the views of the constituencies that they hope to represent. But the electoral process provides one additional reason: When given a choice between candidates, constituencies tend to elect the candidate who best represents their views.[79]

This chapter has dealt with the representative as an individual who is faced with the task of participating in the making of public policy and who must act as the spokesman for his or her constituency. Despite substantial research, many questions remain concerning the representative's resolution of how and when to weigh public opinion in the decision-making process.

The simple alternatives of trustee and delegate are devoid of subtlety, and probably unrealistic for the problems faced by the representative. Furthermore, the device for assuring representative accountability—public elections—fails to threaten those holding safe seats and those lacking ambition for continued public service. While accountability via elections may not always be fulfilled, the knowledge that elected officials occasionally get defeated may buttress the representative's desire to represent. Similarly, the civicly motivated representative, while not fearing electoral defeat, may be offended by the charge that he or she misrepresents constituents, and therefore, would also try to weigh public opinion when making decisions.

But whatever the differences in and motivations of representatives, the opinion they holds as well as the opinions of those surrounding them may be uncharacteristic of public opinion. When specifically charged to do so, both congressmen and legislators prove able to assess constituency opinions with only modest accuracy. Even more difficult is predicting whose opinion within that public will most affect the probability of re-election. Contributor opinion, attentive voter opinion, and mass opinion may differ greatly. Each may see the political world from a different perspective.

If elections served as mandates to representatives for public wants on each legislative program, the difficult process of learning constituency opinion would be unnecessary. Representatives could choose when to reflect public opinion with the complete confidence that they understood it, and they would be confident that heeding this public opinion will ensure future support. But the public's votes in elections depend on many factors beside the support for the positions the winner might have taken during the campaign or while in office. And once in office, even the most strongly motivated, responsive representative faces the difficult process of learning the constituency's wishes.

FOOTNOTES FOR CHAPTER 8

1. Kenneth Prewitt, *The Recruitment of Political Leaders: A Study of Citizen Politicians* (New York: Bobbs-Merrill, 1970). p. 66.

2. Ibid., p. 61

3. James David Barber, *The Lawmakers* (New Haven: Yale University Press, 1965).

4. On the social and economic characteristics of American legislators see Malcolm Jewell and Samuel Patterson, *The Legislative Process in the United States* (New York: Random House, 1966), pp. 106–118; Suzanne Keller, *Beyond the Ruling Class* (New York: Random House, 1963); Prewitt, *The Recruitment of Political Leaders*, Chapter 2; and Roger H. Davidson, *The Role of the Congressman* (New York: Pegasus, 1969). pp. 34–71.

5. Stein Rokkan and Angus Campbell, "Citizen Participation in Political Life: Norway and the United States of America," *International Social Science Journal*, 12 (1960), pp. 69–99.

6. Leon D. Epstein, *Political Parties in Western Democracies* (New York: Praeger, 1967), pp. 167–200.

7. For example, 31 percent of the delegates had family incomes of $25,000 or more in comparison to 5 percent for the nation at large. *Source:* Haynes Johnson, "A Portrait of Democrats' New Delegates," *Washington Post,* July 8, 1972. p. A-1.

8. Seymour Martin Lipset, *Agrarian Socialism* (Berkeley: University of California Press, 1950). p. 166.

9. Within state legislatures, lawyers more frequently vote against no-fault insurance than do not-lawyers. See James A. Dyer, "Do Lawyers Vote Differently? A Study of Voting on No-Fault Insurance," *Journal of Politics,* 38 (May, 1976), pp. 452–456.

10. Within the public, 47 percent of the Democrats and 35 percent of the Republicans favored an increase in "tax on large incomes." Among Convention delegates, only 27 percent of the Democrats and 5 percent of the Republicans did so. Similar breaks were found on the issues of "corporate income tax" and "tax on business." *Source:* Herbert McClosky, Paul J. Hoffman, and Rosemary O'Hara, "Issue Conflict and Consensus Among Party Leaders and Followers," *American Political Science Review,* 54 (June 1960), p. 414.

11. Norman R. Luttbeg, "The Representative Quality of Community Leaders' Policy Preferences: A Study of Prevalent Assumptions," *Research Reports in Social Science,* 12 No. 2 (August 1969), pp. 1–25.

12. V.O. Key, *Public Opinion and American Democracy* (New York: Knopf, 1961), p. 547.

13. In 1970, U.S. senators were also interviewed. Senators displayed slightly more liberal views than either the public or the House members. For an analysis of the 1970 findings, see Charles H. Backstrom, "Congress and the Public: How Representative is One of the Other?" *American Politics Quarterly,* 5 (October 1977), pp. 411–436. For an analysis of the 1978 data, see Kathleen A. Frankovic and Laurily K. Epstein, "Congress and its Constituency: The New Machine Politics," paper presented at the 1979 American Political Science Association convention, Washington, D.C., September 1979.

14. Warren E. Miller and Donald E. Stokes, "Constituency Influence in Congress," *American Political Science Review,* 57 (March 1963), pp. 45–56.

15. Christopher Achen, "Measuring Representation: Perils of the Correlation Coefficient," *American Journal of Political Science,* 21 (November 1977), pp. 805–815.

16. To understand why constituency opinion correlates more positively with the attitudes of congressional winners than with the attitudes of congressional losers, one must remember that constituency electorates determine which candidates become winners and which candidates become losers. In other words, the positive relationship between constituency opinion and the attitudes of winning candidates is enhanced by the choices that constituencies make at the polls.

17. V. O. Key, "Public Opinion and the Decay of Democracy," *Virginia Quarterly Review,* 37 (Autumn 1961), p. 490.

18. John C. Wahlke, et al *The Legislative System* (New York: Wiley, 1962), p. 73

19. Davidson, *The Roll of the Congressman,* p. 128.

20. James H. Kuklinski with Richard C. Elling, "Representative Role, Constituency Opinion, and Legislative Roll Call Behavior," *American Journal of Political Science,* 21 (February 1977), pp. 135–147; Donald J. McCrone and James H. Kuklinski, "The Delegate Theory of Representation," *American Journal of Political Science,* 23 (May 1979). For contrary findings in the Iowa setting, see Ronald D. Hedlund and H. Paul Friesema, "Representatives' Perceptions of Constituency Opinion," in Norman R. Luttbeg (ed.) *Public Opinion and Public Policy,* 2nd ed, (Homewood, Ill.: Dorsey Press, 1974), pp. 390–412. Hedlund and Friesema report the counter-intuitive finding that self-designated trustees had more accurate perceptions of constituency opinion than did self-designated delegates. This same pattern is reported from a Florida

study. See Robert S. Erikson, Norman R. Luttbeg, and William V. Holloway, "Knowing One's District: How Legislators Predict Referendum Voting," *American Journal of Political Science*, 19 (May 1975), pp. 231–246.

21. Donald E. Stokes and Warren E. Miller, "Party Government and the Saliency of Congress," *Public Opinion Quarterly*, 26 (Winter 1962) p. 542.

22. John W. Kingdon, *Candidates for Office: Beliefs and Strategies* (New York: Random House, 1966, p. 24.

23. Ibid., p. 31.

24. Charles L. Clapp, *The Congressman: His Work as He Sees It* (Garden City: Doubleday, 1963), pp. 111–113.

25. Ibid pp. 420–428; See also, Lewis, Anthony Dexter, *The Sociology and Politics of Congress* (Chicago: Rand McNally, 1967), Chapter 8.

26. James H. Kuklinski, "Representativeness and Elections: A Policy Analysis," *American Political Science Review*, 72 (March 1978), pp. 165–177.

27. For Figure 8-3, roll call ideology is measured by the average of the member's support for the liberal position of the Americans for Democratic Action and the member's nonsupport for the conservative position of the Americans for constitutional action.

28. On the relationship between presidential voting in the district and the Representative's roll-call behavior, see John E. Schwartz and Barton Fenmore, "Presidential Election Results and Congressional Roll Call Behavior," *Legislative Studies Quarterly*, 2 (November 1977), pp. 405–422; and Robert S. Erikson and Gerald C. Wright, Jr., "Electoral Marginality and Congressional Representation," paper presented at the 1978 Convention of the American Political Science Association meetings.

29. John W. Kingdon, *Congressmen's Voting Decisions* (New York: Harper and Row, 1973).

30. David R. Mayhew, *Congress: The Electoral Connection*, (New Haven: Yale University Press, 1974).

31. Richard F. Fenno, Jr., *Home Style: House Members in their Districts* (Boston: Little Brown, 1978).

32. Morris P. Fiorina, *Congress: Keystone of the Washington Establishment* (New Haven: Yale University Press, 1977).

33. Over recent years, the electoral advantage in House elections that accrues from being an incumbent has been increasing. See David Mayhew, "Congressional Elections: The Case of the Vanishing Marginals," *Polity*, 6 (Spring 1974), pp. 295–317. For an exploration of the reasons for the concomitant declining popularity of Congress as an institution, see Glen R. Parker, "Some Themes in Congressional Unpopularity." *American Journal of Political Science*, 21 (February 1977), pp. 93–110.

34. For a discussion of the advantages and disadvantages of the two-year term of congressional office, see Charles O. Jones, *Every Second Year: Congressional Behavior and the Two-Year Term* (Washington: The Brookings Institution, 1967).

35. Key, "Public Opinion and the Decay of Democracy," p. 490.

36. Joseph Schlesinger, *Ambition and Politics* (Chicago: Rand McNally, 1966), p. 2.

37. Computed for *Congressional Quarterly* sources.

38. H. Douglas Price, "The Congressional Career—Then and Now," in Nelson W. Polsby (ed.), *Congressional Behavior* (New York: Random House, 1971), pp. 14–27.

39. Prewitt, *The Recruitment of Political Leaders* pp. 176–177, Prewitt suggests (p. 201) that the rate of indifference to re-election among the councilmen studied, is in the neighborhood of 50 percent.

40. David Ray, "Voluntary Retirement and Electoral Defeat in Eight State Legislatures," *Journal of Politics*, 38 (May 1976), pp. 426—433.

41. Prewitt, *The Recruitment of Political Leaders* p. 86.

42. V. O. Key, *Public Opinion and American Democracy*, p. 538.

43. Reports on the frequency of congressional polling can be found in Walter Wilcox, "The Congressional Poll and non-Poll," in Edward C. Dreyer and Walter A. Rosenbaum (eds.) *Political Opinion and Behavior*, 2nd ed., (Belmont, California: Wadsworth, 1970); tabulation by John E. Saloma III, reported in Donald D. Tacheron and Morris K. Udall, *The Job of the Congressman* (New York: Bobbs-Merrill, 1966), p. 288; and Lester Markel, *What You Don't Know Can Hurt You* (Washington: Pacific Affairs Press, 1972), p. 258.

44. Tacheron and Udall, *The Job of the Congressman*, p. 288.

45. Richard A. Brody and Edward R. Tufte, "Constituent-Congressional Communication on Fallout Shelters: The Congressional Polls," *Journal of Communication*, 14 (January 1964), pp. 34—49.

46. Ronald D. Hedlund, "Perceptions of Decisional Referents in Legislative Decision-Making," *American Journal of Political Science*, 19 (August 1975), pp. 527—542.

47. Robert L. Crain, Elihu Katz, and Donald B. Rosenthal, *The Politics of Community Conflict: The Fluoridation Decision* (Indianapolis: Bobbs-Merrill, 1969), p. 138.

48. For a lively account of McCarthy's rise and fall, see Richard H. Rovere, *Senator Joe McCarthy* (New York: Meridian Books, 1960).

49. Nelson W. Polsby, "Toward An Explanation of McCarthyism," *Political Studies* 18 (October 1960), pp. 250—271.

50. Erikson, Luttbeg, and Holloway, "Knowing One's District."

51. Kingdon, *Candidates for Office*, pp. 44—81.

52. For one account of how Congressmen view their mail see Lewis Anthony Dexter, "What Do Congressmen Hear? The Mail," *Public Opinion Quarterly*, 20 (Spring 1956), pp. 16—27.

53. Leila Sussman, "Mass Political Letter Writing in America: The Growth of an Institution," *Public Opinion Quarterly*, 23 (Summer 1959), pp. 203—212.

54. Key, *Public Opinion and American Democracy*, p. 418.

55. Philip E. Converse, Aage R. Clausen, and Warren E. Miller, "Electoral Myth and Reality: The 1964 Election," *American Political Science Review*, 59 (June 1965).

56. Sidney Verba and Richard Brody, "Participation, Policy Preferences, and the War in Viet Nam," *Public Opinion Quarterly*, 34 (Fall 1970), pp. 325—332.

57. One recent study of writers of Letters-to-the-Editor (not writers of letters to public officials) suggests that this group is not particularly unrepresentative of the population in their political viewpoints. See Emmett H. Buell, Jr., "Eccentrics of Gladiators? People Who Write about Politics in Letters-to-the-Editor," *Social Science Quarterly*, 56 (December 1975), pp. 440-449.

58. G. R. Boynton, Samuel C. Patterson, and Ronald D. Hedlund, "The Missing Links in Legislative Politics: Attentive Constituents," *Journal of Politics*, 31 (August 1969), pp. 700—721.

59. Robert S. Erikson, "Constituency Opinion and Congressional Behavior: A Reexamination of the Miller-Stokes Representation Data," *American Journal of Political Science*, 22 (August 1978), pp. 511—535.

60. Ronald D. Hedlund and H. Paul Friesema, "Representatives' Perceptions of Constituency Opinion," *Journal of Politics*, 34 (August 1972).

61. Erikson, Luttbeg, and Holloway, "Knowing One's District."

62. Computed from *Congressional Quarterly* sources. The success rate of incumbents who seek re-election for low-level offices has not adequately been explored. David Ray, however, has discovered the rather surprising finding that electoral defeat accounts for about half of the turnover in state legislatures. In 1967, the average re-election rate of incumbent candidates for the state legislature in eight states was 87 percent. For earlier elections, the re-election rate was somewhat lower. (Ray, "Voluntary Retirement and Electoral Defeat in Eight State Legislatures.") Among the Bay Area councilmen, the return rate was 80 percent, with considerable variation between cities. (Prewitt, *The Recruitment of Political Leaders* pp. 137–138.)

63. Elections for governor (the second most visible office to most voters, after the presidency) have been the focus of surprisingly little systematic study. Turett has shown that the governor's vote margin generally goes down with each term he survives. See J. Stephen Turett, "The Vulnerability of American Governors, 1900–1969," *Midwest Journal of Political Science*, 15 (February 1971), pp. 108–132. The source of this vulnerability is little understood. Pomper has shown that there is no statistical evidence to bolster the common-sense notion that governors lose votes when they raise state taxes. See Gerald W. Pomper, *Elections in America* (New York: Dodd, Mead, 1969), pp. 126–148. Piereson has shown that in recent years, outcomes of gubernatorial elections have become less dependent on the relative party strengths in the states. See James E. Piereson, "Sources of Candidate Success in Gubernatorial Elections, 1910–1970," *Journal of Politics*, 39 (November 1977), 939–959.

64. Stokes and Miller, "Constituency Influence in Congress," p. 537.

65. Following the 1966 election, 44 percent said the Republicans has "elected the most Congressmen"; 21 percent said the Democrats did; the remainder said they did not know. *Source:* Survey Research Center, 1966 Election Study Codebook, p. 76.

66. Roger H. Davidson, David M. Kovenock, and Michael K. O'Leary, *Congress in Crisis: Politics and Congressional Reform*, (Belmont, Calif.: Wadsworth, 1968) pp. 60–63.

67. Part of the Miller-Stokes representation study was intended to be an examination of local newspapers coverage of congressional campaigns. But this aspect was dropped when the discovery was made that campaign information was "printed *only* sporadically and then was usually buried in such a remote section of the paper that the item would go unheeded by all but the most avid readers of political news." See Philip E. Converse, "Information Flow and the Stability of Partisan Attitudes," *Public Opinion Quarterly*, 26 (Winter 1962), p. 587n.

68. Stokes and Miller, "Constituency Influence in Congress," pp. 536–540.

69. Barbara Hinkley, "Issues, Information Costs, and Congressional Elections," *American Politics Quarterly*, 4 (April 1976), pp. 131–152; Alan I. Abromowitz, "Name Familiarity, Reputation, and the Incumbency Effect in Congressional Elections," *Western Political Quarterly*, 28 (September 1975), pp. 558–684.

70. Close inspection of Table 8-7 shows a minority must have been aware of their congressman's SST vote: the perception that one's congressman opposed the SST rose when the congressman actually did so. Still even SST proponents were more often seen by their constituents as opponents than as supporters. Since most voters opposed the SST themselves, they may have "projected" this preference onto their congressman.

71. Miller and Stokes, "Constituency Influence in Congress" p. 54.

72. Robert S. Erikson, "Is There Such a Thing as a Safe Seat?" *Polity*, 8 (Summer 1976), pp. 623–632. A relevant unpublished paper is Robert Weissberg, "Congressional Elections as Random Terror."

73. Mayhew, *Congress: The Electoral Connection*, p. 37.

74. Miller and Stokes, "Constituency Influence in Congress", p. 55.

75. Walter Dean Burnham, "Insulation and Responsiveness in Congressional Elections," *Political Science Quarterly*, 90 (Fall 1975), pp. 411–436.

76. *1964 Congressional Quarterly Almanac,* pp. 1014, 2578–80; *Congressional Quarterly,* (June 19, 1964), p. 1216. See also Robert A. Schoenberger, "Campaign Strategy and Party Loyalty: The Electoral Relevance of Candidate Decision Making in the 1964 Congressional Elections," *American Political Science Review,* 63 (June 1969), pp. 515–520.

77. Erikson, "Constituency Opinion".

78. Miller and Stokes, "Constituency Influence in Congress," pp. 51–56.

79. Erikson, "Constituency Opinion".

CHAPTER 9

Parties and Pressure Groups: Mediating Institutions and Representation

Democratic theorists concerned with the political linkage between public opinion and the behavior of elected leaders often posit an important role for the mediating institutions of political parties and pressure groups. In its own way, each of these institutions can provide a means for a less than fully attentive public to attain its desired policy goals. If political parties take distinctive stands on issues, party labels provide a mechanism for voters to elect government leaders in accord with their own views. Pressure groups have resources at their disposal which are not normally available to the mass public. To the extent pressure groups reflect public opinion, their vigilant eye on the behavior of elected officials can help promote accountability. We begin our discussion with political parties.

9-1 POLITICAL PARTIES AND REPRESENTATION

According to the Political Parties Model, party labels clarify the political choices available to the voters. First, each political party would outline the program it would enact its candidates were elected; thus the candidates' party labels signify what they will do if elected. Second, each voter would make his selection at the polls on the basis of the party that best represented his views. This model simplifies the task of the policy-oriented voter. Instead of monitoring each candidate's campaign statements and hoping that they reflect what the candidates would do if elected, the voter would need only to learn the differences between the parties' programs and use party labels as a cue to rational voting.[1]

We have seen that voters do not always behave according to the prescription of the Political Parties Model. Although most voters identify with a political party and party identifiers generally vote for their party's candidates, as we saw in Chapter 3, there is only a modest tendency for Republican and Democratic identifiers to differ from one another on issues. Moreover, voters perceive only modest policy differences between the two major parties. Thus, party voting by the mass public only to a limited degree can be considered policy voting.

Whether voters are rational in selecting candidates on the basis of party labels depends on the differences between the programs of the two parties. Strong party voting is not meaningful if the policies of the two parties are indistinguishable. Only when parties offer different programs does the public have a valuable guide to voting. Here, we examine the extent to which Republican and Democratic leaders actually differ in their policy preferences and in their behavior in office.

Ideological Differences Between Republican and Democratic Leaders

Do the labels "Democratic" and "Republican" signify anything about the policy preferences of party leaders? Typically, one associates Republicans with the conservative ideological viewpoint and Democrats with the liberal viewpoint. Although ideology is not a major source of partisan division between Republican and Democratic voters, one might suspect that ideology motivates the party choice of the political activists who become the leaders of their party. However, noting the pragmatism and singular interest in winning office of American political parties as compared with the ideological and often well-disciplined European parties, many observers see American parties as devoid of ideological purpose and program. As we will see, the proper view of the policy option that American political parties offer lies between the two extremes. Although the Republicans and Democrats seldom offer the public a clear set of policy alternatives, the partisan affiliation of a political leader provides some clues about personal policy preferences and behavior.

The earliest comparison of the personal beliefs of Republican and Democratic leaders is a study by Herbert McClosky, Paul Hoffman, and Rosemary O'Hara.[2] In 1957 and 1958 they gathered identical kinds of data from a public sample of supporters of the political parties and from delegates to the 1956 political party conventions. For each of 24 policy issues the researchers reported the percentages of both leaders and followers preferring an increased government commitment. They found that issue differences were greater between Republican and Democratic convention delegates than between Republican and Democratic party identifiers: Republican delegates were farther to the right than Republican identifiers, while Democratic delegates were farther to the left than Democratic identifiers. Interestingly, Democratic delegates were closer to Democratic identifiers on the issues than Republican delegates were to Republican identifiers. In fact, on the average across the issues, Republican delegates were less representative of Republican iden-

tifiers than Democratic delegates were representative of Republican identifiers. As McClosky, et al note, "Republican leaders are separated not only
from the Democrats (both leaders and followers) but from their own rank
and file members as well.[3]

Although the McClosky et al study is the most thorough comparison of
convention delegates and party rank-and-file, it was conducted more than
two decades ago. Studies of delegates to the 1972 party conventions suggest
that the Democratic rather than the Republican delegates were the least representative of the views of party rank-and-file. For example, majorities of
Democratic delegates to the 1972 convention that nominated McGovern for
president favored such policies as busing for racial balance, marijuana legalization, abortion upon demand, amnesty for draft evaders, and a guaranteed
annual income, which were opposed by most Democratic as well as most
Republican identifiers at the time.[4] In fact, in 1972 Democratic identifiers
were closer to the Republican than to the Democratic delegates on the issues—the exact reverse of the 1956 pattern.[5] Republican delegates, however, were still more conservative than the Republican rank-and-file.

Other studies report that policy difference between Democratic and
Republican activists at a lower level in the party hierarchy than national
convention delegates are greater than those between the two parties' rank-
and-file voters.[6] Figure 9-1 shows the changing differences between each
partys' ordinary identifiers and its activists (defined as partisans who scored

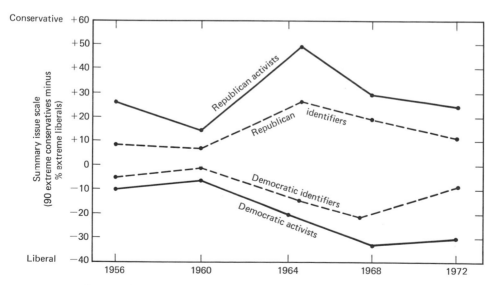

Figure 9-1. Policy positions of party activists identifiers, 1956–1972. [Adapted from Norman H.
Nie, Sidney Verba, and John R. Petrosik *The Changing American Voter* (Cambridge: Harvard
University Press, 1976), Figure 12-3, p. 203.]

very high on an index of campaign activity) for each presidential election year from 1956 through 1972. The data are consistent with the studies of convention delegates. Although the gap was once greatest between the views of Republican activities and identifiers, in 1972 it was between Democratic activists and identifiers. In each comparison of the four groups, the Republican activists are the most conservative and the Democratic activists the most liberal.

People often say that to win elections, political parties must appeal to the moderate voter. But to win elections, parties must also appeal to their loyal activists who, as we have seen, tend to represent their parties' extreme. The party leaders' dilemma is, as David Butler states, "to conciliate those who support them with money or with voluntary work, without alienating that large body of moderate voters whose attitudes make them more likely to swing to the other party."[7] Additionally, while the classic role of party leader is to do what is pragmatically necessary for winning elections, party activists may be more concerned with ideological correctness than with electoral victory. Increasingly, with the decline of traditional party organizations and the growing openness of party conventions brought about by recent reforms of party rules, ideologues are moving into party leadership positions and determining the nominations of party candidates. There is an irony here. As the leadership structures of the political parties are becoming more democratic, the potential for greater policy choice between the parties is created. This results in greater differences between the parties' policies and the preferences of their rank-and-file supporters.

The Relevance of Party Platforms

At national conventions every four years, each party devotes considerable time to spelling out the details of its platform to form the party's "official" position on the issues of the day. Party platforms are often dismissed as mere ritualistic documents since they are rarely read, quickly forgotten, and not officially binding on a party's candidates. Nevertheless, as research by Gerald Pomper and by Benjamin Ginsberg shows, careful readings of party platforms provides some clue to what the parties would do if they came to power.

Pomper examined the content of the Democratic and Republican platforms from 1944 to 1964.[8] Table 9-1 presents his evaluation of the content of these twelve platforms. At one extreme are such statements as platitudes applauding American uniqueness ("The American Free Enterprise System is one of the great achievements of humankind and spirit") or statements about the issues but with unclear meanings ("The Anti-Trust Laws must be vigorously enforced"). The bottom three categories of statements listed in the table, however, provide information on the policies the parties intend to

Table 9-1 Content of Party Platforms (in Percentages of Total Platform)

	Dem. 1944	Rep. 1944	Dem. 1948	Rep. 1948	Dem. 1952	Rep. 1952	Dem. 1956	Rep. 1956	Dem. 1960	Rep. 1960	Dem. 1964	Rep. 1964
Unusable in the Parties Model												
General Rhetoric	22	11	12	23	18	9	14	15	20	21	20	11
General Approval	23	3	11	3	11	3	5	15	4	7	14	5
General Criticism	0	7	3	4	1	18	11	4	7	1	1	12
Policy Rhetoric	17	24	17	32	22	20	15	14	20	16	5	16
Usable in the Parties Model												
Policy Approval	13	2	10	8	16	11	9	26	4	13	48	2
Policy Criticism	0	10	8	1	3	14	17	2	11	1	1	25
Fairly Detailed Policy Positions	25	44	39	29	29	25	29	24	33	40	10	28
Percent of Platform												
Consistent with Model	38	56	57	38	48	50	55	52	48	54	59	55

Source. Data recomputed from Gerald M. Pomper, *Elections in America: Control and Influence in Democratic Politics* (New York: Dodd, Mead, 1968) pp. 159, 164, and 176.

implement or have already implemented and thus are consistent with the parties model. Policy approval statements, for example, include, "In the Nuclear Test Ban Treaty, we have written our commitment to limitations on the arms race," and a detailed policy position is, "The security of the American Trade Unions must be strengthened by repealing section 14B of the Taft-Hartley Act." Pomper notes the Republicans emphasize defense and government issues while the Democrats stress labor and welfare issues, but neither party proves deficient in providing a meaningful platform for voter evaluation. Typically the parties' platforms include about one statement in five that state an evaluation of past policies and about three in ten that offer fairly detaided information on the party's policy intention. Although the platforms are seldom read, platform statements reach voters indirectly, "through interests groups, mass media, candidates' speeches, and incomplete popular perceptions."9

We must also consider whether parties keep their policy promises once in office. Although the answer to this question involves many complexities, Pomper offers a "bottom line" count of the frequency with which the detailed policy pledges in party platforms are successfully implemented by actions of Congress or the president during the following four years. Even though elected leaders are free to ignore their party's platforms if they so desire, Pomper finds that almost three-quarters of all policy promises are kept, with the remainder defeated or ignored. Not unexpectedly, the party holding the presidency experiences much greater success in achieving its platform promises, succeeding four out of five times as compared with the better than 50 percent success of the out party. Many of these successes, of course, occur when both parties promise the same thing. In the crucial instances when the two parties take opposite platform stands on an issue, Pomper finds that the party controlling the presidency achieves its pledge with at least partial success 80 percent of the time, while the out-party is at least partially successful 18 percent of the time. The remaining 2 percent are cases of non-action.10

Pomper's data should not be given extreme interpretations. Platforms serve as symbolic appeals to the elements of the party's coalition rather than as ideological dogma. But the platforms are far from meaningless rhetoric since three-fourths of the policy pledges are fulfilled. Policy pledges constitute only 27 percent of the statements in the platforms and the parties take alternative stands on only 10 percent of these pledges. Thus fewer than 3 percent of all platform statements afford the voter a clear choice of alternative partisan positions.11 Pomper finds a middle ground, rejecting both the conclusion that platforms are irrelevant rhetoric and that they are "inspired gospel to which the politicians resort for policy guidance."12

Pomper's findings are paralleled by Benjamin Ginsberg's study of party platforms. Ginsberg attempts to quantify the extent of party conflict between the two parties' platforms in each presidential year from the 1840s through 1968. He finds the highest amount of what he calls "critical conflict" during periods of partisan realignment—the 1850s, 1896, and 1932.[13] Periods with the greatest policy differences between the parties (measured from their platforms) are generally followed by short periods of unusually high policy change (measured by an index based on U.S. statutes).[14] Although Ginsberg's data contain elements of ambiguity, his interpretation is intriguing: When party platforms signify that voters are given a clear choice between widely divergent programs, their electoral verdict can determine the course of future policy.

Party Voting in Legislatures

Ideally, from the standpoint of the Political Parties Model, the electorally dominant party would not only have articulated a program that achieves voter approval, but would be in a position to enact that program once in power. The dominant congressional party, for example, would be able to enact its preferred legislation, particularly if the president is of the same party and gives encouragement. As is well known, however, events do not always work out this way in the American system. As the developments during the Carter Administration illustrate, the president often has difficulty pushing his proposals through Congress even when a decisive majority is of his party. For example, a Democratic president with a "liberal" program can find his policies blocked in Congress by the so-called "conservative coalition" of conservative Democrats (mainly Southerners) and Republicans.

Table 9-2 shows the party breakdown (Republicans, Northern Democrats, and Southern Democrats) in the U.S. House on selected key roll calls of 1977—the first year of the Carter Administration. On the first three issues shown (common-site picketing, defense spending, federal funding of abortions), the liberal side failed. On the final three issues shown (natural-gas regulation, the B-1 bomber, and the minimum wage), the liberal side prevailed. Although this table illustrates that neither party in Congress acts as an all-cohesive unit, it also shows that party affiliation can sometimes predict roll-call voting. Each of the six issues shown in Table 9-2 is a "party vote" (defined as a vote in which a majority of Democrats oppose a majority of Republicans). In modern Congresses, some 30 to 50 percent of roll-call votes are party votes.[15] On party votes, parties are only modestly cohesive: two-thirds of each party's members will generally vote with their party and one-third with the opposition.

Party voting in Congress is most prevalent on issues with a discernable liberal versus conservative content, especially those dealing with the government's role in the economy and social welfare legislation.[16] On virtually any congressional issue with some ideological content, supporters of the liberal

Table 9-2   Party Voting in the U. S. House of Representatives on Six Selected Roll Calls in 1977

		Republicans	Northern Democrats	Southern Democrats	All
Vote on Labor-backed bill to allow common-site picketing	For:	14	171	20	205
	Against:	129	23	65	217
Vote to raise defense spending from $116.2 billion to $120.3 billion	Against:	20	149	15	184
	For:	119	35	75	225
Vote to outlaw use of federal funds to pay for abortions, even if the mother's life is endangered	Against:	21	97	37	155
	For:	98	65	38	201
Vote on Carter-opposed amendment to energy bill that would end price regulation of newly discovered natural gas	Against:	17	169	41	227
	For:	127	25	47	199
Vote to cancel $1.4 billion appropriation for B-1 bomber	For:	33	145	24	202
	Against:	103	32	64	199
Vote to reduce minimum wage for young workers, 18 years or younger	Against:	12	156	43	211
	For:	130	53	47	210

Source. House Key Votes, 1977, *Congressional Quarterly* (December 31, 1977), pp. 2685 – 2688.

position are disproportionately Democratic and supporters of the conservative position are disproportionately Republican. In fact, party affiliation is generally considered to be the best predictor of the liberal or conservative tendency of a congressman's roll-call behavior. This is especially true if we exclude Southern congressmen, as in Figure 9-2. For Northern House members in 1977, this figure shows party differences in liberalism measured by ratings of ideological pressure group: The average of the member's support for the positions of the liberal Americans for Democratic Action and the member's opposition to positions of conservative Americans for Constitutional Action.

In state legislatures, the average rate of party voting is slightly higher than in Congress, but there is considerable variation.[17] While systematic party differences on issues are virtually non-existent in some state legislatures, in other legislatures, parties actually behave as somewhat disciplined units. The source of this occasional discipline sometimes is a powerful presiding

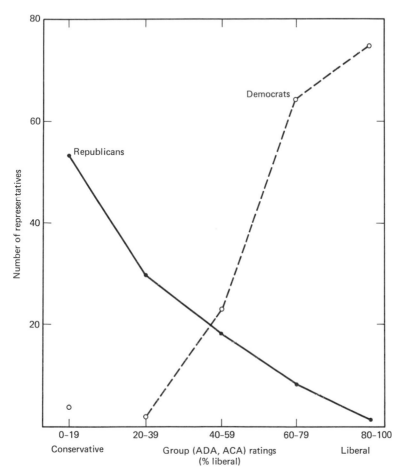

Figure 9-2. Liberalism-conservatism of northern Democrats and northern Republicans in the U.S. House of Representativies, 1976.

officer who can penalize members of his party for not supporting his positions, and sometimes is the party caucus. When a legislative party operates according to the "strong caucus" system, members of the party democratically decide a party position on certain issues, which is sometimes binding on its members.

Party discipline is seldom evident in Congress, because it is not in the members' interest: If all Republicans in Congress were forced to vote with their party's conservative majority and all Democrats were forced to vote with their party's liberal majority, many would be kicked out of office by their local constituencies.[18] Interestingly, however, congressional parties once acted as cohesive units. In the latter part of the nineteenth century, party discipline was maintained in the U.S. House because the Speaker of the House held broad powers over the members. When the Speaker's powers were diluted in the "revolution of 1910-11," power reverted for a short time to the parties' caucusses. Especially during Woodrow Wilson's Administration (1913-1920), each party's caucus regularly voted on issues and members were often bound (with the rarely exercised excuse of a matter of conscience) to vote for the majority position. The strong caucus system, however, was short-lived. Given the diversity of viewpoints within the congressional parties and a heightened sensitivity to constituency interests (due in part to increased congressional ambitions to stay elected), to hope that the strong caucus system would return in Congress would be unrealistic.

Party Labels as a Basis for Electoral Choice

As we have seen, there exists diversity both between and within congressional parties. Democrats and Republicans in Congress diverge on issues because within the political elite they tend to share different sets of values and ideologies.[19] But within each congressional party, there remains considerable diversity of viewpoint, largely because different members represent different kinds of constituencies.

At this point, we can consider the nature of the choice that congressional constituencies face when they elect congressional candidates. Their choice is not between the typical congressional Democrat and the typical congressional Republican, for the reason that congressional candidates often adjust their issue stances according to the prevailing constituency views. As a result, a liberal district will generally be given a choice between a relatively liberal Democrat and a relatively liberal Republican. Similarly, a conservative district will generally be given a choice between Democratic and Republican candidates who are both relatively conservative for their party. We are interested in the extent to which candidates at the district level diverge from each other and give the constituency voters a meaningful choice.

John Sullivan and Robert O'Connor demonstrate that U.S. House candidates at the district level offer a choice—at least in the 1966 election.[20] From a eight item questionnaire they ascertained the relative liberalism-conservatism of all major-party candidates running for the U.S. House in 1966. Comparing views of Republican and Democratic candidates the same district, they find that in only 19 of the 400 competitive races was the Republican more liberal than the Democratic. Upon entering Congress winning candidates generally voted consistently with the values expressed in their answers to the questionnaires. Thus, partisan differences appear to extend to actions in office as well as to personal beliefs.

Sullivan and O'Connor's evidence shows that voters are given a mechanism by which they can choose a candidate on the basis of policy issues without having to pay attention to the policy views of the particular candidates: "If a voter in 1966 wanted to vote conservatively, he only had to know that the Republican party is generally more conservative than the Democratic party in order to cast his ballot correctly in light of his values."21

Sullivan and O'Connor also compared the ideological distribution of the Congress actually elected with those of some hypothetical Congresses that could have been elected. Table 9-3 shows their findings for domestic (social welfare) issues. (Parallel findings—not shown here—were found on civil rights and foreign policy.) Comparison of the first two columns of the table shows there was no nationwide pattern of ideological choice since the winners' opinions cannot be distinguished from the losers'. At first glance, this might seem to indicate that the voters randomly select among liberal and conservative candidates. But the proper interpretation is that some districts regularly elect conservatives and others regularly elect liberals—resulting in an ideological standoff at the national level. The extent of the policy differences offered by the parties can be seen from the last four columns of the table. Hypothetical Congresses consisting of either available Democratic candidates or the most liberal candidates from each district would differ considerably from the most Republican or most conservative Congresses.22

Clearly, the parties present a meaningful policy choice to the public. For example, if the public desired a much more conservative Congress, they would simply need to elect a greater number of Republicans. Although the numbers of Republicans and Democrats in Congress will vary from one election to the next, these changes generally can be traced to such factors as economic conditions, presidential coattails, and Watergates; not to changes in policy preferences by the public. Yet the mechanism of choice is available if the public were to desire a policy shift in Congress. We can see the policy result of a large net shift in congressional party strength from the example of 1964. In that election, an unusually high number of Democrats were elected to Congress on the coattails of President Johnson's landslide victory. The combination of a large Democratic majority (in fact a Northern Democratic majority) and an activist president resulted in the passage of a lot of liberal legislation (Medicare, federal aid to education, the Voting Rights Act) that had been delayed for years.23 One can even speculate that a major partisan shift in Congress is a necessary condition for major policy change at the national level. Realigning elections provide a special case of electoral change producing policy changes that perhaps can be traced directly to public demands. Realigning elections—1896 and 1932 are the best examples—produce not only changes in the party strengths in Congress, but also increased cohesiveness within the dominant party.24

The assertion that parties provide a choice need not be restricted to the congressional arena. The party that wins the presidency is an obvious influ-

Table 9-3 Hypothetical Congresses—Domestic Policy Issues

Score	Winners	Unchallenged and Losers	Most Democratic[a]	Most Republican[a]	Most Liberal	Most Conservative
4 Liberals	79	57	129	7	130	6
5-6 Moderate-liberals	81	105	161	25	160	26
7-9 Moderates	43	85	64	64	67	61
10-11 Moderate-conservatives	70	90	28	132	33	128
12 Conservatives	162	98	53	207	45	214
	435	435	435	435	435	435
Mean	8.7	8.3	6.6	10.5	6.5	10.5
Median	10	8	6	11	6	11

Source. John L. Sullivan and Robert E. O'Connor, "Electoral Choice and Popular Control of Public Policy: The Case of the 1966 House Elections," *American Political Science Review* (December 1972) p. 1260.
[a]Most Democratic Congress includes Democrats plus unchallenged Republicans; most Republican Congress includes Republicans plus unchallenged Democrats.

ence on policy direction, even if the influence is not as great as the rhetoric of presidential campaigns would have us believe.[25] Also, the party in control can make a difference in government below the national level. For example although the statistical evidence is not clear on this point, a state will probably get more liberal policies if it elects a Democratic governor and legislature than if it puts Republicans in control.[26] The importance of parties is evident during circumstances when parties cease to play a meaningful role—either because elections are held on a truly non-partisan basis (as in many American cities) or because one party is totally moribund (as was once true in the South). In such settings, voters find it more difficult to get their preferred policies enacted and to hold leaders accountable for their actions.[27]

Conclusion. Many elements of the Political Parties Model are confirmed. Although neither the Republican nor the Democratic party is a disciplined organization, the leaders and activists within the two major parties are somewhat ideologically different from one another. The task of the party in assuring the elective representatives support for party positions is greatly facilitated by the similarity of opinion among its elected leaders that makes their action on the basis of their own beliefs quite compatible with party policy. The person with sufficient political motivation to work for a political party or to run for public office usually holds strong political views. The activist will normally choose to work within the political party that best represents his personal beliefs unless there is a compelling reason not to, such as the party being so weak locally that it has little chance for victory. Although candidates generally avoid their party's ideological extreme in order to get elected, their own strong views and those of their ideologue supporters help push their public positions away from the political center. Thus, the Republican and Democratic candidates will ordinarily offer the voter some choice of policies. Probably, party labels would supply voters with a still greater choice if the public shared the ideological commitment of partisan activists and candidates.

The choices that the parties presently afford the voters may be overly restrictive. In a typical partisan election, the voter is asked to choose between a somewhat liberal Democrat and a somewhat liberal Republican. The relatively few voters at the extreme left and extreme right may find this selection unsatisfactory. But any failure of the Political Parties Model appears to come more from the public's failure to respond to the choices offered by the political parties than from the parties' failure to satisfy the conditions of the model.

9-2 PRESSURE GROUPS AND REPRESENTATION

Like the Political Parties Model, the Pressure Groups Model allows for an intermediate agent (in this case groups) between individuals and their government leaders. Leaders, according to the model, can satisfy public opinion by responding to group pressures. Group members need not engage in extensive activity themselves, but can instead rely on their group's leaders and lobbyists to represent their interests. Members may be called upon, however, to contribute to the group's strength by giving money, writing letters to officials, demonstrating, or voting for the group's endorsed candidates.

For the model to work, the influence of different pressure groups should be in ratio to their membership and the intensity with which their views are held. Conflicting demands of different pressure groups might then result in a compromise with each side getting its way in proportion to the strength of its membership support.[28]

To evaluate the Pressure Groups Model, we need to know whether its suppositions are correct. First, in what ways can pressure groups get officeholders to respond to their demands? Unless combinations of individuals can influence policy by engaging in pressure group activity, the Model cannot work. Second, do the leaders of pressure groups know and support the preferences of their members? If there is no linkage between an organization's mass membership choices and the behavior of its leaders, pressure groups cannot furnish any linkage between public opinion and public policy. Third, to what extent does group opinion represent public opinion? The Model cannot hold if many individuals possess strong political views that are unexpressed by groups. If, as many suspect, certain pressure groups succeed for reasons other than a strong mass following, then public opinion is not being satisfied.

Pressure Group Influence

No scholar has attempted to give any kind of quantitative assessment of the net impact of pressure group activity on public policy, and offering one here would be beyond our capabilities. Although to assert that public policy is always (or most always) the result of group influence would be an overstatement, most observers agree that group influence in the policy process is considerable. While pressure groups are noted for their influence at the administrative level (the general public pays the least attention at the policy-implementation phase) their influence at the legislative level is of central concern here.

The possible sources of group influence are several. A group will be more influential if its lobbyists share the same values as the legislators with whom they interact, its lobbyists have relevant information to offer the legislature, or perhaps if its lobbyists are simply more visible than others. Everything being equal, legislators try to please interested parties, or at least those who do not alienate them. Other sources of pressure-group influence stem from groups' potential influence on the electoral process. Legislators tend to be more responsive to a group's interests if the group has contributed or will contribute money to their political campaigns. Also, the legislator will be more responsive if the group can give a creditable claim that it represents a sizeable and attentive voting block. In rare cases, a group may achieve influence by the anticipated threat that they can go over the legislature's head to influence the views and votes of the general public.

How important is lobbying activity in determining legislative outcomes? Despite obvious drawbacks, one way to try to answer this question is to ask legislators or lobbyists. When congressmen are asked to make such an assessment, they rank lobbying activity among the least important of possible influences on congressional decisions. For example, it is more influential than party leadership positions, but less important than constituency opinion.[29] Washington lobbyists also assess their influence as modest.[30] Ambiguous results are obtained from the responses of state-level legislators and lobbyists. For example, Table 9-4 shows the answers to questions about lobbyist influence, asked of both legislators and lobbyists in four states in a study by Harmon Zeigler and Michael Baer.[31] The table shows substantial numbers (but rarely a majority) of legislators admitting to at least occasional

Table 9-4   Extent of Influence: Percentages of Legislators and Lobbyists Believing Legislators Have Been "Frequently" or "Occasionally" Influenced

	Extent of Influence			
	Questioning a Previously Held Opinion (%)	Leaning More Toward the Views of the Lobbyist (%)	Changing from One Position to Another (%)	(N)
Massachusetts				
Legislators	34	31	20	(244)
Lobbyists	51	39	26	(185)
North Carolina				
Legislators	22	20	18	(164)
Lobbyists	76	70	39	(132)
Oregon				
Legislators	45	42	51	(84)
Lobbyists	79	52	41	(193)
Utah				
Legislators	32	38	42	(90)
Lobbyists	77	66	48	(134)

Source. Harmon Zeigler and Michael Baer, *Lobbying: Interaction and Influence in American State Legislatures* (Belmont, California: Wadsworth, 1969), p. 155.

influence by lobbyists. But this extent of perceived influence varies. In Oregon, for example, both legislators and lobbyists candidly admit to the influential role of lobbyists. For this and other reasons, Zeigler and Baer suggest the Pressure Group Model may be more viable in Oregon than in other states.

The strict lobbyist registration law in Iowa, that requires lobbyists to signify which bills they are interested in, gave Charles Wiggins and Samuel Skare an unusual opportunity to obtain hard evidence regarding lobbyist activity in that state.[32] Studying a randomly chosen 20 percent of the bills considered by the 1971 Iowa legislature, Wiggins and Skare found less lobbying activity than one might expect. About 25 percent of the bills had no groups listed as lobbyists and only 16 percent had more than four lobbying groups listed. On only 16 percent of the bills did different groups take conflicting opinions. Lobbyists were found to have only limited influence on passage. Although a mere 22 percent of bills passed when they were *opposed* by all interested lobbyists, the rate of passage was only slightly higher, 35 percent, when all interested lobbyists *favored* enactment. The positions of the governor and the majority party leader appeared to be more decisive than the lobbyist positions. One can certainly question whether Iowa is typical among American States, but in Iowa at least lobbyists have influence but do not shape all policy outcomes.

A more fruitful endeavor than attempting to assess the net impact of lobbying is to locate the *kinds* of issues on which lobbyists are most successful. Generally, a group will be most purposeful in its efforts (and perhaps successful) if its goal would greatly benefit the group and cost little to others.[33] Examples of such benefits include tax breaks, agricultural subsidies, oil import quotas, veterans' benefits, and tariffs on various commodities. Unfortunately, from the standpoint of the Pressure Group Model, the beneficiaries of such policies are "special interests" that cannot claim to represent public opinion. Narrow but specialized interests have an advantage not only because of their unity of purpose but also because the public is often not aware of them. This is not to say, however, that large mass-based groups cannot also be effective when they claim to represent significant segments of public opinion. Judged at least by the reports of lobbyists and legislators, the extent of a group's impact on public policy is often determined by the size of its membership and its electoral muscle.[34]

Groups sometimes attempt to influence policy by influencing election results or by mobilizing public support for their cause. These activities can have a direct and an indirect impact. When groups are able to elect their desired candidates or are able to influence the results of public referenda, their need for lobbying diminishes. But also, if the group's threat of imposing electoral sanctions on nonsupportive candidates is believable, this enhances their lobbying effectiveness as well.

Pressure groups are a major source of campaign contributions to political candidates. For example, via their subsidiary "political action committees" (PACs) in 1976 the AFL-CIO contributed $8.2 million to congressional candidates, while various business groups and corporations contributed $7.1 million.[35] The PAC of the American Medical Association added an additional $1.6 million to congressional campaign coffers.[36] Issue-oriented and ideological groups contribute as well. Although liberal groups (notably the National Committee for an Effective Congress) were once better financed than conservative ("New Right") groups, the latter appear to have caught up.[37] A group's rating may itself be an electoral factor. For example, although Environmental Action gives no money it regularly condemns twelve members of Congress to a hit list called the "dirty dozen," who are supposedly enemies of the environment. Although the causal connection cannot be proved, most of the House members named to this list since its origin in 1970 have left Congress.[38]

The apparent effect of group contributions to campaigns is mixed. The best study to date of the effect of campaign spending on House election outcomes suggests that incumbents' electoral success is not influenced by their rate of spending; but nonincumbent candidates' spending levels make considerable difference.[39] Moreover, the candidate's need for cash is most crucial at the nomination phase when he or she must establish initial credibility.

The crucial importance of group financing of campaigns is that except for the independently wealthy, all legislative candidates need contributions to spend the amount they believe necessary to run an effective campaign. U.S. House members, for example, spend about $60,000 on the average, per campaign, even though this amount may not be necessary. Nonincumbent House candidates generally must spend about twice this amount in order to have a chance at victory. While recent reform legislation has set a $5,000 per candidate limit on group contributions ($1,000 for individual contributors), this limit results in candidates seeking smaller amount from a wider range of sources. Although legislators may prefer to view their contributors as altruistic citizens most contributors regard their behavior as an investment. Otherwise, why would groups contribute to unopposed candidates or concentrate their contributions upon members of congressional committees that must pass upon legislation relevant to the group? Since contributions are often given in gratitude for legislative support for the group's position in the past rather than for explicit future favors, the legislator can enhance his expectation of future group support if he supports the group position in advance. But when groups donate to legislators who support their favored positions the causal connection is not always clear. As Carol Greenwald states, "in most cases the contribution suggests a close relationship between politician and interest group based on a shared identification of values, friends—indeed the common ground that led to contributions in the first place."[40]

While money buys *access*, the necessary entree to obtain a resceptive legis-lative audience, access does not always result in successful *influence*. As Greenwald states, "money alone cannot assure continued meaningful access to officials unless other factors such as commonality of interests, useful in-formation, and friendship develop to supplement the campaign donation.[41]

Beginning with the 1976 election, presidential campaigns are financed by the public, thereby reducing group influence at the presidential level. A pos-sible additional reform step will be public financing of congressional cam-paigns, and perhaps campaigns in some states. Such changes would reduce campaign finance as a potential source of group effectiveness. But those who follow pressure groups closely think these changes may not greatly diminish the role of groups in the policy process, since organized groups would still possess the advantage of information, expertise, and direct monitoring of government officials which the general public does not possess.[42]

In addition to giving campaign contributions, groups sometimes attempt to influence public opinion directly, via propaganda campaigns. The pressure groups with a large mass-membership base, such as labor unions, place the greatest emphasis on public relations as a technique for influencing legisla-tive and administrative action.[43] The public relations efforts of labor unions are largely aimed at influencing the opinions and voting behavior of its members. The success of these efforts are limited, but visible. For example, Table 9-5 shows that in the 1950s, rank and file AFL-CIO members were more opposed to the Taft-Hartley Act than their nonunionized counterparts of the same occupational class. But most union members either did not sup-port their union's views on Taft-Hartley, or failed to offer an opinion on this

Table 9-5   Opinions of Respondents in White-Collar and Blue-Collar Households with and without Union Members on Taft-Hartley Issue

Opinion	White-Collar[a]		Blue-Collar	
	Union[b]	Nonunion	Union	Nonunion
Repeal or change pro-labor	23%	12%	29%	10%
Leave as is or change pro-management	20	20	12	9
Change, NA how	22	25	18	9
No opinion	35	43	41	72
	100%	100%	100%	100%
N	60	413	333	292

Source. V. O. Key, Jr., *Public Opinion and American Democracy* (New York: Knopf, 1961), p. 509.
[a]That is, the head of the household of the respondent was white-collar: professional, business, or clerical.
[b]The respondent falls in the union column if he or she, or some other member of the household belongs to a union.

issue that stimulated such strong concern from union leadership. Union leaders also have some influence on the voting behavior of their members. The best study of union influence on member voting finds that union members are about 20 percent more likely to vote Democratic than the nonunion counterparts in similar life situations.[44] Also unions devote considerable effort to stimulating voter *turnout* among members.

Since most pressure groups do not have a large mass membership, their efforts to indoctrinate their members cannot affect the mass opinion distribution very much even if their indoctrination efforts are entirely successful. However, ordinary pressure groups often spend vast amounts of money to influence the opinion of the general public. Such efforts hold the greatest promise of immediate rewards to the group when the public affects policy directly via referendum. Since public opinion on an issue is largely unformed at the time it is put to a referendum, the propaganda effort of interested pressure groups can sometimes greatly influence the outcome. For example, flouridation referenda often go down to defeat, even though most people favor fluoridated water at times when it is not a "hot" issue in their community. Largely responsible for fluoridation defeats is the fear-exploiting propaganda of the antifluoridation forces, which overcome the more "establishment-oriented" propaganda from the other side. Facing a referendum decision on fluoridation, the previously uninvolved voter may ask a friend for the pros and cons and be told that one side says fluoridation minimizes tooth decay, while the other side says it causes unanticipated medical hazards and, besides, may be the first step toward the poisoning of our water supply by the Communists. Not being able to sort out the credibility of the arguments, our voter will assign them equal weight and go for the one that promises the least risk.[45]

The frequent and important referenda on pollution control are also subject to effective fear-invoking propaganda, emanating from business groups that don't want stricter controls. When the issue is control of pollution, the propaganda antidote that can sometimes reverse public opinion is the exploitations of fear of losing jobs and, perhaps, higher prices.[46]

Not all propaganda efforts are successful however, as sometimes the intended audience manages to avoid the message entirely. Or the effort may backfire by alerting the intended audience to the issue without winning it to the intended side of the issue. For example, one recent study suggests that propaganda efforts in favor of school bond issues actually have the unintended consequence of provoking a stronger anti-bond issue vote.[47]

Organized propaganda efforts are not limited to referenda alone, since a pressure group may try to rally mass opinion to influence the outcome of a legislative issue. Nationally, the past activity of the American Medical Association to reverse public support for Medicare proposals is the most visible example. Provoked by President Truman's proposal for a national health care

program, the AMA launched a campaign to label it "socialized medicine."
The AMA propaganda machine went to work once again in an attempt to
overturn public support for President Kennedy's Medicare program, suggesting that the benefits from a private plan would be better. Although not prova-
ble, AMA propaganda may have been responsible for the temporary erosion
of public support for Medicare during 1962.[48] Although Medicare narrowly
failed congressional passage in 1962, it was voted into law three years later
despite further opposition by the AMA.

Scholarly observers generally agree that except when the public is
alerted to its responsibility to vote in a referendum, pressure group activity
is of little consequence in the shaping of mass opinion. As V.O. Key observes:

The broad conception of pressure groups as activators of general public
opinion which in turn softens up government seldom conforms with the reality. . . . The scale of operation necessary to have substantial impact on public opinion is beyond the resources of most groups. They may reach selected
groups of political activists through one channel or another with considerable effect, but by and large their lone efforts to mold mass opinion must be
of small consequence.[49]

The impact of pressure groups on policy, which is often considerable,
does not rest with the success of propaganda efforts except for the possibility of an indirect effect when policy makers mistakenly measure the success
of pressure group propaganda by its volume.

Representation within Pressure Groups

We have studied some of the ways in which pressure groups try to influence
public policy. Shortly we will evaluate the extent to which opinion within
organized groups reflects public opinion. First, however we shall examine a
further aspect of the Pressure Groups Model. For the model to work, the
positions advocated by group lobbyists must be shared by the members.
This may not be an easy condition to fulfill, since the internal decision-making structures of organized groups seldom function in the manner of ideal
democracies.

If the group's reason for organization is the sharing of a common ideology or common point of view on a single issue, the group's leaders should
have no difficulty discerning the members' positions on those issues that
were the source of the group's mobilization. One study of two women's
groups with opposite positions on the Equal Rights Amendment (National
Organization of Women and Women Who Want to be Women) found the
two membership groups not only held *opposite* views on the ERA (no sur-

prise) but, interestingly, were also sharply divided on other issues as well. Members of the pro-ERA group were generally ideologues of the left who supported liberal causes generally, while members of the anti-ERA group tended to be ideologically committed to right-wing issue positions.[50] In general, groups that organize because they share a common political viewpoint draw heavily from ideological and issue-oriented citizens. In this way, the intensity aspect of public opinion gets represented in the political process via the group process.

Not all organized groups, however, stimulate and maintain membership because the members share commitments to common political views. Such politically active organizations as trade unions and professional associations form for nonpolitical reasons and only incidentally make forays into the political arena. Leaders of these groups have a politically diverse membership that is difficult to represent. For example, a study of the Oregon Education Association (a teachers' group) found that the leaders were decidedly more liberal and activist than the members, but interestingly, they saw their members as even more conservative than they actually were.[51] Similarly, union leaders are more liberal and activist than union rank-and-file members, especially on issues peripheral to the trade-union cause. An example is civil rights, on which leaders show a strong liberal commitment that is not shared by their rank-and-file white membership.[52] However, leaders of conservative business groups and professional groups (such as the AMA) are probably more *conservative* than their members.

The ability of group leaders to assess member opinion is enhanced if group members are at least relatively homogeneous in their opinions on germane issues. Two of the authors sought to ascertain the distinctiveness of group opinion within a sample of Florida residents. The Florida respondents were asked to indicate their memberships in an extensive list of possible organized groups and were also asked their opinions on 20 state issues ranging from protection of alligators to state support to cities for law enforcement. If all members of each group shared the same opinions, one could predict a person's opinions by knowing his group affiliation. Technically, this would mean that 100 percent of the variance in individuals' opinions is explained by knowing their group memberships. Conversely, if groups were totally nondistinct in their opinions, 0 percent of opinion variance would be explained by knowledge of group memberships. Our findings much more closely parallel the latter extreme, since across the 20 different state issues an average of only four percent of the variance in individual opinion can be explained by group membership.[53] The logical conclusion is that groups contain a diverse variety of opinions. The vision of numerous groups unified in their opinions on the issues with their leaders accurately articulating the group opinions seems unrealistic.

Does Group Opinion Equal Public Opinion?

Pressure group activity only satisfies the model if the opinion of groups corresponds to the opinion of the public. In a typical poll, 62 percent of the respondents reported that they belong to at least one voluntary association such as a club, union, or business organization. Only 31 percent reported membership in an organization where political discussions take place.[54] As with other forms of political participation, people are more likely to belong to groups if they are among the most wealthy or most educated. For example, whereas most Americans in the lowest third in socioeconomic status belong to no groups, most in the upper third are *active* members of one or more organizations.[55] To the degree that persons of differing status levels prefer different policies, group opinion would appear to be biased.

Generally, a person's group memberships do not provide a focus for his or her political activity. This can be seen from further analysis of our Florida poll. Respondents were asked whether, on local, state, and national issues, they would turn to a group, person, or other source of information and advice that they felt they could trust. Table 9-6 indicates that despite this open solicitation to mention groups in answering this question only 23 percent of the sample were conscious of or admitted to forming their opinion on the advice of groups. And only 44 percent of the groups mentioned as sources of advice were those to which the individual belonged. In conclusion then, only about 10 percent of this Florida sample concede that they formed their opinions on the basis of advice from groups to which they belonged.

We have seen that certain people are more likely than others to join organized groups, with the most frequent joiners being among the wealthy and better educated. We can also observe that most lobbyists represent business, labor, professional, or agricultural groups—to which most people do not belong.[56] Many opinions clearly do not receive articulation by organized

Table 9-6   Sources of National State, and Local Advice and Information (in Percent)

Source	Not Mentioned	Mentioned, Unspecific[a]	Mentioned, Specific
Public persons	55	17	28
Agency of government	63	10	27
Media source	75	22	3
Group	77	7	16
Private person	78	6	16

[a]A specific mention would be to say "my senator," instead of "an official"; the "Department of Agriculture", instead of "city hall"; *Newsweek*, instead of "reading about it", UAW instead of "seeing how farmers react": and "my doctor", instead of "seeing how my friend reacts".

groups while others are amply represented by group spokesmen. Is there any way then to save the Pressure Groups Model as a means by which pressure groups advance the preferences of *public* opinion? One might argue that people with the most intense views on public policies organize into pressure groups, so that group views are at least representative of people who care the most. By this argument, if a set of unorganized individuals were to perceive a strong common interest, they would form an organized pressure group. If potential groups that are not organized remain so, they are reasonably content with the way things are.

The flaw in this argument is that spontaneous organization for political actions is too costly to expect the effective mobilization of a group simply because its potential members share an intense concern. To form an organization some individuals must play the difficult entrepreneural role of recruiting members.[57] More importantly, the incentive to join a dues-paying political group is limited because potential members can obtain the same benefits of the group's potential activity whether they join or not. Mancur Olson calls this the "free rider" problem.[58] As Olson has shown, most politically powerful interest groups did not originally organize over a common political cause. Instead, key interest groups such as labor unions, professional groups, business groups, and farm groups, developed their memberships because of common incentives to share nonpolitical benefits from organization. Only after the groups grew from offering nonpolitical services to their members did they become effective in the political arena. Olson's insightful analysis suggests a further problem with the Group Model. Because politically oriented groups are difficult to organize, existing organizations tend to be defenders of the status quo.

Some observers see the problem as a difference in resources between the organized special interest group and a disorganized public. In recent years, so-called "*public* interest groups" (Common Cause and Ralph Nader's organizations, for example) have entered the political arena in order to restore a balance. Although these groups have not mobilized the general public into a cohesive political force, they have not been without their political influence as they lobby for their versions of "the public interest." Also in recent years, there has been a proliferation of organized groups representing such causes as the advancement of women, consumers, taxpayers, and the environment. Although these groups receive financial support from only a fraction of the people they claim to represent, they are recognized as an important new force in the political arena. A model is provided by the activities of the NAACP and other civil rights groups which for years have articulated the grievances of American blacks. Although civil rights groups had been underfinanced and often ignored, their persistent activities were in large part responsible for the political advances blacks have made over the past two decades.

Conclusion. Because the positions voiced by influential organized groups do not neccessarily correspond to even the most strongly held views within the general public, the actual group process seldom follows the prescription of the Pressure Groups Model. If group activity were the sole input into governmental decisions, it seems unlikely that decisions would follow public opinion. The problem is that the group process results in some opinions carrying more weight than others.

Although some people obtain more representation from group activity than others, observers do not all agree that pressure groups operate against the public interest. A fact of political life is that some people—particularly the wealthy, educated, articulate, and already politically powerful—are in the best position to advance their political preferences. This fact is only made clearer when we examine the role of pressure groups in politics. Although the Pressure Group Model may not describe reality, perhaps we should ask whether we would prefer if all pressure group access to government officials could somehow be eliminated. While the "special interest" would lose access, so would the spokesmen for the general public. Rather than wish pressure-group influence could be reduced, perhaps we should concentrate on ways to make the process more equitable.

FOOTNOTES FOR CHAPTER 9

1. This has been a controversial suggestion. See Committee on Political Parties of the American Political Science Association, "Toward a More Responsible Two-Party System," *American Political Science Review,* 44 (September 1950), supplement.

2. Herbert McClosky, Paul J. Hoffman, and Rosemary O'Hara, "Issue Conflict and Consensus among Party Leaders and Followers," *American Political Science Review,* 59 (June 1960), pp. 406–427.

3. Ibid., p. 411

4. John W. Soule and Wilma E. McGrath, "A Comparative Study of Presidential Nomination Conventions: The Democrats 1968 and 1972," *American Journal of Plitical Science,* 21 (August 1975), pp. 501–518; Jeane Kirkpatrick, "Representation in the American National Conventions: The Case of 1972," *British Journal of Political Science,* 5 (July 1975), pp. 262–322.

5. Kirkpatrick, "Representation in the American National Conventions."

6. Norman Nie, Sidney Verba, and John R. Petrocik, *The Changing American Voter* (Cambridge: Harvard University Press, 1976), Chapter 12; Samuel J. Eldersveld, *Political Parties: A Behavioral Analysis*(Chicago: Rand McNally, 1964), Chapter 8.

7. David Butler, "The Paradox of Party Difference," *American Behavioral Scientist,* 4 (November 1960), pp. 3–5.

8. Gerald M. Pomper, *Elections in America: Control and Influence in Democratic Politics* (New York: Dodd, Mead, 1968), Chapters 7 and 8.

9. Ibid., pp. 177–178.

10. Ibid., p. 187.

11. Ibid., p. 194.

12. Ibid., p. 201.

13. Benjamin Ginsberg, "Critical Elections and the Substance of Party Conflict: 1844–1968," *American Journal of Political Science*, 16 (November 1972), pp. 603–625.

14. Benjamin Ginsberg, ' Elections and Public Policy," *American Political Science Review*, 70 (March 1976), pp. 41–49.

15. For trends in party voting in Congress, see Malcolm E. Jewell and Samuel C. Patterson, *The Legislative Process in the United States*, 3rd ed. (New York: Random House, 1977), pp. 389–391; Joseph Cooper, David William Brady, and Patricia A. Hurley, "The Electoral Basis of Party Voting: Patterns and Trends in the U.S. House of Representatives, 1887–1969," in Louis Maisel and Joseph Cooper, eds., *The Impact of the Electoral Process* (Beverly Hills: Sage Publications, 1977) pp. 133–165.

16. Aage Clausen, *How Congressmen Decide: A Policy Focus* (New York: St. Martin's Press, 1973), Chapter 5.

17. Hugh L. LeBlanc, "Voting in State Senates: Party and Constituency Influences," *Midwest Journal of Political Science*, 13 (February 1969), pp. 33–57; Samuel C. Patterson, "American State Legislatures and Public Policy," in Herbert Jacob and Kenneth N. Vines, *Politics in the American States: A Comparative Analysis*, 3rd ed., (Boston: Little Brown and Co., 1976), pp. 139–195. As the case with Congress, social welfare and economic issues are among the issues that most divide parties at the state legislative level. See Malcolm E. Jewell, "Party Voting in American State Legislatures," *Midwest Journal of Political Science*, 49 (November 1955), pp. 773–791.

18. For a good discussion of this point, see David Mayhew, *Congress: The Electoral Connection* (New Haven: Yale University Press, 1974), Chapter 1.

19. An additional reason for party differences in congressional voting may be that Representatives obtain voting cues from others within their party. This process may explain the finding that the party is a better predictor of roll-call votes that of congressional attitudes. See Helmut Norputh, "Explaining Party Cohesion in Congress: The Case of Shared Policy Attitudes," *American Political Science Review*, 10 (December 1976), pp. 1156–1171.

20. John L. Sullivan and Robert E. O'Connor, "Electoral Choice and Popular Control of Public Policy: The Case of the 1966 House Elections," *American Political Science Review* 66 (December 1972) pp. 1256–1268.

21. Ibid., p. 1264.

22. Similar findings to Sullivan and O'Connor's were observed for the 1974 House Elections in Gerald C. Wright, Jr., "Issue Strategy in Congressional Elections: The Impact of the Primary Electorate," paper presented at the 1978 Meetings of the Midwest Political Science Association.

23. David W. Brady and Naomi B. Lynn, "Switched-Seat Congressional Districts: Their Effect on Party Voting and Public Policy," *American Journal of Political Science* 17 (August 1973), pp. 528–543: Theodore R. Marmor, *The Politics of Medicare* (Chicago: Aldine, 1970), Chapter 4.

24. David W. Brady, "Critical Elections, Congressional Parties, and Clusters of Policy Changes," *British Journal of Political Science*, 8 (January 1978), pp. 79–99; Barbara Deckard Sinclair, "Party Realignment and the Transformation of the Political Agenda: The House of Representatives, 1925–1938, *American Political Science Review*, 71 (September 1977), pp. 940–953.

25. As we have seen from Pomper's analysis of party platforms, the platform positions of the president's party are more likely to be enacted than the platform positions of the losing presidential party. In a careful statistical analysis Douglas Hibbs has shown that the party controlling the presidency influences the unemployment rate: with the Democrats in power, the unemployment rate is more likely to go down. The reason, of course, is that the Democratic party gives greater emphasis to employment as the criterion of national economic health. See

Douglas A. Hibbs, Jr., "Political Parties and Macroeconomic Policy," *American Political Science Review,* 71 (December 1977), pp. 1467–1487.. However, the party in power does not appear to affect the level of government expenditures in various categories such as health or defense. See Paul Burstein, "Party Balance, Replacement of Legislators, and Federal Government Expenditures, 1941–1976," *Western Political Quarterly,* 32 (June 1979).

26. Attempts to see whether a state's policies change when party control of the governorship and legislature changes have produced conflicting results. See Robert S. Erikson, "The Relationship between Party Control and Civil Rights Legislation in the American States," *Western Political Quarterly,* 24 (March 1971), pp. 178–182; and Richard Winters, "Party Control and Policy Change," *American Journal of Political Science,* 20 (November 1976) pp. 597–636.

27. On the impact of nonpartisan elections, see Willis D. Hawley, *Nonpartisan Elections and the Case for Party Politics* (New York: Wiley, 1973); and Susan Welch and Eric H. Carlson, "The Impact of Party on Voting Behavior in a Nonpartisan Legislature," *American Political Science Review,* 67 (September 1973), pp. 854–867. The classic study of politics in the one-party South is V.O. Key, Jr., *Southern Politics* (New York: Random House, 1949).

28. Actually, we know of no author who presents the Pressure Groups Model in its pure form. For a concise discussion of the different theories about groups, see Norman J. Ornstein and Shirley Elder, *Interest Groups, Lobbying and Policymaking* (Washington: Congressional Quarterly Press, 1978), Chapter 1. The reader may note we use the term "pressure groups" instead of the more common term "interest groups." We prefer the former because groups in general have a variety of functions in addition to seeking favorable action from government. By "pressure groups" we are referring more specifically to the political role of these groups.

29. John W. Kingdon, *Congressmen's Voting Decisions* (New York: Harper and Row, 1973), Chapters 1, 5. Kingdon finds that with other motivations controlled, congressmen are no more likely to vote with interest-group positions than would be expected by chance.

30. Lester W. Milbrath, The *Washington Lobbyists* (Chicago: Rand McNally and Company, 1963).

31. Harmon Zeigler and Michael Baer, *Lobbying: Interaction and Influence in American State Legislatures* (Belmont, California: Wadsworth, 1969).

32. Charles W. Wiggins and Samuel E. Skare, "The Structure of Lobbying within a State Legislative System," paper presented at the 1977 meetings of the American Political Science Association.

33. For the development of this theme, see James Q. Wilson, *Political Organizations* (New York: Basic Books, 1973), Chapter 16.

34. Zeigler and Baer, pp. 195–197; John C. Wahlke, Heinz Eulau, William Buchanan, and Leroy C. Ferguson, *The Legislative System* (New York: Wiley 1962), pp. 334–335.

35. "Interest Groups' Gifts to 1976 Congressional Campaigns," *Congressional Quarterly Weekly Report* 35 (April 16 1978), p. 710.

36. Ibid.

37. "New Right: 'Many Times More Effective Now,' " *Congressional Quarterly Weekly Report* 35 (October 24, 1977), pp. 2649–2653.

38. "Dirty Dozen," *Congressional Quarterly Weekly Report,* 34 (August 3, 1976), p. 765.

39. Gary C. Jacobson, "The Effects of Campaign Spending in Congressional Elections," *American Political Science Review,* 72 (June 1978), pp. 469–491.

40. Carol S. Greenwald, *Group Power,* (New York: Praeger, 1977), pp. 158–159.

41. Ibid., p. 159.

42. Bruce Ian Oppenheimer, "Interest Groups in the Political Process," *Current History,* 67 (August 1974), pp. 75–78.

43. Lester Milbrath, "Lobbying as a Communications Process," *Public Opinion Quarterly*, 24 (Spring 1960), p. 45.

44. Angus Campbell, Philip E. Converse, Donald E. Stokes, and Warren E. Miller, *The American Voter* (New York: Wiley, 1960), p. 306.

45. Robert Abelson, "Computers, Polls, and Public Opinion: Some Puzzles and Paradoxes," *Trans-Action*, 5 (September 1968) pp. 20–27.

46. For an interesting example, see William H. Rodgers, Jr., "Ecology Denied: The Unmasking of a Majority," *The Washington Monthly*, 2 (February 1971), pp. 39–43.

47. M. Kent Jennings and L. Harmon Zeigler, "Interest Representation in School Governance," Paper presented at meeting of American Political Science Association, September 1970, pp. 42–43.

48. Data reported in Mark V. Nadel, "Public Opinion and Public Policy," in Robert Weissberg and Mark V. Nadel (eds.), *American Democracy: Theory and Reality* (New York: Wiley, 1972).

49. V. O. Key, *Public Opinion and American Democracy* (New York: Alfred Knopf, 1961), p. 515.

50. Kent L. Tedin, et al. "Social Background and Political Differences Between Pro- and Anti-Era Activists," *American Politics Quarterly*, 5 (July 1977), pp. 395–408.

51. Norman R. Luttbeg and Harmon Zeigler, "Attitude Consensus and Conflict within an Interest Group: An Assessment of Cohesion," *American Political Science Review*, 60 (September 1966), pp. 655–665.

52. Derek C. Bok and John T. Dunlop, *Labor and the American Community* (New York: Simon and Schuster, 1970), p. 134.

53. The percentage of explained variance varied between 2 percent on strengthening state air and water pollution laws and 7 percent on making all church property taxable. For a full enumeration of the issues examined, see Norman R. Luttbeg, "The Structure of Public Beliefs on State Policies: A Comparison with Local and National Findings," *Public Opinion Quarterly*, 31 (Spring 1971), pp. 114–116.

54. Sidney Verba and Norman H. Nie, *Participation in America* (New York: Harper and Row, 1972), p. 176.

55. Ibid., pp. 203–204.

56. For example in the 1969 Congress, 53 percent of all organizations represented by lobbyists in Washington weer business organizations, 11 percent were labor organizations, 6 percent were farmers' organizations, and 6 percent were professional organizations. Similar figures obtain at the state level. See Malcolm E. Jewell and Samuel C. Patterson, *The Legislative Process in the United States*, 3rd ed. (New York: Random House, 1977), p. 283.

57. On the role of entrepreneurs in the formation of political groups, see Robert H. Salisbury, "An Exchange Theory of Interest Groups," *Midwest Journal of Political Science*, 13 (February 1969), pp. 1–32.

58. Mancur Olson, Jr., *The Logic of Collective Action* (New York: Schocken Books, 1968).

CHAPTER 10

Public Opinion And The Performance Of Democracy

According to democratic theory, the health of a democracy depends on the existence of a politically informed and active citizenry. By carefully monitoring government affairs, citizens could develop informed opinions about policies that would represent their interests. By working for and voting for candidates who represent their views, and by making their views known to elected leaders, citizens could collectively translate their various policy preferences into government action. The resulting set of policies that governments would enact would represent a reasonable compromise between competing claims of equally powerful and informed citizens. This description represents the democratic ideal. In this concluding chapter we assess the degree to which American democracy approaches this democratic ideal and speculate about possible ways to achieve improvement.

10-1 ASSESSING THE IMPACT OF PUBLIC OPINION ON POLICY

We have discussed five models that have the potential to provide public policy consistent with what the public would prefer. By voting for leaders who share its views, the public can fulfill the basic needs of the Rational Activist Model. If reliable voting cues are furnished by political parties, policy-oriented voters can fulfill the Political Parties Model by choosing the party platform most compatible with their views. Aside from voting, the public can influence policy makers by bringing the policies of the groups to which they belong to bear on officials, thus fulfilling the Pressure Group Model. In addition, linkage between opinions and policy can be furnished by two models that do not demand public coercion of leaders. If policy makers try to follow public opinion because they believe they should and if they perceive that opinion accurately, the Role Playing Model would be fulfilled. Finally, because leaders and followers share many of the same political beliefs, even the Sharing Model provides political linkage in many circumstances.

By itself, each of these sources of political linkage may provide only a small increase in the degree to which officials are responsive to the public. Their total effect may, in fact, be slight, since to show that public opinion can influence policy is not a demonstration that public opinion is followed all or even most of the time. Perhaps the evidence we need is some sort of counting of the frequency with which government policies are in accord with public opinion. A truly definitive study following this design would need information at the national, state, and local levels across a broad range of policies as to whether the process of political linkage results in public policy that is consistent with public opinion. We would want to be able to say which of the linkage models proves most viable and on what issues. Hopefully, we would be able to assess the consequences of linkage failure for the public's opinions about its government, for its participation in political affairs, and ultimately for political stability. Unfortunately such a study does not exist.

Since presently available evidence of the frequency of political linkage is limited, conclusions based on it must be very tentative—perhaps limited to only the specific issues studied, the level of government considered, and the time period involved. Moreover, congruence between majority opinion and government policy may not always be the best indicator of political linkage, since government decisions can be responses to the intense opinions of a minority rather than to the preferences of the majority. Also, as we have seen, "majority" opinion on an issue fluctuates with the exact wording of a survey question. Keeping these cautions in mind, let us see what the evidence shows about the congruence between public opinion and government policy.

Evidence at the National Level

If acts of Congress were determined by the demands of public opinion, then Congress would act whenever public opinion built to majority support or higher behind a proposed program. Because polls do not regularly monitor opinions on specific proposals before Congress, we seldom know how much support the public gives to a policy prior to its enactment. However, polls can offer clues regarding how well Congress serves the broad policy guidelines preferred by the public. One issue on which we can assess this consistency between opinion and policy is Medicare—which became law in 1965. As early as 1935, a presidential commission had proposed a plan for national health insurance that would have covered more people than the present plan. In 1945, President Truman endorsed such a plan. Twenty years later Congress passed a comprehensive health insurance plan, but only for the elderly. Why was there such a delay? One reason was that although most people favored government assistance, they were not insistent. For example, consider the results of an SRC poll in 1956 (when the health care issue was dormant) that asked people whether the government should "help people get doctors and health care at low cost" and also asked for an appraisal of government performance to date (too far, less than it should, about right, or "haven't heard yet what the government is doing"). Although opinion was more than two to one in favor of government participation, only 30 percent said government was doing less than is should. The crystallized opposition to government participation and those who said the government either was doing about right or going too far made up only 15 percent of the sample.[1] Most people apparently did not have a coherent opinion one way or the other. Even when Medicare became a central issue in the 1960s, few were attentive. According to a 1962 quiz of the public, only 57 percent said they had heard of Medicare and had any understanding of it. In fact, only 7 percent knew the basic facts—that it would be financed by Social Security and limited to people receiving old age insurance.[2]

Perhaps if people had become politically mobilized by their views on medical care, Medicare or something even more extensive would have been enacted much sooner. As things stood, the powerful American Medical Association was able to forestall satisfaction of a feeble-voiced public. In fact, neither Medicare nor its predecessors even emerged from the House Ways and Means Committee in more than very diluted form until the 1964 Democratic landslide tipped the committee's balance in favor of such legislation.[3]

While how important public opinion was in the enactment of Medicare is not clear, we need to analyze more than a single issue. To develop a strong statistical argument that policy corresponds (or seems to follow) public opinion we need to find such a pattern over many issues. One approach is to conduct a "time series" analysis; that is, to follow several issues over time to determine if changes in public opinion are generally followed by policy changes. Evidence that opinion influences policy would exist when new government policies follow abrupt shifts in opinion, perhaps from a majority in opposition to a majority in support. Or one might find that the government spends more money on a given program (for example, foreign aid) at times when public opinion is most favorably disposed to that program.

Doing this type of time-series analysis is more difficult than it might seem, in part because analysis must be restricted to issues on which extensive over-time poll results exist. Also, instances of abrupt shifts in public opinion are relatively rare. Robert Weissberg, in the most thorough time-series examination of the opinion-policy relationship to date, has investigated several issues but with ambiguous results. He reports ". . . a wide variation in the amount of congruence between public opinion and public policy. In some instances, e.g., the admission of Communist China to the United Nations, government and public are in nearly complete accord; on other issues, for example, income tax rates, considerable incongruity occurs."[4]

Rather than examine only issues which are monitored by polls over an extended time interval, an alternative approach is to examine opinion-policy congruence on national issues for which polls report opinions, even if only occasionally. Alan Monroe has used this approach for Gallup Poll questions over the period from 1960 to 1974.[5] Each usable poll question ascertained whether or not the public preferred a specific change in national policy. For each of the issues, Monroe then determined whether the specific policy change eventually took place. His basic findings are shown in Table 10-1. On the 74 issues for which the public favored the status quo, the desired outcome of no change occurred 76 percent of the time. On the 48 issues on which the public preferred change, the desired outcome of designated change occurred 59 percent of the time. Evidently, the public is less likely to get its way when it prefers change than when it prefers the status quo. Of course, that the American political system tends to be status quo oriented has often been observed. That is, an intense minority (for example, opponents of gun control) can often block change. But in either case, the public's preference becomes policy more often than not. Over all cases—preferences for change and preferences for the status quo—Monroe finds policy corresponding to public opinion almost two-thirds of the time.

Evidence at the State Level

At the state level, the opinion-policy linkage can be analyzed by seeing whether states where the public is most in favor of a given policy tend to be the states that enact the policy. Unfortunately, this kind of analysis is limited by the fact that polls rarely report reliable state-by-state breakdowns of opinion for comparison. Surprisingly, the best state-level opinion data is from polls conducted in the 1930s when national polls were based on much larger samples than is the case today. One study examined three state-level issues for which there were available state opinion data in 1936.[6] On each of

Table 10-1   Congruence Between Policy Preference Among the Mass Public and Policy Outcomes at the National Level

	Preference	
Outcome	Status Quo	Change
Status Quo	76%	41%
Change	24	59
	100%	100%
	(*N*=74)	(*N*=148)
Consistent = 64%		

Source. Alan D. Monroe, "Consistency Between Public Preferences and National Policy Decisions," *American Politics Quarterly,* 7 (January 1979), p. 9.

these issues—capital punishment, child labor regulation, and women jurors—a strong correlation between state opinion and state policy was found. Table 10-2 shows the opinion-policy relationship for capital punishment. States in which opinion was most favorable to the death sentence in 1936 were the states with the most consistently pro-capital punishment policies between the 1930s and the 1970s. While suggestive of opinion-policy linkage, this type of analysis is limited by lack of available state opinion data. Some studies have attempted to remedy this gap by examining the relationship between state opinion that is estimated ("simulated") from the state's population characteristics.[7] These studies also find some evidence that state policy can be predicted from state public opinion.

Evidence at the Local Level

At the local level of government we know very little about the relationship between public opinion and policy decisions. There appear to be no studies that systematically attempt to determine whether existing differences among local policy choices are related to local political opinions. One study, however, examined the relationship between political participation levels and "policy congruence" for citizens and leaders in 55 American cities. Policy congruence is a measure of the extent to which citizens and elected officials agree on what are the most important local problems. A study by Sidney Verba and Norman Nie,[8] and a further analysis of the same data by Susan Hansen,[9] reveal that the higher the community's level of public participation—particularly its level of voting participation—the greater the congruence between mass and elite perceptions of community problems. Of further consequence are competitive elections. Hansen finds the combination of high

Table 10-2 Relationship Between State Opinion and Capital Punishment and State Policy Toward Capital Punishment, 1936-1974

Composite Capital Punishment Policy Score[a]	Percent of Public Favoring Death Penalty in 1936		
	49-63%	64-71%	72-84%
Weak Commitment to Death Penalty	82%	48%	0%
Strong Commitment to Death Penalty	18	52	100
	100% (N=17)	100% (N-21)	100% (N=10)

[a]A state is scored as having a relatively strong commitment to the death penalty if it retained the death penalty uninterrupted between 1936 and 1972 and restored the death penalty by mid-May 1974, following the Supreme Court ruling that existing capital punishment statutes were unconstitutional.

voting turnout *and* close local elections produces the greatest citizen-leader congruence scores. Unfortunately, the Verba-Nie data does not contain information which allows an investigation into the factors responsible for this congruence. But their data do suggest that when the public is active in a community, it can influence leaders about what problems should be placed on the agenda for solution.

Summary

Although the evidence is certainly incomplete, the few relevant studies that test for an opinion-policy linkage suggest that public opinion is far from inconsequential. At the national level we find that opinion and national policy are in agreement more often than not. At the state level we find that state opinion can be a good predictor of state policy. At the local level we find that high citizen participation is associated with citizen-leader agreement on important problems, although we have no data concerning solutions to those problems.

Such findings should not be surprising, because as we have seen there are several linkages at work translating even feebly voiced public opinion into public policy. This information, however, should not be cause for complacency about the current state of American democracy. Other forces besides public opinion shape government decisions. In addition, the opinions that sometimes influence policy may not be informed or, from our point of view, enlightened opinions. On the positive side, the evidence that a rather inattentive public can sometimes influence policy suggests that a more attentive public would have even greater control over policy decisions.

10-2 INTERPRETING THE PUBLIC'S ROLE IN DEMOCRACY

As this book describes, the public generally does not live up to its prescribed activist role. Moreover, while public opinion can often influence government policy, in reality public opinion is not the sole determinant of policy outcomes. Why not? Public control of government decisions depends on both the extent to which people actually participate in policies and the equality of peoples' resources for effective participation. The first point is obvious. That the more people participate in politics, the more they can influence government decisions seems logical. But some people can participate more effectively than others because they command a greater share of the necessary resources such as money, information, articulateness, and access to decision makers. How inequitable one views the distribution of these political resources can determine one's view of how democratic the political system actually is. Some observers see effective political power concentrated in the hands of a "power elite" who control policy outcomes for their own interests. Others more optimistically see the inequality in the distribution of power limited basically to the different political skills that individuals have and their interest in using them.[10] Because this debate over the equality of the distribution of political power is not easily decided by scientific inquiry, we shall not enter it directly here. But, taking into account that the tools of effective political participation are not equally distributed, how can we assess the less than active political role of the public? We shall discuss four different plausible conclusions.

Public Apathy as Mass Political Incompetence

Perhaps the easiest view of the public's limited role in government affairs is that people are simply incapable of doing any better. The frequency with which people fail to hold political opinions, the rarity of the liberal or conservative "ideologue," and the difficulty in locating rational policy-oriented voters may all indicate that people generally lack the skills necessary to make sophisticated judgments about their political leaders and policies. Worse yet, the political views that people do hold may be intolerant, naïve, or simply wrong. Viewed from this perspective, an increase in public participation would only make the situation worse because "bad" public opinion would drive "good" policy makers toward undesirable acts.

If the mass public is viewed as being inherently incapable of playing a useful role, then the remedy of trying to "uplift" public opinion becomes ineffective. Instead, one might have to rely on the proper training or careful recruitment of political leaders as a means of producing desired outcomes. If such desired outcomes include the preservation of the substance of democracy, then one must prescribe both a limited public role and the instillation of a heavy dose of democratic values among political elites. Thomas Dye and Harmon Zeigler, who arrive at this position, call it the "irony of democracy."[11]

Public Apathy as Rational Disengagement

Possibly the reason that most people do not allow politics to intrude far into their lives is that to do so would be irrational. From a strict cost-versus-benefit standpoint, one should not follow public affairs closely, since the investment would get one nowhere. One's vote is useless because it is fantasy to assume that one vote can decide an election's outcome except in the most extraordinary circumstances. Even when one's economic interests are directly at stake in the political arena (which may be rare), organizing like-minded people for collective political pressure is irrational because the costs of organization outweigh the possible benefits one could expect.[12] The cynic might also suggest that increased public knowledge of governmental affairs would only produce greater political withdrawal, as people who learn about their leaders' corruption and unresponsiveness will feel even more helpless at the prospect of changing things.

If this logic is correct, then people who do participate in politics usually are motivated by something other than tangible personal gains. Perhaps they "irrationally" participate in order to gratify a felt obligation or civic duty. If the major determinant of an individual's sense of obligation to participate is preadult political socialization, then a reformer might hope to increase public participation by improving the "training" of the next generation of citizens. Alternatively, one might hope to eliminate rational withdrawal from politics by somehow increasing the rewards of political participation.

Public Apathy as Elite Manipulation

One can also interpret the public's low participation in politics as the result of manipulation by leaders and their allies. When one observes political docility on the part of people who seemingly should have strong reasons for political protest, one can easily draw the conclusion that the individuals are being misled by propaganda. Whether or not one can support such an interpretation depends on one's convictions that the individuals in question are actually oppressed. A convinced Marxist, for example, can readily view the lack of class consciousness on the part of American workers as a sign of deception by the existing power structure. Similarly, a member of the John Birch Society might attribute the public's lack of concern about what he sees as a pervasive communist conspiracy to be a sign of the effectiveness of that conspiracy.

One does not have to believe in a complex conspiracy in order to view political quiescence as the result of elite manipulation. Because most political events are remote from people's everyday lives, people willingly view these events through the interpretation of their leaders. Also, since people want to believe that their political system is benign rather than corrupt or evil, they readily find reassurance from optimistic interpretations of the existing order and resist the voices that tell them otherwise[13] This may be why most Americans will deny any immorality to America's role in Vietnam and will support the police in any violent confrontation with political protestors.

If one sees people as unwilling to accept "truth" because they do not want to disturb their cherished beliefs, the obvious remedy would appear to be heavy doses of correct information. But how to make this remedy effective remains unclear.

Public Apathy as Public Contentment

Rather than viewing public apathy as a sign that the classical democratic model does not hold, one can interpret apathy as an indicator of public contentment. If people do not concern themselves with political matters, then they must not have any additional demands to make on their government. Conversely, when many people do participate in politics, it is a distressing signal either that government has ignored public needs or that conflicts between societal groups are no longer being successfully resolved by political leaders.[14]

Actually, the view that public apathy means public satisfaction rests on the assumption that the public is rather politically sophisticated. It assumes that people are capable of articulating any grievances they might have, that people feel that their expression of grievances would be effective, and that people are not easily led to ignore their interests. Only if these assumptions are made can one conclude that the lack of political participation indicates that people's needs are met by the proper working of a democratic system.

Although they contradict one another, each of these four possible explanations of the public's lack of political participation contains a grain of truth. For example, the public may not be capable of participation in all government decisions, particularly when the decision depends on proper evaluation of advanced technical knowledge. Equally obvious, is that people can take only limited time from their personal affairs to participate in politics. Moreover, people may decide not to participate because they feel (perhaps mistakenly) that they can trust their political leaders. Finally, people may sometimes retire from the political arena because they have no particular grievances.

Simply holding them up to the light of scientific evidence cannot determine which of the explanations of low participation in politics is most valid, since every observer will view the evidence through the filter of his own preconceptions and values. How the observer views such matters as human nature, people's basic interests, and the benevolence of government can shape how strongly he concludes that political inactivity signifies incapability, rational withdrawal, manipulation, or contentment. Similarly, the extent to which the observer sees his own opinions in harmony with majority opinion might influence his view of whether public control of government should increase or decrease.

10-3 THE EXPANSION OF POLITICAL PARTICIPATION

Whether increased public political participation is desirable also depends on the type of political participation. Few would applaud the increased mass participation that would result in civil war or mass mobilization in support of an antidemocratic movement. But few would fear an increase in informed, democratic participation—particularly if we ignore possible disagreements over what "informed democratic participation" means. When there is little mass participation, the burden of responsibility falls on the political elites— both to insure the continuation of the democratic rules and also to make policy decisions that are fair and equitable. But if one agrees that the purpose of democracy is to insure that political leaders are held accountable to the people, one can hardly applaud when people do not actively seek to protect their own interests. Are there any ways to increase the number of active participants while at the same time insuring that this participation will be rational and democratic?

Seemingly part of the answer would involve some way of creating a more politically informed public. Since the public can hardly be blamed for its political ignorance when it is given little information on which to make its political judgments, we can favor more thorough political reporting by the news media and the efforts of various "public interest" groups (such as Ralph Nader's organizations and Common Cause) to increase public awareness. Hopes should not be set too high, however, because information campaigns do not always reach the people who are most in need of them. Also, we must recognize the possibility of side effects produced by increased public knowledge, such as greater public cynicism or an intensification of conflict between politically aroused mass groups.

Possibly, an increase in mass political participation could be brought about by the difficult task of creating a culture or climate of opinion that encourages more participation. The place to start would be with children, whose political values and expectations are not yet formed. Since to politicize American families that are not already politically active would be difficult, the public schools would be a more plausible agent than the family for the encouragement of greater participation—perhaps, as some suggest, by instituting greater student participation in classroom decision making. But even if this would work in principle, it may be politically impossible to implement, since people generally see the proper role of schools as instilling loyalty and respect for authorities rather than permitting premature sharing of classroom authority by pupils. Of course, even more than early schooling, the college experience prepares young people for activist political roles. Thus the trend toward increasing attendance in institutions of higher education may provide some increase in public activism without large-scale reform programs. But events might channel the "idealism" of college youths into cynical withdrawal or violent participation rather than into participation in "normal" political activities.

Simply changing the laws in certain ways may be the most realistic means of bringing about at least modest increases in political participation. For example, the voting rate might increase considerably if obstacles to voter registration are eliminated so that each voter could register automatically rather than having to take the time and effort to do this on his own. Political influence would become more evenly distributed if laws to limit and regulate campaign contributions can effectively weaken the influence of wealthy special interest groups.

Perhaps the existing methods for translating public opinion into government policy are inaccurate relics from a technically primitive time when ballot casting, face-to-face communication, and geographic representation were the only feasible conduits for public expression. A novel but simple way to encourage greater participation would be to increase the number of decisions in which the public can play a greater role. Participation might increase not only from the increase in the public's options to participate but also from a resultant growth in the public's perception that its opinions count. Participation could be encouraged by giving people greater opportunity to participate directly in local decisions, including perhaps more participatory democracy in nongovernmental organizations such as the factory, school, or church. Also the public can play a more direct role by deciding policy questions in referenda instead of letting their elected leaders decide them. There have even been proposals for more direct democracy at the national level, such as by the attachment of electronic devices in every home that would allow the public to pass laws by instantaneous referenda.[15] There is little question that extensive public participation is a desired democratic value. But it is debatable whether additional opportunities to participate would lead to wiser government decisions than elected leaders presently make. While proposals for expanding participation deserve serious consideration, their practicability and desirability remain uncertain.

FOOTNOTES FOR CHAPTER 10

1. Recomputed from V. O. Key, Jr., *Public Opinion and American Democracy* (New York: Alfred A. Knopf, 1967), p. 269.

2. Mark V. Nadel, "Public Policy and Public Opinion," in *American Democracy: Theory and Reality,* by Robert Weissberg and Mark V. Nadel (eds.), (New York: Wiley, 1972), p. 540.

3. Theodore L. Marmor, *The Politics of Medicare* (Chicago: Aldine, 1970).

4. Robert Weissberg, *Public Opinion and Popular Government* (Englewood Cliffs: Prentice-Hall, 1976), p. 169.

5. Alan D. Monroe, "Consistency Between Public Preferences and National Policy Decisions," *American Politics Quarterly,* 7 (January 1979), pp. 3–21.

6. Robert S. Erikson, "The Relationship between Public Opinion and State Policy: A New Look at some Forgotten Data," *American Journal of Political Science,* 20 (February 1976), pp. 25–36.

7. Richard L. Sutton, "The States and the People: Measuring and Accounting for State Representatives," *Polity,* 3 (Summer 1973), pp. 28–37; Ronald E. Weber and William R. Shaffer, "Public Opinion and American State Policy Making," *Midwest Journal of Political Science,* 16 (November 1972), pp. 457–482.

8. Sidney Verba and Norman Nie, *Participation in America* (New York: Harper and Row, 1972).

9. Susan Blackall Hansen, "Participation, Political Structure, and Concurrence," *American Political Science Review,* 69 (December 1975), pp. 1181–1191.

10. The most widely cited representatives of these opposing viewpoints are C. Wright Mills, *The Power Elite* (New York: Oxford University Press, 1956); and Robert A. Dahl, *Who Governs?* (New Haven: Yale University Press, 1961).

11. Thomas R. Dye and Harmon Zeigler, *The Irony of Democracy*, 4th ed. (Belmont, California: Wadsworth, 1978).

12. For the development of this particular point, see Mancur Olson, Jr., *The Logic of Collective Action* (Cambridge: Harvard University Press, 1965).

13. For a provocative discussion of opinion manipulation, see Murray Edelman, *The Symbolic Uses of Politics* (Urbana: University of Illinois Press, 1965).

14. For an articulation of this view, see Francis Graham Wilson, *A Theory of Public Opinion* (Chicago: Greenwood Press, 1962).

15. This proposal may be technically feasible. See Leo Bogart, *Silent Politics: Polls and the Awareness of Public Opinion* (New York: Wiley, 1972), Chapter 1.

APPENDIX **A**

The Theory of Sampling Political Opinions

Most surveys of public opinion are based on samples. When the *Gallup Poll* reports that 50 percent of adult Americans approve of the way that the President is handling his job it is obvious that the Gallup organization has not gone out and interviewed 140 million American adults. Instead, it has taken a sample. In fact, the analysis of samples is the method employed in the vast majority of public opinion studies.[1] The reasons for sampling are fairly straightfoward. First, to interview everybody would be prohibitively expensive. The current estimate is that the 1980 census (in which presumably everyone is interviewed) will cost over $1 billion. Second, to interview the entire population would take a very long time. Months might pass between the first and last interview. Public opinion may, in that period, undergo real change.

Sampling provides a practical alternative to interviewing the whole population. Furthermore, when correctly done sampling can provide very accurate estimates of the political opinions of a larger population. The theory of sampling is a branch of the mathematics of probability, and the error involved in going from the sample to the population can be known with mathematical precision. Unfortunately many surveys of public opinion do not meet the demanding requirements of sampling theory. The attendant result, of course, is a loss in accuracy. To introduce the reader to sampling theory we shall begin by defining key terms and by describing a scientifically drawn sample. We shall then analyze reasons for some of the better known mistakes made by political pollsters. Finally, we shall outline how the major survey organizations like the SRC/CPS, Gallup, and Harris currently draw their samples.

A-1 THE TERMINOLOGY OF SURVEY SAMPLING

The *population* is that aggregate about which we want information. In a survey of presidential vote preference the population would be all the registered voters in the United States. But populations can be more specialized. For example, one might be interested in the political views of lawyers on the question of no-fault insurance. The population would then be all licensed attorneys in the United States.

A *variable* is some particular characteristic of the population. An example is age. We might want to know what percent of the population is under 30. Another example is vote intent. What percentage of the population plans to vote? What percent prefers the Republican candidate?

The *sample* is that part of the population that is chosen for study. Usually the sample is considerably smaller than the population. In nationwide surveys where the population is about 140 million, samples are usually less than 2000. When samples accurately mirror the population they are said to be *representative samples.*

The term *randomness* refers to the only method by which a representative sample can be scientifically drawn. In a random sample each unit of the population has exactly the same probability of being drawn as every other unit. If the population is attorneys in the state of Texas each attorney would be required to have exactly the same probability of being selected for the sample to be random. This situation obviously requires a very detailed knowledge of the population. In the case of Texas lawyers one could get a list from the bar association and then sample from that list. But suppose the population was unemployed, male adults. To specify the population in such a fashion as to be able to draw a random sample would be very difficult. As a consequence obtaining a representative sample of the unemployed is not easy. A *probability* sample is a variant on the principle of random sampling. Instead of each unit having exactly the same probability of being drawn, some units would be more likely to be drawn than would others. But this would be a *known* probability. For example, if one were sampling voter precincts in a state it is of consequence that some precincts contain more people than others. To make the sample of people in those precincts representative, the larger precincts would have to be assigned a greater likelihood of being drawn into the sample. Probability samples correctly executed are considered to be scientific.

A *purposive sample* is a nonrepresentative sample drawn to study some particular phenomenon. An example might be a study contrasting the political attitudes of blacks and whites in the United States. If a representative sample were drawn it would consist of about 12 percent blacks and 88 percent whites. Therefore, for purposes of the study, to oversample blacks might be desirable; that is, the sample would be drawn in such a way that it is 50 percent blacks and 50 percent whites. Using this strategy the blacks in the sample should be representative of black adults and the whites representative of white adults, but the combined sample could not be used to make inferences about the American population. If you asked such a sample who they preferred for president in the next election the result would be a very inaccurate predictor of the actual election result.

One of the most important strengths of random sampling is that the accuracy of the sample as an estimate of the population value can be precisely known. That any sample will estimate the true population value exactly is unlikely. In the 1976 presidential election Jimmy Carter got 50.0 percent of the vote. If we had taken a random sample of 1500 voters on election day we probably would have come very close to the actual vote, but not have estimated it exactly. Our sample estimate might have been something like 51.6 percent for Carter. The difference between the sample estimate and the actual election day result is due to sampling error. *Sampling error is the difference between the population value and the sample estimate that is due strictly to the workings of chance.* Sampling error can be illustrated with simple coin flips. We know theoretically that if we flip an honest coin an infinite number of times it will come up 50 percent heads and 50 percent tails. But suppose we flip it only 10 times and it comes up heads 8 times (80 percent). What do we conclude? That the coin is dishonest? Probably it is not. Even though the coin is honest it could come up eight heads simply by chance alone. The difference between the theoretical limit of five and the eight heads we got in our ten flips is due to sampling error — simple chance. The same principle works in sampling from a population. Suppose we took a random sample of 1500 registered voters shortly before the presidential election. For our sample we estimate that candidate "A" will get 48 percent and candidate "B" will get 52 percent. But our sample estimate will not be exactly precise so we say that candidate A will get 52 percent of the vote *give or take 3 percent.* The 3 percent is the sampling error. In other words, we know that 95 out of 100 times (the 95 percent figure is a standard for accuracy that is agreed upon by statisticians) we can be sure that the true value of the population variable, the percent that plan to vote for candidate "B", lies between 49 and 55 percent (a sampling error of 3 percent is added to and subtracted from our sample estimate of 52 percent). Given a random sample of 1500 we would know that 95 out of 100 times that we took such samples the real value of the population variable would lie in an interval, called the *confidence interval,* which is plus or minus 3 percent of our sample estimate. Thus most of the time we should be pretty close to the true population value. Occasionally, however, due to simple chance, we might miss our estimate of the population value by more than 3 percent. We need to emphasize that the term "error" in sampling error does not mean that we have made a mistake in our sampling procedure. Rather, sampling error is a technical term that refers to the workings of chance. If we make a mistake in the sampling procedure which results in an unrepresentative sample the term that is used is *bias.*

Sampling error is basically related to the size of the sample.[2] The larger the sample, the smaller the sampling error. Examples of the relationship between sample size and sampling error are presented in Table A1-1.

Table A1-1. The Relationship Between Sample Size and Sampling Error (Based on Experience with Gallup Poll Samples)

Sample Size	Sampling Error
4000	±2%
1500	±3
1000	±4
600	±5
400	±6
200	±8
100	±11

Source. Charles W. Roll, Jr., and Albert H. Cantril, *Polls* (New York: Basic Books, 1972), p. 72.

The table demonstrates that as samples get larger, sampling error gets smaller. But the relationship between the two is not a direct proportion. Doubling the size of the sample will usually not cut the sampling error in half. In fact, after a certain point increasing the size of the sample leads to only very modest decreases in sampling error. As can be seen from the table, a sample size of 1500 seems to be about optimal.[3]

An important point that many people find hard to understand is that there is usually no significant relationship between the size of the population and sampling error. If we wished to estimate the percent of the public that favors no-fault insurance a random sample of 1500 would be just as accurate for making that estimate in the entire United States as it would be for making the same estimate for the state of California.[4] To conduct a statewide poll requires about as large a sample as to conduct a nationwide poll.

In an ideal survey employing simple random sampling the investigator could clearly identify each person in the population. An example might be the students at large university, all of which were listed in the student directory. If there were 20,000 students each would receive a number from 1 to 20,000. Then using a table of random numbers[5] 1500 students would be drawn from the population. We might then ask them, "Do you approve of the way the President is handling his job?" If 53% of the sample said "yes," we would then add and subtract 3 percent from our sample value. We could say therefore that we are 95 percent sure that 53 percent of the students approve of the way the President is handling his job, give or take 3 percent.

The technique just described, however, is not practical for most large surveys. One reason is that there is no master list of all Americans from which a sample could be drawn. Also, such a tactic would result in the sample members being widely dispersed geographically, making the survey unduly expensive and time consuming. But there are methods for overcoming these difficulties and still maintaining scientific standards. We shall discuss these shortly, but first we will analyze some of the better known polling disasters and the lessons we can learn from them on how *not* to conduct a public opinion poll.

A-2 PITFALLS IN SAMPLING POLITICAL OPINIONS

While we normally think of public-opinion polls as being of fairly recent origin, commerical publications were forecasting the outcome of presidential contests as early as 1920. The best known of these publications was the *Literary Digest*. The *Digest* accurately forecast the winner (if not the exact percent) of each presidential election between 1920 and 1932. However, in 1936 the *Digest* made a gigantic error and forecast that Alf Landon would be a landslide winner over President Franklin Roosevelt. The *Digest* was, of course, wrong; and partly as a result of this went out of business two years later. The following excerpts from the *Digest* depict the flavor of their public-opinion pollings operation.[6]

August 22, 1936

THE *DIGEST* PRESIDENTIAL POLL IS ON!

Famous Forecasting Machine Is Thrown into Gear of 1936

The 1936 nation-wide *Literary Digest* Presidential Poll has begun. Unruffled by the tumult and shouting of the hottest political race in twenty years, more than 1,000 trained workers have swung into their accustomed jobs. While Chairmen Farley and Hamilton noisily claim "at least forty-two States," and while the man in the street sighs "I wish I knew," the *Digest's* smooth-running machine moves with swift precision of thirty years' experience to reduce guesswork to hard facts.

This week, 500 pens scratched out more than a quarter of a million addresses a day. Everyday, in a great room high above motor-ribboned Fourth Avenue, in New York, 400 workers deftly slid a million pieces of printed matter—enough to pave forty city blocks—into the addressed envelopes. Every hour, in the *Digest's* own Post Office Substation, three chattering postage metering machines sealed and stamped white oblongs; skilled postal employees flipped them into bulging mail-sacks; fleet *Digest* trucks sped them to express mailtrains. Once again, the *Digest* was asking more than ten million voters—one out of four, representing every county in the United States—*to settle November's election in October.*

Next week, the first answers from those ten million will begin the incoming tide of market ballots, to be triple-checked, verified, *five times* cross-classified and totaled. When the last figure has been totted and checked, if past experience is a criterion, the country will know to *within a fraction of 1 percent* the actual popular vote of forty millions.

As in former years, the *Digest* Poll will be marked by three distinctions: Impartiality—A half century's reputation as the oldest and greatest news magazine in the world precludes any thought of bias; the *Digest* has not stake in the outcome. . . Accuracy—the Poll represents thirty years' constant evolution and perfection. Based on the "commercial sampling" methods used for more than a century by publishing houses to push book sales, the present mailing list is drawn from every telephone book in the United States, from the rosters of clubs and associations, from city directories, lists of registered voters, classified mail order and occupational data. . .

Trained experts have been constantly keeping [a] master-list up to date, checking names against the latest directories and organization rosters. Thousands of telephone books piled to the ceiling have been combed through for "revises," and new names have filtered in to keep the total at ten million. Soon, the first of the marked ballots will begin to trickle in, tho the tide reaches thousands upon thousands a day at its peak.

August 29, 1936

DIGEST POLL MACHINERY SPEEDING UP

First Figures in Presidential Test to be Published Next Week

In election after election, as the public so well knows, the *Literary Digest* has forecast the result long before Election Day. For this journalistic feat and public service it has received thousands of tributes during many years. Today the praise is continuing. For instance, Percy B. Scott, Editor, writes in the September issue of *The American Press*, "a magazine for makers of newspapers." "With the advent of the Presidential election campaign comes the *Literary Digest* Poll—that oracle, which since 1920, has foretold with almost uncanny accuracy the choice of the nations's voters. . ."

October 31, 1936

LANDON, 1,293,699 (57%); ROOSEVELT, 972,897 (43%)

Final Returns in the *Digest's* Poll of Ten Million Voters

Well, the great battle of the ballots in the Poll of ten million voters, scattered throughout the forty-eight states of the Union, is now finished. These figures are exactly as received from more than one in every five voters polled in our country— they are neither weighted, adjusted nor interpreted.

November 14, 1936

WHAT WENT WRONG WITH THE POLLS?

None of Straw Votes Got Exactly the Right Answer—Why?

In 1920, 1924, 1928, and 1932, the *Literary Digest* Polls were right. Not only right in the sense that they showed the winner; they forecast the actual popular vote with such a small percentage of error (less than 1 percent in 1932) that newspapers and individuals everywhere heaped such phrases as "uncannily accurate" and "amazingly right" upon us . . . .

Well, this year we used precisely the same method that had scored four bull's eyes in four previous tries. And we were far from correct. Why? We ask that question in all sincerity, because *we want to know.*

In 1936 Franklin Roosevelt got 62.5 percent of the vote and carried every state except Maine and Vermont. The *Literary Digest* not only failed to pick the winner, it missed the popular vote by over 19 percent. Why did the poll fare so badly? One reason that can be discounted is sample size. The *Digest* claims to have polled ten million people. Thus a large sample is no guarantee for accuracy. Rather, there were four fundamental defects which resulted from their sampling procedure. First, the sample was drawn in a biased fashion. Even though questionnaires were sent to ten million people, a large part of the sample was drawn from telephone directories and lists of automobile owners. During the Depression this was a decidedly upper-middle-class group—one which was predominantly Republican in its political sentiments. A second factor that contributed to the *Digest's* mistake was time. The questionnaires were sent out in early September, making impossible the detection of any late trend favoring one candidate over the other. Third, 1936 was the year that marked the emergence of the "New Deal coalition." The *Digest* had picked the winner correctly since 1920 using the same methods as in 1936, but in 1936 voting became polarized along class lines. The working class and the poor voted overwhelming Democratic while the more affluent classes voted predominantly Republican. Since the *Literary Digest's* sample was heavily biased in the direction of the more affluent, it is not surprising that their sample tended to favor Landon. Finally, there was the problem of self-selection. The *Digest* sent out its questionnaires by mail. Of the ten million they mailed only a little over two million responded—about 20 percent. Those people who self-select to respond to mail surveys are often quite different in their political outlooks than those who do not respond. They tend to be better educated, to have higher incomes, and to feel more strongly about the topics dealt with in the questionnaire.[7] So even if the sample of ten million had been drawn in an unbiased fashion, the poll probably still would have been in error due to the self-selection factor. One very fundamental principle of survey sampling is that *one cannot allow the respondents to select themselves.*

Despite the failure of the *Literary Digest,* several public opinion analysts did pick Franklin Roosevelt as the winner. Among them was George Gallup, Jr., who built his reputation on his correct forecast in 1936. Percentagewise, Gallup did not get particularly close. He missed by almost seven percent (see Table A1-2), but he at least got the winner correct. The technique used by Gallup in 1936 and up until 1950 is called quota sampling. This technique employs the census to determine the percentage of certain relevant groups in the population. For example, what percentage is male, Catholic, white, and college educated? Interviewers are then assigned quotas. They must interview a certain percent women, a certain percent with less

Table A1-2.   Record of the Gallup Poll

Year	Gallup Final Survey[a]		Election Result[a]			
1976	48.0%	Carter	50.0%	Carter		
1974	60.0	Democratic	58.9	Democratic	Average deviation for	
1972	62.0	Nixon	61.8	Nixon	21 national elections	
1970	53.0	Democratic	54.3	Democratic	2.3 percentage points	
1968	43.0	Nixon	43.5	Nixon		
1966	52.5	Democratic	51.9	Democratic	Average deviation for	
1964	64.0	Johnson	61.3	Johnson	14 national elections	
1962	55.5	Democratic	52.7	Democratic	since 1950, inclusive:	
1960	51.0	Kennedy	50.1	Kennedy	1.5 percentage points	
1958	57.0	Democratic	56.5	Democratic		
1956	59.5	Eisenhower	57.8	Eisenhower	TREND IN DEVIA-	
1954	51.5	Democratic	52.7	Democratic	TION REDUCTION	
1952	61.0	Eisenhower	55.4	Eisenhower		*Average*
1950	51.0	Democratic	50.3	Democratic	*Elections*	*Error*
1948	44.5	Truman	49.9	Truman		
1946	58.0	Republican	54.3	Republican	1936-49	4.0
1944	51.5	Roosevelt	53.3[c]	Roosevelt	1950-58	1.7
1942	52.0	Democratic	48.0[b]	Democratic	1960-68	1.5
1940	52.0	Roosevelt	55.0	Roosevelt	1970-76	0.9
1938	54.0	Democratic	50.8	Democratic		
1936	55.7	Roosevelt	62.5	Roosevelt		

Source. Gallup Opinion Index.
[a]The figure shown is the winner's percentage of the Democratic-Republican vote except in the elections of 1948, 1968 and 1976. Because the Thurmond and Wallace voters in 1948 were largely split offs from the normally Democratic vote, they were made a part of the final Gallup Poll pre-election estimate of the division of the vote. In 1968 Wallace's candidacy was supported by such a large minority that he was clearly a major candidate and the 1968 percents are based on the total Nixon-Humphrey-Wallace vote. In 1976, because of interest in McCarthy's candidacy and its potential effect on the Carter vote, the final Gallup Poll estimate included Carter, Ford, McCarthy, and all other candidates as a group.
[b]Final report said Democrats would win control of the House, which they did even though the Republicans won a majority of the popular vote.
[c]Civilian vote 53.3 Roosevelt soldier vote 0.5=53.8 Roosevelt Gallup final survey based on civilian vote.

than high school education, a certain percent black, etc. Once the interviews are completed the sample is weighted so that it will be representative of the population on those variables. If 15 percent of the population is male, high school educated, and making over $15,000 a year the sample will be weighted so that it reflects those same proportions. Quota samples are a clear improvement over the methods used by the *Literary Digest,* but they also suffer important shortcomings. The most serious of these is a variant on the self-selection problem. The interviewer has too much opportunity in determining who is selected for the sample. If an interviewer must get a certain number of "female blacks," he or she may avoid certain areas of town or may get the entire quota from a single block. There is a natural tendency to avoid shabby residences, long flights of stairs, and homes where there are dogs. Experience with quota samples demonstrates that they systematically tend to underpresent the poor, the less educated, and racial minorities. Members of those groups which are interviewed tend not to be "typical." These defects in quota sampling were a primary factor in the Gallup Poll's prediction that Thomas Dewey would defeat Harry Truman in 1948. Gallup erred in estimating the turnout and vote preference of minorities and poor people. They turned out in larger numbers than anticipated and voted overwhelmingly for Truman. Gallup predicted that Truman would get 44.5 percent of the vote; he got 49.5 percent. Thus he actually missed the Roosevelt-Landon election by a *greater* percentage than he missed the Truman-Dewey race. However, errors in terms of percent are easily forgotten. Errors in terms of who wins and who loses are long remembered. A second factor which contributed to Gallup's failure in 1948 was that, as was standard practice, he quit polling about two weeks before the election. He missed what was apparently a strong last-minute trend in the direction of Truman. Gallup, Harris, and others now poll up until the day of the election. They also take pains to insist that they are not trying to forecast the outcome of the election, that they can only portray opinion at the point which it is taken, and that inferences to election day must be made with great caution.

A-3 CONTEMPORARY METHODS OF SAMPLING

As a result of the error in the 1948 election, major polling organizations abandoned quota-sample methods. Most reputable polls now use scientific probability sampling down to the block level. At the block level a rigorously defined quota system is used. One exception to this practice is the SRC/ CPS. They use scientific probability techniques all the way down to the selection of the individual respondent.

What follows is a general description of probability sampling. However, that individual firms may employ a number of ideosyncratic variations should be understood. Modern probability sampling is done by household, not by individual. There is simply no up-to-date list of all Americans from which a sample could be drawn. The first step is to use the census to divide the country into a number of regions. This procedure insures that the proper proportion of respondents in a region gets into the sample. For example, if we know that 22 percent of the population lives in the West, and that 60 percent of these live in cities with populations of over 100,000 that percentage would be reflected in our sample. Note that this is *not a quota sample* since the respondents are ultimately selected by chance. This is simply a stratification procedure designed to help eliminate some of the fluctuations in the sample due to chance. If we picked a purely random sample we might, simply by chance alone, get 50 percent of the respondents from New York. Stratification prevents this possibility and still maintains the scientific nature of the sample. Within each of these regions smaller geographical units are selected by probability sampling. That is, they are selected randomly with the probability of their selection being proportionate to their size. These areas, called *primary sampling units* (PSUs), normally consist of either cities, or in less populous areas, counties. The PSUs once selected are often used for several years before they are replaced. The reason is economic. Interviewers are expensive to train, but once they are trained they can be used over and over. Normally PSUs are replaced on a gradual basis so it may be ten years before they are all completely changed.[8]

The primary sampling unit is divided into city blocks or areas of equivalent population in rural areas. These areas are then randomly sampled. Usually three to twelve individuals are interviewed in the block-area. Once again this saves time and money by keeping the geographic area compact. Most survey organizations then abandon probability methods at the block level and rely on some sort of quota.[9] The problem is that specifically selected individuals are often hard to locate. The interviewer may have to return five or more times to find the person at home. Again, this is time-consuming and costly. Survey organizations vary in the method they use to select individuals at the block level. The one we shall describe is that used by the *Gallup Poll*. A starting point on the block is randomly selected. The interviewer is then instructed to take every nth household throughout the defined area (either a block or a precinct). The interviewer then goes to the house and asks to speak to the youngest man of voting age. If he is not at home the interviewer asks to speak to the youngest woman of voting age. If neither of these is at home or refuses to be interviewed the interviewer then goes to the next adjacent dwelling and tries again. If successful, he or she then resumes the count from the original dwelling selected as the starting point. Each interviewer has a male-female quota, so once the male quota is reached the interviewer begins only asking for females. The procedure is continued until a predetermined number of people are interviewed in a particular geographical area.[10]

The major criticism of this procedure is that it suffers from a self-selection bias. Those who rarely "select" to be at home are clearly under-represented in the sample. To compensate, many polling organizations use a weighting procedure where individuals who are typically not at home are given a heavier weight in the sample. Another self-selection factor that detracts from the representativeness of the sample is that a certain percentage will refuse to be interviewed. Evidence indicates that this proportion has been increasing in recent years and now ranges close to 20 percent.

Nevertheless, the procedure seems to work reasonably well, at least if measured in terms of forecasting the vote in presidential and off-year elections. The accuracy of the Gallup Poll since 1936 is presented in Table A1-2. Note that in recent years, with improved sampling techniques, the polls have been quite close.

The sampling techniques we have just described, however, apply only to the major polling organizations such as Gallup, Harris, CBS, the National Opinion Research Center, SRC/CPS[11] and a few others. Many other polling organizations are run on a shoe string, and do not employ methods anywhere close to being scientific. Unfortunately, there is often no way of knowing the nature of the sampling procedures employed. The field of survey research is completely unregulated, by either government or any professional organization.

APPENDIX A FOOTNOTES

1. Some populations, however, are so small that all members can be interviewed. An example might involve a study of a state legislature. Rather than sampling, an attempt would be made to interview everyone.

2. It is also related to the variability of the population value. The greater the variability, the larger the sampling error. Thus if the true population value in terms of candidate preferences were 80/20 in election A and 50/50 in election B sampling error would be greater in election B. Also, sampling error would normally be larger if inferences about a population were being made with respect to age (which can take on a wide range of values) as opposed to sex (which has only two values). For an excellent discussion see Earl Babbie, *Survey Research Methods* (Belmont, California: Wadsworth Publishing Company, 1973), chapter 5

3. That this table applies to a variable that can take on only two values should be emphasized. Sampling error would be slightly greater if the variable could take on more values.

4. Since the United States as a whole is more heterogeneous than any one state there might be more variation in key variables for a nation-wide study than for a state-wide study. If that is the case, the sample would have to be somewhat larger for the nation-wide study to maintain equivalent sampling error.

5. Random numbers are created in a fashion such that the value of each numeral is not influenced by any previously created numeral in the table. As the name suggests, the numerals are created in a "random" fashion. Computer routines are available to generate random numbers; also, many statistics books have a table on random numbers in the appendix. To draw the sample, one simply uses the first 1500 numbers in the Table and selects the appropriate respondents from the population.

6. The following passages are from *Literary Digest,* 122 (August 22, 1936), p. 3; (August 29, 1936), p. 5; (September 5, 1936), p. 7; (October 31, 1936), p. 5; (November 14, 1936), p. 7.

7. For a good discussion see Don A. Dillman, *Mail and Telephone Surveys* (New York: Wiley, 1978).

8. Much of this discussion has come from Norval D. Glenn, "Trend Studies with Available Survey Data: Opportunities and Pitfalls," in Phillip K. Hastings and Jessie C. Southwick (eds.),

Survey Data for Trend Analysis (Williamstown, Mass., The Roper Public Opinion Research Center, 1974), pp. 6–45.

9. The one survey organization that uses random selection down to the individual level is the CPS/SRC. A specific individual is selected and that person must be interviewed; there can be no substitutions, as Gallup uses.

10. Paul Perry, "Election Survey Procedures of the Gallup Poll," *Public Opinion Quarterly* 20 (Fall 1960), pp. 531–541.

11. As we just noted, the SRC/CPS uses probability sampling down to the individual level.

APPENDIX B

1976 CPS
Opinion Items

In several places, this book examines the responses to opinion questions asked by the Center for Political Studies in its 1976 election survey. Because these questions are lengthy, the text usually presents their content only in abbreviated form.

The format of these questions is somewhat elaborate. After respondents were presented with the extreme positions on the issue, they were asked to place themselves on a scale from one to seven. Shown the scale, respondents were asked, "Where would you place yourself on this scale, or haven't you thought much about it?" For each question, the scale position "1" represents the extreme liberal viewpoint and the scale position "7" represents the extreme conservative viewpoint. Generally, in the text we combine the responses of "1," "2," and "3" as "liberal" responses and the responses of "5," "6," and "7" as "conservative" responses. We generally omit the midpoint scores of "4" along with the "no opinion" responses.

Below are the complete wordings of these questions. Responses are labeled as [L] for liberal and [C] for conservative according to how these terms are applied to the response alternatives within the text.

GUARANTEED JOB AND A GOOD STANDARD OF LIVING

Some people feel that the government in Washington should see to it that every person has a job and a good standard of living. Others think the government should just allow each person to get ahead on his own . . . Where would you place yourself on this scale . . . ?

[L] Government see to job and good standard of living.
[C] Government let each person get ahead of his own.

TAX RATE

As you know, in our tax system people who earn a lot of money already have to pay higher rates of income tax than those who earn less. Some people think that those with high incomes should pay even more of their income into taxes than they do now. Others think that the rates shouldn't be different at all—that everyone should pay the same portion of their income, no matter how much they make . . . Where would you place yourself on this scale. . .?

[L]   Increase the taxes for high income.
[C]   Have the same tax rate for everyone.

MARIJUANA LEGALIZATION

Some people think that the use of marijuana should be made legal. Others think that the penalties for using marijuana should be set higher than they are now . . . Where would you place yourself on this scale. . .?

[L]   Make use of marijuana legal.
[C]   Set penalties higher than they are now.

BUSING

There is much discussion about the best way to deal with racial problems. Some people think achieving racial integration of schools is so important that it justifies busing children to schools out of their own neighborhoods. Others think letting children go to their neighborhood schools is so important that they oppose busing . . . Where would you place yourself on this scale. . .?

[L]   Bus to achieve integration.
[C]   Keep children in neighborhood schools.

MEDICAL CARE

There is much concern about the rapid rise in medical and hospital costs. Some feel there should be a government insurance plan which would cover all medical and hospital expenses. Others feel that medical expenses should be paid by individuals, and through private insurance like Blue Cross . . . Where would you place yourself on this scale. . .?

[L]   Government insurance plan.
[C]   Private insurance plan.

WOMEN'S RIGHTS

Recently there has been a lot of talk about women's rights. Some people feel that women should have an equal role with men in running business, industry, and government. Others feel that women's place is in the home . . . Where would you place yourself on this scale . . .?

[L]   Women and men should have an equal role.
[C]   Women's place is in the home.

RIGHTS OF ACCUSED

Some people are primarily concerned with doing everything possible to protect the legal rights of those accused of committing crimes. Others feel that it is more important to stop criminal activity even at the risk of reducing the rights of the accused . . . Where would you place yourself on this scale. . .?

[L]   Protect rights of accused.
[C]   Stop crime regardless of rights of accused.

AID TO MINORITIES

Some people feel that the government in Washington should make every possible effort to improve the social and economic position of blacks and other minority groups. Others feel that the government should not make any special effort to help minorities because they should help themselves. . . Where would you place yourself on this scale?

[L]   Government should help minority groups.
[C]   Minority groups should help themselves.

MILITARY SPENDING

Some people believe that our armed forces are powerful enough and that we should spend less money for defense. Others feel that military spending should at least continue at the present level. How do you feel. . .?

[L]   Continue spending at least at present level
[C]   Cut military spending

(Only two—rather than seven—alternatives were offered respondents on this issue.]

DOMESTIC SPENDING

The government should spend less even if it means cutting back on programs like health and education.

[L]   Disagree
[C]   Agree

[Unlike the previous items, this one has a simple agree vs. disagree format.]

AUTHOR INDEX

SUBJECT INDEX

DATE DUE

APR 2 9 1989			